Paul's Letter
to the
Romans

A Commentary

Paul's Letter
to the
Romans

A Commentary

Peter Stuhlmacher

Translated by
Scott J. Hafemann

Westminster/John Knox Press
Louisville, Kentucky

Translated from the German *Der Brief an die Römer* (Das Neue Testament Deutsch), ©1989 Vandenhoeck & Ruprecht, Göttingen.

Book design by Susan E. Jackson

Cover design by Drew Stevens

First edition

Published by Westminster/John Knox Press
Louisville, Kentucky

This book is printed on acid-free paper that meets the American National Standards Institute Z39.48 standard. ∞

PRINTED IN THE UNITED STATES OF AMERICA
9 8 7 6 5 4 3 2 1

Library of Congress Cataloging-in-Publication Data

Stuhlmacher, Peter.
    [Brief an die Römer. English]
    Paul's letter to the Romans : a commentary / by Peter Stuhlmacher ;
translated by Scott J. Hafemann. — 1st ed.
        p.   cm.
    Translation of: Der Brief an die Römer.
    Includes bibliographical references and indexes.
    ISBN 0-664-25287-7 (alk. paper)
    1. Bible. N.T. Romans—Commentaries.   I. Title.
BS2665.3.S8413   1994
227'.1077—dc20   93-40128

To D. Gerhard Friedrich
(8–20–1908—1–18–1986)
in grateful memory

Contents

Translator's Preface and Introduction to the Commentary   xi

Abbreviations   xv

Introduction   1

   1. Encountering the Letter to the Romans Today   1

   2. The Letter to the Romans as a Historical Problem   3

     2.1 The Status of the Problem   3

     2.2 Paul's Situation   5

     2.3 The Situation of the Roman Christians   6

     2.4 The Letter to the Romans as a Statement of Accountability   8

   3. The Theme and Significance of the Letter to the Romans   10

The Letter to the Romans

An Outline of the Letter   13

1:1–17.   The Introduction to the Epistle   17

1:18–8:39.   Part One: The Righteousness of God for Jews and Gentiles   33

9:1–11:36.   Part Two: The Righteousness of God for Israel   142

12:1–15:13.   Part Three: The Testimony of the Righteousness of God in the Life of the Community   185

15:14–16:27. Conclusion   235

Select Bibliography   259

Index of Names and Subjects   265

Excursuses

1. "Apostle of Jesus Christ"   20

2. The Gospel in Paul's Thought   22

3. God's Righteousness in Paul's Thought   29

4. The Natural Knowledge of God   44

5. Judgment according to Works   45

6. Justification in Paul's Thought   61

7. The Meaning of Faith according to Paul   76

8. Justification and Reconciliation   82

9. The Pauline Understanding of Baptism   97

10. The "I" in Rom. 7:7–25   114

11. The Pauline Doctrine of the Law   122

12. Paul and Israel   177

13. Christian Life under the Power of the State   205

14. The Nature of the Pauline Exhortation to the Church (*Paraklesis*) 214

15. Does Chapter 16 Belong to the Letter to the Romans?   244

Translator's Preface
and Introduction to the Commentary

Peter Stuhlmacher has been Professor of New Testament at the University of Tübingen for over twenty years. During this time, one of the central goals of Prof. Stuhlmacher's work has been to develop an understanding of the writings of the New Testament, especially Paul, from the perspective of the biblical and Jewish postbiblical traditions which influenced them most. A prolific writer, his works include the previously translated *Historical Criticism and Theological Interpretation of Scripture* (1977); *Paul: Rabbi and Apostle* (with Pinchas Lapide, 1984); *Reconciliation, Law and Righteousness: Essays in Biblical Theology* (1986); and *The Gospel and the Gospels* (1991), which he edited. Most recently Prof. Stuhlmacher's ongoing development of a biblical theology of the New Testament has culminated in the first of a two-volume work entitled, *Biblische Theologie des Neuen Testaments, Band 1: Grundlegung: Von Jesus zu Paulus* (1992). This translation of his commentary on Paul's letter to the Romans (originally published in German in 1989), because of the nature of Romans itself, offers the English reader a summary of Prof. Stuhlmacher's thinking not only concerning Romans but also concerning the broad contours of Paul's theology. Written primarily with students in mind, the former is presented in a verse-by-verse exposition of Paul's argument, while the latter is summarized, above all, in a series of fifteen excursuses on the central aspects of Paul's life and thought.

The commentary is characterized by a twofold structure. For every paragraph of Paul's letter, *Section A* presents an overview of the text's essential logical structure and any essential issues concerning its history, together with the most important biblical, Jewish, Greco-Roman, and early church traditions and/or historical information needed to understand Paul's thinking. Following this discussion of the structure, traditions, and historical background of Paul's thought, *Section B* offers the commentary on the text proper. But unlike the more traditional commentary format in which verses are dissected into their grammatical-syntactical parts and then commented upon in isolation from one another, Stuhlmacher presents Paul's train of thought in an ongoing essay style that traces and restates Paul's thinking in an expanded form. In so doing, he weds the theological meaning of the text together with the historical situation behind Romans in order to make Paul's meaning clear. Paul's argument is thereby explained, at times subtly, by its recapitulation as part of an amplified restatement of the text itself.

As in his work on Paul's life and writings as a whole, Prof. Stuhlmacher's approach in this commentary is marked by three central convictions. First, Stuhlmacher consistently stresses the Old Testament and postbiblical Jewish traditions as the primary backdrop to Paul's thought, as these traditions were known by Paul himself or mediated to him through Jesus and the early church. In this regard the commentary offers a biblical theology of Romans. Second, the themes of the righteousness of God and the corresponding justification of both Jews and Gentiles are viewed as the center of Romans. Romans 9–11 are therefore not considered to be merely an excursus or theological aside in Paul's thinking or in the structure of the letter as a whole, but to be at the very center of Paul's concern. For Stuhlmacher, a central, driving question of Paul's gospel was how God's righteousness in Christ becomes effective not only for Gentiles, but also for Israel as well, to whom the promise of salvation was first given. In addition, in explaining the meaning of God's righteousness and the justification of the ungodly in Paul's thought, the emphasis throughout the commentary is on the inextricable link between justification and sanctification in Paul's theology. Chapters 12–16 are therefore also not to be regarded as an appendix to Paul's thinking in chapters 1–11, but as the essential outworking of justification itself. Finally, Stuhlmacher's commentary seeks at every turn to place the theology of the apostle within its historical context, making clear that the grand themes of Romans must all be viewed within the occasional nature of the letter and understood against the backdrop of the opposition that Paul continually faced, an opposition that had preceded Paul to Rome. Stuhlmacher thus destroys the false dichotomy that has often characterized the study of Romans between those who view it as a general theological treatise, which functions as Paul's last testament to his Christian faith, and those who simply treat it as one particular and completely occasion-bound expression of Paul's thinking. For Prof. Stuhlmacher, Romans is the product of Paul's consistent and abiding theology, now expressed within the context of Paul's need to defend his gospel in Rome in preparation for his future visit on his way to Spain.

The translation of this work has not been without its challenges. The most difficult among them has been the translator's desire to please both the author, whose intention the work expresses, and English readers, who will be grappling with this intention. On the one hand, the author desired to have as literal as possible a translation for the sake of accuracy and clarity. On the other hand, readers need some accommodation to their literary customs, so that some dynamic equivalence is required. By way of comparison, the result of steering a course between these two poles has been a translation much closer in style to the New American Standard Bible than to the New Revised Standard Version, not to mention the New International Version! Such a compromise of style for literal accuracy and brevity has thus been intentional. Since every translation is also a commentary, thanks go to Prof. Stuhlmacher himself and to Jonathan Whitlock, one of his current doctoral students, for their willingness to read through and correct the translation where needed. Their labor has added to the quality and surety of the work. Of course, I alone am responsible for any errors of judgment or translation.

Those who know the translator personally also know that he is a grateful student of Prof. Stuhlmacher, who owes so much to his tutelage and influence, both personally and theologically. This translation is thus offered as a token of deep appreciation for the author and his exegetical-theological work in the hope that many more students will profit from his method and insights.

Scott J. Hafemann

Abbreviations

Abbreviations and Sequence of the New Testament Writings Followed in This Work

Mk.	Mark	Phlm.	Philemon
Mtt.	Matthew	1 Tim.	1 Timothy
Lk.	Luke	2 Tim.	2 Timothy
John	John	Tit.	Titus
Acts	Acts	Heb.	Hebrews
Rom.	Romans	James	James
1 Cor.	1 Corinthians	1 Pet.	1 Peter
2 Cor.	2 Corinthians	2 Pet.	2 Peter
Gal.	Galatians	1 John	1 John
Eph.	Ephesians	2 John	2 John
Phil.	Philippians	3 John	3 John
Col.	Colossians	Jude	Jude
1 Thess.	1 Thessalonians	Rev.	Revelation
2 Thess.	2 Thessalonians		

Old Testament (Including the Apocrypha)

Bar.	Baruch	Jer.	Jeremiah	Num.	Numbers
Dan.	Daniel	Josh.	Joshua	Prov.	Proverbs
Deut.	Deuteronomy	Jud.	Judith	Ps.	Psalms
Eccl.	Ecclesiastes	Judg.	Judges	1, 2 Sam.	1, 2 Samuel
Esth.	Esther	1, 2 Kgs.	1, 2 Kings	Sir.	Sirach
Exod.	Exodus	Lev.	Leviticus	Tob.	Tobit
Ezek.	Ezekiel	1, 2 Macc.	1, 2 Maccabees	Wis.	Wisdom of
Gen.	Genesis	Mal.	Malachi		Solomon
Hab.	Habakkuk	Mic.	Micah	Zech.	Zechariah
Hos.	Hosea	Nah.	Nahum		
Is.	Isaiah	Neh.	Nehemiah		

Jewish Writings from 2nd Century B.C. to 2nd Century A.D.

1 Enoch	Ethiopic Enoch (2nd cent. B.C. to 1st cent. A.D.)
Jub.	Jubilees
3, 4 Macc.	3, 4 Maccabees
Ps. Sol.	Psalms of Solomon (LXX, Pharisaic, 1st cent. B.C.)
1Q, 4Q, etc.	Writings from caves 1, 4, etc. from Qumran (3rd to 1st cent. B.C.)
1QH	Thanksgiving Hymns from Qumran
1QM	War Scroll from Qumran
1QS	Rule of the Community from Qumran
2Qflor.	Florilegium from Qumran
1QpHab.	Habakkuk Commentary from Qumran
4QpPs.	Psalms Commentary from Qumran
T. Ab.	Testament of Abraham (1st/2nd cent. A.D.)
T. Ash.	Testament of Asher (2nd cent. B.C.)
T. Benj.	Testament of Benjamin (2nd cent. B.C.)
T. Dan	Testament of Dan (2nd cent. B.C.)
T. Gad	Testament of Gad (2nd cent. B.C.)
T. Job	Testament of Job (1st cent. B.C. to 1st cent. A.D.)
T. Jos.	Testament of Joseph (2nd cent. B.C.)
T. Jud.	Testament of Judah (2nd cent. B.C.)
T. Levi	Testament of Levi (2nd cent. B.C.)
T. Naph.	Testament of Naphtali (2nd cent. B.C.)
T. Sim.	Testament of Simeon (2nd cent. B.C.)

Jewish Writings from 1st and 2nd Centuries A.D. and Later

Adam and Eve	Life of Adam and Eve (1st cent. A.D.)
Apoc. Mos.	Apocalypse of Moses (1st cent. A.D.)
Apoc. Zeph.	Apocalypse of Zephaniah (1st cent. B.C. to 1st cent. A.D.)
b. Ber.	Babylonian Talmud, Tractate Berakot
b. Sabb.	Babylonian Talmud, Tractate Shabbat
b. Yeb.	Babylonian Talmud, Tractate Yebamot
2 Bar.	Syriac Baruch (an apocalypse, beginning of 2nd cent. A.D.)
2 Enoch	Slavonic Enoch (end of 1st cent. A.D.)
Ep. Arist.	Epistle of Aristeas
4 Ezra	4th Ezra (end of 1st cent. A.D.)
Josephus	Josephus Flavius (Jewish historian, born A.D. 37/38, died after 100)
Ant.	Josephus, Antiquitates Judaicae
Bell.	Josephus, De bello Judaico
Contr. Ap.	Josephus, Contra Apionem
Vit.	Josephus, Vita Josephi

m. Abot	Mishna, Tractate Abot
m. Ber.	Mishna, Tractate Berakot
m. Qidd.	Mishna, Tractate Qiddushin
m. Sanh.	Mishna, Tractate Sanhedrin
m. Tamid	Mishna, Tractate Tamid
Midr. Teh.	Midrash Tehillim
Pesiq. R.	Pesiqta Rabbati
Philo	Philo of Alexandria (ca. 20 B.C. to A.D. 50)
Abr.	Philo, *De Abrahamo*
Conf. Ling.	Philo, *De Confusione Linguarum*
Decal.	Philo, *De Decalogo*
Leg. All.	Philo, *Legum Allegoriae*
Leg. Gai.	Philo, *Legatio ad Gaium*
Plant.	Philo, *De Plantatione*
Rer. Div. Her.	Philo, *Quis Rerum Divinarum Heres sit*
Som.	Philo, *De Somniis*
Spec. Leg.	Philo, *De Specialibus Legibus*
Vit. Cont.	Philo, *De Vita Contemplativa*
Ps.-Philo, *Lib. Ant.*	Pseudo-Philo, *Liber Antiquitatum Biblicarum* (1st/2nd cent. A.D.)
S. Num.	Sifre on Numbers
Sifra	Sifra (Leviticus)
Tg. Is.	Targum of Isaiah
Tg. Neof.	Targum Neofiti
Tg. Yer. I, II	Jerusalem Targum I, II
y. Ber.	Jerusalem Talmud, Tractate Berakot

Non-Christian Greek and Roman Writings

Aelius Aristides, *Or.*	Aelius Aristides (A.D. 129–189, Greek rhetorician), *Orationes*
(Pseudo-)Columella, *Arb.*	L. Junius Moderatus Columella, agricultural author from the time of Seneca (1st cent. A.D.), *Liber de arboribus*, either from him or an unknown author
Corp. Herm.	Corpus Hermeticum
Dio Chrys., *Or.*	Dion of Prusa (ca. A.D. 40–120), later called Chrysostomus, *Orationes*
Empedokles, *Fr.*	Empedokles (ca. 495–435 B.C., Greek philosopher), *Fragments*
Epictetus, *Diss.*	Epictetus (ca. A.D. 50–130, the main representative of earlier Stoicism), *Dissertationes*
Euripides, *Hipp.*	Euripides (480–406 B.C., Greek writer of tragedies), *Hippolytus*
Liv.	Titus Livius (59 B.C. to A.D. 17, Roman historian)
Ovid, *Metam.*	Publius Ovidius Naso (43 B.C. to ca. A.D. 18, Roman poet), *Metamorphosen*
Tacitus, *Hist.*	Cornelius Tacitus (Roman writer of history, end of 1st cent. A.D.), *Historiae*

Christian Writings from 1st and 2nd Centuries A.D. and Later

Barn.	The Epistle of Barnabas
1 Clem.	1 Epistle of Clement to the Corinthians (ca. 96, from Rome)
Did.	The Didache
Justin, *Apol.*	Justin Martyr (Ephesus, Rome, died ca. 165), *Apology*
Orosius, *Hist.*	Orosius, Paulus (Spanish presbyter, died after 418), *Historia adversus paganos*
Tertullian, *Adv. Marc.*	Tertullianus Q. Septimius Florens (church writer in Carthage, born ca. 160, died after 220), *Adversus Marcionem*

Lexicons and Collected Works

Bauer	W. Bauer, *Griechisch-deutsches Wörterbuch zu den Schriften des Neuen Testaments und der frühchristlichen Literatur*, 6th, completely reworked edition, ed. K. Aland and B. Aland, 1988.
Bill.	(H. L. Strack-) P. Billerbeck, *Kommentar zum Neuen Testament aus Talmud und Midrasch*, I–IV, 1922–1961.

Introduction

1. Encountering the Letter to the Romans Today

In all of the editions and translations of the Bible available today, the letter to the Romans introduces the series of Paul's letters. Moreover, the destiny of the apostle Paul is bound together most closely with this letter, while the path taken by the church has also been tied to its interpretation. From Origen (A.D. 185 to around 254), to John Chrysostom (A.D. 347–407), Augustine (A.D. 354–430), and Thomas Aquinas (1225–1274), through the period of the Reformation, and up until the present, interpreters of all confessions have again and again taken Romans as their starting point whenever they desired to confront the church with the message of the apostle Paul.

Protestantism, in particular, has a special relationship to Romans, since the encounter with this letter marks both the turning and high points of its history. Indeed, it was through Luther's study of Romans, or more precisely through the reading of Rom. 1:16–17, that he arrived at his understanding of the gospel of the salvific righteousness of God, who, for the sake of Christ, justifies the sinner on the basis of faith alone without works of the Law. Luther's high esteem for the letter to the Romans found expression, above all, in his "Preface to the Letter of S(aint) Paul to the Romans" contained in his translation of the New Testament, which originated in Wartburg near Eisenach, and appeared in September 1522 in Wittenberg as "The New Testament in German." There he writes,

> This epistle is really the chief part of the New Testament, and is truly the purest gospel. It is worthy not only that every Christian should know it word for word, by heart, but also that he should occupy himself with it every day, as the daily bread of the soul (*Luther's Works*, vol. 35, 1960, p. 365).

Luther subsequently went on to explain that whoever wished to understand the letter to the Romans must first learn what Paul meant by the central theological

1

concepts of "Law," "Sin," "Faith," "Righteousness," and so on that repeatedly emerge in the letter. After expounding these concepts, Luther outlines the content of the letter and then concludes his preface with these words:

> In this epistle we thus find most abundantly the things that a Christian ought to know, namely, what is law, gospel, sin, punishment, grace, faith, righteousness, Christ, God, good works, love, hope, and the cross; and also how we are to conduct ourselves toward everyone, be he righteous or sinner, strong or weak, friend or foe—and even toward our own selves. Moreover, this is all ably supported with Scripture and proved by St. Paul's own example and that of the prophets, so that one could not wish for anything more. Therefore it appears that he wanted in this one epistle to sum up briefly the whole Christian and evangelical doctrine, and to prepare an introduction to the entire Old Testament. For, without doubt, whoever has this epistle well in his heart, has with him the light and power of the Old Testament. Therefore let every Christian be familiar with it and exercise himself in it continually. To this end may God give his grace. Amen (*Luther's Works*, vol. 35, 1960, p. 380).

Luther's friend, Philipp Melanchthon, interpreted Paul's letter as a compendium of Christian doctrine in his "Loci Communes," which appeared for the first time in 1521; and continued to do so in his commentary on Romans from 1532. Ever since, it has been perceived to be such a compendium.

The Anglican pastor John Wesley (1703–1791), one of the founders of Methodism, had his "heartwarming experience" at the public reading of Luther's "Preface to the Letter to the Romans." The new awakening of Protestant theology and church life in Europe after World War I was marked by Karl Barth's famous inaugural work, *The Letter to the Romans* (1st edition 1919, 2nd edition 1921). Then, in his 1935 Romans commentary, programmatically entitled *The Righteousness of God*, Adolf Schlatter developed the thesis that Paul's message must not be simply identified with the interpretation of Luther and his followers. Rather, it extended beyond it. However, Rudolf Bultmann's portrayal of Paul in his *Theology of the New Testament* (1953) is still strongly determined by Luther, while Ernst Käsemann, in his 1973 Romans commentary, consistently pursued the path further which had been opened up by Schlatter. For Käsemann, the theme of Romans is also the righteousness of God, which he sees to be "the reign of God over the world which has revealed itself in Christ." Käsemann's interpretation has convinced not only Paul Althaus, who before his death in 1966 once again fundamentally reworked his 1932 commentary (which preceded the present commentary in the Das Neue Testament Deutsch series), but also Ulrich Wilckens, whose three-volume commentary on Romans (1978–1982) has established criteria for the interpretation of the letter which will remain unsurpassed for a long time.

Yet, the time is already long since past in which the interpretation of the letter to the Romans has been merely a Protestant domain. At the moment, in the

German-speaking sphere, this is documented, above all, by the extensive commentaries of Otto Kuss (1957–1978) and Heinrich Schlier (1977). From the standpoint of the church as a whole, it is satisfying to experience that, precisely through work on the letter to the Romans, the confessional fronts that were hardened for centuries have been loosened up. Moreover, it is equally gratifying that a common conviction has been achieved concerning the fact that the church of Jesus Christ lives from the gospel and that her only justification for existence resides in testifying to this gospel. Today, Catholics and Protestants no longer dispute the fact, but rather hold in common, as Paul develops it in his letter to the Romans, that the gospel is the message of God's righteousness in and through Jesus Christ.

2. The Letter to the Romans as a Historical Problem

2.1. The Status of the Problem

Interpreting the letter to the Romans today, however, can no longer simply mean working out the doctrine that the apostle presents in his letter. Of course, this doctrine must never be overlooked in the interpretation of Paul. But if attention is paid only to Paul's theology, one easily loses sight of the fact that the biblical gospel, which comes from God, first took on its unmistakable historical form in the person and history of Jesus from Nazareth, and then, after Easter, in the testimony to Jesus through the apostles. The letter to the Romans could therefore only become a compendium of Christian doctrine for the church because it originally was a letter that Paul had written in order to inform the Christians living in Rome concerning the true nature of his gospel. It thus becomes detrimental whenever one forgets the time and situation in which Romans originated due to the powerful effect that the letter to the Romans has had and will continue to have in the church. God's ways with the church and with individual believers are not simply transtemporal, but are experienced in history. The more clearly we trace the history of Jesus and the history of the apostles, the deeper we comprehend these ways. In the last century, nobody has emphasized this in relationship to Romans more persistently than the church historian Ferdinand Christian Baur (1792–1860), who taught on the Protestant theological faculty in Tübingen beginning in 1826. According to Baur, the letter to the Romans can only be appreciated theologically if one has first examined precisely the historical circumstances surrounding its composition. When one does this, in Baur's view, the danger no longer exists, for example, of still understanding Romans 9–11 as merely a Pauline discourse concerning the providence of God (as Luther did), or of speaking of Romans 9–11 as merely an excursus on the problem of Israel that is superfluous for the understanding of the doctrine of justification (as several modern interpreters do). On the contrary, when placed within its historical context, one realizes that it is precisely in these chapters that the apostle is contending with the Judaizers in Rome in order to establish that his universal gospel of the righteousness of God is valid and full of promise for Israel as well. As a result of this type of historical consideration, these three chapters thus move into the very center of the letter and present one of its high points. Hence, Baur's model founded a school of thought around the idea and established the fact that any interpretation of the things written by the apostle in those letters that we have received, to be really taken seriously today, must always ask itself a twofold question, namely, that of their historical profile, on the one hand, and of their pertinent significance, on the other.

The towering significance of the letter to the Romans for the church and the fact that in this letter Paul actually deals in detail with the gospel and its consequences make it difficult to decide, however, which intention the apostle is pursuing with his letter of instruction. An important group of interpreters are of the opinion that the destination "Rome" is only of subordinate significance for Paul's letter. They point to the fact that Paul, according to his own testimony, is writing to a Christian congregation that is still unknown to him personally and concerning which he was only informed thirdhand. They consider Romans 16 to be a secondary addition to the letter, which originally ended with chapter 15. In their view, Paul reports in 15:25–32 that before he can come to Rome, he still desires to see the work of the collection through to a good end (cf. Gal. 2:10), with which he was commissioned at the Apostolic Council, by bringing the offering that has been gathered to Jerusalem himself. In this context he expresses the request that the Christians in Rome might pray for him, "in order that [he] might be rescued from those who are not obeying [the gospel] in Judea, and that [his] service to Jerusalem might be acceptable to the Saints [there]" (v. 31). On the basis of these statements, this interpretation determines that the purpose of Romans is as follows: In view of the difficulties and dangers that await him in Jerusalem, Paul outlines a comprehensive statement of accountability concerning his preaching in order to take it with him to Jerusalem. But he then also sends this report to the Christians in Rome because he expects from them not only intercession, but also intervention on his behalf with those in Jerusalem. From this perspective, Rome is, as it were, merely the verifiable address for the doctrinal statement that was essentially addressed to the representatives of the early church in Jerusalem.

This solution to the problem cannot escape a certain artificiality. Therefore a second group of interpreters seek the motive for the composition of the letter to the Romans primarily in Rome itself. They point to the fact that the apostle certainly must have had knowledge of the life and problems of the Roman congregation, especially since in 14:1–15:13 he summons the so-called "strong" and "weak" in Rome "to accept" one another in brotherly respect. According to more recent textual-critical investigations, chapter 16 can also no longer be considered an addition that was subsequently attached to the letter; one should much rather start from the fact that the letter originally encompassed all sixteen chapters (see below, pp. 244–246). Thus, in reality, the fact must be reckoned with that through his friends and acquaintances mentioned in 16:3–16 Paul was oriented concerning the situation of the Christians in Rome. The swift postal connections between Italy and Greece in the ancient world facilitated such an orientation. On this basis it is advisable, historically, to seek the reason for the writing of Romans first in Rome (which in no way can or should exclude the fact that the apostle had also presented in Jerusalem some of the fundamental ideas that he expresses in the letter to the Romans).

As simple as this supposition is, it too requires a historical grounding and foundation, that is, a historical grounding that goes beyond references to the concrete instructions of the apostle in 14:1–15:13 and to the circle of Paul's friends in 16:3ff. This foundation can also by all means be given. One must only think through further and make more precise the enlightening indications that F. Chr. Baur's successor in Tübingen, Carl Weizsäcker, gave for a historical understanding of the letter to the Romans in his book, *The Apostolic Age of the Christian Church* (*Das Apostolische Zeitalter der Christlichen Kirche*), which had already appeared in 1886. Stimulated by Baur's work, Weizsäcker proceeds from the supposition that in the letter to the Romans Paul defends his gospel from the attacks of "Judaistic doctrine": "The Letter to the Romans is a polemic not only against Judaistic doctrines but also, without a doubt, against Judaistic forces" (*Apostolic Age*, p. 440). According to Weizsäcker, Paul has an urgent need to write to Rome because he had learned that Judaizers are at work among the Roman Christians, "who wanted to secure an entrance for the gospel of the Law by showing, in reference to Paul, where the gospel leads when it is preached without the Law" (*Apostolic Age*, p. 441). If one takes into consideration the situation in which Paul found himself at the composition of the letter to the Romans, and moreover, if one keeps in mind the situation of the Roman Christians as Paul wrote to them, then the view represented by Weizsäcker proves, in reality, to be true.

2.2. Paul's Situation

When Paul dictated the letter to the Romans (probably in the spring of A.D. 56) in Corinth in the house of Gaius (cf. Rom. 16:22f. with Acts 20:3f.), he found himself at a decisive turning point in his missionary activities. He had fully deployed the gospel of Christ that had been entrusted to him in the eastern Mediterranean world and had carried out the work of the collection in accordance with his commission to do so. He therefore planned, from then on, to missionize in the West and to push forward as far as Spain. In doing so, Rome was to become his new point of departure (cf. 15:15–29). Of course, the work of

Paul in the East had not remained undisputed. Not only did the apostle come into conflict again and again with the guardians of the public order and with the representatives of Jewish congregations in his missionary region (cf. 2 Cor. 11:24–27), but he also had to experience, to a growing degree, the criticism of ritually oriented Jewish Christians who held more tightly to the Law of Moses than he did. Indeed, they were not able to prevail against Paul and Barnabas at the Apostolic Council in Jerusalem in A.D. 48 (cf. Gal. 2:3f.; Acts 15:1f., 24). After the Apostolic Council, however, when Paul came into contention in Antioch with Peter (and with those sent from James, the Lord's brother) over the question of table fellowship between Jewish and Gentile Christians, his standpoint concerning the freedom of the Gentile Christians from all legal duties could not prevail. As a result, Paul continued his mission among the Gentiles without Barnabas (Gal. 2:11–14; Acts 15:36–41), and his opponents considered that their hour had come. With the tolerance or even support of the Lord's brother, James, and with reference to the apostles who were actually called before Paul—most of all Peter—they put into effect a kind of countermission from Jerusalem and Antioch. First they attempted to alienate the congregations that Paul had founded in Galatia from the gospel of the apostle (cf. Gal. 1:16ff.; 3:1ff.; 5:7ff.; 6:12). Then they followed Paul to Thessalonica (cf. 1 Thess. 2:5ff.) and Philippi (cf. Phil. 3:2ff., 18f.), stirred up great unrest in Corinth with their "other gospel" (2 Cor. 11:4, 21ff.), and, without the apostle being able to hinder it, finally also began to establish a front against Paul and his gospel in Rome, which in their opinion was accommodated too much to the lax desires of the Gentiles (Gal. 1:10; 2 Cor. 5:10). According to Rom. 3:8, "certain people slander" Paul in Rome with the insinuation that he preaches, "Let us do what is evil (unhindered), in order that (from it) good might come!" In doing so, they are stirring up "dissensions and irritations contrary to the teaching which you have learned" (16:17). From a distance, all the apostle can do is reject this defamation with an extreme severity and advise the Christians from Rome not to have anything to do with these people (cf. 3:8; 16:17). Naturally, if the opponents are able to gain a footing in Rome before Paul himself can travel to the world capital, his missionary plans, with their goal of reaching Spain, would be seriously endangered. Paul writes the letter to the Romans in order to instruct the Roman Christians concerning his gospel and his true intentions. He does this in the hope of being able, with his writing, to squelch the agitation of his Jewish-Christian opponents, now beginning in Rome, while there is still time.

2.3. The Situation of the Roman Christians

Unfortunately, we do not know who brought Christianity to Rome. As a result of the demonstrably very considerable mobility of people in the first-century A.D. Greco-Roman world, it would have most probably been merchants and artisans who came from Jerusalem and Antioch to Rome. It is also possible that the apostolic (married) couple praised in Rom. 16:7, Andronicus and Junias, participated in the mission in Rome. As in the other large cities of the Mediterranean world, the Christian faith first gained its footing among the numerous Jews who were settled in Rome and the "God-fearers" who congregated around the synagogues. When as a result of the Christian mission in the Roman synagogues a tumult finally erupted, the Roman emperor Claudius banished the instigators of this unrest from the city; among them were also found Aquila and Priscilla, whom Paul encountered in Corinth (cf. Acts 18:2). In his biography of Claudius (§ 25), the Roman historian Suetonius reports the following concerning the Edict of Claudius: Claudius "Judaeos impulsore Chresto assidue tumultuantes Roma expulit" (Caesar Claudius "banished the Jews from Rome who were constantly in unrest as a result of the instigation of Chrestus"). In all probability, what is meant by "Chrestus" is not a Roman agitator, but Jesus Christ, whose name caused unrest among the Roman Jews. According to the thoroughly credible dating attained through the Roman historian Orosius (*Hist.* 7.6.15), the edict fell in the year A.D. 49. Claudius's measures had decisive consequences for nascent Christianity in Rome. As the example of Aquila and Priscilla shows, not only Jews, but also Jewish Christians were affected by the edict. When they had to leave, it was the Gentile Christians who, above all, remained in the city. They now no longer had any possibility of meeting in their congregational gatherings as a "special synagogue" under the protection of the Jewish religious and legal privileges, but had to form their own freely constituted assemblies without leaning on the Jewish synagogues. They were consequently much more vulnerable than before to the Roman suspicion of all forms of Eastern superstition. Moreover, they had to observe the prohibition against all private and public associations, which was binding since the time of Caesar (murdered in A.D. 44), in order to refrain from every kind of political or quasi-political agitation. An offense against this prohibition would have resulted in the immediate disbanding of the congregations. As Romans 16 documents, at the time of the letter to the Romans the Roman Christians were still organized in the form of individual house churches; they had not yet formed a united congregation to which Paul could have written. Rather, the letter to the Romans was passed along from house church to house church and each time read aloud and discussed anew.

The Edict of Claudius was binding only during his lifetime. Thus, after the inauguration of the reign of his successor, Nero (A.D. 54–68), the expelled Jews and Jewish Christians could gradually return once again to Rome. For example, according to 16:3f., Priscilla and Aquila, together with other Jews and Jewish Christians, had taken advantage of this opportunity. But the return of those who had been banished presented the Roman Christians with new problems. The Gentile Christians, who in the meantime had become established, saw themselves all at once confronted with the task of integrating the returning Jewish

Christians into the house churches, with all of their unfamiliar customs. Moreover, they were now also exposed to the criticism of all those Jews who had
been expelled from Rome because of the Christian mission. In addition, those
who were returning had experienced firsthand during their exile those disputes
that had existed in regard to the Pauline gospel in Galatia, Ephesus (cf. 2 Cor.
1:8ff. with Acts 19:23–20:2), Philippi, and Corinth, and in doing so they had encountered not only Paul and his co-workers, but also the "countermissionaries"
who followed them. If the Gentile Christians who were settled in Rome could
already hold divided opinions concerning Paul's mission, then it would certainly
be true of the house churches which were permeated with those who had returned in A.D. 56, when Paul wrote to them. If his mission to Spain was really to
succeed, for which he was dependent on the support of the Roman Christians
(15:24), then with his letter the apostle had not only to refute his opponents,
who had pressed forward to Rome, but at the same time, and above all, to convince the Christians in the Roman house churches of the truth of his gospel.
From this perspective, the letter to the Romans is to be seen as more than
merely a polemical document; it had to be a doctrinal writing if it were to accomplish its purpose for the history of missions.

2.4. The Letter to the Romans as a Statement of Accountability

If one takes into consideration the situation in which Paul and the Christians
in Rome found themselves when the apostle wrote to them, then the special
features of the letter to the Romans which have already been repeatedly emphasized can be easily explained. The first things which strike one's attention
are the detailed nature and the tone of the letter. From the beginning of the letter to its last chapter, Paul takes pains, almost assiduously, to render recognition
to the Christians in Rome, since it is due them for their strong standing in the
faith, which is known throughout the entire ancient world (cf., e.g., 1:8ff.; 6:17;
7:1; 15:14f.; 16:17–19). At the same time, he argues in such a way that his recita-
tion of doctrine appears enlightening and in accordance with the faith-convic-
tions of the Roman Christians, while the assertions of his opponents are nothing
more than slander and errors that have little or nothing to do with the faith-tra-
ditions that are valid in Rome. We are able to say this so precisely because the
critical objections that were brought forward against the preaching of Paul from
the opposing side appear behind the rhetorical questions that again and again
introduce the apostle's train of thought. For precisely this reason the apostle
asks in 3:31, "Do we then nullify the Law through faith? By no means!" Or in
6:1: "Should we remain in sin that grace might increase? By no means!" Or in
6:15: "Should we sin because we are not (any longer) under the Law, but under
grace? By no means!" Or in 7:7ff.: "[I]s the Law sin? By no means! . . . The Law

is holy, and the commandment is holy and righteous and good"; and so on. The dialogue that Paul carries on here, and into which he incorporates the reader of his letter, is a genuine dialogue. Paul is contending for the hearts and the understanding of the Roman Christians and is doing so in view of the critical objections against his gospel that are being voiced in Rome and that have, above all, Jewish-Christian roots. If the letter of James was sent out from Jerusalem into the Mediterranean world already during Paul's lifetime, for which there is much support historically, then one can gather from James 2:18–26 how the opponents of Paul, protected and encouraged by the brother of the Lord, argued in reference to justification. The apostle is just as willing in his letter to meet the Christians in Rome halfway, and to make it clear with the aid of quotations and allusions to traditions, which are repeatedly interwoven into the text of the letter, that his teaching agrees with the doctrinal and confessional tradition received by the Roman Christians (cf. merely 1:3f.; 3:25f.; 4:25; 6:17; 8:3; 10:9; 13:8f.; 14:17; 15:14f.), as he is unrelenting in one regard: Paul cannot and will not change anything concerning the gospel of Jesus Christ which has been entrusted to him. The gospel is bestowed upon him (and all Christians) through the divinely orchestrated mission of the messiah, Jesus Christ, in history, through his atoning death, his resurrection and exaltation to the right hand of God, and in his appointment as savior and judge on the day of judgment. In this gospel the salvific righteousness of God is revealed. Hence, there is nothing to be explained away concerning the gospel. When the apostle emphasizes in 1:16 that he is not ashamed of the gospel, this sentence signals at the very beginning of the letter, for friend and foe alike, that in Rome as well Paul will stand by that which has been entrusted to him, no matter who or what might also come against him. The apostle also does not conceal the flip side of being obligated to the one gospel of God, and he is no less unrelenting concerning it here than he was in Galatians and 2 Corinthians. There he cursed the preachers of "another gospel" or "another Christ" and unmasked them as disguised messengers of Satan (cf. Gal. 1:9; 2 Cor. 11:4, 13–15). It is similar in Romans: Whoever insinuates that Paul merely preaches "cheap grace" (D. Bonhoeffer) is guilty of divine judgment as a servant of Satan (3:8; 16:17f., 20). As severe as this renunciation of the opponents is, the reason for it is just as apparent. Whoever doubts in the least or would like to modify the fact that God justifies godless transgressors in and through Christ without the works of the Law, on the basis alone of the faith granted them (cf. 3:28; 4:5, 24f.), calls into question the eschatological salvation of Jews and Gentiles. But it is precisely this that Paul, who as an apostle stands and falls with the gospel (1 Cor. 9:16; Rom. 1:1–7, 16), cannot and will not allow. Paul makes it clear that he does not teach cheap, but "expensive Grace" (D. Bonhoeffer) in that he teaches one to see in the gospel the message of both the act of deliverance and the lordship of Christ (cf. 2:16). At the same time he draws out the implication from it that faith stands in the service of righteousness and in the fulfillment of the will of God (6:17ff.; 8:4ff.; 12:1ff.). A. Schlatter was completely right when he emphasized that Paul does not dissect divine grace "into two gifts which follow one another," called "Justification and Sanctification." Rather, "for Paul the connection to the Lord through faith completely (determines) one's knowledge and desire and (places) one in his or her entire manner of life under the efficacy of Christ."

3. The Theme and Significance of the Letter to the Romans

In view of the artistically stylized epistolary introduction in 1:1–7 and the conclusion to the letter in 16:25–27, which once again refers back to this prescript and is no less carefully formulated, the theme of Romans cannot be contested. It concerns the gospel entrusted to Paul, which as the gospel of Christ is the revelation of the salvific righteousness of God for Jews and Gentiles (1:16–17). Indeed, the letter to the Romans, throughout all of its chapters, deals with God's righteousness (A. Schlatter, E. Käsemann, U. Wilckens, etc.). But it does this not as an abstract treatise, but in the form of a large-scale, urgent dialogue with the Roman Christians concerning the content and true dimensions of the Pauline gospel, which is being criticized by Jews and Jewish Christians as far as Rome. As he stands on the threshold of a new chapter in his mission among the Gentiles (15:23f.), the apostle writes a statement of accountability to the Christians from Rome in which he defends his position and attempts to make it as strong as possible.

What the apostle could not yet suspect while he was dictating his letter was that he would only come to Rome as a Roman prisoner (Acts 28:11–31) and that he would never be allowed to reach Spain. Paul suffered martyrdom in Rome under Nero at the beginning of the sixties (1 Clem. 5:4–7). His letter, with which he wanted to push open the door to the West for the gospel, has become for the church, as Günther Bornkamm beautifully formulated it, the "Testament of Paul."

Even his opponents were ready to concede that Paul was a great composer of letters (2 Cor. 10:10). As far as the letter to the Romans is concerned, his missionary mandate, good friends, and the opponents who provoked him, led the apostle to formulations that have become spiritually authoritative for the church of all ages. Nowhere in the entirety of Holy Scripture is the nature of the gospel more clearly and exactly worked out than in the letter to the Romans. This is precisely what constitutes the theological significance of this letter.

In view of the different ways in which Paul and Jesus have been pitted over against one another, what has just been said must be made more precise. From the letter to the Romans one is able to do more than observe how Paul understood and testified to the gospel. His expositions also make clear what the gospel is in general. Paul knows and affirms that the teaching praised by him in Rom. 6:17 is the same "gospel" quoted by him verbatim in 1 Cor. 15:3–5 as that which belongs to all of the apostles who went out from Jerusalem. This gospel, together with the traditional texts cited by Paul in Rom. 1:3f., 3:25, and 4:25, which likewise can be traced back to Jerusalem, truly attest to who Jesus himself wanted to be and how he understood his sacrificial action, which culminated on the cross at Golgotha. Jesus saw himself as sent to Israel as the Son of Man-messiah. As God's Servant destined for this work (cf. Is. 52:13–53:12), he first wanted, through his sacrificial action on the cross, to lead the chosen people of God, and in their train the Gentiles, back to peace with God, out of which they had all fallen as a result of their sins. Mark 10:45 par. and the words at the Lord's Supper in Mark 14:22–25 verify this. Inasmuch as Paul explicitly quotes the Lord's Supper tradition in 1 Cor. 11:23–25 (according to the Lukan version) and designates the message of the destiny of suffering of the Servant of God, Jesus Christ, as the gospel preached by all the apostles and by Paul himself (cf. 1 Cor. 15:11 and Rom. 10:16f.), the circle is closed. Who Jesus was and what he accomplished for Jews and Gentiles in the name of God, namely, salvation as fellowship with God through the atoning death of God's Servant, is preserved as valid not only in the traditional formulas quoted by Paul but also and above all in his own formulations of the gospel. The Pauline gospel, concerning which the apostle gives account in the letter to the Romans, is the key to the understanding of Jesus; conversely, Jesus' messianic existence assists in understanding the gospel in the way in which Paul taught it.

Luther ranked the letter to the Romans with those biblical books "which show you Christ and teach everything that is blessed and necessary for you to know, even though you never again see or hear any other book or doctrine." Luther's judgment remains valid until this very day.

A short word concerning the dedication of the commentary is in order. Gerhard Friedrich's legacy for the exegesis of the (Old and) New Testament may be seen above all in the monumental work, *Theological Dictionary of the New Testament*, which Gerhard Kittel began in 1933 and Friedrich continued after World War II, bringing it to completion in 1979. Friedrich's most important essays appeared under the title, *Auf das Wort kommt es an: Gesammelte Aufsätze zum 70. Geburtstag herausgegeben von Johannes H. Friedrich*, published by Vandenhoeck & Ruprecht in Göttingen. In that volume there is also a bibliography for the years 1973–1978, which extends the bibliography for 1934–1972 which was published in the 1973 festschrift for G. Friedrich, *Das Wort und die Wörter*, edited by H. Balz and S. Schulz. Since I came to know G. Friedrich in 1967 in Erlangen, he has become a fatherly mentor for me. Originally he wanted to write the commentary on Romans himself in the commentary series

Das Neue Testament Deutsch (cf. his article "Römerbrief," in *RGG*[3], vol. 5, pp. 1137–1143), edited by P. Althaus and him and named after Luther's "Septembertestament" (see above, p. 1). After I, at the instigation of Friedrich, had become co-editor of the series, he turned over the composition of the volume to me. Now that the commentary is finally finished, there is nothing better I can do than to dedicate it to the grateful memory of this great man (cf. Heb. 13:7).

The Letter
to the Romans

An Outline of the Letter

The composition of letters in the ancient world, much more so than today, was an ability one had to acquire. In doing so, what mattered was not only the art of writing as such, but also, and to an even greater degree, the capacity to be able to express oneself to others well and accurately in specific situations. While it is indeed true that Paul was born in the commercial city of Tarsus in Cilicia, he received his upbringing in Jerusalem and was educated in the school of Gamaliel I, the scribe (cf. Acts 22:3). Hence, Paul did not acquire the training and rhetorical competence which he possessed at one of the elite ancient academies in Pergamon or Alexandria, nor in one of the higher Greek schools of rhetoric. Instead, he gained it through the basic instruction he received in Jerusalem, which he enjoyed before and in conjunction with his entrance into the school of Gamaliel. Yet it was common in Hellenistic training, already in the elementary grades, to undertake the discipline of learning rhetorical models and to practice the composition of specific types of texts. The rabbis also knew of and valued such "Progymnasmata." Evidently, Paul had successfully submitted himself to such a training, since even his opponents acknowledged that the letters which he wrote were "weighty and strong," even though they found his personal appearance hardly convincing (cf. 2 Cor. 10:10).

If one attempts to understand the letter to the Romans rhetorically, then following David Aune and Klaus Berger it may be characterized most likely as a "Logos Protreptikos." The Greek verb προτρέπειν (*protrepein*) means "to call someone's attention to something," or "to interest someone in something." A Logos Protreptikos is thus essentially "an advertisement which primarily attempts to win adherents to the pursuit of a certain discipline, especially philosophy" (K. Berger). Moreover, the genre Logos Protreptikos was flexible and open enough to be adapted to a carefully considered and detailed letter such as the letter to the Romans, which Paul had dictated to his amanuensis Tertius in an effort which lasted over a period of weeks (see below, p. 254).

Ancient letters followed a certain literary scheme. At the beginning of the letter, the sender and addressees were named and greetings were given, sometimes together with expressions of gratitude. Then the actual letter followed, after which, at the closing of the letter, greetings and wishes were once again expressed. Paul knew and used this form. While the actual writing down of the letter on papyrus was laborious and time-consuming, it was not yet common to divide a letter into chapters. In addition, no superscriptions were inserted in order to make the units of meaning recognizable. The way in which a letter is to be outlined and which subjects are to be handled must therefore be determined by the reader and the recipient(s) from the text itself, written without demarcations, and from its internal structural characteristics. When one pays attention to and follows these characteristics in the text of Romans, a carefully structured outline of the writing emerges:

1:1–17. The Introduction to the Epistle

I. 1:1–7		Introductory Greeting
II. 1:8–17		The Letter's Introduction and Announcement of Its Theme: The Pauline Gospel of God's Righteousness for All Those Who Believe

1:18–8:39. Part One: The Righteousness of God for Jews and Gentiles

I. 1:18–3:20		Gentiles and Jews under the Wrath of God
	1. 1:18–32	Gentiles under the Wrath of God
	2. 2:1–29	Jews under the Wrath of God
	2.1. 2:1–11	God's impartial Judgment
	2.2. 2:12–16	The Criterion of Judgment
	2.3. 2:17–29	The Guilt of the Jews
	3. 3:1–8	Objections
	4. 3:9–20	Jews and Gentiles under Sin
II. 3:21–5:21		The Righteousness of God as the Righteousness of Faith and the Ground of Reconciliation
	1. 3:21–26	God's Righteousness in the Atoning Death of Christ
	2. 3:27–31	The Universal Scope of Justification
	3. 4:1–25	The Righteousness of Faith Already Promised to Abraham
	4. 5:1–11	The State of Reconciliation

5. 5:12–21   The Reign of Grace

III. 6:1–8:39   The Righteousness of God as the Ground and
                       Power of the New Life

1. 6:1–23   Freedom from the Power of Sin and Service to
                       Righteousness
1.1. 6:1–14   The Change of Lordship in Baptism
1.2. 6:15–23   In Service of Righteousness
2. 7:1–8:17   The End of the Reign of the Law and the New
                       Service in the Spirit
2.1. 7:1–6   The End of the Reign of the Law
2.2. 7:7–25a   The Law and Sin
2.2.1. 7:7–12   The Perversion of the Law into an Instrument of
                       Sin
2.2.2. 7:13–25a   The Reign of Sin by Means of the Law
2.3. 7:25b–8:1   An Interim Statement
2.4. 8:2–17   The New Service in the Spirit as Life in Relation
                       to God as His Child
2.4.1. 8:2–11   Liberation from Sin and the New Service in the
                       Spirit
2.4.2. 8:12–17   The Spirit and Life as a Child of God
3. 8:18–39   Suffering in the Certainty of Salvation
3.1. 8:18–30   Suffering in Hope
3.2. 8:31–39   God's Unshakable Love in Jesus Christ

9:1–11:36. Part Two: The Righteousness of God for Israel

I. 9:1–5   Lament for Israel

II. 9:6–29   The Election and Mercy of God

1. 9:6–13   God's Free Election
2. 9:14–29   God's Free Mercy

III. 9:30–10:21   Israel's Rebellion against the Righteousness of
                       God in Christ

1. 9:30–33   Israel's Offense at the Stone of Stumbling
2. 10:1–13   Israel's Failure to Recognize the Righteousness
                       of God
3. 10:14–21   Israel's Disobedience to the Gospel

IV. 11:1–32   The Way of God's Mercy

1. 11:1–10   The Chosen Remnant
2. 11:11–24   The Temporal Hardening of Israel

3. 11:25–32 The Mystery of the Salvation of All Israel

V. 11:33–36   Praise for the Way of God

12:1–15:13. Part Three: The Testimony of the Righteousness of God in the Life of the Community

  I. 12:1–2   Worship as the Testimony of One's Life

  II. 12:3–8   Community according to the Measure of Faith

  III. 12:9–21   The Way of Life in Love

  IV. 13:1–7   The Christian's Relationship to the Institutions of the State

  V. 13:8–10   Love for One's Neighbor as Fulfillment of the Law

  VI. 13:11–14   Christian Conduct in View of the Coming Salvation

  VII. 14:1–15:13 Mutual Acceptance within the Community

    1. 14:1–12   One Lord and Judge for both the Weak and the Strong
    2. 14:13–23   The Edification of the Community through Respect
    3. 15:1–6   Self-Denial in Accordance with the Model of Christ
    4. 15:7–13   Mutual Acceptance of Those Who Have Been Accepted

15:14–16:27. Conclusion

  I. 15:14–21   The Ministry of the Apostle to the Gentiles

  II. 15:22–24   Through Rome to Spain

  III. 15:25–33   The Trip to Jerusalem with the Collection

  IV. 16:1–2   A Recommendation for Phoebe

  V. 16:3–16   A List of Greetings

  VI. 16:17–20   A Warning against False Teachers

  VII. 16:21–23(24) Greetings from Paul's Co-Workers

  VIII. 16:25–27 A Concluding Doxology

1:1–17. The Introduction to the Epistle

Within the biblical canon, the letter to the Romans has become a "textbook" for the Christian faith. But it can appropriately be appreciated as such only if one has first recognized that the letter was originally written by the apostle Paul from Corinth to the Christians in Rome in the middle of the first century A.D. Moreover, the occasion for it was a matter of pressing importance: Paul wanted to inform the recipients of the letter firsthand concerning his gospel, which had suffered repeated hostile criticism, and through this information to win their friendship and support for his ongoing missionary plans.

On the basis of Rom. 16:22 it becomes evident that the apostle had dictated the letter to the Romans to his Christian amanuensis, by the name of Tertius, in a laborious work that probably demanded weeks to finish. In doing so he took into account that the letter would be read aloud to the members of the Roman house churches mentioned in 16:5, 14f., and to other such groups, and that it would be discussed by them. As the preceding outline of the letter indicated (see above, pp. 14–16), Paul thus constructed his argument very carefully. This careful structure and the Greek textual tradition, which uniformly attests to the letter in its entirety, demonstrate that in dealing with the letter to the Romans we are not concerned with a composition which was first produced after the time of Paul on the basis of several Pauline letters (sent to Rome and Ephesus) by a second or third hand (so W. Schmithals, among others). Instead, the letter was originally a unity, including chapter 16.

The apostle formulated the introduction to his letter and thought it through rhetorically with special care. In accordance with ancient literary custom, he divided it into two sections. After a greeting (1:1–7), there follows an introduction to the letter, which then overflows, without a seam, into a statement of the letter's theme (1:8–17).

I. 1:1–7. Introductory Greeting

(1) Paul, a servant of Christ Jesus, a called apostle, set apart for the gospel of God, — (2) which he promised ahead of time through his prophets in (the) Holy Scriptures, (3) (which concerns) his Son, who came forth from the seed of David according to the flesh, (4) who was appointed Son of God in power

according to the Spirit of holiness on the basis of the resurrection of the dead,
Jesus Christ, our Lord, (5) through whom we have received grace and the
commissioning to bring about the obedience of faith among all the Gentiles
on behalf of his name, (6) among whom also you are as those who are called
by Jesus Christ, — (7) to all the beloved of God, called to be saints, who are in
Rome: Grace (be) with you and peace from God, our Father, and from the
Lord Jesus Christ.

Verses 2f.: 2 Sam. 7:12ff.; Ps. 2:7; 89:27f.; 110:1ff.

A. Like all Paul's letters, the letter to the Romans begins with a deliberately
formulated introductory greeting. At the public reading of the letter within the
gathering of the church (cf. 1 Thess. 5:27; Col. 4:16) these headings gave the
pronouncements of the apostle an official tone. Instead of simply conforming to
the usual Greek custom of beginning a letter with only a single, short sentence
of greeting (cf. James 1:1; Acts 15:23; 23:26), Paul follows a model that we find
in Dan. 3:31 (4:1) and contemporary Jewish letters. The sender presents his
title, takes up the rank and position of his addressees just as explicitly, and then
offers them his greeting in a new sentence. The introductory greeting of the letter to the Romans is more detailed, however, than all the other introductions in
the Pauline letters. It describes Paul's mandate, message, and aim in carefully
linked sentences, and thereby intends to signify to the Christians in Rome,
whom Paul does not yet know personally, that in this letter they are dealing with
a man and a matter that are of great significance for them. In order to give still
additional emphasis to his well-formed sentences, Paul refers in verses 3f. to a
catechetical and confessional formula which was presumably already known in
Rome. With it Paul affirms that the gospel entrusted to him concerns Jesus
Christ, the Son of God, who, according to his (lowly) earthly existence, comes
from the tribe of David (which bore the promise of the coming messiah), and
who, by virtue of his resurrection and ascension to the right hand of God, has
been appointed to the sovereign rule of the messianic Son of God. The language and style of verses 3f. betray the fact that Paul is taking up a tradition.
Verses 3 and 4 together create a parallelism like those we often encounter in the
Psalms or in the wisdom poetry of the Old Testament. Nowhere else does Paul
speak of Jesus' origin from the family of David or of the "Spirit of holiness" (the
Jews' term for the "Holy Spirit"), and the contrast between "according to the
flesh" and "according to the Spirit of holiness" is comparable to the small
Christ-hymn from 1 Tim. 3:16, where the earthly and heavenly worlds are also
placed in contrast to one another. In v. 7 Paul addresses "all who are beloved in
God" and not, as for example in 1 Thess. 1:1 or 1 Cor. 1:2, "the church of God"
in Rome. There is a simple historical reason for this distinction. When Paul
wrote the letter to the Romans there were still a number of house churches in
the world capital of Rome, distributed throughout the various quarters of the
city, which had not yet been able to come together into one unified congregation

(cf. Rom. 16:5, 12ff.). The letter to the Romans was thus passed on from house church to house church and there read aloud and discussed. The apostle's mode of address (which is comparable to Phil. 1:1) fits this situation exactly.

B. The introductory greeting, with its extremely careful formulation, makes it possible to recognize Paul's concerns in his letter from the beginning. As his greeting shows, Paul is concerned with his apostolic commissioning with the gospel of Christ, which has been entrusted to him, and with the agreement of all Christians in Rome in regard to this gospel and Paul's apostolic office.

[1] Paul introduces himself to the Romans by pointing to his threefold characteristic as an apostle. Just as Moses, Joshua, David, and the prophets were servants of God (cf. Josh. 14:7; 24:29; Ps. 89:4, 21; 2 Kgs. 17:23), Paul is a "servant of the messiah Jesus." His commission continues the work of the prophets. On the road to Damascus he was "called" to be an apostle, in accord with the fact that God had already determined him ("set him apart") from his mother's womb to be an envoy of the message of salvation which God had established. Paul's reference to his call in v. 1 thus recalls the more detailed exposition of his calling in Gal. 1:11–17 and 2 Cor. 4:5f. and counts on the fact that the Christians in Rome know his story. [2] The gospel entrusted to Paul is entirely the work of God: God had already caused this gospel to be declared prior to the earthly appearance of Jesus through his prophets in the Holy Scriptures (of the Old Testament) (cf., e.g., Is. 9:1–6; 11:1–9; Jer. 23:5f.; 31:31–34). These promises have been fulfilled in the mission of Jesus, the messiah (2 Cor. 1:20), and therefore the gospel has a clear content: [3] it tells of the earthly way and work of the messianic Son of God, who as a man came from that tribe of David which is the bearer of the promise of 2 Sam. 7:12–14; [4] and upon whom, after his passion and burial, God brought about, in fulfillment of his promise, the realization of the eschatological resurrection of the dead by the creative power of the Holy Spirit (cf. 1 Cor. 15:20 with Rom. 6:4). With the resurrection Jesus was "exalted" to the right hand of God in accordance with Ps. 110:1, which means that he was appointed to that appropriate sovereign rule which appertains to the Son of God. From this time on he is called "the Lord" (cf. Phil. 2:9–11). Verses 3 and 4 contain the history of Christ told in the Gospels in short form, and emphasize that the entire way of Jesus, from his birth to his exaltation, stands under the sign of the promises of God (cf. esp. Lk. 1:55; 24:24ff.; Acts 2:30ff.; 4:24ff.; 10:36–43; 13:23, 32ff.). The apostle will return once again to this theme in 15:8. At the beginning of his letter he is satisfied with using confessional and formal language to which the Christians in Rome will be able to assent without hesitation (see above). [5] He continues: Through the exalted Lord we have (with this so-called plural of majesty Paul is referring to himself) grace and a commissioning, which means that he has received the authority granted by grace and the ability to bring about the obedience of faith among all the Gentiles on behalf of the sovereign name of Jesus. The expression "on behalf of the name" becomes understandable when one considers that according to biblical

thought the name of Jesus is the essence of his salvific act and presence (cf. Acts
4:10–12; 1 Cor. 6:11). As an apostle Paul is to awaken the "obedience of faith"
on behalf of and in the Spirit of Christ (cf. 2 Cor. 5:20). By this expression Paul
means the conversion and subordination to the sovereign authority of Jesus,
which is the result of the preaching of the gospel.

[6] With v. 6 Paul turns directly to his addressees. The Christians from Rome
also live among the Gentile peoples. As Paul is called to be an apostle, so too
they are called by Christ to faith. But there is still more: [7] Because God has
demonstrated his love to them in the sending of Jesus, and has freed them from
their sins and sanctified them through the sacrificial death of his Son (1 Cor.
6:11), they are the "beloved of God" in faith and those who are "called to be
saints." Paul thus explicitly emphasizes that with his letter he is focusing his attention on "all" the Christians in Rome. The apostle's letter and greetings are
meant not only for those friends and acquaintances listed in chapter 16, but for
all his fellow believers, whether they are inclined to be friendly or unfriendly to-
wards him. The greeting "Grace and peace be with you" is built upon the Jewish
greeting-formula, "Mercy and peace be with you" (2 Bar. 78:2 and Gal. 6:16)
and reminds one of the common introduction to Greek letters, "Greetings!"
Paul wishes the Christians in Rome that they might participate in the grace and
peace which God has brought about through Christ (cf. Rom. 5:1ff.). Everything which Paul has to say from here on stands under this rubric.

Excursus 1:
"Apostle of Jesus Christ"

With the claim to be an *apostle* of Jesus Christ, which is already expressed in the first lines of the book of Romans, Paul aligns himself with
that group of men (and women) who preach the gospel by virtue of their
Easter-commission by the resurrected Christ (in Rom. 16:7, Junia is engaged, together with [her husband?] Andronicus, in missionary service).

The only thing the New Testament title "apostle" has in common with
the Greek concept of ἀπόστολος (*apostolos*), meaning "admiral" or
"leader of a navy expedition," is the word. It is based, instead, on Old Testament and Jewish examples and received its decisive character from
Jesus. It is already said of Moses and the Old Testament prophets that
they were called by God and "sent" to preach (cf. Exod. 3:10, 13; Is. 6:8;
Jer. 1:7; Is. 61:1, etc.). According to Mk. 6:7ff. par. and Lk. 10:1ff. par.,
Jesus sent out the Twelve chosen by him and others of his disciples to
preach the reign of God as he himself was doing (according to the Jewish
law concerning messengers, "the one sent by a person is like that person
himself" [*m.* Ber. 5.5]). Before Easter, this was a temporary obligation.
After the Easter appearances, which Paul (in 1 Cor. 15:5ff.) and the

Gospels narrate, this temporally limited commission to preach is changed into a lifelong mission for those to whom Christ appeared (cf. Mtt. 28:16–20; John 20:21–23; Acts 1:8; Rom. 10:14–17). Paul had contended all his life to be considered a part of this circle of apostles. His main hindrance was twofold: He had not known the earthly Jesus, and he had also not immediately joined the church of Christ in Jerusalem as James, the Lord's brother, had done. Rather, he had persecuted the Christians who followed Stephen from Jerusalem to Damascus and attempted "to destroy" their churches (cf. Gal. 1:13; 1 Cor. 15:9; and Acts 8:3; 9:1f., 21). Whether to consider Paul an Easter witness and an apostle of equal status with Peter and the Twelve because of his vision on the road to Damascus of the resurrected Christ as the Son of God, concerning which he reports in Gal. 1:16; 1 Cor. 9:1; 15:8; 2 Cor. 4:6, remained a matter of dispute in early Christianity. Paul explicitly claimed this status (cf. Gal. 1:1, 11ff.; 1 Cor. 9:1f.; 15:9–11; 2 Cor. 4:1–6) and firmly maintained the divine revelatory quality of his gospel from the beginning of his ministry down to the book of Romans (cf. Gal. 1:8f., 11f.; Rom. 1:1f., 16f.; 2:16; 15:16, 19f.).

But Paul's Jewish-Christian opponents disputed his right to this claim, beginning in Galatia (cf. Gal. 1:10), Philippi (cf. Phil. 3:2ff.), and Corinth (cf. 1 Cor. 9:2ff.; 2 Cor. 2:14–17; 4:1–6; 10–13), and as far as Rome (cf. Rom. 3:8). In comparison with the elder apostles from Jerusalem such as Peter, John, and so on, Paul appeared to them to be merely a later offspring who was an assistant to Barnabas in his mission (cf. Acts 11:22–26; 13:2) and had accompanied him to the Jerusalem Council (cf. Acts 15:1ff.; Gal. 2:1ff.). In their view he accommodated his preaching of the gospel to the wishes and criteria of the lawless Gentiles (cf. Gal. 1:10), despised the Law, and made Christ to be a "servant of sin" (Gal. 2:17). Accusations of this kind are reflected every step of the way in the letter to the Romans (see, e.g., merely Rom. 2:16; 3:8, 31; 6:1, 15; 7:7, 13, etc.).

Yet the accusations of Paul's opponents were better founded than we wish to acknowledge today. For Paul himself admits in 1 Cor. 15:7 that he is later than "all the apostles" and that his being deemed worthy of Christ's appearance was entirely unmerited. Moreover, it can hardly be disputed that he accompanied Barnabas to Jerusalem in the role of a "church apostle" (cf. 2 Cor. 8:23), and that the Pauline critique of the Mosaic Law is more fundamental than all of the other early Christian opinions concerning the question of the Law.

In the book of Acts, Luke chooses for his presentation of Paul's commission a historical perspective which places him both between and above these fronts. In the original sense of the word, only the Twelve chosen by Jesus, together with Matthias, who was chosen later to take the place of Judas (Acts 1:2ff., 15–26), are apostles. Paul does not yet belong to this circle. But besides and after the Twelve, he is the most significant witness to the gospel, whom the resurrected Christ himself had chosen for the mission to the Gentiles (cf. Acts 9:15f.; 26:16–18). Yet Paul is an "apostle" only in the sense that he was sent out, together with Barnabas, by the church in Antioch (as a "church apostle," see above) and discharged with a special mandate (cf. Acts 13:1–3; 14:4, 14). But for Paul it is at the same time true that, by virtue of the grace of God, he accomplished more in his mission than the apostles before and besides him (1 Cor. 15:10). Luke makes this clear through his overall presentation of Paul's path, leading as it does from Jerusalem to Rome.

The example of Paul the apostle and his history confronts us with the highly important fact theologically that the message of the gospel obtained its form as a human word of witness which is unmistakable historically. The church and theology remain founded on this original witness and are thereby at the same time instructed that there were original historical witnesses to the gospel who cannot be replaced. Among them is Paul, who was the most effective of these witnesses both in terms of his mission and (through his letters) literarily.

Excursus 2:
The Gospel in Paul's Thought

Paul's apostolic office is inseparably connected to his *gospel*. The twofold definition of the gospel which Paul gives in Rom. 1:1ff. and 1:16f. makes it necessary to draw out the contours of the understanding of the "gospel" which the apostle defends in the letter to the Romans. As Paul describes in detail in Gal. 1:11–16 and 2 Cor. 4:1–6, he received the gospel at his call through the revelation of Jesus Christ to him. The gospel is a power of revelation (Rom. 1:16) which, for better or for worse, has the apostle in its grasp, just as the prophet Jeremiah was once grasped by the word of God with which he had been commissioned (cf. 1 Cor. 9:16 with Jer. 20:9). Paul can expound the gospel, he can argue with it and in its service, but he cannot change it, let alone place it under discussion. Whoever impugns the gospel and dares to preach a "different Christ" than the one who appeared to Paul on the road to Damascus is under a curse (cf. Gal. 1:9 and 2 Cor. 11:3f.). The authority of the Pauline gospel is the authority of God; in the "gospel of God" Paul preaches God's own word (1 Thess. 2:2, 8, 9, 13; 2 Cor. 11:7; Rom. 1:1; 15:16).

In terms of its content, the Pauline gospel is the "gospel of Christ" (1 Thess. 3:2; 1 Cor. 9:12; Rom. 15:19, etc.). It concerns the salvific act of God which took place in history in the sending, atoning death, and resurrection of Christ (Rom. 1:3f.), and in it Christ appears as the redeemer and Lord. For this reason, "to preach Christ" (1 Cor. 1:23; 15:12) and "to preach the gospel" (1 Cor. 1:17; 15:1) are interchangeable in Paul's writings. On the road to Damascus Paul beheld Christ as the Son of God who had been exalted in glory to the right hand of God (Gal. 1:16; 2 Cor. 4:5f.). For Paul, the persecutor of the Christians, this meant a profound turnabout. As a persecutor of the church, the young, fanatic Pharisee Paul saw in Christ a messianic deceiver of the people who justly died the death of disgrace on the cross (in accordance with Deut. 21:22f.). He now saw precisely this same Christ as the one whom God had declared just and upon whom he had bestowed all glory. As a result, he was summoned into service by him. Christ encountered him, the one who was a zealot for the Law and the opponent of faith (Gal. 1:14), as the messianic Lord, and as the redeemer who accepted Paul, the one who was opposing him, and pardoned him, the sinner, in order to make him his messenger (1 Cor. 15:10; 2 Cor. 2:14f.; Rom. 1:5). Instead of the Law, from this point on Paul preached Christ as the "end of the Law" (Rom. 10:4) and faith in him as the way of salvation. He himself confessed about himself that, "If we once also knew Christ in a fleshly manner, from now on we know him thus no longer" (2 Cor. 5:16). And in the churches it was explained that, "the one who formerly persecuted us, now preaches the faith which he once tried to destroy" (Gal. 1:23; cf. also Acts 9:19–21). Because of his preaching of Christ, with its criticism of the Law, from the very beginning of his calling Paul was embroiled in difficult arguments with the synagogues and Jewish courts (cf. 2 Cor. 11:24ff.). In addition, those Jewish Christians who were faithful to the Law began to be suspicious of and to criticize his preaching of the gospel (cf. Gal. 2:4f.; Acts 15:1f., 5, 24). The main evidence of this conflict for us today is the letter to the Galatians; but it continues in the Corinthian epistles and in Philippians, and the situation of strife in which Paul finds himself is also reflected in Romans (cf. Rom. 3:8; 15:20f.; 16:17f.).

Hence, from the beginning, the Pauline gospel of Christ was disputed. But together with the elder apostles from Jerusalem, Paul preached the gospel of Jesus' atoning death, burial, resurrection on the third day, and his Easter appearances before Peter and the Twelve (1 Cor. 15:3–5, 11). Paul also completely adopted the doctrine of Jesus' atoning death (cf. 2 Cor. 5:21; Rom. 3:25f.; 4:25; 8:3). And Paul held high the Lord's Supper tradition, which originated from Jesus himself (cf. 1 Cor. 11:23ff.), and he instructed his churches to follow his own example by leading a way of life which was pleasing before God and mankind, and which was worthy of the gospel (1 Thess. 2:9f.; 4:1; Phil. 1:12f., 16, 20; 3:12–17, etc.). What made Paul's opponents suspicious, therefore, were the following central Pauline affirmations: "Christ has redeemed us from the curse of the Law, in that he himself became a curse for us, for it stands written, 'Cursed is everyone who hangs on the cross' " (Gal. 3:13; cf. Deut. 21:23); "For freedom Christ has set us free, remain steadfast therefore, and do not submit anew to the yoke of slavery," that is, to the Law (Gal. 5:1); and above all, "[N]o flesh is justified (before God) from works of the Law" (Gal. 2:16; Rom. 3:20), and likewise, "We are of the opinion that a person is justified (by God) by faith (alone), without the works of the Law" (Rom. 3:28). Paul defended these insights from the beginning of his ministry down to the book of Romans.

It was the apostolic tradition, of which Paul saw himself a part (for this, see too above, pp. 20–22), which caused the apostle to designate his missionary message his κήρυγμα (kerygma) (cf. 1 Cor. 1:21; 2:4; 15:14), his "gospel" (i.e., his message of salvation or good tidings), or even in a more engaged sense, "my (our) gospel" (1 Thess. 1:5; Gal. 1:11; Rom. 2:16). This apostolic tradition was given its decisive character by Jesus. Isaiah 52:7 speaks of the messengers of peace, "who cause peace to be heard, preach good tidings, cause salvation to be heard," and preach to Zion the inauguration of God's reign as king with the call, "Your God is king" (similarly in Nah. 2:1). In Is. 61:1f. it speaks of the one who is anointed with the Spirit of God that he is sent "to bring good news to the poor." Early Judaism explained these scriptural texts as referring to the coming messiah. We can see from Lk. 4:16–21 and Mtt. 11:2–6 par. that Jesus understood himself, on the basis of Is. 61:1f., to be the promised messianic evangelist to the poor; as such he was at the same time the preacher of the approaching reign of God (Mk. 1:14f. par.). Jesus' message was therefore already referred to early on as "the gospel of God('s reign)," and in certain cases it was even so designated by Jesus himself and his disciples (cf. Mk. 1:15 with Is. 52:7; furthermore, Mtt. 4:23; 9:35; 24:14). Already during his lifetime, Jesus gave his disciples a share in his preaching; according to Lk. 9:6 they moved out and wandered from place to place as "evangelists and healers." With Easter and Pentecost, their commission to preach was transformed into a lifelong mandate; since then the apostles understood themselves as evangelists who must preach the "gospel of Jesus Christ" by order of the exalted Christ (Rom. 10:14–17). From 1 Cor. 15:3ff. it is possible to know how this gospel sounded. Without discussing in full the question of the distinct spheres of mission and the problem of the Law represented there, one can distinguish at the Apostolic Council in Jerusalem between the "gospel to the circumcision" (i.e., for the Jews and proselytes) confided to Peter, and the "gospel to the uncircumcision" (i.e., for Gentiles and God-fearers), with which Paul and Barnabas were entrusted (Gal. 2:7). It is for this gospel that Paul stands up in his letters, and in 1 Cor. 15:8–11, as well as Rom. 10:14ff., he emphasizes the equality of his commission to preach with that of the rest of the apostles or "preachers (= evangelists) of good tidings" (cf. Is. 52:7; Nah. 2:1).

Paul thus took over his language concerning the "gospel" from the apostles before and beside him. The particular accents which he gives to it become recognizable when he calls his gospel "the word of the cross" in 1 Cor. 1:18 and "the word of reconciliation" in 2 Cor. 5:19. God's salvific work through the cross of Christ and its consequences for faith and life stand in the center of the Pauline preaching of Christ. What the actual preaching of Paul looked like in particular situations can be known only through a few intimations from his writings. Like other Christian missionaries, Paul called people to faith and repentance (cf. 1 Thess. 1:9f.). He worked as a teacher of Holy Scripture, having also taken over for himself and passed on to others the (Jesus-) tradition (cf. 1 Thess. 4:1; 1 Cor. 11:23; 15:1ff. with Acts 18:7, 11; 19:9f.). He wrote letters to churches and individual Christians (cf. Philemon) and was consumed by his deliberations on their behalf (cf. 2 Cor. 11:28f.). He accepted financial support only occasionally (cf. Phil. 4:10–20). For the most part, he attempted to earn his own living as a (leather-) tent maker (cf. 1 Cor. 9:6; 2 Cor. 11:7ff., 28; Acts 18:1–3).

The use of the word "gospel" in the Greek royal inscriptions to refer to the good news concerning the birth, inauguration, victories, or good deeds of the emperor may have been known to Jesus, the apostles, and to Paul. But it had no influence on the meaning of the language they used to describe their preaching. Moreover, the influence that it exerted on the understanding of the message of Christ in the churches is not significant enough to be mentioned.

II. 1:8–17. The Letter's Introduction and Announcement of Its Theme: The Pauline Gospel of God's Righteousness for All Those Who Believe

(8) Now first, I thank my God through Jesus Christ for you all, that your faith is being proclaimed in the entire world. (9) For God is my witness, whom I serve with my spirit in the gospel of his Son, that I mention you unceasingly: (10) In my prayers I always ask whether I will finally indeed one day succeed in coming to you by virtue of the will of God. (11) I long, namely, to see you in order to share some spiritual gift of grace with you for your strengthening, (12) that is, in order to experience among you a common encouragement through the mutual exchange of your faith and mine. (13) But I would (also) not like to leave you in ignorance concerning the fact, (dear) brothers, that I have already often undertaken to come to you, and yet I have been hindered from also obtaining some fruit among you, as I do among the other Gentiles as well. (14) I am under obligation (in the same manner) to Greeks and barbarians, to the wise and uneducated; (15) therefore my readiness to preach the gospel also to you in Rome. — (16) I am, namely, not ashamed of the

gospel, for it is a power of God for salvation for everyone who believes, for the Jew first, but also for the Greeks. (17) For in it God's righteousness is revealed from faith to faith, as it is written: "But the righteous will live from faith."

Verse 16: Ps. 98:2f.; Verse 17: Hab. 2:4.

A. At the time of Paul it was common among Greeks and Jews to follow the introductory greeting with yet another introduction to the letter in which one assured the addressees of one's reciprocal remembrance and eventually also of one's intercession. Paul adopts this custom, but also gives this part of the letter's introduction its own character. With carefully chosen words, Paul first takes up in v. 8 the matter of the worldwide reputation of the Christians in Rome, assures them in vv. 9 + 10 of his long-cherished desire to come to them, indicates in vv. 11 + 12 what he hopes for in his visit, and then comes in vv. 13–15 to speak of the (obviously acute) question of why he had not yet been able to make it to the world capital, although as the apostle to the Gentiles he should have wanted and been able to conduct his mission in Rome as well. In vv. 16 and 17 the introduction to the letter widens out into two thematic verses which announce the content of Romans: It concerns the gospel of the righteousness of God in Christ for all who believe.

Once one clarifies the structure of the text, a problem can be solved which has repeatedly confronted interpreters of this passage in view of the fact that at the closing of his letter, in 15:14–33, Paul returns once again to speak of his travel plans and intentions to visit Rome. In doing so he declares with much pride that he has always considered it his honor to preach the gospel only in those places where no other missionary before him has yet been; in his mission he does not want to build on a foundation laid by others (15:20f.). If one sees Rom. 1:13–15 merely to be the continuation of 1:10–12, and then (with Wilckens, among others) translates v. 15 to read, "So I am ready, as far as it concerns me, also to preach the gospel to you in Rome," a serious contradiction then exists with 15:20f. While Paul boasts there of a missionary practice which excludes building further upon a foundation laid by others, he declares in 1:15 that his intention in Rome is exactly this very practice. But the contradiction is resolved when one takes seriously the structure of vv. 8–15, from which one can discern precisely that in vv. 11f. Paul is merely speaking of his desire to come to an agreement concerning the faith during his visit with the Christians in Rome. He then expresses the same thing once again in 15:24. In 1:13–15 he adds that he would have liked very much to have been the pioneer missionary in Rome as well, but that he was hindered from it (by God). Verse 15 also belongs to precisely this explanation. In Greek the verse avoids a direct main verb and says only that at the time it was Paul's intention to preach the gospel also in Rome (as the first one). Now, however—this is the way it is to be understood in view of 1:11f. and 15:20ff.—Paul is only concerned to foster a fellowship of faith with the Romans. Hence, Paul does not desire to visit the Roman Christians in order to preach the gospel to them anew. Rather, he desires with his letter and his personal visit to create clarity concerning his gospel (disputed all the way to Rome) and in this way to secure the support of the Roman church for his mission plans, with their goal of reaching Spain (cf. Rom. 15:22–24). Verses 16 and 17 indicate that the Pauline gospel is disputed, but Paul is determined to stand by the message with which he was commissioned.

B. At the beginning of the letter's introduction Paul lets the Roman Christians know that [8] he boasts of their standing in faith in his thanksgivings, which are directed to God and mediated by Christ (cf. Rom. 8:26). He then adds that their standing in faith is being told throughout the whole world. Although this too may be formulated in a way that is a bit flattering, it is clear that the gaze of the world does rest on the Christians from Rome and that Paul has nothing to find fault with concerning the sincerity of their faith! [9, 10] In vv. 9 and 10 Paul asserts that he serves God in the spread of the gospel of God's Son (cf. 1:3f.), that he continuously remembers the Roman Christians before God, and that he constantly entreats God in his petitions for the possibility of a trip to Rome. [11] What he hopes for in his coming together with the Roman Christians is a mutual give and take. He himself would like to strengthen the Romans in their faith on the basis of the authority to proclaim the gospel which has been bestowed on him by grace (cf. 1:5). [12] He understands by this not a one-sided missionary endeavor, but a mutual exchange concerning the content and obligation of faith which will also strengthen and encourage him. Verses 11f. are formulated in an unusually careful manner, but they allow one to recognize sufficiently what Paul is seeking in Rome, namely, a mutual understanding with the Christians who live there. This understanding will help him to carry the gospel further, from Rome to Spain (cf. 15:24). [13] With v. 13 Paul begins to address the question of why he did not come sooner to the metropolis. What hindered him from also harvesting missionary fruit in Rome, as elsewhere in the Gentile world, in spite of his numerous and cherished travel plans, was the will of God. The passive formulation, "I have been hindered from it," is to be understood, as is often the case in Paul's letters, as "God hindered me from it." It is thus not personal negligence nor a lack of interest that has kept Paul from traveling to Rome thus far! Whether with this statement the apostle intends to fend off criticism from the side of some of the Roman Christians cannot be unequivocally determined; it is thoroughly possible. [14] In the following two sentences Paul makes it known just how much he would have liked to have come as the first missionary witness to Rome. As the apostle to the Gentiles, he is equally obligated to those who have experienced the (much-desired) Hellenistic education, as he is to the barbarians who have not enjoyed it; he is indebted under the gospel both to the educated and to the uneducated. [15] Paul's readiness to be the first to preach the gospel to the people in Rome also results from this obligation, entrusted to him by the resurrected Christ (cf. Rom. 1:5 and 1 Cor.

9:16f.). But as reported in v. 13, the situation is simply that this readiness did not accord with the will of God. In view of his missionary plans, Paul thus had to hold back. What he does intend to hold fast before God and mankind, however, is the gospel which has been entrusted to him.

[16] According to 2 Tim. 1:8 and Mk. 8:38, the expression "I am not ashamed (of the gospel)" derives from the language of confession associated with Jesus and early Christianity. It means that the apostle stands unflinchingly by the gospel. There can hardly be a doubt concerning which problematic situation Paul has in view. His gospel and his person are "slandered" all the way to Rome (cf. Rom. 3:8). Paul will not give in to this criticism. On the contrary, he desires to remain faithful in Rome as well to the gospel advanced by him. A clear signal is thereby given to Paul's critics in Rome. At the same time it becomes clear why vv. 16 and 17 paraphrase the theme of the letter to the Romans, since with the help of this letter, which anticipates his visit in Rome, Paul would like to come to an understanding concerning his gospel with the Christians in the city. There is nothing to change in this gospel. Why not? Paul gives the answer himself in language which is modeled on Ps. 98:2f. and which the apostle had already tried in his correspondence with the Corinthians (cf. 1 Cor. 1:18, 23f.). The gospel is the power of God. In it God works through the Christ who has been exalted "in power" to his right hand (1:4) on behalf of every person who believes in Jesus as the redeemer and Lord to keep them from being submitted to destruction in the final judgment. Moreover, the precedence of Israel over the Gentiles in terms of salvation history, established by God through election (cf. Rom. 3:2; 9:4f.), is not annulled by the gospel, but confirmed. The gospel addresses itself first to the Jew, in order to show him or her the messianic redeemer promised to Israel (cf. Rom. 9:5; 11:26; 15:8; and 2 Cor. 1:20), and then, in addition, to the Greek (Gentiles), who likewise may recognize in Christ his or her savior and Lord (cf. Rom. 15:9ff.). By virtue of the gospel, Jews and Gentiles together may live on the basis of the grace of God, that is, the Jew who experiences in Christ God's faithfulness to his promises (Rom. 1:2), and the Gentile (Greek), over whom in Christ the order of grace is extended. The next sentence speaks of this order of grace: God's righteousness is revealed in the gospel from faith to faith. "To be revealed" means that a (long-hidden) state of affairs, one which will still be valid on the final day of judgment, is now disclosed by God in the message of the gospel. This state of affairs is called here, God's righteousness. In the Old Testament, "God's righteousness" is the embodiment of God's activity as creator and judge, with which he arranges the world and holds it in order (see below). The New Testament sees this activity as coming to fulfillment in Christ. Paul can therefore say in 1 Cor. 1:30 that "Christ has become for us our righteousness from God" (cf. with Jer. 23:6). The mission, sacrificial offering, and exaltation of Jesus are the high points in the line of those historical acts of salvation which Judg. 5:11 signifies to be the "righteous deeds of God." If one takes the definition of the gospel which Paul

gives in 1:3f., together with 1:16 and 17, it becomes clear that in v. 17 the right-eousness of God is used as a summary expression for God's (promised) salvific activity in the mission and exaltation of Christ. Christ is God's righteousness in person, which has now been made known to us. It is received on the basis of faith and stays open to faith, or as Rom. 3:22 comments, "for all those who be-lieve." God's righteousness is experienced as salvation simply and solely by faith. For Paul everything depends on the connection between the righteousness of God and faith in that this connection opens up the possibility of being saved for every person and is indicated by God himself in the Scripture. As he did earlier in Galatians (3:11), here too the apostle refers to Hab. 2:4 in order to make clear that according to the witness of the Scripture it is the one who has ob-tained a share in the righteousness of God in Christ by faith who may and will live before God. Paul reads the prophetic text in the light of the revelation of Christ, but he does not distort it. In the Hebrew text it reads, "but the righteous one shall live on the basis of his (trusting-) faithfulness"; and in the Septuagint (i.e., the Greek translation of the Old Testament) which lay before Paul it says, "but the righteous one shall live on the basis of my (= God's) faithfulness." The apostle thus offers, as it were, the summation of both textual versions and states that it stands written as God's will (in Habakkuk) that the one who is righteous before God on the basis of faith (which has been opened up to him by God's grace through the preaching of the gospel) shall live. The gospel rests on this promise, and it became the act of God in history in the sending of Jesus.

Verses 16 and 17 make it possible to recognize what it is that concerns Paul in Romans, namely, the gospel of the righteousness of God in Christ, which is experienced on the basis of faith and which characterizes the life of faith before God. If one wants to summarize it in even shorter terms, one can say (with A. Schlatter) that the theme of Romans is God's righteousness. But whether the righteousness of God really incorporates the entire gospel was already disputed at the time of the letter to the Romans (and remains disputed until today). In the midst of this controversy, the apostle is determined to stand up for the gospel which predated him and to convince the Roman Christians of the legiti-macy and truth of his message through the arguments of his letter.

Excursus 3:
God's Righteousness in Paul's Thought

If one designates *God's righteousness* to be the theme of Romans, one must then clarify the meaning of the expression. It is found repeatedly in Paul's letters: 2 Cor. 5:21; Rom. 1:17; 3:21, 22, 25, 26; 10:3; and in Phil. 3:9 Paul speaks of "the righteousness by/from God." The Gospel of Matthew uses the term in the Sermon on the Mount (Mtt. 6:33), and it appears in the book of James in a statement which is reminiscent of Sir.

1:22: "The wrath of a person does not work the righteousness of God"
(1:20). Whether 2 Pet. 1:1 should also be considered part of the textual
evidence depends on the translation of the passage. The material as a
whole shows that the concept is especially important for Paul (in Romans), but that it is also used by other New Testament authors.

The prior history of the expression sends us back into the Old Testament and early Judaism. According to (Deut. 33:21) Judg. 5:11; 1 Sam.
12:7; Mic. 6:5; Ps. 103:6; and Dan. 9:16, the history of Israel is filled with
"demonstrations of the righteousness of God" in procuring salvation and
deliverance. The Essene community from Qumran on the Dead Sea also
praises God for these deeds (cf. 1QS 10:23). In the second part of the
book of Isaiah (cf. Is. 45:8, 23f.; 51:6, 8) and in the Psalms (cf. Pss. 71:19;
89:17; 96:13; 98:9; 111:3) God's righteousness is praised as that absolute
activity of God which creates the order of salvation and well-being. But
also in the situation of judgment the righteousness of God is evidenced as
salvific, since it enables those without rights to gain justice and the repentant to gain new recognition (cf. Is. 1:27f.; 49:4; 50:8f.). The best perception of God's righteousness is thus offered by the Old Testament and early
Jewish prayers of repentance (e.g., Dan. 9:16, 18 and 4 Ezra 8:36). Moreover, prayers have been found among the Essenes from Qumran which
approach quite closely Paul's own use of the concept, for example, 1QS
11:11–15: "(11) [A]nd I, when (12) I waver—God's demonstrations of
grace are my help for ever! When I blunder through the guilt of the flesh,
my right remains through God's righteousness, enduring (certainly) for
the duration, (13) when He relieves my affliction and saves me from per-
ishing, steers my foot along the path, draws me near in His mercy. —
Through His grace comes (14) my right, and in His true righteousness He
judges me, and in His great goodness He atones for all my sins and in His
righteousness He cleanses me from human impurity (15) and from the sin
of men, God be praised (for) His righteousness and the Highest (for) His
glory!" In the Old Testament and early Judaism, God's righteousness thus
means the activity of God through which he creates well-being and salvation in history (specifically that of Israel), in creation, and in the situation
of the earthly or eschatological judgment.

As Jews by birth, the New Testament witnesses have taken over this
language tradition. With its help they confess and extol the salvific act of
God in and through Jesus Christ, which enables them to be saved in view
of God's approaching judgment. Paul is picking up Jewish-Christian tradition in 2 Cor. 5:21 and Rom. 3:25f. (and makes their statements into his
own): "God made the one (= Christ) who did not know the guilt of sin to
be a sacrifice for sin for us, so that we might become the righteousness
of God through him" (2 Cor. 5:21); and, "God publicly appointed him

(= Christ) to be the place of atonement by virtue of his blood as a demonstration of his (= God's) righteousness because of the forgoing of sins
which previously took place (26) under the forbearance of God" (Rom.
3:25f.). Paul is thus not the first early Christian witness to speak of God's
righteousness. The one expression, "the righteousness of God," was already understood in the Christian tradition which existed before Paul to
refer at the same time both to God's own salvific activity (Rom. 3:25f.)
and to its effect in the form of the righteousness which is allotted to those
who, in faith, confess Christ (2 Cor. 5:21). This twofold possibility of
meaning for one and the same word can be explained once one considers
that already in (deutero-) Isaiah there is talk not only of God's own righteousness (see above), but also of the righteousness which proceeds from
God (cf. Is. 54:17). In exactly the same way, it says in the targum, that is,
the Aramaic paraphrase and explanation of this passage, that God's righteousness will manifest itself to the servants of God in "demonstrations of
righteousness, (which proceed) from (me and are effective) before me"
(Tg. Is. 54:17). In the Old Testament, in the early Jewish tradition, and in
the New Testament, God's righteousness thus means the salvific activity
of God the creator and judge, who creates for those concerned righteousness and well-being.

In this way Paul made the expression "the righteousness of God" the
center of the gospel in that, together with the Christians before and beside him, he spoke of God's salvific activity for the sinful world in and
through Christ and related God's righteousness strictly to faith. Through
faith in Jesus Christ as redeemer and Lord, every individual Jew and Gentile obtains a positive share in the work of the one, just God who brings
forth through Jesus Christ peace, salvation, and deliverance for Israel, the
Gentile nations, and the (nonhuman) creation. For Paul and his apocalyptic view of history and creation, the final judgment of the entire world is
soon approaching. To obtain a share in God's righteousness by virtue of
faith means to be acquitted of all guilt and to be accepted in the new
world of God in which death (and with it all distress) will be overcome (cf.
Rom. 8:18ff.; 1 Cor. 15:50ff.). But in Paul's gospel this righteousness of
God is already being revealed before the beginning of the day of judgment and made possible for those who believe.

It has long been a matter of debate in Pauline exegesis whether
one should understand the righteousness of God in Paul's thought above
all, on the basis of Phil. 3:9, as the gift of God, the righteousness of faith,
or "the righteousness which is valid before God" (Luther); or whether the
accent is to be placed, with Schlatter among others, on God's own juridical and salvific activity (in and through Christ) (cf. Rom. 3:5, 25f.; 10:3).
According to our reflections concerning the history and meaning of the

concept, one should not establish a false alternative between the two. The expression incorporates both, and it must be determined from passage to passage where Paul places the accent.

In looking for such a nuance, however, one must take into consideration the fact that Paul did not develop his message of justification from the standpoint of the question posed by Luther. While Luther sought comfort for the assailed conscience of the individual sinner, and saw the portals of paradise opened up for him when he found in Rom. 1:16f. the message of the "righteousness which is valid before God" revealed as a gift for those who believe in the gospel, it is precisely in the letter to the Romans that Paul pursues the goal of showing how God, the creator and judge, brought about deliverance for Jews and Gentiles through the sending of his Son into the world. Only when one follows this perspective and sees that God causes his righteousness, which creates salvation, to be effective for Jews and Gentiles, that is, for all of humanity, in the sending, death, resurrection, and lordship of Christ, does the gospel of the righteousness of God which the apostle preaches take on a real worldwide dimension as well as taking on relevance from the perspective of the theology of creation. But that is not all. If one takes as a starting point this cosmic dimension of the gospel, then Romans can be understood as a whole in that it deals from chapters 1 to 16 with God's righteousness in Christ for the salvation of the entire world. This comprehensive interpretive perspective includes that of Luther's within it, but also goes far beyond it. It has been tested out exegetically and insightfully carried through by various modern interpreters of Paul (above all by A. Schlatter, E. Käsemann, and U. Wilckens). This perspective makes plain the soteriological breadth of the Pauline view of justification, together with the breadth of its creation theology.

1:18–8:39. Part One: The Righteousness of God for Jews and Gentiles

After the apostle has designated the theme of his letter in 1:16–17, he now desires to present the individual components of his controversial gospel and to defend it against the criticism which has become voiced against Paul's message all the way to Rome. He does this with carefully thought through argumentation. First, he makes it clear that Gentiles and Jews are equally affected by God's judgment of wrath and therefore are both in need of deliverance.

I. 1:18–3:20. Gentiles and Jews under the Wrath of God

Verses 1:18–32 speak primarily about Gentiles. Following them in 2:1–29 is a parallel, but more detailed indictment, which beginning in 2:1 is first implicitly, and then, from 2:17 on, explicitly directed toward the Jews. After the apostle has set forth in 3:1–8 the objections that are being brought forward against his argument, he brings his accusatory speech against Jews and Gentiles to a climax in 3:9–20. In 1:18–3:20 Paul is speaking as a preacher of repentance; the various kinds of generalizations that he makes can be understood from the perspective of the broad sweeping style of the (prophetic) judgment speech.

1. 1:18–32. Gentiles under the Wrath of God

(18) God's wrath is revealed, namely, from heaven against all ungodliness and unrighteousness of mankind, who suppress the truth through unrighteousness. (19) For what is known about God is evident among them; God has made it, namely, evident to them. (20) For that which is not visible about him becomes visible for the eye of reason from the creation of the world on through the works (of creation), his eternal power and deity, so that they are without excuse. (21) For in spite of the knowledge of God, they have certainly not honored him as God or given thanks to him, but they were given up to futility in their thinking, and their foolish hearts were darkened. — (22) While they claimed to be wise, they became fools (23) and exchanged the glory of the immortal God for an image of the form of a mortal man and of birds and

animals and snakes. (24) Therefore God gave them up in the lusts of their
hearts to the impurity of the profaning of their bodies by means of their bodies themselves. — (25) They are the ones who exchanged the truth of God for
a lie and have rendered honor and service to the creation rather than the creator. — He be praised forever, Amen. — (26) For this reason, God gave them
up to sinful passions. Their women, namely, have perverted natural (sexual)
intercourse into the unnatural; (27) in the same way, the men have also abandoned natural (sexual) intercourse with the woman and have become in-
flamed in mutual lust, men with men they promote shamelessness and receive
the payment in themselves which is due their aberration. — (28) And because
they have not found it to be good to keep God in mind, God gave them up to
an incompetent understanding in order to do what is not proper: (29) Filled
with every kind of injustice, evil, avarice, wickedness; full of envy, murder,
strife, cunning, craftiness; a gossip, (30) slanderer, God-hater, evildoer, arrogant, braggart, intent on wickedness, disobedient to parents, (31) imprudent,
unreliable, loveless, merciless. — (32) They, to whom God's just demand is
known, that those who act in such a way are guilty of death, not only do this,
but they, moreover, also applaud those who do it.

Verses 19f.: Wis. 13:1–9; Verses 22f.: Wis. 11:15;
Jer. 2:5; Verses 24–32: Wis. 14:12–14, 22–31.

A. The introductory section of the apostle's indictment is artistically structured rhetorically. Verse 18 offers the overall heading for the explanations from
1:18–3:20. In vv. 19–21 they are supported twice in regard to the Gentiles (vv.
19 and 21). In vv. 22–24 and 25–27 Paul expounds in a parallel manner why and
in which way God gives those who refuse to recognize him and pursue serving
idols up to their own lusts. In vv. 28–31 the giving up of the Gentiles to godless
thinking and behavior is presented as a whole in reference back to vv. 19–21.
Verse 32 then summarizes by making the point that whoever thinks in this manner and behaves in this way has, without fail, fallen under the judgment of God.
Paul thus picks his words in the introductory section of his letter with much reflection. The repeated use of "God gave them over" in vv. 24, 26, and 28 cannot
be overlooked by any reader or hearer of the letter.

The sharp contrast that Paul draws between the Gentiles' fallen state of guilt
(and from 2:1ff. on also that of the Jews) and the revelation of God's saving
righteousness in 3:21ff. calls to mind the preaching of repentance and conversion conducted (before Gentiles) by the early Christian missionaries according
to the scheme of 1 Thess. 1:9f. This preaching led to baptism, and for this reason is also characteristic of the baptismal admonition (cf. 1 Cor. 6:9–11; Rom.
6:17). Paul thus argues in Rom. 1:18ff. on the basis of his missionary experience.

In terms of content, Paul follows closely the way of thinking found in the
(Hellenistic) Jewish wisdom tradition, as it is represented, for example, in the
Wisdom of Solomon, which the apostle found in his Greek Bible. In the wisdom

tradition, the creation of the world through the creative word of God (cf. Gen. 1:1–3, 6, 9, etc.; Ps. 33:9; Is. 48:13) is understood as creation through the wisdom of God (cf. Wis. 9:1–3; Sir. 24:3ff.), which is also revealed in the Torah (the Law) (cf. Sir. 24:23ff.; Bar. 4:1ff.). This double equation allows one to speak of the reflection of wisdom (or of the creative will of God) in the works of creation and to interpret the Jewish Law in a way that concerns the entire creation, while at the same time meeting with the Greek way of thinking. That part of Judaism interested in mission has already used these interpretive possibilities, and the Christian mission did the same. Paul is one of its most striking representatives. In Acts 17:22–31 we have before us a famous example of a positive connection to Gentile religiosity on the basis of the wisdom tradition, while in Rom. 1:18ff. we see a similar paradigmatic connection, but this time in a critical reference to the religion of the Gentiles on the basis of the same wisdom tradition. The two models do not contradict, but complement one another. For Paul the existing world is based on God's creative wisdom and at the same time makes it evident.

The paradigm for the apostle's concrete invective is the criticism of the idolatry of the Gentiles (of Egypt) attested in Wis. (11:15 and) 13:1–9, together with the following exposition in Wis. 14:12–14, 22–31 of the corruption of all morals that goes hand in hand with Gentile idolatry. Wisdom 14 already makes use of a broad sweeping "catalog of depravity" for its presentation and also offers a direct prototype for the apostle's summary accusation in v. 32. In Wis. 14:22 it states that, "As if it were not enough to err concerning the knowledge of God, they also still call, in fierce discord, that which brings ignorance into their life, so great an evil, peace." Paul takes over in 1:18–32 the generalizing language of the Hellenistic Jewish critique of the immoral Gentiles. The legitimation for this polemic (which with its generalizations is by no means free from danger!) lies in the recognized, high Jewish ethic of the ancient world, which was oriented on the Ten Commandments and taken over by the apostle in his admonitions to the church (cf. chapters 12ff.).

B. The connection between v. 18 and v. 17 is very close, being formulated by Paul as a conscious contrast. While the righteousness of God is revealed in the gospel to all those who believe, the wrath of God is revealed from heaven against all ungodliness. God's righteousness and God's wrath, from the standpoint of the Old Testament, are antithetical concepts. The former denotes the activity of God, the creator and judge, which establishes an order of well-being; the latter refers to his authority to penalize, or also to God's judgment of destruction as a whole (cf. Ps. 90:9, 11; Is. 66:15f.). The wrath of God is at work where his gift and love are disdained, while the righteousness of God creates this love itself, though still within the context of judgment (cf. Is. 63:1–6). According to early Jewish apocalyptic expectation, the entire world is quickly approaching God's judgment of wrath (cf. Dan. 7:26f.; 12:2f.; 1 Enoch 91:14–17). Paul also cherishes this imminent expectation. He anticipates the eschatological arrival of Christ to be soon, the so-called parousia, which precedes the final judgment, and sees in Christ the savior from the approaching judgement of wrath (cf. 1 Thess. 1:10; 4:16; 2 Thess. 1:7ff.; 1 Cor. 15:23; Rom. 14:10). [18] While the revelation of the righteousness of God in the gospel comes about through the (faith-opening) word of proclamation, the judgment of God is revealed "from heaven," that is, from God's judgment seat (cf. Ps. 76:9; 2 Thess. 1:7ff.). The end events are near at hand, and for those who believe, to whom Paul is writing, the anticipatory signs and criteria of judgment are already clearly evident and explicable from the perspective of the gospel. God's wrath directs itself against every kind of godlessness, that is, against the recognition that is withheld from God; and against every injustice of mankind, that is, against the disregard for his holy will. Godlessness and injustice are characteristic for the behavior of the wicked (cf. Ps. 73:6ff.); they signify the offense against the Ten Commandments as a whole. In vv. 21, 23, 25, 28 Paul outlines, above all, the disregard for the first and second commandments (Exod. 20:2–6); in vv. 24, 26–27 the transgression of the sixth commandment (Exod. 20:14) is signaled; and in vv. (21) 28–31 the offense against the rest of the commands of the so-called second tablet (Exod. 20:12–17) is portrayed. [19] The wicked suppress the revealed reality of God through their unjust actions, although God has made himself evident to them, which people should perceive from his work. [20] Ever since the foundation of the world, namely, God's creative power and greatness are reflected in the works of creation and thus become visible to the eye of reason. Wisdom 13:5 classically formulates this truth when it states, "For one can judge its creator from the greatness and beauty of the creation." Paul shares this perspective, but applies it here in a critical manner. Because the wicked have closed themselves to this (indirect) revelation of God, they are without excuse and justifiably encounter God's wrath. [21] Because they have not assented with praise to the judgment of God that, ". . . behold, it was very good" (Gen. 1:3; cf., e.g., Ps. 104 or 139), God gave them up in their thinking to futility and darkened their foolish heart (cf. Eph. 4:17f.). Whoever follows after that which is nothing, becomes nothing himself (Jer. 2:5)!

[22] This point is now illustrated more closely in two passages (vv. 22–24 and 25–27). [23] In spite of their claim to be wise, the Gentiles became fools. Instead of the creator, they have elevated his creatures to the level of gods. For the reader of Romans, the ancient statues of idols and heroes, together with the religious symbols made of animals, offered abundant material from which one could gain a perspective on the Pauline statements. The apostle did not stop, however, with merely a preliminary condemnation of Gentile idol worship. The passive verb forms, "gave up to futility," "were darkened," and "became fools" already indicate a judicial act of God. [24] Verse 24 (with 26, 28) make(s) this evident. Those who transgress God's will must bear the consequences of their sin, and the judgment takes place precisely in these consequences: God "gave them up" (to the effects of that which they themselves desire to do). The

everyday scenery of the Gentile way of life becomes the place of the divine judgment, but only those who believe recognize that the Gentiles are left to profane themselves with their perverted sexual lusts.

[25] The apostle then repeats the point. Whoever exchanges the truth of God for a delusion and puts the cult of the creation in place of honoring the creator, loses one's standard and destroys oneself. After he has named the name of God, the creator, Paul follows the Jewish and Jewish-Christian custom of adding a short declaration of praise (cf., similarly, Rom. 9:5; 2 Cor. 11:31). The only way one can speak of God, of his greatness, and of his work, is with praise. [26, 27] The renewed expression "for this reason God gave them up" makes precise what was already said in v. 24. With every indication of his loathing, the apostle now pictures how the Gentiles profane themselves (in a sinful reversal of Gen. 1:27f.) in lesbian love and sodomy. There was also a sufficient conception in Rome of what this was like to make Paul's point clear. What the Gentiles do is contrary to creation and characteristic of their fallen state of guilt. In the context of his general judgment speech, Paul had no occasion to go into detail or to be concerned with the problem of homosexuality from the perspective of the gospel. But now that in the course of the history of the church Paul's general formulations have led simply to excommunicating homosexuals, instead of getting to the root of their distinct behavior, accepting them, and helping them, there does exist for us today a reason not to repeat Paul's statements without reflection!

[28] In the fourth passage, Paul turns away from the problem of the perversion of sexuality into a behavior that is contrary to creation and directs his attention toward the general failure of Gentile life. God has given up the Gentiles who refuse to acknowledge him and to respect his will to an incompetent understanding (cf. thus also Eph. 4:18f.), so that they do "what is not proper." In Hellenistic Judaism, this expression refers to that which contradicts God's will (cf. 2 Macc. 6:4; 3 Macc. 4:16). [29f.] The catalog of depravity fills out the subject matter in view. Paul desires to speak in a broad-sweeping way (as he also does at other times, cf. Rom. 13:13; Gal. 5:19–21) in order to bring to expression that "the honoring of the nameless idols (is) the beginning, origin, and high point of all evil" (Wis. 14:27). Injustice, evil, avarice, and wickedness describe the general depravity of life. There then follows a list of ways of thinking and acting which damage the community. Within this Jewish and Jewish-Christian context, with its focus on community, rebellion against one's parents thus carries much weight (cf. Deut. 21:18ff.). [31] Imprudence, unreliability, lovelessness, mercilessness then provide the contrast to the behavior of the pious Jew (or Jewish Christian). The pious one must not be lacking in wisdom and in the fear of God (Sir. 1:11ff.), may not be characterized by the breaking of covenants, and should be filled with the love of neighbor and compassion which corresponds to God's conduct (cf. Lev. 19:18; Sir. 4:1–19). The lack of all of these ways of acting indicates an exemplary godlessness. The catalog of depravity in

this passage is thus oriented on the commandments of God and is intended to show Paul's reader, who is well acquainted with them (cf. Rom. 7:1; 13:8ff.), that God's judgment is also effective in an exemplary fashion there where one abandons the way and sphere of life which his commandments mark out. [32] The concluding sentence offers a serious summation. The fact that the Gentiles, instead of repenting, continue to confirm one another in the doing of evil (cf., similarly, Wis. 14:22; Ep. Arist. 152; T. Ash. 6:2) makes them fully worthy of judgment. The just demand of God to respect his will is known to them by virtue of the wisdom of God which permeates the entire creation (see vv. 19f.). The philosophical ethic of the ancient world, to which the Jewish and early Christian mission related differently (cf. in Paul, e.g., Phil. 4:8f.; Rom. 12:2), justifies the apostle in this judgment. His readers in Rome could also carry out this sentence. According to the Old Testament and Jewish thought, only such sins could be forgiven which were begun unknowingly; the one who knowingly sins must bear his guilt all the way to destruction (cf. Num. 15:22–31). According to this criterion, the Gentiles who intentionally sin have irretrievably fallen under God's judgment of wrath (see v. 18). There is deliverance for them only through the righteousness of God revealed in the gospel, and this is precisely the goal at which the apostle's argument aims in 3:21ff.

2. 2:1–29. Jews under the Wrath of God

After Paul has outlined in 1:18–32 the Gentiles' state of having fallen under the judgment of God, he now proceeds to his accusation against the Jews. In doing so, his argumentation is more differentiated than it was earlier and is divided into three sections: 2:1–11 deals with God's impartial judgment, 2:12–16 with the criterion of judgment, and 2:17–29 with the guilt of the Jews. Only in the last discourse is the "man" who is addressed from 2:1 on identified as a Jew (2:17).

2.1. 2:1–11. God's Impartial Judgment

(1) Therefore you are without excuse, O man, you who judge, whoever you are. You judge yourself, namely, by that concerning which you judge another, for you, as judge, do the same thing (as he). (2) But we know that the judgment of God befalls on those who do such things. (3) Do you by chance suppose, O man, you who judge those who do such things and do it indeed (yourself), that you will escape the judgment of God? (4) Or do you despise the riches of his goodness and patience and forbearance and take no notice of the fact that God's goodness leads you to repentance? (5) In accordance with your hardening and unrepentant heart, you are heaping up wrath for yourself on the day of wrath and of the revelation of the righteous judgment of God, (6) who "will give back to each one according to his works": (7) to those who

strive after eternal life with the persistent doing of good, glory and honor and immortality; (8) but to the others, who on the basis of selfishness, and because they are disobedient to the truth but belong to unrighteousness, wrath and rage. (9) There will be distress and anxiety over every human soul which does evil, for the Jew first, but also for the Greek; (10) but glory and honor and salvation for every one who does good, for the Jew first, but also for the Greek. (11) For God is no respecter of persons.

Verse 4: Wis. 11:9f.; 15:1–3; Verse 6: Prov. 24:12
(Ps. 62:13); Verse 11: Sir. 35:12f. in the Septuagint.

A. The textual tradition gives no reason to consider v. 1 to be a gloss by a later reviser of Romans. Paul is consciously working rhetorically—similar to Nathan according to 2 Sam. 12:7—to bring about a surprise effect. The dialogical formulation of the text in questions and answers is also to be understood rhetorically. Like his contemporary Greek authors, Paul loosens up his didactic statements. Of course, Paul did not choose the stylistic means of the so-called *Diatribē* (= conversation) without a concrete reason (see below). The verses pick up formulations from 1:18–32 and work, moreover, with word-pairs which are known from the Septuagint (and based on this source, also from elsewhere in the New Testament): "wrath and rage" (cf. Deut. 29:27; Ps. 69:25; 78:49), "distress and anxiety" (cf. Is. 8:22; 30:6), "glory and honor" (cf. Pss. 29:1; 96:7).

The structure of the argument is as follows. After the surprising judgment of v. 1, v. 2 contains a statement which draws attention to community knowledge (and refers back to 1:32). It functions to declare that the still-unnamed discussion partner of v. 1 and vv. 3–5 is worthy of judgment by raising two critical questions and then drawing a conclusion. The catchword "(righteous) judgment of God" connects v. 2 with v. 5 and is defined by the relative pronoun clause in v. 6 as a judgment according to works. Verses 7–10 unfold the rules of this judgment in two pairs of sentences which are (chiastically) related to one another according to the scheme a–b/b–a. Verse 11 supports this double rule with a statement which is analogous to v. 6 and draws upon Sir. 35:12f.: God judges impartially. Paul thus once again formulates his thoughts with extreme care and concentration.

The tradition which lies at the foundation of these verses is, above all, that of wisdom (as already was the case in 1:18ff.). In the Wisdom of Solomon, God's judgment on Israel and on the Gentiles is spoken of differently. While God strikes the Gentiles (= the Egyptians) as an example, he still holds back his judgment of wrath concerning his chosen people. He punishes them only temporarily as a warning and invites them to be led to repentance through the example of his present judgment on the Egyptian Gentiles. "You have put them (= the Israelites of the Exodus generation) to the test like an admonishing father, but judged and condemned the evildoers (= the Gentile Egyptians) like a strict king" (Wis. 11:10; cf. also 15:1–3). Paul does not flatten out the difference between

Jews and Gentiles established by God's election either in regard to the gospel
or in regard to the (final) judgment (cf. Rom. 1:16; 2:9f.; 3:1; 9:1ff.). He again
takes up the doctrinal tradition concerning wisdom and with its help argues as
follows: While God's judgment of wrath is already at work among the Gentiles
(cf. 1:24, 26, 28), Paul's conversation partner belongs to the group of those
whom God still desires to lead to repentance through his forbearance, but who
will bring judgment upon themselves all the more "on the day of wrath" in the
case of their impenitence. The conversation partner thus belongs to the Jews
and is then also addressed as such in v. 17. But he can derive profit from his
privileged position only if he gives up his conduct worthy of judgment and re-
pents. If he does not do this and hardens his heart, God's wrath falls on him
more than ever. In view of these verses it is impossible to maintain that Paul
underrated the Jewish tradition of repentance or pushed it entirely to the side.
God's judgment of wrath does not yet fall on Israel to the degree that it does
over the Gentiles. In contrast to them, the Jews still retain the opportunity to
repent until the day of judgment. In this way, Paul already corrects here the
standpoint he expressed in 1 Thess. 2:16 (cf. further below, pp. 164ff., 177ff.). Romans 2:16 and 3:8 will show us why, that is, because he desires to give the
(above all, Jewish-Christian) objections against his gospel as little basis for attack as possible. In Romans, the (Christian) Gentiles are not the problem for
Paul, but the Jewish-Christian critics and their sympathizers. These circumstances surrounding Paul's discussion also explain the extensive detail of 2:1–29
over against 1:18–32.

B. With his critique of the Gentiles (1:18–32), Paul could count on the agreement of the Roman Christians. In view of the position of the Jews, the matter
was more difficult. In order to prevent the suspicion that he denies or levels out
Israel's privileged position with his type of preaching, which was relatively easily
supported by 1 Thess. 2:14–16, Gal. 2:14–16, and Phil. 3:2ff., Paul argues in
chapter 2 like a Jewish preacher of judgment. [1] Verse 1 begins with a surprising, inferential "therefore." The conversation partner, who at first remains
anonymous, obviously agrees with Paul's argument up to this point. But in the
opinion of the apostle, in his agreement with God's judgment over the Gentiles
he has already caught himself (similar to David in Nathan's famous parable
from 2 Samuel 12), because he does the same as they do: He sins intentionally
(see above). Paul reserves the more precise support for this assertion until vv.
17ff. [2] First, he continues his rebuke. The fact that God judges the sinner who
(intentionally) does evil is not a matter of dispute among Jews and Christians.
They know it from the Holy Scriptures which are read by both (cf. v. 6). [3, 4]
Therefore Paul can pose two critical questions to his conversation partner,
which everyone who is versed in Scripture would recognize as typical questions
from one Jew to another. If the conversation partner does the same thing as the
Gentiles, it is impossible for him to hope to escape the judgment of God. He
should not deceive himself away from the fact that the patience of God which

still holds sway over him is only intended to provide him with an opportunity for repentance! [5] If he does not exercise such repentance, the wrath of God will be unleashed against him all the more because of his impenitence. The guilt of the conversation partner thus consists in Israel's well-known attitude of "hardening and impenitence" (cf. Deut. 31:27). It will find its response on the day of judgment. In accordance with early Jewish apocalyptic tradition, Paul calls this day, which is termed by the prophets the "day of God" (Joel 2:1f.; Amos 5:18ff.), the day of wrath and revelation of the righteous judgment of God. On this day, no repentance, prayer, intercession, or advocacy from the Fathers, prophets, or the righteous will find favor any more before God; at that time there remains only the judgment of destruction over the wicked and the verdict concerning the righteous (cf. 4 Ezra 7:33ff.; 2 Bar. 85:12–15). [6] Or, as Paul says with a citation from Prov. 24:12 (Ps. 62:13), God will then give "to each one according to his works" what is due him. In one's works it becomes evident whether a person obeys or not. On the day of the righteous judgment of God, that is, of that judgment which destroys all evil, every individual will receive in accordance with his works: [7, 8] The one who toiled patiently for the good, which is God's will, will receive glory and honor and an immortal nature; in contrast, destruction threatens the evildoer (Dan. 12:2f.), who opposes the claim of God out of haughty selfishness (cf. 2 Bar. 48:40). [9, 10] Or, as Paul once again enjoins, affliction and inescapable destruction will strike the doer of evil, but the doer of good will share in glory and salvation. Both times the apostle adds, "to the Jew first, but also to the Greek." Because the Jew belongs to God's chosen people (cf. Sir. 17:17), the judgment of God strikes him first (cf. Amos 3:2). But the Greek (Gentile) also cannot avoid this judgment, because he too owes worship and obedience to the creator. [11] God's judgment is impartial. The Jew carries no more weight in this judgment than the Greek; the only thing that counts is the weight of the good and bad works. With this evaluation, Paul sharpens the expectation of judgment in a radical way that is similar to that of the apocalyptic tradition (see above) and to John the Baptist (cf. Mtt. 3:9 par.). Nothing indicates that Paul intends his statements only to be taken hypothetically. The final judgment according to works is and remains the point of departure, and (also), at the same time, the overall horizon for his preaching of justification. The next verses demonstrate this.

2.2. 2:12–16. The Criterion of Judgment

(12) Whoever, namely, has sinned without the Law, will also come into ruin without the Law; and whoever has sinned under the Law, will be judged by the Law. (13) For the hearers of the Law are not just before God, but the doers of the Law will be justified. (14) If Gentiles, namely, who do not have the Law, do on the basis of nature what the Law demands, then they, who do not have the Law, are a Law unto themselves; (15) they, the ones who show the work of the Law as written in their hearts, when their conscience bears

witness for them and their thoughts reciprocally accuse and defend them, —
(16) on the day when God will judge that which is hidden within man according to my gospel through Jesus Christ.

A. Verse 16 presents a problem for the interpretation of the text in regard to
its content; but this is no reason to regard it as a gloss from a later copier of Romans who has in mind 1 Cor. 4:5 (see below). These verses refer back to 2:1–11,
comprise a self-contained context, and explain the criterion according to which
God will judge Jews and Gentiles on the day of judgment, namely, according to
the demands of the Law. Verse 13 offers the apostle's main thesis, v. 16 his
pointed concluding observation.

The main thoughts of the text have been prepared for by Jewish tradition.
The fact that God will judge the world according to the criterion of the Law is a
common Jewish perspective (cf. 4 Ezra 7:37, 70–73; 2 Bar. 48:27, 38–40, 46f.).
With the help of the equation already known to us of the creative word, wisdom, and the Law (see above, pp. 35f.), early Judaism accepted the philosophical thesis of the Stoics that the truly wise person has no need of any written Law
when he or she follows the unwritten Law of nature, which rules through reason. In 2 Bar. 57:2 it says concerning Abraham's time that "at that time the unwritten Law was generally known among them, and the works of the
commandments were accomplished at that time, and faith in the future judgment was born at that time." According to rabbinic reckoning, the Law consists
of 248 commands and 365 prohibitions, 613 instructions all together. Correspondingly, it says in the Targum to Gen. 1:27 that a person is created out of
248 members and 365 arteries (Tg. Yer. to Gen. 1:27). "On the basis of nature,"
that is, with every fiber of his being, the person must thus follow the Law. What
the person does and what he or she neglects to do, truth and falsehood, cannot
remain hidden before God, because they are written concerning the person on
(in) the heart (cf. T. Jud. 20:3f. with Jer. 31:33). It is a matter of the conscience
to weigh out reasonably between the good and the evil, to accuse the person inwardly, and to admonish one to repent (T. Jud. 20:1f.; Philo, *Decal.* 87). Moreover, the way in which the Gentiles will accuse and defend themselves with
their deliberations on judgment day before the judgment seat of the Son of
Man can be beautifully illustrated on the basis of 1 Enoch 63:1–12.

Paul stands at the point where this early Jewish tradition comes together and
argues by using it in favor of his gospel. What is striking is the detail with which
the apostle enters into the judgment (also) of the Gentiles in vv. 12, 14 + 15.
This copiousness, together with the pointed speech concerning "my gospel" in
v. 16, is explained by the acute circumstances surrounding the discussion (in
Rome). Ever since the controversy in Galatia, his Jewish-Christian opponents
have reproached Paul with the rebuke that he accommodates his gospel to the
wishes of the morally weak Gentiles and thus makes Christ into a "servant of
sin" (Gal. 1:10; 2:17) with his doctrine of grace. He declares in these verses that

this is precisely what he does not do. With his accusation against "the" Jew (in Rom. 2:1, 17), Paul has that Jewish Christian in view who is criticizing his preaching all the way to Rome.

B. Verse 12 forms a carefully crafted antithetical parallelism: [12] Whoever has sinned without knowledge of the Jewish Law, will be delivered up (by God) to corruption as a lawless evildoer. Every pious Jew could affirm this statement, which was aimed against the Gentiles; it is verified in a Jewish context in 2 Bar. 48:38–40. But the pious Jew must also accept the second half of the parallelism: Whoever has sinned under the knowledge of the Law (revealed to Israel at Sinai), will be judged according to this very Law, given by God (or by the one who has been messianically commissioned by God). The Law is the eschatological criterion of judgment. The Law will determine which of the deeds done by mankind will experience recognition or rejection before the judgment seat of God. [13] As a result, the following legal maxim holds good: at the judgment what counts is not simply the knowledge of the Law and the determined desire to keep it (cf. for this Sir. 15:15), but only the completed deed, which the Law requires. This too corresponds to the Jewish-apocalyptic view (cf. 4 Ezra 7:35; 2 Bar. 85:12f.) and was clearly known to the Christians from John the Baptist (Mtt. 3:9f. par.) and Jesus (Mtt. 25:31–46). "To be justified" means for Paul to receive the verdict of being "just" before God's eschatological judgment seat and with it to obtain a share in God's glory and his eternal kingdom.

[14] Paul now continues to speak more precisely of God's incorruptible judgment of the "lawless" Gentiles (v. 12) with a sentence clearly connected to vv. 12f. with "namely." While Israel was deemed worthy of the revelation of the Law (cf. 9:4), the Gentiles lack the Law's revelation. But by virtue of their having been created according to the standard of wisdom (which according to Sir. 24:23ff. is manifest in the Law), they themselves can by all means declare what is good and evil. [15] The Lord God has written for them in their hearts what the Law demands (already at the creation). The testimony of this will be the stirrings of the Gentiles' consciences when they launch forth into critical reflection, either out of regret or despair, [16] on that day when God will judge through Jesus Christ that which people would gladly keep hidden. Paul then adds to this that "my" gospel, that is, the gospel which is entrusted to me to preach, speaks, by all means, of precisely this judgment of God through Jesus Christ! If one takes into consideration the acute situation of dialogue which surrounds the letter to the Romans, v. 16 can be easily understood in the sense of a rhetorical (sarcastic) remark against Paul's critics (from 3:8). Paul does not preach cheap grace for the Gentiles, as they maintain, but according to his gospel God will judge Jews and Gentiles through Jesus Christ in accordance with the legal demand of the Law. In v. 16, 1 Cor. 4:4f. (and 2 Cor. 5:10) are again taken up. But rather than being a gloss from a later copyist of Romans, as many exegetes suppose, we have here before us, as Schlatter already saw, an emphasized remark from the apostle. Also according to Paul's gospel, Christ is

the judge of the world who will carry out the judgment according to works in accordance with the criterion of the Law. It is impossible and unthinkable for the apostle to conceive of a proclamation of justification without the expectation that Gentiles, Jews, and Christians must appear before the judgment seat of Christ and there be responsible for their deeds.

This concise text gives reason to consider two questions by way of summary. First, there is the question of the "natural" knowledge of God and the consciousness of good and evil among the Gentiles. Second, there is the question of the judgment according to works, which is even more important for an understanding of the Pauline gospel of justification.

Excursus 4:
The Natural Knowledge of God

For Paul and his time the question concerning the Gentiles' natural knowledge of God was not yet a fundamental theological question, but a practical problem for missions. Because the apostle distinguished himself and the Christian community not only from the way of thinking and life of the Gentiles, but also from those Jews who reject the gospel (cf., e.g., 1 Cor. 5:7f.; 6:2, 9–11, 20; 2 Cor. 6:14–7:1), he had to ask himself how he should encounter the Gentiles in his mission and what stand he should take concerning their piety and morals. Many missionaries to the Gentiles adopted the principle from the Jewish mission that a critical evaluation of Hellenistic education and its philosophical ethic was necessary. This was also true for Paul and his co-workers. The apostle demanded from the Gentiles the strict renunciation of idol worship and the turning to the one and only true God (1 Thess. 1:9). He severely condemned the (in-part) lax morality of the Gentiles (cf. 1 Cor. 5:9ff.; Gal. 2:15; Rom. 1:18–32). But he also recognized that there is a pronounced consciousness of good and evil among the Gentiles that even Christians can take as an example (cf. 1 Cor. 5:1; Phil. 4:8f.). Because Paul adopts the view of the early Jewish wisdom theology, according to which God created the world through his creative word (which is identical with wisdom) and thus imprinted all of his creation with a sense of God and of that which he desires (cf. Prov. 8:12–36; Job 28; Sir. 24:1–6; Wis. 7:15–8:1; 9:1–3), he can positively address the Gentiles on the basis of the knowledge of God from the works of creation, which they neglect (1 Cor. 1:21; Rom. 1:18ff.; 2:14f.). Or else— as worked out literarily in an artistic manner by Luke in Acts 17:16–31— he could attempt to lead their thinking, already formed by an understanding of God the creator, over to the obedience of faith in Christ (2 Cor. 10:5). Because Paul recognized in Christ the creative wisdom of God (1 Cor. 1:30; 2:6ff.), he confessed, as a result of his faith in Christ,

God as the creator and Jesus Christ as the mediator of the old and new creation (1 Cor. 8:6; Col. 1:15–20). In 2 Cor. 4:6 he describes the knowledge of God and of Christ which has led him since his calling to be an apostle in the following way: "For the God who spoke then, 'Let light shine from the darkness!' (Gen. 1:3), he has shone in our hearts for the illumination of the knowledge of the glory of God on the face of Jesus Christ." It is this knowledge of Christ and of God that gives the apostle the possibility of speaking, in a critically reasonable way, of the natural knowledge of God and of the good which is granted to the Gentiles and of viewing the created world as upheld by the wisdom of God.

Excursus 5:
Judgment according to Works

The expectation of the return (= parousia) of Christ at the end of time and of the final judgment according to works, which takes place on "the day of the Lord" (1 Thess. 5:2; 1 Cor. 5:5; 2 Cor. 1:14; Phil. 1:6, 10; 2:16), characterizes Paul's letters as a whole (cf. besides Rom. 2:1–16, 1 Cor. 3:12–15; 4:4f.; 2 Cor. 5:10; Rom. 14:10–12, to name just a few). Paul looked forward eagerly to these final events throughout his life (cf. 1 Thess. 4:15ff.; 1 Cor. 7:29ff.; Rom. 13:11ff.) and expected from them the definitive realization of salvation for those who believe (Phil. 3:20f.; Rom. 8:23; 13:11), for Israel (Rom. 11:26ff.), and for creation as a whole, which was subjected to futility with Adam's Fall (Rom. 8:19–22). In a typically biblical manner, the final judgment is also for the apostle not a divine act of revenge, but the longed-for event in which the salvific righteousness of God is definitively carried through over against all the powers of evil (cf. 1 Cor. 15:24–28, 54f.; Rom. 8:38f.).

Inasmuch as the apostle shares this (positive) expectation of judgment with the late strata of the Old Testament and the Jewish-apocalyptic tradition, the language in which he speaks of judgment is cast entirely in terms of those sources. Paul can speak of "the judgment seat of God" (Rom. 14:10 compared with Dan. 7:9) and of "the judgment seat of Christ" (2 Cor. 5:10 compared to 1 Enoch 62:2ff.) at the same time because he takes as his starting point, together with the Jewish tradition and the Jesus tradition (cf. Mk. 13:26 par; Mtt. 25:31–46), that the final judgment will be accomplished through God's chosen messiah. Jesus, who is exalted at the right hand of God, is this chosen messiah (cf. Phil. 2:6–11; Rom. 1:3f.). That God will judge every individual according to his or her conduct is just as characteristic of the Old Testament (cf. Ps. 62:13; Prov. 24:12; Job 34:11; Sir. 16:14) as it is of early Jewish literature (cf. Jub. 5:15; 1 Enoch 100:7) and of early Christian tradition in general (cf. Rev. 2:23; 20:12f.).

The same is true concerning the language of God's impartiality (cf. Deut. 10:17; Sir. 35:12; Ps. Sol. 2:18; 1 Pet. 1:17). Against this same background, "works" are those deeds which show a person to be righteous or godless. The "works of the Law" refer in Paul's writings (Gal. 2:16; Rom. 3:20, 28), as also in the Jewish tradition (cf. 4Qflor. 1:7 and 2 Bar. 57:2), to the fulfillment of individual commandments, while "the work" of a Christian (1 Cor. 3:13) designates the totality of his works. Paul is just as sure that one's good work will be rewarded by God on judgment day and that evil will be requited by the same God, as he is familiar with the (Jewish) conception that the works of mankind are recorded in heaven (Dan. 7:10; Rev. 20:12). In this way, the unrepentant person is storing up for himself or herself wrath for the day of wrath (Rom. 2:5), while the apostle hopes that he and all those who do God's will will receive from God a reward (1 Cor. 3:8, 14; 9:17f.), praise (1 Cor. 4:5), and honor (1 Cor. 9:15f.; Phil. 2:16). Paul's letters give no reason to abolish this conceptual world as "pre-Christian" or "merely Jewish." The apostle did not perceive it as a contradiction to his preaching of justification. Rather, he developed his gospel within precisely this horizon of expectation. But the interpretation of Paul must also remain faithful to Paul in showing, without hiding it, that nowhere in his extant letters does he draw a systematically rounded out picture of the final judgment. He limits himself much more to making clear individual aspects of his expectation concerning the last judgment.

The criterion of the last judgment will be the will of God as it is expressed in the Law (Rom. 2:12-16). The Jews know the Law from the revelation on Sinai (cf. Exod. 19:1-20:21); the Gentiles can perceive God's will from the works of creation and be led by their conscience to that which is good; the Christians satisfy the instruction of Christ by the power of the Holy Spirit (Gal. 6:2) and thereby fulfill the just requirement of the Law (Gal. 5:14; Rom. 8:4). Paul can thus justifiably say that Jews, Gentiles, and Christians will be judged according to the criterion of the Law, that is to say, by Christ (Rom. 2:16).

In the final judgment, one's works, as a visible expression of the nature of a person, are evaluated. What is pleasing before God is rewarded; what is evil or was neglected, will be punished. Paul reckons with good and bad works among Christians and non-Christians (1 Cor. 3:14f.; 2 Cor. 5:10; Rom. 2:9f.) and expressly summons his congregations to do that which is good (Gal. 5:16-26; 1 Cor. 6:7-11; Phil. 2:12f.; Rom. 12:2).

But the apostle is also acquainted with the Old Testament and Jewish perception of God as "the one who makes hearts known" and sees what is hidden (cf. Rom. 2:16 and 1 Cor. 4:5 with Acts 1:24; 15:8; Jer. 17:10; Prov. 17:3; Sir. 23:19f.). On this basis he already knows that in God's presence a person is more than individual works or the sum of his or her deeds as they become known in the final judgment (1 Cor. 3:15; 5:5; 11:32). This means that the one who is under the power of sin cannot be freed from his or her sinful nature and attain a pardon at the final judgment through individual good works and the "works of the Law" (Gal. 2:16; Rom. 3:20; 9:32). The only one who can hope for such a pardon, or indeed "glory and honor" (Rom. 2:10), is the one to whom God the creator grants, as an act of free grace, a new nature in righteousness and the spiritual ability to do what is right, and then establishes at the judgment an advocate at his or her side, against whom no accuser can appear.

According to Paul, this is precisely what happens in Christ. By virtue of the atoning death of Jesus, sinners obtain liberation from sin and acquire a new nature in righteousness (cf. 2 Cor. 5:17, 21). The Spirit then enables the Christian to fulfill the just requirement of the Law (Gal. 5:18, 22ff.; Rom. 8:4ff.). And finally, Christ, the one who was given over to death and then raised "for us," steps in at the final judgment as an advocate for those who believe (cf. Rom. 8:34; Heb. 7:25; 9:24; 1 John 2:1f.; Rev. 3:5). The gospel thus proclaims salvation from destruction under God's judgment of wrath to everyone who believes.

Paul was not yet, by far, confronted with the phenomenon of Christian sin to the degree that Augustine was, or the Reformers were, or we are in the present. But he had already clearly experienced it with the Corinthians (1 Cor. 5:1–5; 6:1–11) and with his opponents (cf. Phil. 1:15–17; 3:18ff., to give just one example). For Paul there was no salvation possible in the case of a believer who impugns or repudiates the gospel (Gal. 1:8; 2 Cor. 11:4, 13–15; Phil. 3:18f.). But as long as faith and the gospel remain valid, Christ also remains at work for sinners (Rom. 8:39). They may therefore anticipate their acceptance at the judgment, after they have borne the punishment for their sins and omissions (cf. 1 Cor. 3:15; 5:5; 11:32). Hence, in view of these bold statements, the apostle did not grant a license to sin, nor did he mitigate the sharp point of his declarations concerning judgment. For Paul, God, the Lord, and Christ, his messianic Son, will not allow themselves to be mocked (1 Cor. 12:3; Gal. 6:7ff.; Rom. 3:5–8). God has entrusted the final judgment to his Son (Rom. 2:16). This means that no one can enter into glory by bypassing Christ. Entering into the glory of God depends, rather, on every individual seeking and finding in Christ his or her merciful Lord and judge. It is this fact which gives inner suspense to the life of all those who approach judgment day (Phil. 2:12; 3:12–21).

2.3. 2:17–29. The Guilt of the Jews

(17) But whenever you call yourself a Jew and entrust yourself to the Law and boast concerning God (18) and know God's will and, as one who has been instructed by the Law, test what matters, (19) and trust yourself to be a guide to

the blind, a light for those in darkness, (20) a correcter of those who do not understand, a teacher of those not yet of age, someone who possesses in the Law the fundamental framework of knowledge and truth —: (21) You who teach another, do you not teach yourself? You who preach not to steal, do you steal? (22) You who demand that marriage not be broken, do you commit adultery? You who abhor idols, do you rob temples? (23) You who boast in the Law, do you dishonor God through the breaking of the Law? (24) Truly, "The name of God is blasphemed among the Gentiles because of you," just as it is written! (25) For circumcision is indeed of value, if you obey the Law; but if you are a transgressor of the Law, your circumcision has become uncircumcision. (26) Now, if the uncircumcision keep the legal demands of the Law, will not then the uncircumcision of such a (one) be regarded as circumcision? (27) And the uncircumcised according to their natural condition who carry out the Law will judge you who, with the letter and circumcision, are nevertheless a transgressor of the Law. (28) Because he is not a Jew who is (one) visibly, and also the circumcision which takes place visibly in the flesh (is) not (circumcision); (29) but the one who (is a Jew) inwardly is a Jew and the circumcision of the heart, in the Spirit and not according to the letter, is circumcision; whose praise (comes) not from men, but from God.

Verse 24: Is. 52:5.

A. The structure of the text is easy to recognize. Verses 17–20 comprise a rhetorical unit whose content crescendos as it sketches out the claim of the Jews over against the Gentiles. In v. 21 the sentence construction changes to a direct accusation in the form of rhetorical questions. In v. 24 the accusation is supported with a quotation from Scripture. Verse 25 begins a paragraph which runs parallel to vv. 12–16 and places the Jew next to the Gentile from the vantage point of the final judgment: Only the one who has kept the legal requirements of the Law will receive praise from God. But who this will be is determined not on the basis of the external condition of circumcision or uncircumcision, but from the perspective of the circumcision of the heart, which is demonstrated in deeds of obedience.

Paul again argues here as a preacher of judgment, in accordance with an exact knowledge of Jewish claims and tradition. The claim of the Jewish mission, reflected in vv. 17–20, to lead Gentiles out of darkness, the worship of idols, and impurity, into the light and truth is based on Is. 42:6f.; 49:6 and may be directly verified from Hellenistic-Jewish missionary writings such as Joseph and Aseneth (cf. there 8:5–9). The esteem for the Law in v. 20 is attested in Bar. 3:37–4:4; 2 Bar. 44:14; 48:22–24. The arguments in vv. 21–23 correspond to inner Jewish judgment speeches as we know them from the so-called Deuteronomic tradition, prayers for penitence, and testamentary admonitions (cf., e.g., Ps. Sol. 8:7–13; T. Naph. 4:1; 8:6; 4 Ezra 8:20–36; Josephus, *Ant.* 4.207). Deuteronomy 30:6, Jub. 1:23, and 1QS 5:5f. already refer to the necessity of circumcision of the heart. But the fact that Paul extensively relativizes circumcision, which was viewed by the Jews as a seal of the Abrahamic covenant (cf. Gen. 17:1–27), and elevates those Gentiles who follow God's will as judges over the Judaism which departs from the Law, goes beyond even the most radical Jewish texts on judgment such as 4 Ezra 7:33ff. and 2 Bar. 85:12ff. It has its model, rather, only in John the Baptist's preaching of repentance (Lk. 3:7–9 par.) and in the message of Jesus. According to early Jewish expectation, the righteous will one day execute judgment over sinners (and the Gentile nations) (cf. Dan. 7:22, 27; Wis. 3:7f.; 1 Enoch 90:19; 95:3). Jesus speaks, however, of the judgment of repentant Gentiles over unrepentant Jews (Lk. 11:31f. par.) and promises his followers participation in the reign of the Son of Man (cf. Lk. 12:32 with Dan. 7:18, 22). As 1 Cor. 6:2 indicates, Jesus' promise is carried over in Paul's mission to Christians who have been sanctified by virtue of their baptism (cf. 1 Cor. 6:11 and Rev. 20:4). In our context, Paul returns to this Christian expectation. With his argument Paul intends not only to demonstrate the guilt of the Jews, but also implicitly to silence the claims of those Jewish-Christian opponents who, according to 3:8, are "slandering" him.

B. Ever since 2:1f., Paul has left it open in what way the person whom he addressed critically "does the same thing" as the Gentiles who deliberately violate God's demand. The apostle now clarifies this point. [17–20] Paul's conversation partner is that Jew who fulfills the claim characteristic of the Jewish mission of Paul's day. He desires to bring to the Gentiles the light of the knowledge of God (cf. Is. 42:6f.; 49:6); through his teaching he would like to lead them from a position of immaturity and lack of understanding to an understanding of the truth of God as it has been prescribed and entrusted to him in the Law of Sinai. [21–23] But in doing so he overlooks the glaring contradiction between his claim and his own behavior. He himself lives at this time in "all the depravity of the Gentiles" (T. Naph. 4:1). He boasts, over against the Gentiles, in the Law: "We Israelites are fortunate, because it has been made known to us what pleases God!" (Bar. 4:4), and then dishonors God through his transgression of the Law. [24] In Paul's Greek Bible such behavior is branded as Israel's blaspheming the name of God (i.e., his holy reality) among the Gentiles (Is. 52:5). Naturally, these sentences are formulated just as generally as the accusations against the Gentiles in 1:18–32. Moreover, they derive their severity from the inevitability of the coming judgment of God, to which the Jewish sources already point.

The following statements of Paul are also formulated in view of the final judgment, which gives his accusations against the Jews their final edge. [25] Circumcision, that is, the sign that one belongs to God's chosen people, is only effective for salvation when the covenant obligation in the form of the Law is also kept. Where it is transgressed, circumcision becomes a burden (see below to 3:3). [26] If, on the other hand, uncircumcised Gentiles fulfill the legal requirements of the Law, God will value their uncircumcision as circumcision; that is, they will be incorporated into the chosen people of God (made up of Gentiles and Jews). But there is still more. [27] The Gentiles who are obedient to God will sit in judgment over those Jews who, in spite of their knowledge of the Law, which has been written and entrusted to them, and in spite of their circumcision, are transgressors of the Law. Here Paul develops further what Jesus had already proclaimed (Lk. 11:31f. par.). [28, 29] The true Jew, who will receive praise before God, is not simply the Jew who bears in his flesh circumcision as the sign of the covenant, but is that Jew who has received from God the Spirit and circumcision of the heart so that he no longer turns away from his creator (cf. Jub. 1:23).

These verses have been misused in Christian ecclesiastical tradition as an anti-Semitic placard for describing a heretic. As a result of their relativizing of the Jewish claim to election they go to the limit and beyond that which is bearable for Jews. But as spoken by the Jew, Paul, over against Jews, their original purpose is not to declare the election of Israel simply null and void, but to direct the Jews to the reality of the coming God, who indeed demands more from his chosen people than merely external obedience. The following verses demonstrate this with unmistakable clarity.

3. 3:1–8. Objections

Paul does not write the letter to the Romans as an abstract essay concerning his gospel, but as an account which is designed to convince the Roman Christians concerning the content and legitimacy of his gospel. This gospel appears to have been criticized all the way to Rome by Paul's Jewish-Christian opponents and their sympathizers as a message of cheap grace and the disavowal of Israel's election as God's own people. In view of this situation of critical dialogue between Paul and his opponents, it is completely understandable that in the course of his judgment speech against Gentiles and Jews (= 1:18–3:20) the apostle would take his stand not only indirectly (see above to 2:16), but also directly against the objections which have been made known to him. This is precisely what takes place in this paragraph. In the manner of thinking and arguing which has come to be associated with Paul, he will return once again to the theme of Israel's election in chapters 9–11, and to the rebuke that he preaches cheap grace in chapters 6 and 7. The present flow of Paul's argument thus merely clarifies the fronts for the first time, but precisely for this reason it is of special interest for the letter to the Romans as a whole.

(1) What then is the advantage of the Jew, or what good is circumcision? (2) Much in every respect! Above all, that they have been entrusted with the words of God. (3) To what end? If some have become unfaithful, will not their unfaithfulness then nullify the faithfulness of God? (4) By no means! Rather, may God show himself to be true, though every person be a liar, as it is written, "So that you are justified in your words and win the victory when one disputes

with you!" (5) But if our unrighteousness demonstrates the righteousness of God, what should we say: Is God then not unjust when he inflicts the judgment of wrath? I am speaking in a human manner. (6) By no means! For how should God (otherwise) judge the world? (7) But if the truthfulness of God has shown itself to abound to his glorification through my lies, why am I then still being judged as a sinner? (8) And (is it) perhaps (valid), as we are slandered and certain people maintain about us, that we have said, "Let us do evil, so that (thereby) good might come!"? Their condemnation is just!

Verse 4: Pss. 116:11; 51:6.

A. The structure of the text is as follows. In vv. 1 and 2 Paul responds to the questions which present themselves in connection with 2:25–29, namely, whether the privileged position of the Jews in relation to the Gentiles has henceforth become entirely untenable. To this is attached in vv. 3–4 and vv. 5–8 two rhetorical dialogues. In both cases they are concerned with the faithfulness and righteousness of God. Verse 8 shows that Paul must resist the slander of those people who maliciously condense his preaching into the statement, "Let us do evil, so that (thereby) good might come!" Paul's critics are most likely Jewish-Christian missionaries as we know them from Galatians, 2 Corinthians, and Philippians. They consider Paul's gospel to be a message which is tailored to the desires of the lawless Gentiles (Gal. 1:10), which renders harmless the judgment of God (see above to 2:16), and thus degrades Christ, or even God himself, as a "servant of sin" (Gal. 2:17). Because in his mission to the Gentiles Paul programmatically rejected circumcision (Gal. 2:3f.; 5:2, 6, cf. with Acts 15:1f., 28f.), almost as a matter of display devalued his own prior Jewish title of honor (Phil. 3:4–11), and apparently renounced the Law (Gal. 2:19; 1 Cor. 9:20), they also accused him at the same time of annulling Israel's privilege of election in relation to the Gentiles and of despising the Law. Against this background these verses become readily understandable. Paul is emphatically rejecting the objections of these people, who are striving to gain a hearing in Rome as well.

In so doing, Paul makes use in v. 4 of the early Jewish tradition of repentance and of Psalm 51, in which this tradition is employed and to which Jesus also alludes in Lk. 18:13. The one who prays in this psalm confesses before God, the judge, his misdeeds and guilt. But he also considers God's legal demand to be just (and hopes precisely thereby to receive mercy). Paul employs the Greek translation of Ps. 51:6 in order to establish that God is justified in his lawsuit with sinners and the manner in which it comes about. Verse 6 reads in the Septuagint: "Against you alone have I sinned and done evil before you, so that you are justified in your words and win the victory when one disputes with you." The "words of God" spoken here and in v. 2 are, according to their use in the language of the Greek Old Testament, above all the commandments of God, which were entrusted in a special way to Israel (cf. Exod. 20:1ff.; Deut. 4:30; 10:4; 33:9; Ps. 119:11, 67; Rom. 9:4).

B. The sharp argumentation of the apostle in 2:25–29 provokes the objection concerning [1] the remaining privilege of the Jews (over the Gentiles) and the advantage of circumcision under these circumstances. Paul does not formulate this objection on his own, but in view of the conflict with the Jewish-Christian missionaries that has been forced upon him by those who have established fronts against him as far as Rome. But his answer is now precisely not that the Jew no longer has any privilege over the Gentile and that circumcision is no longer of any value, but rather, [2] "Much in every respect!" The relativizing of the special claims of the Jews in view of the final judgment according to works in no way means for Paul that Jews and Gentiles were equal in terms of the history of election. Rather, the Jew enjoyed over against the Gentile, "above all," the continuing privilege that "the words of God" (= commandments) were entrusted to him (cf. 2:20; 9:4 and Acts 7:38). (Paul spares himself the naming of Israel's further privileges until 9:4f., where he picks up anew the thread of conversation which is begun here.) Within the context of the judgment speech this one statement is sufficient: Israel knows God's legal demands from the Law, and circumcision aligns Israel symbolically with her God. [3] Both place Israel especially under obligation and do not create for her a particularly generous right to freedom (cf. Amos 3:2). On the basis of this (prophetic) argumentation Paul can reject the first objection of his critics, that is, that he leaves out of consideration God's special relationship of faithfulness to his chosen people. In view of the coming judgment the exact opposite is the case: The unfaithfulness of some of the Jews, whom Paul branded in 2:1–29, in no way nullifies God's faithfulness and reliability toward Israel. [4] Just the opposite! It is precisely in the judgment that God will show himself to be true, though every sinner is shown to be an unreliable liar in accordance with the witness of the Scripture. According to Ps. 51:6, God will be victorious in his lawsuit with the sinner, and his words (= commandments) will be recognized as just and dependable! [5] Paul thus holds fast to God's faithfulness (expressed to Israel in the exhortation of the Law) and to his words (= commandments).

In a second discourse, Paul now takes up the issue surrounding the fact that he does not preach cheap grace by circumlocuting God's judgment. But with the expression, "I am speaking in a human manner," Paul indicates that the following question was forced upon him: If according to Ps. 51:6 God's righteousness is brought into clear light in view of the injustice done by sinners, then is God not unjust if he nevertheless still inflicts his judgment of wrath on the sinner? Must he not rather forgive (cf. similarly 9:14)? The objector desires to establish that Paul makes God and his Christ into a "servant of sin" (Gal. 2:17). For years Paul preached the justification of the godless by God's free grace and presented himself as an example of it (cf. Gal. 2:15ff.; Phil. 3:7–11 with 1 Cor. 1:26–31; 2 Cor. 5:19–21). How can he then still speak seriously of God's judgment? [6] Paul goes on the defense anew: By no means is God unjust! How else other than in his righteousness, by which he creates the order of the world,

should God judge the world? That God is the just judge remains for Paul unshakably firm (cf. Gal. 6:7f.; Rom. 14:10). [7] The opponent of Paul persists in
his inquiry and even sharpens it further: If in the final judgment God's veracity
is only enhanced to his glory by the lies of the evildoers, then why is the sinner
still judged (rather than being saved)? The apostle then increases the present
objection still more, rhetorically, [8] by citing at this point the slanderous assertion which those from the side of his critics have attempted to hang on Paul. It
runs: "Let us simply do evil, so that good (in the form of God's grace) might
come!" Paul's answer is clear (and no less blunt than in Gal. 1:18): God's condemnation justly falls on whomever attributes to Paul this perspective! Paul
thus insists on the reality of God's judgment as in v. 6, only this time he does so
in order to consign his slanderers to this judgment. Nobody attributes to him
the message of cheap grace without being punished! God's righteousness is for
Paul, in good Old Testament fashion, closely related to God's faithfulness and
truthfulness (cf. Ps. 98:2f.). This righteousness first really comes to the fore in
God's lawsuit with sinners as that mode of behavior with which God creates
order in the world as its creator and judge and accomplishes the good. Only the
ones who acknowledge God and his commandments as trustworthy and just and
trust in Christ, who (by virtue of his atoning death) is established for those who
believe as their righteousness, sanctification, and redemption (1 Cor. 1:30), and
who is preached in the gospel as savior and Lord (Rom. 1:3f.; 16f.), escape the
destructive wrath of God. *This* is the Pauline message! Whoever maintains that
it is something different is a slanderer who has earned God's condemnation.

As a whole, the (Jewish-Christian) critics of Paul are thus harshly rejected.
But the apostle takes their statements so seriously that he will enter into debate
with them from now on again and again. Paul shows in detail in chapters 9–11
that he maintains Israel's privilege of election even beyond the judgment. Paul
has made it evident up to this point that he is indeed speaking about a final
judgment (according to works), and he will strengthen this point in the future.
From 3:21 until the end of chapter 8 the topic will repeatedly be that of respect
for God's commandments and of the grace of God, which is in no way cheap,
but costly. Finally, from chapter 12 on, the apostle expounds the obligation of
the congregation to a new way of life. His entire letter, therefore, is characterized by the effort to refute the accusations which have been raised against his
preaching and to show, moreover, what his gospel of the righteousness of God
in and through Christ is really about. But first, Paul brings his judgment speech
to an end by drawing out the final result of his argument as a whole.

4. 3:9–20. Jews and Gentiles under Sin

(9) What now? Are we making excuses? For sure, not! For we have already
raised the accusation that Jews and Greeks are both likewise under sin, (10)
as it is written, "There is no righteous person, not even a single one. (11)

There is no person of understanding; there is no one who seeks after God. (12) They have all turned away, they are depraved together. There is no one who acts with integrity; there is no one, not even one. (13) Their throat is an open grave. With their tongues they have deceived; venom (is) under their lips. (14) Their mouth is full of curses and bitterness. (15) Their feet (are) quick to shed blood, (16) desolation and misery (are) in their path, (17) and they have not known the way of peace. (18) There is no fear of God before their eyes." (19) But we know that what the Law says it says to those who (stand) under the Law, so that every mouth might be stopped and the whole world might be culpable before God. (20) For on the basis of the works of the Law no flesh will be justified before him, (rather), through the Law (comes only) the knowledge of sin.

Verse 10: Eccl. 7:20; Verses 11 + 12: Eccl. 7:20;
Ps. 14:1–3 (53:2–4); Verse 13: Pss. 5:10; 140:4; Verse 14:
Ps. 10:7; Verses 15–17: Is. 59:7 + 8 (Prov. 1:16); Verse 18: Ps. 36:2.

A. Paul brings his accusations (judgment speech) against Gentiles and Jews to a climax in these verses. Verse 9 is directly attached to 3:1–8 and at the same time casts an arc back to 2:12. Verses 10–18 offer scriptural proof for the Pauline accusations in the form of a chain of quotations. Verses 19–20 then draw the conclusion that the entire world is culpable before God; it is brought to the knowledge of sin through the Law, without being able to free itself from its entanglement in sin by virtue of the works which the Law itself commands.

The chain of quotations is ingeniously formed from citations from Ecclesiastes, Psalms, and the Prophets. It sketches in an intentionally generalized way the activity and omissions of the sinner and may have been taken over by Paul as a preformed tradition. In Justin's dialogue with the Jew, Tryphon (27:3), an almost identical chain of quotations is used in an accusation against the Jews. It is thus possible that Paul and Justin are both drawing from the treasure of citations used in Jewish and early Christian judgment speeches. It is certainly no accident that in vv. 19f. the apostle returns to theses which he had already advocated in Galatians (cf. Gal. 2:16; 3:22). The apostle continues to insist on his controversial teaching before the Christians in Rome!

B. Interpreters are divided over whether one should translate the introduction to these verses, [9] "What then? Do we have an advantage?" (so Wilckens and many others), or, as rendered above, "What now? Are we making excuses?" There are no lexical Greek parallels for the common translation chosen by Wilckens. Moreover, it clashes strongly with 3:1f., where Paul has just emphasized that the privileged position of the Jew persists before God. In contrast, the translation chosen here corresponds to common Greek usage and, in addition, fits in smoothly into the context. Paul has just entered explicitly into the objections of his Jewish-Christian opponents. With the (rhetorical) question of whether he intends to lose himself in a series of excuses, which is so easily understandable in this context, Paul turns back to the judgment speech which was broken off in 2:29 and comes to the conclusion of his accusations. Hence, there can be no talk of excuses. Rather, the accusation which was raised earlier by the apostle is that both Jews and Greeks are fallen under sin without exception. [10] That which the Scripture laments in the Psalms and through Isaiah is undeniably a present reality. [11] There are no righteous ones, no people of understanding, and no one who truly seeks after God. [12] They are all depraved by sin and no one does what is just before God. [13, 14] The sinners are full of fatal injustice in what they say and think. [15, 16] In the same way, their behavior is marked by violence and destruction. [17] They trespass in word (vv. 13f.) and deed (vv. 15f.), and accomplish nothing which is good. They do not desire to know anything concerning the divinely prescribed "way of peace," that is, concerning the way of life which leads to general well-being and serves salvation (cf. Lk. 1:79). [18] The fear of God is missing among sinners and with it—in terms of the Old Testament conception—the fundamental presupposition for being wise and acting justly (cf. Prov. 1:7).

[19] As a result, Paul can draw his conclusion. Because he knows that he has addressees before him in Rome who are well versed in the Law (cf. 7:1), Paul now resumes the "we" style: We know, that that which the Law says is said to those who live under and with the Law. According to 2:17–24 this is first of all the Jews. But according to 1:20f., 32; 2:14f., 26 this also includes the Greek Gentiles. "What the Law says" in this case means everything which is addressed in the testimony of Scripture in vv. 10–18. According to the Jewish conception, the entire Scripture interprets the Law testified to in the five books of Moses and therefore on occasion can simply be called as a whole, "the Law." For example, Paul adopts this use of language here and in 1 Cor. 14:21. The word of Scripture as an attestation of the Law thus makes it clear that the entire world is culpable before God. [20] In v. 20 Paul then answers the question of why the world is in this condition. He does so with the thesis which he already expressed in Gal. 2:16, which in turn is based on Ps. 143:2, and which was unusually provocative for his previous Jewish contemporaries in the flesh, as well as for his Jewish-Christian adversaries: "No flesh (i.e., no human being) will be declared righteous before God on the basis of works of the Law." Works of the Law are for Paul, as for the Judaism of his time (cf. 4Qflor. 1:7; 2 Bar. 57:2), the fulfillment of the commandments of the Law. This means, in Paul's day, concretely, that the observance of the Law's instructions as a whole, "the observance of the Torah in a comprehensive sense" (O. Hofius), does not lead, according to God's own will, to one's justification in the final judgment. With this view Paul goes beyond other similar-sounding early Jewish texts such as 1QH 4:29f.; 9:14f.; and 1 Enoch 81:5. They too explicitly acknowledge the guilty condition of humanity and are moved by it to repentance and trust in God's forgiveness, which provides

those who repent with new power for the fulfillment of the Law. But according to Paul, this continuously renewed conversion is not sufficient in view of God's unrelenting final judgment. According to the insight which he attained on the basis of Christ, the works of the Law can never free a person, before God, from the power of sin which determines one's life. Indeed, for the apostle the Law is and remains the special gift of God to Israel and to humanity as a whole (cf. 2:20; 3:1f.; 7:12, 14; 9:4). But it provides in and of itself neither the power for repentance, nor the ability to overcome sin. The Law cannot make a righteous person out of a sinner insofar as a righteous person—as the Targum to Is. 7:3; 10:21f.; 26:2 formulates it—is a person who "has not sinned" or "has turned away from sin" and "has kept the Law with one's whole heart." To the same degree that the legal maxim of 2:13 is valid, the Law is also unable to bestow upon the sinner the capacity to do the works which it commands "with the whole heart." To strive after or to hope for justification from works of the Law is therefore a dangerous illusion and misconstrual of mankind's fallen condition of guilt. A consideration of 1QpHab. 7:17–8:3; Ps. Sol. 9:4f.; 4 Ezra 13:23; 2 Bar. 84:5f.; 85:11f.; Tg. Is. 26:2f., on the one hand, and James 2:20–26; Heb. 11:17–19, on the other hand, indicates that with these statements the apostle has in view the counterclaims of Jews and Jewish Christians.

Paul will repeatedly take up the theme of the "Law and sin" throughout the letter to the Romans, a theme which was hotly contested between him, the Jews, and his Jewish-Christian opponents (cf. 4:15; 5:20, and above all, 7:7–25). But already at this point he makes clear where the real problem lies: The Law of God convicts people of sin. As long as sin reigns, it does not enable one to become righteous. For Paul (in this context and otherwise in his letters) sin is always more than merely an individual transgression against God's command. What is merely being expressed in the individual transgression is the fact that, ever since the Fall of the first human pair (cf. 5:12ff.; 7:7ff.), every person has been delivered over to sin as a deadly power. The Law makes one conscious of having been delivered over to sin, without being able itself to help one out of this distress. Jesus had already taught that it is impossible for people in the last judgment to pay God back a ransom for their forfeited lives before him (cf. Mk. 8:36f. with Ps. 49:8f.). Paul views the situation in exactly the same way. In the face of the Law's declaration of guilt, all people appear as sinners who will irretrievably fall under God's judgment of destruction.

With this, the apostle has reached the end of the accusation and judgment speech begun in 1:18. Without equating Gentiles and Jews in a way that is biblically untenable, he has established that both parts of humanity are inescapably subject to God's judgment of destruction. This judgment is already presently at work among the Gentiles, while it is still being withheld from Israel only because of God's patience. Paul's gospel, which was contested all the way to Rome, infers this precipitous insight from the fallen nature of all people, but it also proclaims and inaugurates the deliverance of all people through the righteousness of God for all those who believe. What he only indicated tersely in 1:16f., Paul thus now develops more precisely.

II. 3:21–5:21. The Righteousness of God as the Righteousness of Faith and the Ground of Reconciliation

The apostle now presents in five paragraphs the fact that the righteousness of God has been revealed in the atoning death of Jesus (3:21–26), that it applies in the same manner to Jews and Gentiles (3:27–31), that, according to Paul, Abraham is the father of the righteousness of faith (4:1–25), that those who have been justified may boast in the midst of suffering in God, who has reconciled them with himself in Christ (5:1–11), and that they stand under the reign of grace, which is stronger than death and sin (5:12–21).

1. 3:21–26. God's Righteousness in the Atoning Death of Christ

In the following six verses Paul expounds the definition of his gospel, which he gave in (1:1ff. and) 1:16f. One can thus designate Rom. 3:21–26, with good grounds, to be the heart of the letter to the Romans.

(21) But now, without the Law, the righteousness of God has been revealed, testified to by the Law and the Prophets, (22) that is, the righteousness of God through faith in Jesus Christ for all who believe. There is, namely, no difference: (23) They have all sinned, and all are missing the glory of God; (24) (but) they are justified freely by virtue of his grace through the redemption which (takes place) in Christ, (25) whom God publicly appointed to be the place of atonement, (which is accessible and effective) through faith by virtue of his blood, as a demonstration of his righteousness because of the forgoing of sins which previously took place (26) under the forbearance of God—for a demonstration of his righteousness at the present time, so that he (himself) might be just and declare the one to be just who (lives) from faith in Jesus.

Verse 25: Lev. 16:14–15 (Exod. 25:17–22).

A. Romans 3:21–26 is one of the most difficult passages to understand in the letter to the Romans in terms of its content. Nevertheless, the structure of its argument is clear. In vv. 21 and 22 Paul again picks up the formulations from 1:16f. and explains how to understand God's righteousness in a way which makes the gospel the saving power of God. In order to explain it, Paul attaches a sentence which extends from vv. 22–24. In it he establishes the necessity of justification and names as its ground the redemption brought about by God in Jesus Christ. Paul then explains in v. 25 and the beginning of v. 26, with the help of early Christian creedal statements, what is meant by "redemption in (or also: through) Christ Jesus." With the repetition of the phrase "for a demonstration of his righteousness . . ." (from v. 25), Paul then arrives at the goal of his statement in v. 26: God is the just one in that he himself has brought about redemption and justifies the one who lives from faith in Jesus Christ.

This summary text, with its uncommonly dense formulation, can be understood only if one takes into consideration that early Judaism conceived the consequences of the Fall in Genesis 3 to be the loss of (or also divestment of) the glorious manner of being as the creation of God in innocence and righteousness which belonged to the original human pair in paradise. In the so-called Apocalypse of Moses, Eve complains after the Fall that "in the same hour my eyes were opened, and I knew that I was stripped of the righteousness with which I was clothed. Then I cried and spoke (to the Tempter in the form of the snake): 'Why have you done that to me, so that I am alienated from my glory, with which I was clothed?' " A little while later Adam joins in this complaint when he says to Eve, "[W]hat have you done to us there? You have alienated me from the glory of God!" (Apoc. Mos. 20f.). In Rom. 3:23, Paul proceeds on the basis of this conception.

The ornate style of vv. 25 and 26 and the manner of expression in these verses, which is seldom used by Paul, are best explained when the apostle is seen to be appropriating and commenting on Christian doctrinal tradition, as he has already similarly done in Rom. 1:3f. Paul presumably became acquainted with it in Antioch. The tradition most likely originally went like this: "God publicly appointed (the crucified) Christ to be a monument of atonement by virtue of his blood, (that is) for a demonstration of his (= God's) righteousness because of the forgoing of the sins which took place under the forbearance of God." The Greek expression ἱλαστήριον (hilastērion), translated by us with "the place of atonement," is based on the Hebrew word kapporet (just as it is in Heb. 9:5). According to Exod. 25:17–22, the kapporet is the covering of the ark, which existed hidden in the holy of holies of the Tent of Meeting (and later of the first temple in Jerusalem). Two cherubim were mounted symmetrically on this covering (as bearers of the invisible throne of God). The kapporet served a double purpose. From it God encountered his people with his revealed word (cf. Exod. 25:22), and before it the high priest conducted once a year, on the so-called Great Day of Atonement, the holiest cultic ritual known to Israel, the absolving of the people of God. The basic procedures of this ritual are depicted in Leviticus 16; it was regularly performed in the Jerusalem temple until A.D. 70 (thus long past the time of the composition of the letter to the Romans). All Jews in the motherland or in foreign countries knew Leviticus 16 from their instruction in the synagogue. According to this text, after the high priest brought about atonement for himself, he accomplished atonement for the people through sprinkling the blood of the ram of the sin offering seven times on and before the kapporet. The atonement itself is an act of sacrificial dedication established by God and accomplished by the priest; it is brought about through the medium of blood as the bearer of life (cf. Lev. 17:11). In the blood of the sin offering of the ram, which has been slaughtered as a substitute for Israel, the life of the people of God (through the mediating action of the high priest) is sacrificed to God. On the basis of this sacrifice, Israel receives forgiveness of her sins and new life in fellowship with God.

The creedal text incorporated by Paul uses this famous Old Testament model in order to make clear what took place according to God's will on Golgotha. The yearly ritual of atonement in the temple, hidden from the eyes of God's people, is now replaced by the atonement brought about publicly once for all time by God himself through the cross of Christ. From it the eschatological people of God are born. "Good Friday" becomes the Great Day of Atonement of the Christian community. Moreover, the radical critique of the sacrificial cult of atonement in the Jerusalem temple, which is implicit in this new interpretation, may be traced back to Stephen and his followers (cf. Acts 6:13f.). After his martyrdom and the expulsion of the Stephen-circle from Jerusalem, this tradition appears to have reached Antioch through the dispersed members of this circle (cf. Acts 11:19ff.). It is there that Paul becomes acquainted with it and probably also with those unknown missionaries who brought the Christian faith to Rome. If this is correct, the apostle refers back consciously in Rom. 3:25f. to statements of the faith that unite him with the Roman Christians. Hence, the translation of *hilastērion* with "sacrifice of atonement" or also "means of atonement," often chosen in commentaries and editions of the Bible, has no direct support in the Greek sources and can only be derived hypothetically by reference to the description of the death of the Jewish martyrs on behalf of Israel in 4 Macc. 17:20–22. But because it is philologically uncertain and inadequate in terms of content—throughout the New Testament Jesus is more than merely a Jewish (prophetic) martyr—we do not follow this interpretation here.

B. With the introductory phrase "but now," the apostle intentionally marks the decisive transition from 3:19–20: [21] While Gentiles and Jews have inescapably fallen under the judgment of God's wrath, God has presently raised up salvation in and through Jesus Christ. The righteousness of God has been revealed without the doing of the Law, but it is indeed attested to by the Law and the Prophets. The designation "the Law and the Prophets" refers to the Holy Scripture of the Old Testament (cf. 4 Macc. 18:10; John 1:45; Acts 13:15); their testimony confirms the revelation of the righteousness of God as a valid act of God. Paul may have in view here passages such as Exod. 34:5–7; Is. 11:4f.; 43:25; 45:6–8; Jer. 23:5f.; Hab. 2:4 and naturally also the promise to Abraham from Gen. 15:6 (cf. below under chapter 4). Moreover, according to vv. 25f., Leviticus 16 has found its surpassing fulfillment in Golgotha. The revelation of the righteousness of God conforms therefore to the acts of God described and promised in the Law and the Prophets. As in 1:17, the "righteousness of God" also refers here [22] to the act of God which procures righteousness for the sinner at the judgment, that is, under the aspect of faith. Because the "works of the Law" do not help the sinner attain righteousness at the judgment (3:19f.), God has opened up the way of salvation in the form of faith. The righteousness of God is attained "through faith in Jesus Christ," and it remains open "for all who believe." With this Paul explains what is meant by "from faith to faith" in Rom. 1:17. Whoever believes in Jesus Christ as one's redeemer and Lord is granted righteousness by God on the basis of this faith. Salvation in the final judgment thus consists of the righteousness of God which is granted on the basis of faith, to all who believe, without distinction in regard to their descent or their standing before God. This righteousness of God causes the Pauline gospel to be the saving power of God.

[23] Furthermore, all are in need of it. As Paul established in detail in 1:18–3:20, they are sinners without exception. Ever since the expulsion of Adam and Eve from paradise they have lacked the glory of God, that is, the character of existence of God's innocent creation, which according to Jewish tradition is identical with righteousness (cf. Apoc. Mos. 20f.). This loss cannot be made up for by human endeavor. [24] Instead, sinners are justified on the basis of God's free resolution to extend grace "for free," that is, without one's own action, through "the redemption" which God brought about in and through Jesus Christ. For Israel, God's work of redemption consists essentially of the liberation of Israel from the slavery of guilt in Egypt (cf. Deut. 7:8; 9:26; 13:6, among others); for the new people of God made up of Jews and Gentiles, the foundational event from which everything begins is the redemption through Christ. [25] The apostle now explains how this redemption took place with the help of the doctrinal tradition known to him (and to the Romans, from Antioch or even Jerusalem; see above). Paul affirms this tradition, comments upon it from the perspective of his gospel, and elevates it to the central christological statement of his gospel concerning the righteousness of God. God has thereby completed and brought to an end the sacrificial cult of atonement in the Jerusalem temple in that he has publicly appointed Jesus (on Golgotha) to be the place of atonement for all who believe. The Christian's *kapporet* no longer exists hidden in the holy of holies of the temple, but is revealed to all in the form of Christ hanging on the cross. In this Christ, God draws near to his people and speaks to them as he did previously from the *kapporet* (cf. Exod. 25:22). For the Christians, therefore, there is no longer any need for a priestly mediation between the God who is encountered in secret and the people of God who exist outside in front of the temple. They now encounter God directly in his Christ as the God "who was in Christ and who atoned for (reconciled) the world (to himself)" (2 Cor. 5:19). Through faith in him and through the reception of the atonement from God brought about through Jesus' blood, "once for all time" (cf. Rom. 6:10; Heb. 9:12), the crucified one is active for them as the resurrected one. According to this passage, Jesus is at the same time the God who encounters those who believe from the cross and the Son of God who obediently offers himself up in the name of God, that is, true God and, at the same time, true man. Inasmuch as Jesus gives up his life to death as a substitute for all, he suffers vicariously the

judgment of destruction on behalf of sinners. But because he does this in the name of God as one who is innocent and out of his own love, his blood is the infinitely valuable means of atonement which is effective once for all time and procures for those who believe the forgiveness of their sins, new life before and with God, and consequently the righteousness of God which sinners lack (cf. 1 Cor. 6:20; 2 Cor. 5:21). God has brought about this absolutely decisive salvific work through Christ, who was obedient to God's will "unto death, even to death on the cross" (Phil. 2:8), as a demonstration of his salvation (from the judgment of death) and of his righteousness, which creates well-being. This righteousness becomes effective through the (legally valid) forgoing of those sins which took place [26] under the forbearance of God (which is still holding sway concerning God's chosen people; cf. 2:4) that lasts until the cross and resurrection of Jesus. It becomes completely and clearly visible in this text that the tradition which Paul picks up originally spoke only from the perspective of the salvific community originating out of Israel. Those Gentiles who have converted to faith in Jesus were not yet in view as programmatically as they were after the Apostolic Council (cf. Gal. 2:7ff.). For this very reason Paul now extends the tradition further to include the sense of a mission to the Gentiles and emphasizes that the demonstration of salvation and of the righteousness of God which creates well-being has now ensued "at the present time," that is, at the new time of salvation brought into being through Jesus' cross and resurrection (cf. Gal. 4:4; 2 Cor. 6:2; Rom. 3:21). God now causes this demonstration as the manifestation of the God who justifies *every* person who lives from faith in Jesus and appears before the judgment seat of God in such a faith, without denying his own just judgment or without bending the criterion of judgment itself. The gift of justification on the basis of faith in Jesus is, according to Paul, a gift to the end-times people of God made up of Jews *and* Gentiles. There is no longer any restriction of this gift to the circumcision (i.e. to those who are born Jews and to those Gentiles who are circumcised). According to vv. 25f., "justification" means the leading of sinners back into the glory and righteousness of which they were deprived at their expulsion from paradise (cf. also 1 Cor. 6:11; Rom. 8:30). Justification means acquittal at the judgment for Jesus' sake and the surety of a new existence in righteousness (cf. 2 Cor. 5:21). God, who grants this acquittal, is as the judge thus at the same time the creator, and in this double character the father of Jesus Christ, who takes more pleasure in the life of every sinner converted (to faith) than in his or her death (cf. Ezek. 18:22f.).

Excursus 6:
Justification in Paul's Thought

As Paul's testimony concerning himself in Phil. 3:4–11 shows, the event of *justification* completely determined the life of the apostle. It is therefore

no wonder that he turns again and again to this theme, from Galatians (cf.
Gal. 2:16–21; 3:1–5, 12), to the Corinthian letters (cf. 1 Cor. 1:30; 4:4;
6:11; 2 Cor. 5:14–21), to Romans and Philippians. One can clearly perceive, however, in baptismal texts such as 1 Cor. 6:11 and in christological
formulations such as Rom. 3:25f., 4:25, 2 Cor. 5:21, that Paul was not the
first nor the only one in early Christianity to have spoken about "justification." But the experience of his call, in which he was summoned from persecuting the church of Jesus Christ to be an apostle of Jesus Christ and
appointed to preach the gospel (cf. Gal. 1:11–17; 1 Cor. 15:8ff.), caused
justification to become the essential characteristic of Paul's preaching.
The one who experienced acceptance, reconciliation, and justification
through Christ on the road to Damascus saw himself placed by his new
Lord into the "ministry of righteousness" (in the new covenant) or the
"ministry of atonement (reconciliation)" (2 Cor. 3:9; 5:18) and called to
preach the gospel of atonement and justification among the Gentiles.
Paul asserted this gospel from the day of his calling on (Gal. 1:16; 1 Cor.
9:16). His main declarations are accessible in the citation of tradition in 1
Cor. 15:3ff. and are also reflected in the oldest of the extant letters of
Paul, 1 Thessalonians (cf. 1 Thess. 1:9f.; 2:13; 5:9f.). Right from the beginning of his missionary work within the synagogue communities, in
which he preached Christ, the apostle was whipped and once even
stoned (almost to death) for the sake of his gospel, which went beyond
the horizon of the Law (cf. 2 Cor. 11:24f. with Acts 14:19). Paul defended his Law-free gospel and his renunciation of circumcision for the
Gentiles at the so-called Apostolic Council (cf. Gal. 2:1–10; Acts 15:1–35).
Already in 1 Thessalonians he distinguishes sharply between (Jewish) enmity toward the cross, which occasions God's judgment of wrath, and
that way of life in faith, in relationship to the gospel, which pleases God
(cf. 1 Thess. 2:14–16 with 1:9f.; 2:10; 4:1f.). But we owe Paul's detailed
discussions concerning the theme of justification and reconciliation
through Christ by faith alone in Galatians, Philippians, 2 Corinthians, and
Romans above all to the fact that the apostle's gospel of justification
caused such offense after the Apostolic Council among Jewish Christians
that they inaugurated from Galatia on a formal countermission against
Paul. The Pauline doctrinal declaration found its most provocative crys-
tallization in the divine predication that God is the God "who justifies the
ungodly" (Rom. 4:5).

The conceptual world of "justification" derives from the Old Testament
and early Judaism. In Is. 50:7–9, God's servant speaks of the fact that God
will stand by him in his lawsuit against all his enemies and procure justice
for him. Conversely, the sinner must confess that no human being is just
before God, the judge (Ps. 143:2), or that, according to the Greek version
of the text, "is justified (by God)." "Justification" and "to be justified" refer

to legal acts. They can be used of contemporaneous acts within history, but they can also refer to a legal act at the end of time (cf. Sir. 23:11; Ps. Sol. 8:26, on the one hand, and Is. 43:9; 45:25; Tg. Is. 53:11, on the other). Jesus speaks of "being justified" in the sense of the forgiveness of sins, which in turn is seen as an acceptance by God in the present (Lk. 18:14). Paul was also thoroughly acquainted with such a present-tense use of the expression, but he always linked it with an end-time perspective. The justification experienced in the present establishes the hope and certainty of justification in the final judgment. Within early Judaism, the Qumran community comes the closest to this Pauline language convention (cf. 1QS 11:9–12). The active, "to justify," is reserved in Paul's writings for the activity of God (cf. Gal. 3:8; Rom. 3:26, 30; 4:5; 8:30, 33). The passive, "to be justified," can designate the recognition which the sinner must pay to the just God at the (final) judgment (cf. Rom. 3:4 following Ps. 51:6). Once it also means the act of being vindicated, which is granted to the Christ who was despised on earth at his exaltation to the right hand of God (cf. 1 Tim. 3:16 with the Greek text of Is. 53:11). But usually the passive designates the acceptance which people experience (or continue to be denied) by God at the judgment (cf. Gal. 2:16f.; 3:11, 24; Rom. 2:13; 3:20, 24, 28, etc.). When God pronounces the verdict "Righteous!" over someone at the judgment (Ezek. 18:9), or something is "reckoned as righteousness" to him (Gen. 15:6), new life before God is opened up to him (Gal. 3:6; Rom. 4:2, 20–22). In a postbiblical collection of Jewish homilies it is reported that "God said to the Israelites: Repent in those ten days between the New Year and the day of Atonement and I will declare you to be righteous on the day of Atonement and make you (through the forgiveness of sins) a new creature" (Pesiq. R. 40:169a). In exactly the same way it is already stated by Paul that "if someone is in Christ, (he) is a new creature; the old has passed away, behold, the new has come into being" (2 Cor. 5:17 with 5:21), and this promise of salvation, in a way similar to Rom. 3:25f., can itself be traced back to the missionary church in Antioch. Atonement through Christ as a new creature and justification on the basis of the atoning death of Christ were already intertwined in the early church before Paul (and for this reason then also by him in 2 Cor. 5:14–21 and Rom. 5:1–11). Moreover, Rom. 3:23–26 has already shown us how concretely Paul understands "justification" (see above), and this is confirmed by the parallels between "to be justified" and "to be sanctified" in 1 Cor. 6:11 and Rom. 8:30. According to biblical thought, justification is a legal act of the creator God and therefore at the same time an act of new creation, by virtue of which those who are justified participate in the glory and righteousness which exist in God's presence. Hence, the dogmatic distinction which arose in the history of the church between a justification which is first only reckoned legally (forensic-imputed) and a justification which is creatively at work (effective) is, measured by the examples just named, an unbiblical abstraction.

Already in Is. 53:11 we read concerning the suffering servant of God, "[M]y servant, the just one, makes many just; he carries their guilt upon himself." According to Mk. 10:45 par.; 14:24 par., Jesus understood himself to be this servant of God who suffers vicariously for the many. Under these circumstances it is completely understandable that the Christian community in Jerusalem confessed after Easter, in view of Is. 53:11f., that Jesus was "given up (by God) because of our trespasses and raised up (by God) because of our justification." Paul quotes this old formula in Rom. 4:25. Because of the death (judgment) which Jesus bore vicariously on their behalf, sinners will be acquitted by God at the (final) judgment, and the guarantee of this acquittal is Jesus himself, as the one whom God raised from the dead. Paul shared this conception without qualification. For him as well, Jesus' atoning death is the legal ground of justification (cf. Gal. 2:20; 1 Cor. 1:30; 2 Cor. 5:21; Rom. 3:24ff.; 4:25; 8:3f.). According to the apostle's (experience of his call and) preaching, justification by God is promised to all those who recognize themselves to be "ungodly" (Rom. 4:5), that is, to be transgressors who have violated God's will, and in view of this recognition trust in Jesus Christ as their redeemer and Lord. Such faith is, according to Paul, the sole ground of justification (Rom. 3:28), because it acknowledges God's salvific work in Christ and incorporates in one and the same act of life the confession of Jesus as Lord and savior, repentance, and new obedience (cf. 1 Thess. 1:9f.; Rom. 1:5; 10:9f.).

The primary occasion at which justification is received, according to early Christian and Pauline conviction, is (adult) baptism and the confession of Christ which is bound up together with it (cf. 1 Cor. 6:11; 12:13; Rom. 6:1ff.). The boldness of this preaching lies in the fact that forgiveness of sins and eschatological justification for the sake of Christ are already promised to sinners from among Gentiles and Jews at the time of their baptism. New existence does not first begin for them on judgment day, but already here and now in the life of every individual by virtue of the Holy Spirit which has been poured out upon him or her in baptism (2 Cor. 5:17). However, because the final judgment according to works is still outstanding, misery, suffering, and death still oppress the world, and Israel has not yet obtained the redemption through the messiah promised them by God, the apostle emphasizes that those who believe have only been transferred to the position of hoping for the reception of righteousness in the final judgment (Gal. 5:5f.). It is thus true for all Christians, as it is for Paul himself, that they prepare themselves for judgment day by faith and obedience to the command of Christ and that they must do everything they can not to forfeit again the salvation which has already been granted them (cf. Phil. 3:7–16 with 1 Thess. 3:5; Phil. 2:12f.; Gal. 5:16–25; 1 Cor. 10:1–13; Rom. 6:19–23; 8:3–17). Hence, according to Paul, justification at baptism establishes a Christian state of being in which one is still in the process of "becoming." The fact that the Christ who is now exalted at the right hand of God is also, according to Paul, still underway toward the goal of subjecting all things to the rule of God, including death as the last enemy (1 Cor. 15:20–28), corresponds to this Christian state of being in process here on earth. Consequently, Christians are proceeding toward judgment day together with their Lord and on this side of it must endure the struggle which presently surrounds the carrying out of the reign of God. What fills the apostle himself, and all Christians who follow his preaching, with the certainty and hope along the way that at the last judgment they will be accepted and not condemned is the fact that the Christ who died and was raised for them remains their Lord and redeemer all the way, even when they stand before the eschatological judgment seat of God. Believing Christians may be confident all the way to judgment day of his intercession on their behalf (Rom. 8:34). Because they are chosen by God in Christ in advance to partake in salvation, they may and are able to remain certain in the midst of every temptation that no power of the world can separate them from the love of God embodied in Christ (Rom. 8:38–39).

2. 3:27–31. The Universal Scope of Justification

(27) Where then is boasting? It is excluded. Through what kind of Law, (that) of works? No, but through the Law of faith. (28) For we are of the view that a person is justified (only) by faith, without works of the Law. (29) Or is God only (the God) of the Jews? Not also of the Gentiles? Certainly, also of the Gentiles! (30) If indeed God really is One, who will justify the circumcision on the basis of faith and the uncircumcision through faith. (31) Do we then nullify the Law through faith? By no means! Rather, we establish the Law!

Verse 30: Deut. 6:4.

A. This paragraph picks up the catchword of Jewish boasting from 2:17 and extends the discussion begun in 3:1–8 with a series of rhetorical questions which were nevertheless rooted in the current and pressing situation of dialogue in which Paul was engaged (vv. 27, 29, 31). Once again, with this style of argument Paul is reflecting the accusations against his preaching which have been expressed by his critics. Their charges climax in the supposition that Paul intends to abrogate the Law of God with his preaching of the gospel. Jesus too had to contend against such accusations (cf. Mtt. 5:17); they were raised against Stephen (cf. Acts 6:13f.); and now they are also being levied against the apostle. In fact, in view of Paul's critical statements concerning the Law, such as those found in Gal. 2:21; 5:4; 1 Cor. 9:19–23, and his thesis that Christ is "the end of the Law for everyone who believes," most likely not expressed for the first time in Rom. 10:4, one can reconstruct how such a suspicion came about. These statements were scathing for a native Jew; indeed it states in the Mishnah, Sanhedrin 10:1 that "these are those who have no part in the coming world: the one who says, . . . that the Law is not from heaven . . . ." The apostle, however, energetically rejects the charges. Instead, he sets two ways of encountering and understanding the Law over against one another dialectically, that is, the use of the Law in the sense of works (of the Law), on the one hand, and in the sense of faith, on the other. Paul attaches to this his now famous doctrine of justification by faith alone and then grounds the universality of justification for Jews and Gentiles by referring to Deut. 6:4. During the New Testament era, every Jew had to say, both morning and evening, the prayer of confession from Deut. 6:4; 11:13–21; Num. 15:37–41, which began with the words, "Hear, O Israel! The Lord our God is the only God . . . " (Deut. 6:4). This prayer was considered to be the summation of the Law and was in the ancient world of idolatry the classic mark of the people of God, who acknowledged the one, true God. In conclusion, Paul establishes (in the same pointed fashion as in 2:16; 3:8) that he does not abolish the Law by faith, but rather enforces it. The understanding of the letter to the Romans as a whole depends to a great degree on the interpretation of these verses.

B. With these rhetorical questions, in which the [27] "boasting" (for the meaning of this expression, see below, p. 72) of the Jew in regard to his privileges over against the Gentile (listed in 2:17ff.) still continues, even in view of the God who is just and justifies every person (only) on the basis of his or her faith (3:26), Paul returns to the charges which the Jews and Jewish-Christian missionaries raised against his preaching (cf. 3:1–8). Paul's answer is that boasting is excluded. How so? Through the Law which demands works? No, answers the apostle, since it is precisely upon this Law that the Jew is depending, and on its account boasting before God (2:17). The exclusion of boasting thus takes place through "the Law of faith." This expression has continually caused interpreters great trouble, to the point that they have thought that it is not intended literally, but is to be construed only in the sense of a "rule" or "principle." But in view of the claim expressed in v. 31 that Paul does not nullify the Law, but establishes it, and in the light of the context, which does not suggest any figurative use of the Law, it is more natural to take the expression in the same way that the first readers of Romans must have understood it, namely, as "the Law which is determined by faith (in Jesus Christ)." The meaning of this is threefold. Inasmuch as Paul explicitly designated the "Law and the Prophets" in 3:21 to be witnesses to the revelation of the righteousness of God as the righteousness of faith (cf. the Scripture passages named there), and since the Abrahamic promise from Gen. 15:6, covered in detail in chapter 4, likewise derives from the Law (as the five books of Moses taken as a whole), Paul refers in v. 27 first to the function of the Law as Scripture, which testifies to justification as the promise and work of God. Faith thankfully recognizes this witness. Second, the apostle has in view that Christ has become the place of atonement by virtue of his obedience as the Son (3:25). The obedience of Christ is a "just act" before God (5:18). Hence, with his sacrificial act Christ fulfilled the Law vicariously, and it is precisely from this act that redemption comes into being (3:24). This too, faith is the first to recognize, and Paul will expand this point still further in 5:12–21. But third, and above all, with the expression "the Law of faith" the apostle intends to make unmistakably clear that according to his preaching the Law is thoroughly retained, from the standpoint of faith in Jesus Christ, as the valid will of God. He will explain this in detail in 7:7–8:17 (cf. esp. 8:3f.). There are thus dimensions to the Law which only faith recognizes and which remain hidden to those who take the Law, without faith, only to be a summons to works of the Law, even though this does not lead to justification (3:20).

If we understand v. 27 in this fundamental way, that is, from the perspective of the theology of justification, [28] then Paul's doctrinal statement in v. 28, especially emphasized with the words "for we are of the view," follows organically when taken as a ground or support for v. 27. Here the apostle advocates, in accord with God's will confirmed in the Scripture (cf. the quote from Ps. 143:2 in v. 20), that a person is justified before God by faith alone without works of the Law. No one can free him- or herself from the power of sin with the help of fulfilling individual commandments (see above). The one and only thing which breaks this power is the salvific work of God in the atoning death and resurrection of Christ, and only faith in Jesus as savior and Lord leads to the verdict, Righteous!, before the judgment seat of God. Paul had already represented this view in Galatians (cf. Gal. 2:16; 3:2), and he now also maintains it in Romans over against all opposing criticism. The ground and realization of justification reside in God's grace alone, as it appeared in Jesus Christ, and only the faith awakened by God through the gospel allows a person to participate in it. During the Reformation, Luther's translation of the Pauline expression "from faith" with "by faith alone" was much disputed. Today, even Catholic interpreters of the Bible see that Luther's addition to the text of "alone" is entirely in harmony with the apostle's intention.

The famous expression *sola fide* ("from faith alone") applies to Jews and Gentiles alike. [29, 30] For God is, as Paul adeptly continues, not only the God of the Jews, but also of the Gentiles. God could not be otherwise since, as every Jew confessed daily (see above), he is the one God who created the world and chose Israel to be the people of his own possession. As the one God, he is willing to justify the circumcision, that is, the Israelites, on the basis of their faith and the uncircumcision, that is, the uncircumcised Gentiles, through their faith. [31] Paul then concludes his argument with an inference aimed at his Jewish-Christian opponents which is rhetorically powerful and pointed in terms of its content. He does not nullify the Law with his preaching, as he is accused of doing, but he establishes it as the valid legal demand of God (cf. 2:12–16), which Christ has vicariously fulfilled (5:18), as a witness to justification (3:21; 4:3), and as an instruction for believers to lead them in the Spirit of Christ along the path of righteousness (8:3f.). The apostle's critics, who desire to make him an antinomian (and in so doing to stamp him as a traitor to Israel's holy tradition of faith), are rebuked as liars by the preaching which Paul here lays bare for his readers in the letter to the Romans. The Christians in Rome therefore have every reason to listen to Paul rather than to the voice of that "slanderer" (cf. 3:8). The apostle thus continues the altercation in the next chapter.

3. 4:1–25. The Righteousness of Faith Already Promised to Abraham

(1) What should we then say that Abraham, our forefather, found according to the flesh? (2) For if Abraham was justified on the basis of works, he has a boast—but not before God! (3) What, namely, does the Scripture say? "But Abraham believed God, and it was reckoned to him as righteousness." (4) Whoever does works, to him his wage is not reckoned according to grace but according to what is due him; (5) but whoever does not work, but believes in him who justifies the ungodly, his faith is reckoned as righteousness. (6) As also indeed David pronounces the blessing upon the person to whom God reckons righteousness without works: (7) "Blessed are those lawless ones who are forgiven and whose sins are covered; (8) blessed is a man to whom the Lord does not reckon sin!" — (9) This blessing then, (is it meant) for the circumcision or the uncircumcision? We say indeed: Faith was reckoned to Abraham as righteousness! (10) How was it then reckoned? When he was circumcised or uncircumcised? Not when he was circumcised, but when he was uncircumcised! (11) And he received the sign of circumcision as a seal of the righteousness of faith, (that is), while uncircumcised, on the basis of which he becomes (not only) the father of all those who believe while in the state of un-circumcision, on the basis of which righteousness is also reckoned to them, (12) but also the father of the circumcision for those who (live) not on the basis of circumcision, but also follow the steps of the faith of our father Abraham, which he (exercised) while uncircumcised. — (13) For the promise to Abraham or his seed, that he should be the heir of the world, was not promul-gated through (the) Law, but through (the) righteousness of faith. (14) For if those from the Law (are) heirs, then faith is depleted and the promise is nulli-fied. (15) For the Law brings wrath; but where there is no Law, (there is) also no transgression. (16) Therefore, (it remains valid): from faith, in order that (this also remains valid): according to grace, upon which the promise is valid for all the seed, not merely for the one from the Law only, but also for (the one) from the faith of Abraham, who is the father of us all, (17) as it is written, "I have appointed you to be the father of many nations" before the God, in whom he believed as the one who makes the dead alive and calls into existence

that which does not exist. (18) He believed in hope against (all) hope that he would become the father of many nations in accordance with the statement, "so (many) shall your seed be." (19) And without becoming weak in faith, he considered his body, already deadened—he was already almost one hundred years old—and the deadened nature of Sarah's womb. (20) He did not doubt the promise of God in unbelief, but he gained strength through faith, gave God the glory; (21) and was completely convinced that what he had promised he is also able to perform. (22) Therefore (it) was also reckoned to him as righteousness! — (23) But it was not written for his sake alone that "it was reckoned to him," (24) but also for our sake, to whom (it) will be reckoned, (to us) who believe in him who raised Jesus, our Lord, from the dead, (25) who was given up on account of our transgressions and raised on account of our justification.

Verse 3: Gen. 15:6; Verses 7f.: Ps. 32:1f.; Verse 17: Gen. 17:5;
Verse 18: Gen. 15:5; Verse 23: Gen. 15:6; Verse 25: Is. 53:11 + 12.

[A] We have before us here a long, unified discussion from the apostle concerning the theme "Abraham and the righteousness of faith," which one can outline in four subparagraphs: vv. 1–8; 9–12; 13–22; 23–25. The textual tradition of vv. 1 and 19 offers different readings, that is, variants. In each case the most difficult is probably the most original (see below under B).

This chapter becomes transparent in terms of its content only when one keeps in mind the biblical narrative of Abraham from Genesis 12 and recognizes that Paul makes use of the Old Testament and early Jewish tradition concerning Abraham in an entirely new manner. This special use is provoked by the conception concerning Abraham and the Abrahamic covenant of Genesis 17 held by his Jewish-Christian opponents. These Jewish-Christian "contra-missionaries" have advised the Galatians converted by Paul to allow themselves to be circumcised in addition to faith and baptism, to observe the (Jewish) feast calendar, and to keep the Law (Gal. 4:10, 21; 5:2ff.). In this way they wanted to make it possible for the Gentile Galatians to participate in the promised blessings of the Abrahamic covenant. To them, Paul appears to have left the baptized (Gentile) Christians merely in the outer court of the people of God (i.e., in the state of being a Christian "God-fearer," see below), while, in contrast, by appealing to Abraham, they wanted to make them full-fledged members of God's chosen people (cf. Gal. 3:6ff.; 4:21ff.). Paul had already protested strongly against this seduction of his congregation in his letter to the Galatians. In a bold argument he established that the promise to Abraham of justification by faith (Gen. 15:6), and the promise that in him all nations which share his faith will be blessed (Gen. 12:3), came into being long before the decree of the Law on Sinai. Moreover, Paul wrote in Gal. 3:19ff. that the Law was therefore issued by God, with the support of the angel, through Moses only in order to convict the people of their transgressions of the Law and thereby place them before the

Christ of God, who mediates to sinners the justification by faith (promised to Abraham). This view of Abraham (and of the Law) caused great offense to the opponents of Paul. For precisely this reason Paul returns in Romans 4 once again to Gen. 15:6 in order to clarify the question of how Abraham is to be perceived by Christians. As a Jew called to be an apostle, who preaches the justification of Gentiles and Jews by the one God (3:30), Paul cannot and will not renounce calling Abraham "father" (cf. 4:1, 11f., 16, 18), since, according to Paul, the Christian community also lives on the basis of Abraham, the "root" which God chose and with which he founded the history of Israel in accordance with his promises (cf. Rom. 11:17f.).

For early Judaism the Fathers are the bearers and witnesses to the grace of God in the history of Israel. This results from the introduction of the tradition of the so-called Praise of the Fathers handed down in Sirach 44–50. Here, in the form of the Fathers, Israel is assembled before God and partakes in election, admonition, and guidance down through the ages. The Fathers are therefore not only individual historical persons, but in a certain sense also personifications of Israel as a whole. Inasmuch as Paul comes to speak of Abraham as "father," he joins this early Jewish "personified conception of history" (R. Smend).

The most significant figure among Israel's ancestral fathers is Abraham. Already in Is. 51:2 he is called "father," and in 1 Enoch 93:8 Abraham is the "chosen root" of Israel. In early Judaism, Abraham, as the Aramean called from the land of two rivers (Gen. 12:1ff.), is at the same time the "father" of those Gentiles who have crossed over to Judaism and of those Jews who are descendant from Isaac. The sign of belonging to Israel for both groups is circumcision. Circumcised Gentiles are called "the added ones" or "proselytes," and are to be distinguished during the New Testament period from the so-called God-fearers. God-fearers were Gentiles who joined Israel in confessing the one God and attended the synagogue, but avoided circumcision and were therefore not full citizens of God's people. In Sir. 44:19–21 it says concerning Abraham that "Abraham became the father of many nations, his honor remained untarnished. He kept the commandment of the Highest and entered into a covenant with him. As it was commanded him, he circumcised himself. He was found faithful in the test. Therefore God assured him with an oath that he would bless the nations through his descendants, make them as numerous as the dust on the earth, exalt his descendants as the stars, give them possession from sea to sea, from the Euphrates to the ends of the earth." The "covenant" in this passage refers to Gen. 17:4–14, and the "test" is the trial of obedience of offering up Isaac according to Gen. 22:1–19, which in 1 Macc. 2:52 is also considered to be the proof of Abraham's faithfulness, which was reckoned to him as righteousness. According to Gen. 26:5; Sir. 44:20; 1 Macc. 2:52, and so on, Abraham's faith consists in his unreserved trust in God's promise and in his obedience to God's command. In the Mekilta to Exod. 14:31(40b) this faith is praised in words very close to those used by Paul: "In this way you find that our father Abraham took possession of this and the future world only through the merit of faith (or also: the righteousness of faith), as it says, he believed in God, and he reckoned it to him as righteousness (Gen. 15:6)." On the basis of James 2:20–24 and Heb. 11:8–19, this picture of Abraham also became a constituent part of the Christian tradition. It makes the position of Paul's opponents (in Galatia and beyond) sufficiently clear: Only the one who responds with Abraham to God's call, is circumcised, keeps the Law, and in this way maintains one's faith before God, can be a full member of the eschatological people of God.

Paul encountered the consequences of this Jewish and Jewish-Christian understanding of Abraham in his mission to the Gentiles. In view of the revelation allotted to him on the road to Damascus of the God who elects on the basis of free grace, he considered this view to be narrow. As a result, the apostle takes as his starting point Gen. 12:1ff. (cf. Gal. 3:8) and sees in Abraham the ancestor of faith, who was chosen by God without any merit and experienced justification by grace alone. Paul (in contrast to James 2:21; Heb. 11:17–19) is completely silent concerning "the binding of Isaac" (Gen. 22:9f.). For him, what is important is that Abraham's justification in Gen. 15:6 is narrated earlier than the "covenant" of circumcision in Genesis 17. According to the ancient conception, that which is earlier (older) is superior to what comes later. It is therefore significant that Abraham's election and justification by faith precede his circumcision and test of faith.

The apostle causes his discussion in v. 25 to flow into an old christological formula built on the basis of the Hebrew text of Is. 53:11f. In it Jesus' own self-understanding as the servant of God who suffers vicariously for the many (cf. Mk. 10:45 par. and 14:24 par.) comes together with the confession of the pre-Pauline community (from Jerusalem?) of Jesus as the messiah who died for us and was raised by God (cf. 1 Cor. 15:3–5). Paul agrees with this confession.

[B] With his typical expression, [1] "What should we then say?" (cf. 6:1; 7:7; 9:14), Paul appears to take up the thesis of his opponent, that is, that Abraham found grace before God by virtue of his obedience and the constancy of his faith (cf. Gen. 18:3 with 26:5; James 2:21f.). "To find grace" is a common biblical expression (cf., e.g., Gen. 6:8; the Greek text of Sir. 45:1; and Heb. 4:16). Paul is alluding to the opposing thesis, without previously having used the catchword "grace" himself. The phrase "according to the flesh" can either be related to Abraham (in this case Paul would then be calling him Israel's forefather as a matter of common ground in his dispute with his Jewish-Christian opponents), or as an adverb modifying "found," so that it is then concerned with the question of what Abraham found in accordance with his earthly existence. This second possibility fits with the following text better (and corresponds to the Pauline usage in, e.g., Rom. 8:4f., 12f.). The form of the sentence as a question already shows that the apostle intends to discuss critically what Abraham found and in what way he found it. [2] If, namely, Abraham was justified on the basis of works, then he has a "boast" before God. Paul uses the words "boast," "to boast," and so on, in both positive and negative ways. If sinners attempt to boast before God (and other people) in their privileged position, in their deeds, or even in their possession of the good things of salvation (as the Jew does in Rom. 2:17ff. or as the opponents of Paul do according to Gal. 6:13; 2 Cor. 11:18), then it is true that God destroys such boasting (as the judge) (cf. 1 Cor. 1:29; 3:19–21). One should and may boast only in the Lord (1 Cor. 1:31 and 2 Cor. 10:17, each of which quotes Jer. 9:23), in the cross as the salvific event (Gal. 6:14), in the hope of one's future glorification (Rom. 5:2), and in every work of mission which is done in the Spirit of Christ (cf. 1 Cor. 9:15ff.; 2 Cor. 1:12–14; 10:13–18). The apostle and every Christian with him may expect a reward for such beneficial works (cf. 1 Cor. 9:17; Gal. 6:4; see above, pp. 45–47). But the opponents of Paul see in Abraham one who received a reward from God for the demonstration of his constancy of faith, and therefore they call Christians as well to a perseverance in faith and works by appealing to Abraham (James 2:20ff.; Heb. 11:8ff., 17f.). For his part, Paul considers their view of Abraham to be false and opposes it by asserting that Abraham does not have a boast which leads to justification! [3] For the Scripture explicitly speaks in Gen. 15:6 of Abraham's faith as the ground of justification. A sharp distinction must be made between justification on the basis of works and justification on the basis of faith. [4] It is thus true that whoever does works worthy of recognition, his or her reward is not allocated according to a criterion of grace, but of merit. [5] But the one who, instead of doing works, trusts in the God who justifies the "ungodly," that is, the sinful transgressor (cf., e.g., Ps. 1:1–6; Prov. 2:22; Is. 11:4), that person's faith is reckoned to him or her as righteousness. While on the one hand earthly judges are warned in Is. 5:23 about declaring the wicked to be just, and in the so-called Book of the Covenant it even says concerning God that he does not justify the wicked (Exod. 23:7), on the other hand Ezekiel already also emphasizes that God takes no pleasure in the death of the "ungodly," but in their conversion (Ezek. 18:23). Correspondingly, the wicked themselves appeal in prayers of repentance to God's mercy at the judgment (cf., e.g., Psalm 51; Dan. 9:18ff.; 4 Ezra 8:35f.; 1QS 11:11ff.). Paul is aware of these prayers (cf. 3:4), and based on them he coins a new description of God which is highly paradoxical and of great rhetorical power: God already demonstrated himself toward Abraham to be the God who justifies the ungodly (the wicked) through Christ (cf. 4:25; 5:6). In view of this divine activity, there is no longer any room for the Jewish and Jewish-Christian middle way of justification on the basis of faith and works, that is, on the basis of both God's mercy and the meritorious deeds of the pious (4 Ezra 7:7; 13:23; James 2:20ff.). [6–8] According to Paul, the Scripture already testifies through the mouth (of the Psalmist) David in Ps. 32:1f. that God acts in this way. Methodologically, Paul proceeds here according to the Jewish exegetical principle that two scriptural passages in which the same catchword appears (in this case, "to reckon") explain one another. As a result,

Gen. 15:6 and Ps. 32:1f. mutually interpret each other. With the "reckoning" of his faith, Abraham obtained forgiveness for his transgressions against the Law and for his sins. The formulations of the apostle are provocative. In complete contrast to the Jewish tradition (see above), he sees in Abraham the first "ungodly" one to be justified. Hence, for Paul, "faith" is no longer understood as obedient fear of God, but as the gift of a relationship with God, as he was revealed in Christ. According to Paul, God reveals himself no differently in the history of Israel than in Christ, but always as the same. For this reason the apostle can also no longer allow the concept of faith which governs his opponents to stand (cf. James 2:22; Heb. 11:17–19). For Paul, Abraham's faith is the paradigm of Christian faith in that a person participates in life (through Christ) only in obedient trust in the God who brings about salvation on the basis of free grace.

[9] In Galatia the so-called Judaizers represented the opinion that the Gentile Christians would participate in the blessings of the Abrahamic covenant only through circumcision. Paul protested against this (cf. Gal. 2:3; 3:6ff.; 5:2–6). The question is of such significance for him theologically, and for missions, that he now returns to it once again. Evidently, his "slanderers" (3:8) had contact with Paul's opponents from Galatia. In view of the debate in which he is involved with them, it is no subtlety when the apostle continues in v. 9 with the question of whether the statement in Gen. 15:6, that Abraham was justified on the basis of faith, is related to Israel's forefather while he was in the state of being circumcised or uncircumcised. [10] Since in the Scriptures Gen. 17:9ff. follows Gen. 15:6, the answer must be that Abraham was justified while he was still uncircumcised. [11] His consequent circumcision is thus only the seal and sign of the "righteousness of faith" (for this expression, see v. 13) in which Abraham already lived while he was in the state of being uncircumcised. As a result, Abraham is, according to God's will—in contrast to what Paul's opponents maintain—the father of all those who believe among the uncircumcised Gentiles, who will likewise be justified as Abraham, and [12] the father of those circumcised Jews who do not merely trust in their circumcision (cf. 2:28f.), but who also take the faith of the still uncircumcised Abraham as their model. Abraham is "our father"; that is, he is the forefather of all (uncircumcised) Gentiles and of all (circumcised) Jews who believe in Jesus Christ.

[13] If the issue is Abraham, then the dispute with the Jewish Christians is twofold, namely, the issue of participating in the promise pledged to Abraham (Gen. 15:4f.; 17:4f.) and the issue of the binding nature of the Law. In early Jewish tradition it states that Abraham's descendants "inherit the entire earth" and "will rule over all nations as they desire" (Jub. 22:14; 32:19). Paul shares this expectation, but in doing so thinks of taking part in the reign of Christ to which those saved by Christ look forward (cf. Gal. 3:16; 4:4–7; 1 Cor. 6:2; Rom. 5:17). It is more problematic with the Law. Genesis 26:5 already presupposes Abraham's obedience to the Law, and in Sir. 44:20 it states that Abraham is allotted

the promise of a son because of his faithfulness to the Law (which according to 2 Bar. 57:2 was already present at that time in an unwritten form) and his willingness to offer up Isaac. But on the basis of Gen. 15:4–6 Paul sees it linked only to Abraham's "righteousness of faith." When the apostle uses the expression "the righteousness of faith" here, as earlier in v. 11, he is making use of a Rabbinic conception which refers to Abraham's life of faith in righteousness (cf. Mekilta to Exod. 14:31). But in contrast to his Jewish-Christian opponents, Paul sets this righteousness of faith over against that of (Abraham's) obedience to the Law. [14] But if—as the Jewish and Jewish-Christian interpretation supposes—life on the basis of the Law has something to do with participating in the inheritance of Abraham, then faith is divested of its decisive character (according to Paul) and the promise devalued. [15] For as 1:18–3:20 already showed, the Law makes God's judgment of wrath unavoidable and removes from everyone the prospect of being allowed to enter into the promised inheritance. It can only be otherwise if at the time of Abraham the Law was not yet part of the plan. (In fact, it was first issued on Sinai long after Abraham; cf. Gal. 3:17.) Hence, at the time of Abraham, there was still no formal transgression against the Law, so that from the beginning the promise to Abraham transcended the sphere of the people of Israel, who were directly encountered by the giving of the Law at Sinai. [16] Therefore (according to Gen. 15:4–6) righteousness came to pass for Abraham "on the basis of faith," so that the divine "by grace," and with it the promise, might be valid for all the descendants of Abraham. But these descendants are not only the Jews who live on the basis of the Law, but also the Gentiles who follow the example of Abraham's faith. He is the "father of us all," that is, of Jewish and Gentile Christians who believe as Abraham did (cf. v. 12). [17] In this way Abraham's experience corresponds to the statement of the Scripture that Abraham was appointed to be the "father of many nations" (Gen. 17:5) and to the reality of the one God before whom Abraham lived in faith. This one God is, as the God who justifies the ungodly (v. 5), at the same time also the one who raises the dead and the creator who calls into being that which does not exist. Both characteristics of God correspond to the prior Jewish tradition of faith (cf. 2 Bar. 48:8: "[B]y a word you call to life what does not exist," and the second blessing-formula of the Jewish "Eighteen Benedictions": "Praise be to you, Lord, who makes the dead alive!"). Faith in God in the sense of the three affirmations of vv. 5 and 17 means to be nothing oneself and in precisely this way to experience in oneself creation out of nothing. [18] It is exactly in this sense that the apostle continues: Abraham believed, against all human hope, in hope, that is, in the promise of God that he would become the father of many nations and that his descendants would be as numerous as the stars in heaven (Gen. 15:5). [19] While a whole number of later textual witnesses read "and without becoming weak in faith, he (= Abraham) did not direct his attention to his already deadened body . . . ," thus viewing Abraham's strength of faith to consist in the fact that Abraham managed to overlook his and Sarah's aged condition, the older and better manuscripts omit the explanatory "not." The strength of Abraham's faith, according to this affirmation, shows itself in that he thoroughly considered the fact that he was almost one hundred years old and that Sarah was barren (cf. Gen. 18:11–13) and nevertheless—against all natural hope (v. 18)!—held fast to God's promise. This corresponds to v. 18 and to the biblical narrative in Gen. 17:17. [20] Precisely in a situation that, from a human perspective, appeared hopeless, Abraham did not succumb to unbelieving doubt, but remained strong in faith, gave God the glory, [21] and was entirely convinced that God the creator is powerful enough to transform his promises into reality. Abraham thus remained unshakably faithful to God's word of promise. [22] Because he believed in this way, his faith was reckoned to him as righteousness (cf. Gen. 15:6). With this, Paul has outlined his view of Abraham in a way that is in harmony with the Scripture. He now turns to apply it as a whole.

Abraham is, for the apostle, the "father" of all who believe (see above). He is not, therefore, merely an individual from history, but the historically determinative prototype of what it means to have faith in God, whose promises have become Yes and Amen in Christ (cf. 2 Cor. 1:20). [23] On this basis it holds true that the statement from Gen. 15:6 stands in Scripture not only for the sake of Abraham alone, [24] but also "for our sake," that is, for the sake of the Gentiles and Jewish Christians (in Rome and elsewhere) who read the Scripture for instruction (cf. 15:4) and to whom their faith will be reckoned as righteousness. They are the ones who believe in God, who has documented in the resurrection of Jesus Christ, in a way that is full of promise, his desire to justify the ungodly (v. 5), his creative activity, and his power to resurrect the dead (v. 17). Faith in this God is true faith. It genuinely leads to justification. [25] Verse 25 declares why this is so by a formula of confession which was already structured before Paul's call into two clauses that are arranged in Semitic parallelism and oriented on the Hebrew text of Is. 53:11f. (see above): As it is indicated in Isaiah 53, God delivered Jesus over to his opponents and thus to death on the cross "because of our transgressions" (cf. Mk. 9:31; 10:33f. par.; 1 Cor. 11:23; Rom. 8:32), and he raised him in recognition of his act of sacrifice "because of our justification." Christ's act of sacrifice on the cross, ordained by God and endorsed as valid by the resurrection, is and remains the legal ground for the justification of all those who, as the "ungodly," believe in the God who revealed himself in Christ. God's salvific righteousness comes to pass in the resurrected Christ from "now" (3:21) until the final judgment (8:33f.). The formula found here stands in parallel to 1 Cor. 1:30 and Rom. 3:25f. in terms of its content. By using this formula at the conclusion of his highly controversial argument, Paul consciously places himself on the foundation of that tradition of faith which unites the apostle with his Roman addressees. They (also) can perceive from Romans 4 that with his gospel of justification Paul stands in the tradition of faith that is familiar and precious to them. Hence, they need not cherish any suspicion concerning his teaching.

Excursus 7:
The Meaning of Faith according to Paul

The previous chapter shows especially clearly that the apostle speaks of *faith* with an intensity not reached in the Jewish (and Jewish-Christian) tradition. This is based, above all, on his own experience of faith, which was opened up to Paul at his calling to be an apostle. Nevertheless, the roots of the Pauline conception of faith are found in the Old Testament and early Judaism, on the one hand, and with Jesus, as well as in the mission tradition of early Christianity, on the other hand.

In the Old Testament, Isaiah (eighth century B.C.) is the first to speak, in outline form, of faith as a way of behavior in which one unreservedly and exclusively depends on and has dealings with God, his promises, and his will (cf. Is. 7:9; 28:16; 30:15). Closely related to this is the discourse on Abraham's trust in God's promise, by virtue of which in Gen. 15:6 he is recognized as righteous by God. Habakkuk (2:4) and the Psalms from Israel's preexilic and exilic period also reflect this understanding of faith (cf. Pss. 78:22, 32; 106:12, 24). But it is only in the late Old Testament and early Jewish period that the language of faith gains a wider circulation in Israel. Faith becomes the designation for the devotion of the pious to God and of their faithfulness to his instructions. Abraham is considered to be the model for such an obedient constancy in faith (cf. Gen. 26:5; Sir. 44:19–21). Philo of Alexandria sees in Abraham's faith in God "the queen of the virtues" of the patriarch (*Abr.* 270). The Essene community from Qumran relates Hab. 2:4 to all the doers of the Law who remain faithful to the sharpened interpretation of the Law which was worked out by the "Teacher of Righteousness" (cf. 1QpHab. 7:17–8:3). According to 2 Bar. 54:16, 21, the faith which proves itself true by its love for God's Law will be rewarded in the final judgment and will lead to the eschatological glorification of those who are constant in their faith. The conversion of sinful Gentiles to the one, true, creator God is called "faith" in Jonah 3:5; Wis. 12:2; Jud. 14:10. It is here that we confront early Jewish terminology from the sphere of missions.

Paul knew this Old Testament–Jewish perspective on faith and advocated it as well. But by virtue of his calling to be an apostle of Jesus Christ, he was led beyond it. Since his calling, faith was no longer merely a matter of the conversion to the only true God demanded from the Gentiles and of the faithfulness of the pious to God's commandments. Rather, he sees in faith the absolute way of salvation which God has opened up, on the basis of free grace, for sinners from both the Jews and Gentiles (Gal. 3:23). This way of salvation was disclosed to Paul himself through the appearance of the living Christ on the road to Damascus; conversely, he is

established in the mission to Jews and Gentiles through the preaching of
the gospel, to which the exalted Christ authorized the apostle and sent
him out (cf. Rom. 10:14–17 with Mtt. 28:16–20). On this basis, faith is for
Paul, as the Latin Bible translates Rom. 10:17, *fides ex auditu*, that is, faith
which grows from the obedient hearing of the message in which Christ is
proclaimed as the savior and Lord of the world. Such faith is the gift of
God, which is completely unearned and which leads to justification (Eph.
2:8). The gospel is the message of faith; it demands to be obediently heard
(Rom. 1:5; 6:17; 16:19) and gives, where this happens, the Holy Spirit
(Gal. 3:2). The Holy Spirit fills the heart (2 Cor. 1:22), enables one to gain
the true understanding of Jesus as the Christ of God (1 Cor. 2:7–12), and
assists one to confess him as Lord (1 Cor. 12:3; Rom. 10:9). In the power
of the Spirit, which those who believe receive from the hearing of the
gospel, they fulfill the instruction of Christ, which is identical with the
legal demand of the Law (Gal. 6:2; Rom. 8:4). In this way, love becomes
the dimension of the life of faith, that is, love for God as well as love for
one's neighbor (Rom. 5:5; Gal. 5:5f., 14; Rom. 13:8–10). In accordance
with all of this, faith, for the apostle, is an all-encompassing act of life
which is upheld by the Holy Spirit. Thus, wherever faith is separated from
love, Paul contradicts it just as energetically (1 Cor. 13:1ff.) as he does
those places where one declares that faith is in need of completion by
works of the Law (Gal. 3:1–4). For him, to preach Christ, to preach the
gospel, and to preach faith, are identical (cf. Gal. 1:11, 16, 23; 1 Cor.
1:23f.; 15:1–11; Rom. 1:1–5; 16f.). As the way of salvation opened up by
God through the gospel, which is appropriated with the support of Christ,
faith is the gift of life in the presence of God and "remains" therefore beyond the day of judgment (1 Cor. 13:13).

The apostle could not have talked in this new way concerning faith, if
Jesus had not already spoken of faith in a completely novel way during his
work on earth. Jesus introduced a new way of talking and thinking about
faith into Israel's tradition of faith. With his message of the reign of God
he summoned Israel to conversion and faith (Mk. 1:15f. par.). For him,
faith is faith in God (Mk. 11:22), for whom all things are possible (Mk.
9:23; 14:36). When the disciples believe in God and pray to him with un-
divided hearts, the support of the almighty creator God will be given to
them (Mk. 11:22–24 par.). He grants healing and faith to the sick who
turn to him for help (Mk. 5:34; 10:52); and he does not disappoint the
faith exercised in him by those who are seeking help (Mk. 2:5), but rather,
he calls them explicitly to faith (Mk. 5:36). On the basis of Jesus' way of
talking, and the faith caused and awakened by the Easter appearances,
after Easter the missionary church began to speak, in view of Jesus' completed sacrificial act, of "faith in Jesus Christ" (Acts 10:43), whom God
"made to be Lord and Christ" with the resurrection (Acts 2:36). Such faith

experiences the forgiveness of sins (Acts 10:43). But no longer are merely
the Gentiles called to faith—as in the Jewish mission. Instead, both Jews
and Gentiles are now summoned to it (Acts 2:37–41, 44; 11:21). Paul
stands in this tradition of mission (cf., e.g., 1 Thess. 1:9f.; 2:13; 1 Cor.
15:11); but according to 1 Cor. 13:2 he also knew Jesus' word concerning
the faith which moves mountains.

The book of James and the letter to the Hebrews document the fact,
however, that in early Christianity faith was also spoken of differently by
others than it was by Paul (cf. James 2; Hebrews 11; 12:2). In both cases,
the proximity to the early Jewish tradition (of missions) is close, but, unlike Paul, they too cannot speak, in the sense of Rom. 3:28, of faith as that
which alone justifies.

4. 5:1–11. The State of Reconciliation

(1) Justified now from faith, we have peace with God through our Lord Jesus
Christ, (2) through whom we also received access in faith to the grace in
which we stand, and we boast on the basis of hope in the glory of God. (3) But
not only this, we also boast in afflictions, in the knowledge that affliction
works patience, (4) but patience, that which is proven, and that which is
proven, hope. (5) But hope cannot come to nothing, for the love of God is
poured out in our hearts through the Holy Spirit, who is given to us. —
(6) For Christ died, while we were still weak, at the right time, for those who
were then still godless. (7) Indeed, hardly anyone dies for a righteous person;
it is more likely that one dares to die for the good person. (8) But God shows
his love toward us (in) that Christ died for us while we were still sinners.
(9) How much more then will we, now justified through his blood, be saved
from wrath through him. (10) For if we, as enemies, were reconciled with
God through the death of his Son, how much more will we, as those who have
been reconciled, be saved through his life. (11) But not only this, we also
boast in God through our Lord Jesus Christ, through whom we have now received reconciliation.

A. This paragraph is tightly bound thematically to 3:21–4:25 through the
catchwords "justified" (vv. 1, 9), "boast" (vv. 2f., 11), and "glory of God" (v. 2),
and the theme of atonement and reconciliation through Christ. But Paul now
frees himself from the critical discussion with his opponents and instructs his
readers to see in justification reconciliation with God and the state of hope in
the eschatological deliverance. He does this in two discourses, which cohere together and set forth the gift of justification: vv. 1–5 and 6–11. The first is characterized by a rhetorical chain of syllogisms like we often find in Paul's writings
(cf., e.g., 8:28–30; 10:12–17). The second is marked by a series of inferences
which is likewise frequently encountered in Paul's letters: If this is already
true—then how much more is that the case (cf. 2 Cor. 3:7–9; Phil. 2:12). Such

inferences are a typical characteristic of Rabbinic argumentation and interpretation of Scripture.

On the basis of the Greek textual variants in v. 1, one has the choice of translating the verse either as an indicative, "we have peace with God," or as a hortatory subjunctive, "let us have peace with God." Although the subjunctive is better attested, the indicative is closer in content to Paul's thought and at the same time is the bolder version. Hence, Paul's point is that by virtue of their justification, those who believe already stand in peace with God and need not first strive for it (as the ancient church variously emphasized).

In vv. 3f. Paul refers to the suffering of Christ for the first time in the letter to the Romans. The fact that the pious (righteous) must suffer has been a fixed theme within the Old Testament and Jewish tradition ever since the early Psalms, such as Psalms 18 and 56, the account of the suffering of Jeremiah summarized in Jeremiah 36–45, and the famous poetry of Job. In this tradition, the pious who were persecuted by the enemies of God could endure their suffering only with the help of God. Moreover, according to Sirach 2, suffering serves the purpose of personally purifying the righteous during their time on earth. In early Jewish texts which speak of the suffering of the righteous, the earthly life is transcended: Those pious who have been persecuted on earth and have had their life taken from them need not dread the final judgment. They will be glorified at the resurrection of the dead and will be finally vindicated by God over against their oppressors (cf. Wis. 2:12–20 + 5:1–7; 1 Enoch 103:9–104:5). Jesus thus promised his disciples, who were oppressed together with him, a share in the reign of God (Lk. 12:32; 22:29 with Dan. 7:18, 27). Paul applies both traditions to Christians. As the "suffering righteous," they follow the path of perseverance and are inspired in it by their hope in the future reign of Christ and by their hope of being allowed to participate in the glory of God (1 Cor. 6:2; Rom. 5:17; 8:18ff.; cf. for this topic further pp. 132–134).

B. Now that the apostle has proven the argumentation of his adversary (in 3:27–4:25) to be false, [1] he can, from this point on, unite with his addressees in the "we" style of a letter. He thus states with reference to God's act of deliverance in Christ (called to mind in 4:24f.), which leads "us" to justification, that we, who have been justified from faith (alone), have already received peace with God through our Lord Jesus Christ. While sinners withdraw from God (cf. Gen. 3:8ff.) or, when they do take a stand, confront him as an opponent (v. 10), those who are justified are transferred into a relationship of fellowship with God which brings about their salvation and is therefore designated biblically with the term "peace" (*shalom*). [2] The following sentence says what this peace consists of: Those who believe have received open "access" to grace "through our Lord Jesus Christ." Justification makes it possible for those who believe to live their life before God in grace, freed from their sins. Already in the Qumran texts it says, "Through his mercy he (= God) has brought me near, and through his demonstration of grace comes my righteousness. Through the righteousness of

his truth he has judged me, and through the riches of his goodness he atones for
all of my sins, and through his righteousness he cleanses me from all the un-
cleanness of mankind and from the sin of the children of men; God be praised
for his righteousness and the Highest for his majesty" (1QS 11:13–15). For Paul,
"access" to God has been opened up through the Christ who was given over to
death "for us" and resurrected. In Eph. 2:18; 3:12 this is repeated, and in Heb.
10:19ff. it is described in other words. The "sphere" into which those who believe are led through Christ is called "grace." Those who are justified stand in a
new fellowship with God. They are already protected on earth by his grace and
surrounded by a life full of promise. The hope opened up to them, as those who
have been justified, to be allowed to participate soon in the glorious nature of
the children of God, gives them reason to praise God (cf. v.11). [3] This praise
also need not be silenced by the afflictions which Christians suffer for the sake
of their testimony to their faith. Just the opposite! They know from their own
experience in faith (cf. 2 Cor. 6:3ff.; 11:23ff.), and from the texts of Scripture
which speak of the suffering of the pious (see above), that the afflictions serve
for their good. Through suffering they are led to patience, [4] from patience, to
steadfastness, and from this capacity to stand firm, to hope (in participating in
God's glory, cf. v. 2). [5] The Christians know, by virtue of the Holy Spirit which
has been poured out upon them in their heart through the hearing of the gospel
(cf. Gal. 3:2), that this hope will not cause those who believe to come to nothing
before God (Ps. 22:5–6; Is. 28:16 with Rom. 9:33). In being filled with the Holy
Spirit, the promise from Ezek. 36:26ff. is realized for those who believe, so that
they become capable of returning the love of God bestowed upon them (v. 8),
that is, to love God as their creator and deliverer in accordance with his will. In
this active love, supported by the Spirit, Christians complete the state of grace
into which they are transferred through Christ. [6] By means of a thematic recapitulation of the formula from 4:25 (and as an independent parallel to John
3:16), Paul now explains what the content of the love of God (is) toward sinners
from among both Jews and Gentiles. While they were still weak, Christ died for
godless sinners. God's salvific act in Christ precedes faith and gives it its basis in
history. The history of the sending of Christ, which climaxes in his atoning death,
is thus the absolute realization of the grace of God which exists prior to faith. To
be "godless" is the typical, biblical designation for the wicked who disdain God's
will (cf. the comments to 4:5). They are "weak" before God in two respects: They
cannot accomplish anything in regard to God (Ps. 9:4; 27:2), and they are (without Christ) not in the position to resist temptation and sin (Mk. 14:38 par.). Paul
will work this out once again in 7:14–25. For now he is concerned with Jesus'
vicarious death of atonement for the wicked who are antagonistic toward God. In
addressing this theme, Paul goes beyond all ancient criteria. In the Hellenistic
world, the idea of "dying for someone" had a high moral value and sounded
good ethically. [7] But that one would die for a righteous person (or also for a

just cause) is, however, exactly as Paul notes in v. 7, only seldom attested (cf., e.g., the death of Socrates according to Plato, *Apology* 32a; the readiness to die for the emperor according to Dio Cassius 80.20 and *History of Augustus* 1.14; or the admonition from Sir. 4:28, "[S]tand up for that which is right unto death, then the Lord will fight for you"). Yet there are many examples of the fact that people will go to death for a good cause (cf. 1 Clem. 55:1: "[M]any kings and princes have given themselves over to death on the basis of the saying of an oracle, when a time of disaster ruled, in order to save the citizens through their blood"; and the often misused saying of Horace, *Ode* 3.2.13, "It is sweet and full of honor to die for the Fatherland"). [8] What God did in Christ, however, overshadows these demonstrations of lofty courage and the willingness to sacrifice oneself God proved his love in that, while we were still godless sinners, Christ died for us. God's love in Christ is his free, gracious mercy, which, from the perspective of history, anticipates and precedes all human possibilities and merit.

With an inference from the smaller to the greater (which is typically Jewish, but also not unknown to the Greeks), the apostle now returns to the theme of hope in God's glory (vv. 2, 5). [9] If Christ went to death for sinners in this way, and through his blood brought about atonement for them, then they will all the more be saved through him from wrath in the coming judgment. This matter is so important to the apostle that he repeats it once more in different words: [10] If we were already reconciled with God through the (atoning) death of Jesus as "enemies," that is, as the wicked who rebel against God and despise his will (cf. Ps. 37:20; 68:22; 74:18; 92:10; among others), how much more will we be delivered through the living Christ (from the destruction of the judgment) as those who are already reconciled. By virtue of his sacrificial death, Christ is the living guarantee of the (final) justification of the reconciled (Rom. 4:25), since, as the resurrected one, he intercedes before God for those who believe (Rom. 8:34). In extrabiblical Greek sources, the words "to reconcile" and "reconciliation," used by Paul in vv. 10f. (and in 2 Cor. 5:18–20), refer primarily to the treaty of peace between people who were enemies. "Reconciliation" is the termination of enmity (so too in 1 Cor. 7:11; Rom. 11:15). Paul employs these words in order to establish pointedly the personal and present aspect of the justification which is grounded in the atonement: God gave up his own Son out of pure love for the sinners who were at enmity with him. In so doing, he ended, from his side, the hostility between God and the wicked. As those who are justified, they now stand in peace with and before him (v. 1) and may thus call God "(dear) Father" by virtue of the Holy Spirit which inspires them (Gal. 4:5f.; Rom. 8:15). Instead of being God's enemies, they are already his beloved children in the present through Jesus' sacrificial act and resurrection. [11] Therefore they not only can be certain of their future deliverance through the living Christ, but they can also already boast in God through the mediation of the resurrected one (cf. 8:26f.), who has "now" (3:21) granted them the state of being reconciled with God.

Excursus 8:
Justification and Reconciliation

As P. Althaus already emphasized concerning this passage in earlier editions of this commentary, and F. Lang has recently confirmed in his interpretation of 2 Cor. 5:18–20 (in Das Neue Testament Deutsch, vol. 7, pp. 295–297), for Paul *justification and reconciliation* belong inextricably together. As in 2 Cor. 5:14–21, in Rom. 5:1–11 the language of atonement, justification, and reconciliation also meshes together seamlessly. The abandonment of the Son of God to death on the cross, desired by God himself out of love for his creation and obediently affirmed by Jesus, is the absolute act of atonement which grounds justification (Rom. 3:25f.; 5:8f.; 8:3). God made his own Son, who did not know the guilt of sin, "to be sin" for us, so that we might partake through him in the righteousness of God (2 Cor. 5:21). Because in the Greek Bible the atoning sacrifice offered for the sake of sin is sometimes simply called "sin" for short in the technical language of sacrifice (cf. Lev. 4:21, 24), 2 Cor. 5:21 means that God made Christ "to be an atoning sacrifice" for us. Romans 8:3 confirms this. The blood of Jesus is the infinitely valuable means of atonement for the godless sinner (1 Cor. 6:20; Rom. 3:25; 5:9). God's atoning act in and through Christ forms the historical and legal ground for justification. In turn, "reconciliation" designates the gift of God and the present securing of salvation which are bound together with justification (Rom. 5:11; 2 Cor. 5:20–6:2) viewed from the personal perspective: God has overcome and ended from his side the hostility which prevailed between sinners and himself. He has placed those who have been reconciled with him through Christ in "peace" with himself (Rom. 5:1; Eph. 2:13–16). God is thus the one who creates atonement, grants justification, and establishes reconciliation, on the basis of his free will and grace. Moreover, Rom. 11:15, 32 and Col. 1:19–20 make it possible to recognize that God's act of reconciliation has a worldwide dimension. It affects Gentiles and Jews in the same way and represents the event which establishes the creation anew. Although the doctrinal tradition of the church continues up to the present time to speak of the appeasing of an angry God through the blood of Christ, or also of a satisfaction which takes place by means of Jesus' sacrificial death toward the God who has been injured in regard to his majesty through sin, there is no talk at all of this in the apostle's texts concerning atonement and reconciliation! Nevertheless, the fact that in 2 Cor. 5:18 he calls the apostolic office of proclamation, to which he was commissioned by Christ, the "ministry of reconciliation" shows the high value which the discourse concerning reconciliation has for him. As the ministry of the Spirit and of righteousness, Paul's ministry stands over against the ministry of death and condemnation which Moses had to exercise in the old covenant (2 Cor. 3:7ff.).

5. 5:12–21. The Reign of Grace

(12) Therefore: As through one man sin came into the world and through sin, death, and thus death reached to all men, because all sinned . . . — (13) Up until the Law, namely, sin was already in the world, but sin is not reckoned, if no Law is present. (14) But death reigned from Adam until Moses also over those who did not sin according to the likeness of Adam's transgression (of the commandment), who is the (anti-)type of the one to come. — (15) Yet the case is not the same with the gift of grace as with the trespass: if namely through the trespass of the one the many died, how much more has the grace of God and the gift which consists of grace been granted in abounding measure to the many through the one man Jesus Christ. (16) And the gift of grace (does) not (work) like that which came through the one who sinned! For the judgment (led) from the one to condemnation, but the gift of grace (led) from many transgressions to the gift of righteousness. (17) If namely through the trespass of the one death came to reign through the one, how much more will those who receive the fullness of grace and the gift of righteousness come to reign in life through the one, Jesus Christ. — (18) Therefore, as the trespass of the one resulted in condemnation for all men, so also the righteous act of the one (results) in the justification which bestows life for all men. (19) As namely the many were made sinners through the disobedience of the one man, so will the many also be made righteous through the obedience of the one. — (20) But the Law came in between in order that the trespass might increase. But where sin increased, grace became still more abundant, (21) in order that, as sin came to reign through death, grace also comes to reign through righteousness to eternal life through Jesus Christ, our Lord.

Verse 12: Genesis 3; Verse 17: Dan. 7:18.

A. As the introductory "therefore" and the parallel between 5:8–11 and 5:18–21 make clear, vv. 12–21 still belong to the discussion of 5:8–11. The catchwords "sin," "grace," "Law," and "righteousness" demonstrate, moreover, that in these verses the apostle is bringing his entire discussion from (1:18–3:20) 3:21–5:21 to an end.

The structure of the paragraph is as follows. The contrast begun in v. 12 between Adam and Christ is not brought to an end until vv. 18–21. Verses 13–17 introduce intermediate thoughts, which will once again be taken up in reference to the Law in v. 20. The agitated sentence construction, which repeatedly works with the (Rabbinic) inference from the lesser to the greater, betrays the fact that in his dictation of the letter (cf. 16:22) the apostle is striving for clarity in his argument in regard to form.

From the perspective of the history of tradition, several strands of tradition run together in 5:12–21. In 1 Cor. 15:20–22, 44–49, Paul has already expressed himself in regard to the Corinthians concerning the relationship between Adam and Christ. There the apostle was concerned to show that "as in Adam all die, so also in Christ will all be made alive" (v. 22). In contrast to mortal Adam, created (according to Gen. 2:7) from the earth, Christ is the resurrected Lord and Son of Man (cf. 1 Cor. 15:20–28), "the second man, who is from heaven" (v. 47). The difference between Adam and Christ, together with the sequence from Adam to Christ, dare not be leveled out. Rather, the Corinthians must remain aware of the fact that, as Christians, they are not already simply being transferred spiritually into the kingdom of God prepared by Christ, but that they must still wait for the transformation of flesh and blood into the heavenly body and for the eschatological triumph of the Lord over sin and death (cf. 1 Cor. 15:54f.). The apostle returns to this debate in Romans 5, but at this point works out the relationship between Adam's Fall into sin, its consequences, and the gaining of life through the grace of justification. In view of the fate of sin and death which befell mankind with Adam's Fall, it is not the Law which helps one to progress further, but only the grace made possible through Christ's act of obedience. It is thus under its reign that those who believe now stand.

Paul develops these fundamental thoughts in dependence on the early Jewish interpretation of the Fall in Genesis 3 and the Son of Man tradition as received from Jesus. Concerning the former, in so-called 4 Ezra, just as in Paul's writing, Adam is considered to be the ancestor and the one who determines his descendants' destiny. The author complains in 4 Ezra 7:118, "Oh Adam, what have you done! When you sinned, your Fall occurred not only for you, but for us, your descendants!" In 2 Baruch this is then made more precise, once again in view of the judgment of God: "For when Adam first sinned and brought an untimely death over all, in the same way every one of those who are descended from him also entered into the future torment himself. . . . But now, devote yourself only to corruption, you who are now doers of evil; for you will be severely punished, since you formerly disdained the understanding of the Most High. For his works have not instructed you; the artistic arrangement of his creation, which exists at all times, has also not convinced you. Adam is thus simply and solely the cause of his own life; but we all, each one for himself, have become Adam" (2 Bar. 54:15–19). Hence, according to 4 Ezra 7:128f. and 2 Bar. 85:3–5, the Law and God's grace are the only things available for the pious to overcome the Adamic fate. Paul in turn adopts the main ideas of both of these apocalypses, but in contrast to them does not see in the Law a way out of the Adamic condition of guilt.

In regard to the latter, when in v. 15 (similarly as in 1 Cor. 15:47) Paul calls Jesus Christ "the one man," when he refers in vv. 17, 21 to the participation of the justified in the royal reign (of Christ), and when he speaks in v. 19 of Jesus' obedience, which assists the many to righteousness, this can be explained most

easily in view of the Son of Man tradition. According to Dan. 7:13f., 18, 27, the
"Son of Man" embodies the divine promise that Israel will one day enter into
that dominion over the nations which deserves the predicate "worthy of being a
human being." According to the Enoch apocalypse, the Son of Man is then the
messiah and judge of the world who is set upon the judgment throne by God
(cf. 1 Enoch 61:8; 62:2ff.). According to the presentation of all four Gospels,
Jesus understood himself as the messianic Son of Man sent from God. But instead of already claiming the right to his messianic reign during his life on earth
and allowing himself to be served, he desired to follow the path himself of service and of vicariously giving up his life for "the many" (cf. Is. 53:11f.; Mk. 10:45
par.). He anticipated that his exaltation and installation into the office of judge
would take place only after his passage through suffering and death (Mk. 14:62
par.). But Jesus also promised his followers participation in his eschatological
reign as the Son of Man and judge of the world (cf. Lk. 12:32 and Lk. 22:28–30
par. with Dan. 7:18). Paul had already appropriated this Jesus tradition in 1 Cor.
6:2; 15:20–28, and it is now reflected in Rom. 5:12–21 as well. There are
hermeneutical and missiological grounds, however, for the fact that the apostle
speaks merely of the "man" Jesus Christ in 1 Corinthians and Romans, instead
of the "Son of Man." The biblical expression "son of man" originally refers to
one as a descendant from humanity (cf. thus, e.g., Ps. 8:5; Ezek. 2:1ff.; 3:1ff.). In
order to avoid a misleading contrast between the two titles, "Son of Man" and
"Son of God," and in order to set forth the cosmic significance of Jesus, Paul
and those of his school thus preferred to speak of Jesus Christ as "man" rather
than as the "Son of Man" (cf. thus also in 1 Tim. 2:5f., where Mk. 10:45 is taken
up). The "man" Jesus is the Son of God sent from God into the world, who will
redeem sinners as a whole from the curse of the Law (Gal. 4:4). In contrast to
Adam, the sinner, Jesus is therefore the redeemer sent from God (cf. also
below, pp. 190–192).

B. With the contrast between Adam and Christ, Paul brings his discussion
concerning sin and justification to a close. While, for the apostle, Abraham is already considered the ancestor of all those who believe (4:11f.), it is only on the
basis of Adam that the universality of the justification of Jews and Gentiles by
the one God (3:28–30) becomes completely evident. [12] By pointing to Adam
as the ultimate ancestor who determines the destiny of his descendants, Paul is
able and desires to bring to mind a state of affairs which really does affect all
people. This personal way of viewing history, which Paul already employed in
Romans 4 in regard to our "father" Abraham, is therefore continued in Rom.
5:12–21 and—in a typically Jewish fashion—widened out into a so-called aetiol-
ogy, that is, a historical analysis which explains the origin or founding of something. Paul's point is that what is true for Adam is true for all. In view of the Fall
into sin portrayed in Genesis 3, it holds true that through the one man sin came
over the entire (human) world. Here, in Rom. 7:7ff., and also elsewhere in Paul's
writings, "sin" is much more than an individual offense against God's will. It

concerns—as already indicated in Gen. 3:14ff.—a deadly fate which comes over humanity and its world. The individual sins which people commit are merely an expression of the entanglement in guilt which oppresses everyone and everything. As its consequence, death has become the destiny of all people. The addition, "because they all sinned," shows that, for Paul, death is not simply a matter of the mortality which belongs to being a creature, but at the same time is the exclusion from eternal life as the result of sin. In a way similar to 2 Bar. 54:19 (see above), Paul also means that, beginning with Adam, all people willingly participate in their own way in the fate of the guilt brought about by the sin which has come over them and therefore must suffer death.

Although in 5:12ff. the apostle clearly sees in sin and death an unavoidable human destiny, he does not express here (or elsewhere in his letters) the thought of an original death or of original sin. This notion is to be traced back, above all, to the interpretation of Rom. 5:12 in the Latin church. Here the Latin translation of Paul's phrase, "because all sinned," with *in quo omnes peccaverunt* was understood as a relative pronoun clause and related to Adam, so that the meaning became, "in whom they all have sinned." But more than anything else, the interpretation of the church father Augustine (354–430) became decisive. He takes as his starting point the idea "that all have sinned in that first man, because all were in him at that time when he sinned, and that from then on sin is inherited through birth" (*Contra duas Epistolas Pelagianorum* 4.4, 7). Yet Paul only intends to refer to the fact that death has overtaken all people because they all have sinned (in their own way). For him, sin is at the same time one's fate and one's act, for which one is responsible. While his gospel of justification is to be interpreted without the dogmatic doctrine of original sin and original death, the intention of the apostle's statement must still be maintained. He refers unmistakably to the fact that with and since Adam, death and sin are inescapable. No person can avoid them, not even by performing good deeds of obedience. These deeds may be in themselves valuable and just, but they accomplish nothing against mankind's corporate entanglement in guilt.

Paul does not continue the comparison between Adam and Christ begun in v. 12 until vv. 18ff. He interrupts the contrast in order first to take up the thesis, which was considered equally obvious to Jews and Jewish Christians, that the Law can provide a way out from the Adamic fate of guilt. [13] In Wis. 10:1–2 it says concerning wisdom (which manifests itself in the Law) that "she has freed the forefather of the world . . . from his sin and given him the power to rule over everything"; and in 2 Bar. 85:3–4 we read that "we have nothing now besides the Almighty and his Law. If we thus prepare our hearts and make ourselves ready, in this way we will again acquire everything which we have lost and much better things than we have lost." But according to Paul, the Law comes from Sinai much too late to be able to help and, moreover, it is from the very beginning too weak to restrain sin and to procure righteousness (cf. Gal. 3:21; Rom. 7:14ff.; 8:3). Even before the giving of the Law on Sinai, the guilty fate brought about by sin had already inescapably oppressed the whole world. The only difference between the time before and after the giving of the Law is that only since the decree of the Law is sin reckoned to every person's (eschatological) account regarding his or her guilt in a way that is legally binding (cf. Is. 65:6; Dan. 7:10; 1 Enoch 81:4; 89:62ff.; 98:6ff.; 104:7; Rev. 20:12 for the maintenance of such an account). The Law thus conveys a forensic concept to sin, but it does not help to overcome it. [14] Rather, death already reigned from Adam to Moses over those people as well who had not—unlike Adam (cf. Gen. 2:16f.)—transgressed a clear command of God, but were guilty only of an offense against the order of life laid down by God in creation (cf. Rom. 1:18ff. and 2 Bar. 54:17f.; see above, pp. 35ff.). And since then the reign of death is unbroken. But Adam is also the antitype of the new man of the future, Jesus Christ, and it is this man who makes eternal life possible.

Before the apostle carries through completely the comparison begun in v. 12, he contrasts Adam and Christ with one another in two parallel sentences (= vv. 15 + 16) and then, by way of connection, incorporates in v. 17 the reign of death just mentioned into this contrast. [15] The case of Adam's transgression and Fall is different than that of the gift of grace (from God in Christ). Through the Fall of the one, "the many" have come under the reign of death. (The Semitic expression "the many," as it is used, e.g., in Is. 53:11f., means the innumerable multitude, and is therefore rightly equated by Paul with "all" in v. 18.) The gift of God, which consists of grace, surpasses the effect of Adam's Fall by far. It was brought about in the sacrificial act of the one man (= Son of Man) Jesus Christ, who "came not to let himself be served, but to serve and to give up his life as a ransom for many" (Mk. 10:45 par., cf. with Is. 43:3f.; 53:11f.). [16] The gift of God determined by this sacrificial act is based on other presuppositions and affects more than Adam's sin. God's judgment of Adam led to the condemnation of all people as sinners. In contrast, although the gracious gift of God in Christ has the sin of all people as its presupposition, it nevertheless leads to justification by virtue of Jesus' atoning death, in which all those who believe participate. God's action in Christ is more comprehensive in its effect than Adam's Fall: [17] Death came to reign through the Fall of Adam, but in spite of its reign those who receive God's abounding grace and the gift of (the) righteousness (of faith) will come to reign in eternal life through Jesus Christ. Hence, the promise from Dan. 7:18 pronounced by Jesus to his disciples (in Lk. 12:32; 22:28–30 par.) will be fulfilled for them in that they will judge the world with the Son of Man, Jesus Christ, and share in his reign (cf. 1 Cor. 6:2; 15:23; Rev. 20:4).

[18] Now that Paul has related the Fall of Adam to the Son of Man tradition, which he received from Jesus, in this way (and in doing so anchored his message of justification once more in the doctrine with which the Roman Christians are familiar; see above, pp. 59, 75), he can bring the comparison between Adam and Christ begun in v. 12 to its climax. Just as condemnation came to all people through the Fall of the one man, Adam, so too justification came to all people

through "the righteous act" of the other man, Jesus Christ, which made eternal life possible. The very next sentence explains what Paul means by this. [19] As through the disobedience of the one man Adam "the many" (see above) became sinners before God, in this same way all will become righteous before God through the obedience of Christ. The Christ-hymn of Phil. 2:6–11 speaks in an impressive way of the obedience of Christ, in which he took the death of the cross upon himself (cf. further Mk. 14:32–42 par. with Heb. 5:7–10; 12:2). Christ's obedience makes righteousness possible for all people, because the vicarious atoning death of the righteous Son of God frees all sinners from the curse of the Law, insofar as they believe in Jesus Christ (Gal. 3:13; 4:5). With the repeated "all" and "the many" from vv. 18, 19, Paul has once again clearly expounded the universality of justification for Jews and Gentiles (cf. 3:20; 4:11). [20] He can now also take up and answer the question concerning the function of the Law in relation to justification, which has just been raised for the first time in vv. 13f. Paul's answer is that the Law does not procure righteousness. Just as it did between Abraham and Christ (cf. Gal. 3:19ff.), so too the Law also "came in between" Adam and Christ (at Sinai). The instruction declared by God in the Law makes sin accountable forensically (v. 13) and causes it to appear in all of its severity. When the command of God is explicitly formulated, it raises sin to a conscious and public enmity against God (7:13; 8:7). But it contributes nothing toward the overcoming of sin. For Jewish and Jewish-Christian ears this statement is just as harsh as the formulation of 3:20. Paul has already emphasized in 3:27, 31, however, that with his view he certainly does not intend to impugn the Law as the gift of God, but merely make clear what it can and cannot accomplish. He will once again expound this point in detail in 7:7–8:17. In the present context what concerns him is the contrast between Christ and the Law. For precisely at that point where the Law has increased sin to enmity, God's grace has even more effectively stepped into action. [21] Through its own authority, God's grace has surpassed the reign of sin, which expresses itself in death, that is, through the righteousness which is bestowed to those who believe through the death and resurrection of Jesus and which leads to eternal life (cf. v. 17). Christians who believe in Jesus as their reconciler and Lord have received reconciliation and stand under the reign of the grace of God. Instead of still being placed under the fate of sin and having to anticipate the judgment of death, they live under Christ's reign, who embodies God's righteousness (1 Cor. 1:30), so that they might be filled with the hope of eternal life (cf. v. 5).

III. 6:1–8:39. The Righteousness of God as the Ground and Power of the New Life

After the apostle has brought his discussions concerning sin, the Law, faith, righteousness, and reconciliation to a certain conclusion, he now expresses his views concerning the fundamental questions of the new life which the Christians are to lead under the reign of righteousness (6:13, 18). The critique of the Pauline gospel by the (Jewish-Christian) missionaries who oppose Paul once again stands in the background. Paul consequently develops his argument on the basis of baptism in chapter 6, takes up the matter of the Christian's attitude toward the Law in detail in 7:1–8:17, and beginning in 8:18 outlines the perspectives of hope in which the justified stand who suffer for the sake of Christ. The main themes of 6:1–8:39, that is, life under the reign of grace, the Law, and hope, have already been anticipated in 5:17, 21; 5:13f., 20; and 5:4, 17.

1. 6:1–23. Freedom from the Power of Sin and Service to Righteousness

Paul's remarks concerning justification and reconciliation in chapter 5 have again immediately engaged those critics in battle who are attacking his proclamation of Christian freedom (Gal. 5:1) by accusing the apostle, all the way to Rome, of preaching cheap grace to the Gentiles (cf. 3:8). These objections are of such significance to the apostle that he now takes them up directly in 6:1 and 15 and refutes them in detail. In doing so, he takes as his starting point the view of baptism and the baptismal confession which holds sway in Rome in order to demonstrate anew that his gospel corresponds to the doctrine which is already of great value to the Christians in Rome.

1.1. 6:1–14. The Change of Lordship in Baptism

(1) What shall we now say? "Let us remain in sin, that grace might increase?" (2) By no means! We, who died to sin, how can we still live in it? (3) Or do you not know that we, who are baptized in Christ Jesus, are baptized into his death? (4) We are buried together with him through baptism into death, in order that, just as Christ was raised from the dead through the glory of the Father, we too might walk in the newness of life. (5) If we, namely, are united with the likeness of his death, we will also be with that of (his) resurrection, (6) in the knowledge of the fact that our old man has been crucified together (with him), in order to destroy the body (which is determined) by sin, so that we no longer serve sin. (7) For the one who has died is absolved from sin.(8) But if we have died together with Christ, we believe that we will also live together with him; (9) for we know that Christ, having been raised from the dead, no longer dies; death is no longer lord over him. (10) Inasmuch as he died, he died to sin once for all; inasmuch as he lives, he lives to God. (11) In the same way, consider yourselves as dead toward sin and as alive toward God in Christ Jesus. (12) No (longer) let sin thus reign in your mortal body, in order to obey its lusts, (13) and no (longer) place your members at sin's disposal as weapons of unrighteousness, but place yourself at God's disposal as those who are alive from the dead and your members as weapons of righteousness for

God. (14) On no account shall sin be lord over you any longer, for you are not under the Law, but under grace.

A. With 6:1 Paul begins a new discourse. The catchwords "sin," "Christ Jesus," "righteousness," "rule," and so on show, of course, that the apostle is arguing on the foundation of his statements in 5:12–21.

In v. 1 Paul cites the thesis of his opponents, known to us from 3:8, in a new formulation and in v. 2 contrasts it with his own counterthesis. He explains this counterthesis in vv. 3–10, in order to strengthen it in v. 11. In vv. 12–14 he then draws hortatory conclusions from this affirmation.

In vv. 3, 6, and 9 Paul reminds the Roman Christians of the baptism which they have received and of the confession of Christ (which they have accepted at the occasion of their baptism). In v. 17 the apostle will refer again to that form of the (baptismal) doctrine proper which is recognized in Rome. But his formulations in vv. 2ff., that is, "died to sin," "baptized into the death of Christ," "buried with him in death," "to walk in the newness of life, as Christ was raised from the dead," "crucified with (Christ)," "Christ, having been raised from the dead," and "died to sin once for all," and so on, already make it possible to recognize which confession is in view. In all probability, what is in view is that summary of the instruction associated with baptism which Paul previously cited in 1 Cor. 15:3ff. (and which, according to its original formulation, appears to go back to the first church in Jerusalem): "Christ died for us according to the Scripture and was buried, and he was raised on the third day according to the Scripture and appeared to Cephas (= Peter), and then to the Twelve." Like Paul himself, the Christians in Rome have also adopted this old doctrinal confession (at the occasion of baptism). Just like the apostle, who received his baptism in Damascus (cf. Acts 9:10–19; 1 Cor. 12:13), the Roman Christians have also been baptized "in Christ Jesus," that is, in the name of Jesus, by which the entire salvific work of God is determined (cf. Acts 4:12). In their baptism they have taken part in the fate of the Son of Man and in the fruit of his atoning death. They have died like he did, are absolved through him, can now walk in the newness of life by virtue of the Holy Spirit as "those who are alive from the dead" (v. 13), and hope in their eschatological participation in the glory of the resurrection of Christ.

With this view of baptism, Paul corroborates the position of the Romans. Historically there is no evidence of the practice of a charismatic baptism in Rome, which Paul allegedly banished as beyond the limits in Rom. 6:2ff. (see below, Excursus 9). Rather, the text refers to an entirely different set of circumstances. Ever since the time of his Antiochean mission, Paul had renounced circumcision as a necessary prerequisite for the baptism of the Gentiles and proclaimed to them freedom from the Law. For this reason his doctrine was under suspicion by his opponents. In their opinion, with his practice of baptism Paul was promoting sin within the churches and making Christ into a "servant of sin" who forgives everything (Gal. 2:17). Paul takes up these rebukes and demonstrates that for him the reign of grace established with baptism places one in service to righteousness with the goal of sanctification (cf. v. 19).

B. As elsewhere in Romans (cf. 3:5; 4:1; 7:7; 9:14), here too Paul introduces an assertion with the rhetorical question, [1] "What shall we now say?" which he then subsequently rejects. The assertion clearly refers back to the rebukes of his "slanderers" (3:8). They take offense at the message of the free grace of God in Christ, as the apostle has just developed it once again in chapter 5, and which apparently leads Christians astray into lawlessness. Hence, they maliciously attribute to him the doctrine, "Let us remain in sin, that grace might increase!" [2] Paul wards off the opinion subscribed to him just as clearly as in 3:8 and consciously places himself on the side of his addressees with his argumentation in the "we" form: How should we who have died to sin (through Christ) still desire to live in it!? [3] As proof, he refers to baptism in the form of a reminder. The Christians in Rome know full well that the act of baptism and the baptismal confession associate the ones being baptized completely with their Lord, who died and was raised for them. As believers' or adult baptism—child or infant baptism was not yet generally practiced in the church at the time of the New Testament—the baptism was accompanied in the early church by a genuine change of existence. The candidate for baptism was immersed entirely in flowing or still water and was cleansed from his or her sins in the "washing of rebirth" (Tit. 3:5; cf. Acts 8:36ff.; 22:16; Eph. 5:26). In 1 Cor. 6:11 Paul interprets the process of baptism in terms of the washing away of sins, sanctification, and justification through the name of the Lord Jesus Christ and the Spirit of God. It is entirely similar here. Through baptism the baptismal candidate participates in the Christ-event as it is recapitulated in the baptismal confession. Jesus Christ is the messianic "man" (Son of Man) (cf. above to 5:5ff.) whose destiny affects all those who believe, since according to Dan. 7:13, 18, 27, the Son of Man embodies as a whole the "saints of the Most High," that is, the Israel of God. [4] As a result, the following holds true for baptism in the name of Christ Jesus: It gives one a share in Jesus' death "for our sins," in his burial, and in his resurrection on the third day (1 Cor. 15:3–5). Those being baptized are freed through Jesus' atoning death from their old existence under sin and participate in the life of the Christ who was raised for them. Through their baptism the Christians are buried together with Christ into death in order that, just as he was raised through the glorious power of God (cf. 2 Cor. 13:4), they themselves might also walk in the newness of the resurrection life on the basis of the power of God (cf. likewise 7:4, 6). This state of affairs, though only described for the first time here, is so important to the apostle that in vv. 5–7 and 8–10 he explains it further in two groups of sentences which correspond exactly to one another. In doing so he chooses his words carefully. [5] If we, by means of baptism, "are united with the likeness of his (i.e., Jesus') death, we will also be with that of (his) resurrection." Although the ones being baptized are not literally crucified on Golgotha like Jesus himself, buried close to Calvary, and there on the third day raised from the dead (cf. Mk. 14:21–16:8 par.), in their baptism they have experienced, as did their Lord, being put to death and being raised. In contrast to 1 Cor. 6:11 and Rom. 8:30 (Col. 2:13; Eph. 2:5f.), Paul does not simply say in this context that we are already raised and glorified with Christ. Rather, he consciously makes a distinction between the life of faith and resurrection existence, and thus writes that we will still participate in the resurrection as he has, or, "we believe that we will live with Christ" (v. 8). The basis for this formulation does not lie (as in Corinth, cf. 1 Cor. 10:1–13) in the concern of the apostle that the Roman Christians, by virtue of their baptism, could think that they have already been enraptured spiritually in the glory of the resurrection and with it imagine themselves unencumbered by all earthly cares and responsibilities. Instead, its basis is his opponents' criticism of the Pauline preaching surrounding baptism (see above). Thus, in the letter to the Romans Paul also holds fast unflinchingly to the fact that Christians are already justified through Christ and destined by God for glorification at the side of their Lord (cf. 5:18ff.; 8:30). But at the same time he strives to make it clear that they have responsibilities which grow out of their participation in Jesus' death and resurrection. The reign of grace established at baptism over those who are baptized demands from Christians deeds of confirmation and obedience while in their position of waiting and becoming, which now exists between their change in life brought about by faith and the return of Christ. In this chapter the apostle therefore outlines the main features of his baptismal admonitions (which are also already indicated in 1 Cor. 6:9f.) at the same time that he reminds them of the meaning of baptism. [6] Christians should remember that their old self was defeated with Christ on the cross. Their old body, given over to and yielding sin, has experienced the death sentence on the cross of Christ, so that Christians must no longer be subservient to sin. Hence, in his letters Paul speaks of the "body" of the person when it is a matter of the circumstances involved in one's communication, in a good or evil sense, that is, when it is a matter of that which a person does and accomplishes toward others. According to Paul, there is therefore for the baptized an end to the life which produces sin. [7] Indeed, a widespread Jewish maxim says, "All who die attain atonement through their death" (Sifre Num. §112 to Num. 15:31). Paul applies this premise to baptism: The one who has died (with Christ) is (by virtue of the atoning death of Jesus) absolved from sin (for this terminology, cf. also the Greek text of Sir. 26:29; T. Sim. 6:1; Lk. 18:14). Jesus' death of atonement sets one free from sin and from the compulsion to have to sin.

[8] In the following sentences, which are structured exactly parallel to vv. 5–7, the apostle once again supports his perspective in view of Jesus Christ. If we died together with Christ (in baptism), we now stand at Jesus' side in the hope of eternal life based on faith (cf. 5:17). [9] This faith is grounded in the knowledge that Christ was raised by God from the dead so that, as a result, the reign of death has been taken away forever. Christians depend on being incorporated into this act of God which took place "for us" (cf. 4:24f.) and on being

resurrected just as Jesus was also resurrected (cf. 1 Thess. 4:14). [10] The resurrected Son of God died to sin once for all. Sin leads to the death of the sinner (5:12), but Jesus died as the righteous one in obedience to God's will (5:18). As a result, sin exercised its right once for all on Jesus (Rom. 8:3). Death had to give Jesus up to life before God. [11] With this sentence Paul crosses over to address the Christians in Rome directly. What is true for Jesus, is also true for those who are in him and for whom he died. Christians should and may understand themselves as God's creatures who, like Jesus, were dead in regard to the claim of sin, but have now become alive for God. In and through Christ, the baptized are "new creatures" (2 Cor. 5:17). It is now also their task, therefore, to do justice to their new being through deeds of obedience. Paul is not yet aware of the ecclesiological doctrine of "original sin" (see above, pp. 85f.). But Paul is thoroughly conscious of the fact that during their earthly life even those Christians who are freed from sin remain given to temptation and are entangled in the fight against sin, the passions, and the powers of death. Just as Christ must still fight in heaven against the powers which oppose God, including death (1 Cor. 15:25f.), Christians on earth are also still in battle with those authorities. [12] The apostle therefore summons the Christians from Rome to resist the claims of sin to reign over their bodies, which are still mortal, and not to gratify the lusts of the body. Paul has expounded in 1:24ff. (in an open and far-reaching way) just how devastating the passions have become and can become for the Gentiles (cf. further, Gal. 5:16–21). [13] Christians should no longer place their members, that is, themselves in their bodily existence, at the disposal of sin as weapons of unrighteousness, but they should place themselves—as creatures called by God from the dead into new life!—at the disposal of God to be vanguards of the righteousness which corresponds to God's will. [14] Ever since their baptism in Christ's name, sin has forfeited its right to reign over the very ones who have been baptized. Those who have been baptized no longer live under the guilty verdict of the Law, which brings death, which conveys to sin a forensic notion, and which makes evident the impossibility of overcoming sin (5:13, 20). Rather, they now stand under the reign of the grace of God brought forth and exercised by Jesus (cf. 5:21).

1.2. 6:15–23. In Service of Righteousness

(15) What then? Should we sin because we no longer stand under the Law, but under grace? By no means! (16) Do you not know that the one at whose disposal you place yourselves as slaves for obedience, of this one you are obedient slaves, either of sin unto death, or of obedience unto righteousness? (17) But thanks be to God that you were slaves of sin, but now you have become obedient from the heart to the form of teaching to which you were given over; (18) freed from sin, you were made to be slaves of righteousness! (19) I say that in a human way on account of the weakness of your flesh. Namely, as you

placed your members as slaves at the disposal of impurity and lawlessness for the purpose of lawlessness, in the same way now place your members as slaves at the disposal of righteousness for the purpose of sanctification. (20) For when you were slaves of sin, you were free in regard to righteousness. (21) Indeed, what did you have for fruit at that time? (Fruit) concerning which you are now ashamed, because its end result is death. (22) But now, since you are freed from sin, but have been made slaves for God, you have your fruit for sanctification, but as an end result, eternal life. (23) For the wages of sin (is) death, but the gift of God's grace (is) eternal life through Christ Jesus, our Lord.

A. The structure of the paragraph is clear. In v. 15 Paul repeats the objection from 6:1 and refutes it in two rounds of argument (vv. 15–18 and 19–23) which, in part, run parallel in terms of content. In v. 17 the words, "you have become obedient from the heart to the form of teaching to which you were given over," are explained by some as a marginal gloss by a later transcriber of Romans, but the form of the text in the oldest and best manuscripts of Romans offers no support for this supposition. The formulation from v. 17 is rather very understandable when one considers that in the early Christian mission a certain amount of formalized doctrine concerning the faith was mediated to the churches, which were still in the process of being built, functioning for the new Christians as a plumb line for their thought and life. Paul refers to such apostolic teaching in 1 Cor. 11:23; 15:1–11. Moreover, in terms of that which concerns the Christians' behavior, he calls to mind in 1 Thess. 4:1–3 the fact that from him the Thessalonians "have received handed down, how you should walk and please God," to which he adds, "for the will of God consists in your sanctification." This sounds very closely related to Rom. 6:17ff. As Paul then amplifies it in 1 Cor. 15:1–2, the faith and salvation of the Christians in Corinth depend on the doctrinal tradition in 1 Cor. 15:3–5, called by Paul himself the "gospel." On the basis of the allusions in Rom. 6:2ff., it thus follows that this same tradition also determines the faith of the Roman Christians (see above, p. 90). In addition, a comparison of 6:17 with 10:9f. leads to the recognition of confessional formulations such as found in 1 Cor. 12:3 and Rom. 4:25. Paul thus alludes in v. 17 to doctrine which was taught to the Christians in Rome in their baptismal instruction by the missionaries who brought the gospel to Rome before Paul.

B. The apostle now refers once again to the reproaches of his critics already mentioned in 6:1 (and 3:8). [15] The saying attributed to him, "Let us sin, because we no longer stand under the Law, but under grace!" is both infamous and theologically absurd! [16] To refute it, the apostle first appeals to knowledge gained by the Christians' own experience in Rome and then applies this to baptism. From their observation of the slave market and their own experiences with slavery (cf. the comments to 16:10f.), the Roman Christians know full well that someone who sells himself or herself into slavery owes strict obedience to his or her lord (selling oneself into slavery occurred in Rome and by all means elsewhere as well, cf. 1 Clem. 55:2). The two "lords" which come into question for Christians in view of their baptism are called "sin" and the "obedience (of faith)," "righteousness" (vv. 18f.) or "God" (cf. v. 22). Whoever is a slave to sin reaps death for one's behavior (5:21). Whoever becomes a "slave of obedience" obtains righteousness. This unusual formulation can be explained when one keeps in mind 1:5 and 15:18. In view of these passages, the obedience which Paul means is the obedience of faith. It includes the conversion to the one, true God, the acceptance of the gospel, and the obedient deed of love (see above, pp. 76–78). Hence, just as Paul summarizes the entire message of salvation in the one word, "faith," in Gal. 1:23; 3:25, here he places the entire way of life of the Christian under the sign, "obedience." By virtue of their obedience of faith, awakened by the gospel through the Holy Spirit, Christians thus participate in the righteousness of God (cf. 2 Cor. 5:21; Rom. 3:26). [17] But thanks be to God that for the Christians in Rome the alternative of sin or righteousness is no longer open. The women and men who are now Christians were, to be sure, once slaves of sin, and as a result were surely dedicated to the judgment of death. But on the occasion of their baptism they became obedient "from the heart," that is, according to biblical anthropology, from the foundation of their human nature (cf. comments to 10:18f.), to a form of teaching which made reconciliation and justification possible for them (cf. 5:1, 10f.). In regard to this teaching it is, in all probability, a matter above all of the "gospel" concerning which Paul comes to speak in 1 Cor. 15:1–11 (see above). It was mediated to the Roman Christians by their missionaries, or still better, on the occasion of their baptism they were "given over" to this teaching in which Christ himself comes to the fore (cf. 5:8). The gospel appears here in the function of a living authority which is decisive for life. Since their baptism, it completely determines the life of the Roman Christians. Hence, Paul expresses thanks to God for the fact that God has moved the Christians in Rome to faith in the doctrine of the gospel. Inasmuch as Paul thus explicitly declares his agreement with this teaching, he lays the foundation for the warning with which he closes his letter (in 16:17) that the Christians in Rome must beware to guard themselves from those people who "cause divisions and anger in comparison with the doctrine, which you have learned." It is not the apostle whom the Roman Christians must mistrust, but those "slanderers" (3:8) who attribute to him false views and as a result bring unrest into the (house) churches in Rome! [18] In conclusion to the first round of argumentation, Paul formulates his view crassly and clearly: Christians have been freed (through Christ) from the power of sin. But this has not taken place so that they might from now on have a license to sin, but in order that they might be placed into slavery in regard to the righteousness desired by God (cf., similarly, 1 Pet. 2:16).

[19] The apostle now initiates a second, somewhat more differentiated explanation of the change in lordship which the Christians in Rome have experienced

in their baptism. In so doing he employs in his argument the contrast between "once" and "now" that is typical for baptismal preaching and speaks of the "sanctification" which is not only allotted to the baptized by virtue of the atoning death of Christ, but now determines their way of life (cf., for both ideas, 1 Cor. 6:11). In order not to offend the recipients of the letter, whom he has praised up until now (cf. 1:8 and 7:1; 15:14; 16:19), with the reminder "once," Paul begins with the remark that he formulates his thought in a human way "on account of the weakness of your flesh." He does not draw attention to the past for the purpose of criticism, but in order to make known the propensity which his companions in the church have for temptation (cf. Mk. 14:38 par.). Sanctification is the overcoming of this weakness which still clings to Christians. Once the Roman Christians submitted their members to "impurity" (= immorality) (cf. 1:24) and "lawlessness," that is, to a way of life which has nothing to do with the commands of God. The result was godless and wicked activity. The fact that in such a description the apostle is viewing the Romans as converted Gentiles is obvious in view of 1:18–32 and 1 Cor. 6:9f.; he argues differently in regard to Jews (who are now Christians) (cf. 2:1–24 and Gal. 2:15ff.). Once the Roman Christians were godless transgressors, but now (i.e., since their baptism) they have surrendered their members to the righteousness which God himself exercises and enjoins from his people. Paul agrees here with Mtt. 6:33 and stands entirely within the Old Testament and Jewish tradition (cf. Ps. 15:2; Ezek. 18:5ff.; T. Dan. 6:10). Without any worry about advocating a Christian "works righteousness," Paul demands from baptized Christians a righteous way of life and designates sanctification to be his goal. The transformation of life into a holiness which pleases God is the gift and obligation which baptism makes possible for Christians (cf. 1 Thess. 4:3–8 and 1 Pet. 1:14ff.). As a result of having been atoned for and sanctified by Christ, those who believe must now live as "saints." Justification and sanctification through Christ (1 Cor. 1:30) lead to the sanctification of life, and the ethical characteristic by which it is known is the service of that righteousness which God loves (cf., likewise, 1 Pet. 2:24). [20] Once the Christians in Rome, as slaves of sin, did not stand in the service of righteousness. [21] But their activity at that time also produced in their lives a fruit of which they are now ashamed and which would bring about in them as a result only death at the day of judgment (cf. 1:32). [22] But now, since they are freed from sin's claim to reign and have been placed anew, through Christ, into the service of the righteous God, their life produces a fruit which serves sanctification and whose result is eternal life at the side of Jesus (cf. 5:17). Nevertheless, sanctification itself, together with eternal life, certainly remains, in spite of all the ethical effort which is demanded from those who are baptized, the gift of God (cf. Phil. 2:12f.) [23] Therefore, in the end, the only wages which sin pays is death at the judgment, while God's gift of grace for those who stand in his service consists of eternal life mediated through Christ Jesus. Christ mediates eternal life in that he suffered death for the sinner, is at work as the resurrected

Lord (in the Spirit) in those who believe (cf. Gal. 2:20), and makes intercession before God for those who belong to him, even until the judgment (8:33f.).

With this clear description of the life of the baptized Christian as being in the service of that righteousness which is God's will, Paul has taken the wind out of the sails of the critics of his baptismal preaching who have tracked him from Galatia to Rome. Paul does not preach cheap grace, but the grace of God which is exacting in what it demands!

Excursus 9:
The Pauline Understanding of Baptism

In Rom. 6:1ff. Paul reminds the Roman Christians of their *baptism*, and in so doing he himself shows a most profound understanding of baptism. In baptism the one being baptized is "given over" to the binding doctrine of the gospel, which has been revealed by God (6:17), and at the same time that person is given a share in the gift and mandate of that gospel. Baptism is the symbolic fulfillment of the gospel for those who are being baptized.

Paul himself was baptized in Damascus after his call to be an apostle (cf. Acts 9:17f.; 1 Cor. 12:13). Since then he had the opportunity to appropriate the doctrine of baptism and the baptismal preaching of the Christian missionary churches. Moreover, his own missionary activity among the Gentiles, which extended for many years, and the intensive effectiveness which branched out from Antioch (cf. Acts 11:25–15:35), make it probable that the baptismal formulas and texts which appear in Paul's letters derive, above all, from the sphere of Antiochian Christianity, which was characterized by mission. The texts and subject matter in view are 1 Cor. 6:11; 12:13 (and Gal. 3:28; Col. 3:10f.); Rom. 3:25f.; 4:25; 8:29; Col. 3:12f.; the language and perspective of baptism "in the name" of Christ (1 Cor. 1:13–15; cf. with Acts 2:38); of baptism as a "sealing" with the Holy Spirit (2 Cor. 1:21f.); the baptismal confession and the doctrine of faith which undergirds it (1 Cor. 12:3; 15:1ff.; Rom. 6:17; 10:9f.), as well as the main lines of the preaching concerning baptism and conversion (1 Thess. 1:9f.; cf. with Heb. 6:1f.; 1 Cor. 6:9–11; Eph. 2:1ff.; Col. 3:1ff., etc.). The apostle also carried out the act of baptism in the form of immersion in standing or flowing water (cf. Acts 8:36ff.; 1 Cor. 10:2) like the missionaries did before and beside him. It signified for him participation in Jesus' death and the washing away of sins (1 Cor. 6:11; Rom. 6:3f.).

Paul does not express his opinion concerning the origin of Christian baptism more precisely. But his connections to Peter and the teachers in Antioch make it probable that he saw it as they did. Hence, in the cradle of Christian baptism stands first of all John the Baptist, with his baptism for repentance, which is mentioned not only by the Gospels (Mk. 1:4ff. par.), but also by the Jewish author Josephus (*Ant.* 18.116ff.). It is not by chance that John practiced his baptism for repentance in the river Jordan dressed in the garb of the prophet Elijah (cf. Mk. 1:6 par. with 2 Kgs. 1:8). According to prophetic tradition, the Jordan River corresponds to the flood tides of the Red Sea which opened for Israel's crossing (cf. 2 Kgs. 2:14 with Exod. 13:17–14:31). In the baptism of John, those who repented were "immersed in" or "under" the floods of chaos, and with their reemergence placed in purity before the God who is coming (H. Gese). In 1 Cor. 10:1ff. Paul himself indicates this correspondence between the events within the history of salvation. Jesus and several of his later disciples (cf. John 1:35ff.) submitted to John's baptism. The experience of the Spirit granted to Jesus at this occasion marks the beginning of his public activity as the messianic Son of God and Son of Man (cf. Mk. 1:9–11 par.). Jesus derived his claim to authority and his mandate to suffer from his baptism (cf. Mk. 11:27–33 par. and Mk. 10:38; Lk. 12:50). Jesus' entire work can, in this way, be understood from the perspective of his baptism. For the disciples of Jesus, his baptism with water and the Spirit thus became the model of Christian baptism in general.

On the basis of their renewed and new encounter with the resurrected one, they began to baptize "in the name of Jesus Christ" (in correspondence to the baptism of John) in reference back to the sending of Jesus, which was completed with his passion, and as a result of their having been seized by the Holy Spirit. In other words, they began to baptize on the basis of the work and present activity of the crucified and resurrected Christ (cf. Acts 2:38ff.). By virtue of this baptism those who are baptized are cleansed from their sins, gifted with the Holy Spirit, and aligned with the new people of God, which has its core in the Christian church (cf. Ezek. 36:24ff.; Acts 2:41ff.). Philip even bestowed baptism on an Ethiopian eunuch, who, according to the Jewish perspective, could not become a full-fledged member of the (Jewish) worshiping community because of his disability (cf. Acts 8:26ff. with Is. 56:3ff.). Through Peter and the Antiochian missionaries, baptism was then also granted to Gentiles, without compelling them to be circumcised or to accept the Mosaic Law (cf. Acts 10:44ff.; 11:20f.). Hence, the name "Christian," which came to be used for members of the church for the first time in Antioch (Acts 11:26), betrays a phenomenon which is fundamental for the understanding of baptism. Those who were baptized were distinguished very quickly as "Christians" not only from the Jews, but also from the Gentiles. With their baptism, those who believed in Jesus Christ had to free themselves from their old ties and associations. They entered into a community of faith with new dimensions for living. It was thus probably also in Antioch that one first experienced and then programmatically formulated the fact that with the new relationship to Christ which belongs to all members of the community, the religious and social privileges and disadvantages of Jews and Gentiles, slaves and free, men and women, which until now were valid and separated people from one another, were no longer decisive (cf. Gal. 3:27f.; 1 Cor. 12:13; Col. 3:11). For "Christians," baptism was really "the central 'fact' of the beginning [of their lives] which [subsequently] determined all Christian life and thought" (U. Wilckens). Infant or child baptism was not yet in view as a special duty, not even with the baptism of entire "households," that is, families (cf. Acts 10:44, 48; 11:14ff.; 16:15; 1 Cor. 1:16).

Paul inherited this baptismal tradition. He also baptized "in the name" of the crucified and resurrected Christ (1 Cor. 1:13ff.). For him too, baptism cleansed from sin and caused the person to become new (1 Cor. 6:11; 2 Cor. 5:17). And also according to Paul, those being baptized gained a share in the Holy Spirit and as new people are incorporated into the (life of fellowship of the) salvific community, which he calls the "body of Christ" (1 Cor. 12:13).

In 1 Cor. 1:11ff. Paul criticizes the fact that groups are forming in Corinth with reference to the baptism and teaching of individual apostles and missionaries who dispute and contend with one another. In 1 Corinthians 10 he warns the Corinthians of imagining themselves to be immune from sin and destruction because of their baptism, but lets pass the unusual custom of vicarious baptism for the dead (1 Cor. 15:29). All three times the Corinthians certainly appear to have carried over into their new Christian identity certain religious perspectives still remaining from their Gentile past and environment. But we do not know whether, in doing so, they held specifically to the pattern of the widespread Gentile mystery societies. Historically, we have only fragmentary information concerning the views and customs of the mystery cults, and we know nothing at all about a specific baptismal ritual within the societies. Moreover, in the mystery cults, the perspectives concerning the inclusion of the one who was initiated into the death and resurrection of the mystery deities were so varied that one could hardly interpret Christian baptism in a general sense as participation in the fate of the crucified and resurrected Jesus on this basis. Rather, this interpretation can be seen to come about much more simply and clearly from Christology and the tradition of atonement. The Son of Man represents the people of God made up of the "saints of the Most High" as a whole (cf. Dan. 7:13, 18, 27). As the Son of Man, Christ died for "the many," in other words, for all (cf. Mk. 10:45 par.). For Paul, the Son of Man, the Son of God, and the new Adam are inextricably bound together (cf. Rom. 5:15ff.). By virtue of baptism "in his name," his atoning death on the cross benefits all those who are baptized. Under these conditions, it is therefore wrong to take the Corinthian letters as a model and to suspect that there is a special Hellenistic understanding of baptism which runs throughout the Greek-speaking churches and which leads to a charismatic fanaticism rooted in the Gentile religiosity of the mystery religions, which is then criticized by Paul. That it would be wrong to do so holds true especially for the letter to the Romans. Here the front is an entirely different one than in 1 Corinthians: In Romans 6 Paul refutes a Jewish-Christian misinterpretation of his own teaching concerning baptism, without at the same time correcting the perspective on baptism which the Roman Christians had inherited.

The specifically Pauline understanding of baptism results from the fact that the apostle calls special attention to those assertions concerning justification which determine the meaning of those baptismal texts which had already existed before him (1 Cor. 1:30; 6:11; Rom. 3:25f.; 4:25, etc.). In other words, Paul understands baptism from the perspective of the gospel entrusted to him. He thus emphasizes that those who are baptized obtain in baptism a share in the effect of the atoning death of Jesus on the cross, that they are "sanctified" through him, and that they are aligned with Christ as their living Lord and reconciler. At baptism, those who are baptized are given over to a teaching which for them is determinative for their life and consequently identical with the "gospel" of 1 Cor. 15:3–5 (cf. Rom. 6:17). Baptism, justification, and sanctification are therefore inseparably bound together with one another. By virtue of baptism those who are baptized obtain a share in the atoning power of the death of Jesus and are placed into the reality of a new life which already begins here and now in the church, but which is completed only with the future resurrection of the dead and eternal fellowship with Christ. On the one hand, then, those who believe are crucified together with Christ and buried in death in the act of baptism (Gal. 2:19; Rom. 6:6). On the other hand, the Spirit of the living Christ takes possession of the baptized, who have been freed from their sins and "sanctified," so that, as Paul formatively says, they now live in Christ and he in them (Gal. 2:20). By the power of this Spirit they confess Christ as their new Lord (1 Cor. 12:3; Rom. 10:9f.), obediently follow his command (1 Cor. 7:19; Gal. 6:2), and look forward in certain hope to their final justification and participation in Jesus' resurrection glory (1 Thess. 4:14; Rom. 8:28ff.; Phil. 3:20f.). With baptism as a change in lordship from sin to righteousness, from idols to Christ, those who are baptized have become "new creatures" (2 Cor. 5:17), so that they live henceforth in a life of mutuality with and for one another in the fellowship of the body of Christ (1 Cor. 12:12ff.; Rom. 12:3ff.).

Paul has a profound understanding of baptism, and there can be no talk of the fact that he intends to devalue baptism in favor of justification and faith. To be sure, the main task of the apostle resides in the preaching of the gospel and not in the founding of a "Paul party" by means of baptism

(1 Cor. 1:17). But at the same time, the gospel is for him the living word of God (1 Thess. 2:13) and the effective power of God (Rom. 1:16) that takes possession of those being baptized in the ritual procedure of baptism. Hence, just as for Paul himself, the call to be an apostle possessed a fundamental significance for his life, so that he then subsequently allowed himself to be baptized, so too the encounter with the gospel, which awakens faith, and the baptism that comes about as a result are the decisive beginning points of the new life in faith for every Christian member of the church. Baptism does not put a spell on a person against sin and judgment (1 Cor. 10:1–11), but it gives those who believe, who are accused in the judgment and must anticipate condemnation, the continuing right to appeal to Christ as their redeemer and advocate (1 Cor. 5:5; Rom. 8:31ff.).

2. 7:1–8:17. The End of the Reign of the Law and the New Service in the Spirit

After the apostle's statements in chapter 6, nobody can charge him any longer with preaching cheap grace. But the question of what attitude those who are baptized must have toward the Law was previously answered only indirectly in 6:14. Yet it was precisely this question which was the main problem for his Jewish-Christian critics. Paul knows that and therefore takes up this central problem in chapters 7 and 8 in a train of thought which is both exceedingly bold and impressive. If, at the same time, he should also succeed in refuting the accusation of his "slanderer" (3:8) that Paul intends to nullify the Law (cf. 3:31) in such a way that the emptiness of that accusation clearly stands out, then—so it appears—he has "won" in Rome. Conversely, if Paul is not successful in coming against the criticism, then Paul's cause in Rome is in bad shape. For then the apostle will not be able to count on the Christians in the capital of the ancient (Mediterranean) world for the support for his mission to Spain for which he hopes so much (cf. 15:24). The care with which Paul handles the question of the Law in 7:1–8:17 thus makes sense when one considers what is at stake for him with this question.

2.1. 7:1–6. The End of the Reign of the Law

(1) Or do you not know, brothers—I am speaking indeed to people who know their way around the Law!—that the Law reigns over a person (only) as long as he lives? (2) For the married woman is bound to her husband by the power of the Law (only) during his lifetime; but if the husband dies, then she is freed from the Law concerning the husband. (3) As a result, she is called an adulteress if she belongs to another man during the lifetime of her husband; but if the husband dies, she is free from the Law, so that she is not an adulteress if she belongs to another man. — (4) Accordingly (it is true), my brothers: You

also have died in regard to the Law through the body of Christ in order to belong to another, (namely) to the one who has been raised from the dead, so
that we might bear fruit for God. (5) For when we were in the flesh, then the
sinful passions (aroused) through the Law were at work in our members, in
order to bear fruit for death. (6) But now, because we have died to that
through which we were held fast, we are set free from the Law, so that we
serve in the new nature of the Spirit and not (any longer) in the old nature of
the letter.

Verse 3: Deut. 22:22–24.

A. The structure of the argument is as follows. In v. 1 Paul establishes a thesis (which is in accord with 6:7), which he then explains in vv. 2 and 3 with the
help of an example. In v. 4 he draws the application from vv. 1 and 2 + 3, which
he then expounds more closely in vv. 5 + 6.

The traditions with which the apostle deals in this passage are already known
to us in part. Verse 1 is concerned again with the relationship between death,
the Law, and sin, which was already addressed in 6:7. But whereas in 6:7 Paul
used the Jewish tradition to bring into relief the atoning effect of the death (of
Jesus) (see above), now he is concerned with the principle developed by the
Rabbis from Ps. 88:6 that "[i]f a person has died, he has become free from the
Torah and from fulfilling the commandments" (b. Sabb. 30a). The example adduced in vv. 2 and 3 likewise derives from the Jewish legal tradition: "The (married) woman . . . gains her freedom in a twofold manner . . . through a
certificate of divorce or through the death of the husband" (m. Qidd. 1:1).

In vv. 5 and 6 Paul argues before the Christians from Rome with two pairs of
opposites: (1) flesh and Spirit and (2) Spirit and letter. Both pairs of opposites
appear often in the Pauline letters: (1) From Gal. 5:16–21 it can be clearly perceived that for the apostle "Spirit" and "flesh" present two opposing spheres of
life and power which determine both the individual person and the Christian
church as a whole. The contrast between the perishable, earthly "flesh" and the
imperishable "Spirit" of God is already found in Is. 31:3, and was then developed still further in the Hellenistic period by early Judaism. In the Jewish apocalyptic tradition, perishable, earthly existence in the body and eschatological,
heavenly glory appear in opposition to one another (cf. 1 Enoch 108:7–15). In
the wisdom tradition, the mortal existence of the person, "formed into flesh in
the womb of the mother" (Wis. 7:1), stands in contrast to the imperishable
Spirit of wisdom as the "breath of the power of God" (Wis. 7:25). And the Qumran texts speak of the purification of the wicked flesh by the Holy Spirit, which
is brought about by God at the time of judgment (cf. 1QS 4:20f. with Ezek.
36:25ff.). Paul knows this tradition and sees every person as placed in the
sphere of tension that exists between that which is perishable on earth and
heavenly glory, that is, between flesh and Spirit. In Romans 8 he will take up
this life-situation in detail. (2) As 2 Corinthians 3 demonstrates, the pattern of

contrast between the Spirit and the letter concerns the antithesis between the old and new covenants (cf. Jer. 31:31ff.). The reign of Christ and of the gospel in the new covenant stands over against the reign of the Law in the old covenant. The Law leads to condemnation and to death, the gospel to righteousness and to life (2 Cor. 3:6ff.). This antithesis is also the subject in view at this point in the letter to the Romans.

B. The manner of expression chosen by Paul in 7:1–6 shows that he is concerned further with explaining the change in lordship that the Christians have experienced with their baptism. The catchwords "to reign" in 6:9, 14 and 7:1; "to become free" and "to be free" in 6:18, 20, 22 and 7:3; "to be a slave" and "to serve" in 6:16ff., 22 and 7:6, remove all doubt concerning the intimate connection between Rom. 6:1–23 and 7:1–6. [1] The apostle now forcefully addresses the Roman Christians as "brothers" and as "knowers of the Law." He does this not out of politeness, but as a result of the fact that also in Rome the majority of the Gentiles who have become Christians are likely to have come from the circle of the so-called God-fearers that gathered around the synagogues (see above, p. 70). From their participation in Jewish worship services they knew the Law and the Prophets just as well as they did the interpretation of the scribes. As far as their knowledge of the Old Testament and its Jewish interpretation is concerned, they were hardly inferior to converted Jews such as Paul or Prisca and Aquila (cf. 16:3f.). The apostle can therefore remind his addressees of a Jewish principle (derived from Ps. 88:6) without a problem. The principle is that the Law's claim for adherence, based on its reign, exists only as long as a person lives (see above). [2f.] From their instruction in the synagogues, the Roman Christians could also have been familiar already with the following example, to which (in typical Jewish pedagogical style) Paul refers in order to clarify what has been said: A married woman may only remarry without the reproach of adultery if her husband has died. The apostle does not choose precisely this example by chance. For as can be seen from 2 Cor. 11:2 (and Eph. 5:25ff.), it refers to the fact that after the change in lordship in baptism the community of Christians is brought to their new Lord as a "holy virgin" and is thus prepared for the messianic wedding feast (cf. Mtt. 22:2–14; Rev. 19:9). Yet these aspects remain in the background in the context of this discourse. What matters for Paul in 7:1–6 is the change from the reign of the Law to the reign of Christ. This is indicated by the "application" of the "parable" [4] that Paul draws in v. 4 and that every hearer and reader of the letter would clearly recognize. As amplified in the example that has just been given, so too in baptism have Christians died "through the body of Christ" to the Law's claim to reign. What that means here (as also in 1 Cor. 11:24; Col. 1:22; and 1 Pet. 2:24) is that through Jesus' vicarious giving up of his life on the cross, the baptized Christians are freed from the reign of the Law so that they can belong to another Lord, namely, to the Lord Jesus Christ, who was raised by God and exalted to his right hand. Moreover, those who are baptized, including Paul, live under his lordship in order "to bear fruit" for God. This expression derives from the Christian mission and means that the preaching of the gospel is taken to heart, that the will of God, newly established by Christ, is followed, and that the missionary witness in word and deed is risked before the unbelieving world (cf. Mk. 4:20; Lk. 8:15; and Col. 1:10). Paul thus enjoins here with new words what he has already emphasized in 6:12–23.

[5] The following verses confirm this. In them Paul once again summarizes his entire view of the Christian's change in lordship. The contrast in vv. 5 and 6 between "once" and "now" corresponds to the pattern of preaching at baptism (cf. 1 Cor. 6:9–11 and above, pp. 97f.). Once "we" lived, that is, the Roman Christians and Paul, in the sphere of the power of the flesh. At that time, all the bodily members were governed by the passions (in 6:12 Paul says "lusts") that work themselves out in sinful deeds. Hence, the passions are not somewhat checked or even thwarted by the Law, but rather provoked! As hard as this remark might also sound to the ears of Paul's Jewish-Christian opponents (and to all those in Rome who sympathize with them), Paul cannot renounce it. Already in Wis. 2:1–20 the way in which the righteous one directly provokes the wicked to unjust actions with his faithfulness to the Law is classically portrayed, and in 7:7ff. the apostle will illustrate the same set of circumstances with the example of the command of God from Gen. 2:16f. The fact that the Law first arouses the passions which lead to sin, and then subsequently declares them to be worthy of judgment before God (5:20), thus corresponds to biblical experience. Paul does not deviate from this view of the Law, even in his attempt to convince the Roman Christians of the validity of the content of his preaching. The result of the fact that one's members were being governed by the passions was that one was energetically working for (the unavoidable judgment of) death (as a consequence of sin; cf. 6:23). [6] But with and since one's baptism, this life is over. For "now," through and with Christ, Christians (again including Paul) have died to sin and the Law, which held them captive, so that they can serve God in the new way of life determined by the Holy Spirit (cf. 2 Cor. 5:17; Gal. 2:20). They were set free from the old nature under the letter of the Law, which kills through the pronouncement of judgment (cf. 2 Cor. 3:6ff.).

The apostle formulates the last two verses with programmatic care. They form the outline for his presentation in 7:7–8:17. Verse 5 is further developed in 7:7–25a, while v. 6 is to be made the heading for 8:(1)2–17. For according to Paul, one can only really see and say what the Law is and how Christians relate to the Law (and should relate to it) from the perspective of baptism. In doing so, the time before baptism and the time after baptism must be carefully distinguished.

2.2. 7:7–25a. The Law and Sin

From the beginning of Romans, Paul has been striving to refute the assertion that he preaches a gospel that has been accommodated to the wishes and

weaknesses of the Gentiles, an assertion that his opponents have (also) disseminated among the Roman Christians. For his criticism of the Law was the most
offensive aspect of the Pauline teaching. But if one keeps in mind several of the
polemical and pointed statements from Galatians, such as "Christ has redeemed
us from the curse of the Law" (Gal. 3:13); the Law was first decreed on Sinai
430 years after the promise was issued to Abraham, and then "for the sake of
transgressions" (Gal. 3:17, 19); the Law is not able to make one alive (Gal. 3:21);
and then, in addition, adds to them the statement from 1 Cor. 15:56 that "[t]he
Law is the working power of sin," one can understand Paul's opponents to a
great degree. Their assertion that Paul places the Law and sin on the same level
(Rom. 7:7) does not appear to be fabricated out of thin air! In addition, the argument concerning the Law up until this point in Romans does not yet solve the
problem. To be sure, the apostle has emphatically declared that with his proclamation of faith he does not intend to nullify the Law as the criterion of judgment (2:12ff.), as a witness of Scripture (3:21), or as the will of God fulfilled by
Jesus, but to establish it (3:31). Yet right alongside of these affirmations stand
those statements of Paul which are now, as before, hard to bear for Jews and
Jewish Christians: Works of the Law do not lead to justification before God;
rather, through the Law, came only the knowledge of sin (3:20; cf. Gal. 2:16);
the Law brings about God's judgment of wrath (4:15); it came in between Adam
and Christ in order to increase sin (5:20); and by virtue of their baptism, Christians have died to sin and to the Law (6:14; 7:6). Even from the standpoint of
logic this tension does not appear to dissolve. How can one establish the Law in
faith and at the same time desire to proclaim the end of its reign? In view of this
highly complicated situation surrounding the discussion, Paul thus has every
reason to take up in detail the rebuke which has been raised against him, that is,
that in practice he equates the Law and sin, and to bring clarity to that contradiction. What comes about as a result is an "apology for the Law" (W. G. Kümmel), which the apostle then extends in 8:2ff. into the doctrine that by the power
of the Spirit Christ leads those who believe to fulfill the legal demand of the Law.

On the basis of the structure of the argument, the Pauline "apology for the
Law" can be outlined as follows. In v. 7 and v. 13 questions are raised which in
each case come to the fore in response to the Pauline doctrine. Both times Paul
answers them negatively. In vv. 7–12 he then outlines the relationship between
sin and the Law, and in vv. 13–25 the futility into which sin and the Law place
the Adamic "I."

2.2.1. 7:7–12. The Perversion of the Law into an Instrument of Sin

(7) What then should we say? That the Law is sin? By no means! Indeed, I
would not have known sin except through the Law. For I would not have
come to know lust, if the Law had not said, "Thou shall not covet." (8) Sin
seized (its) opportunity through the commandment and worked in me every

kind of covetousness. For without the Law sin is dead. (9) But I once lived
without the Law, but when the commandment came, sin came to life, (10) but
I died, and the commandment (given) for life, this one was found (to be a
commandment) for death. (11) For sin seized (its) opportunity through the
commandment and deceived me and through it killed me. (12) As a result the
Law is holy, and the commandment is just and good.

Verse 7: Exod. 20:17; Deut. 5:21; Verses 8–11:
Gen. 3:1–24; Verse 9: Gen. 2:16f.

A. As we have already seen, 7:5 is to be regarded as the "heading" and table
of contents for 7:7–12 (+ 7:13–25a). In this verse the apostle depicts the position of the Christian before baptism, with a special view toward one's encounter
with the Law of God. The critical question posed to him in response, that is,
whether the Law is to be identified with sin, is now rejected in v. 7 and cor-
rected through the statement that the Law makes sin recognizable. This statement is then explained more closely with the help of three supporting
sentences, each of which begins with "for" (vv. 7b–8a, 8b–10, and 11), from
which the conclusion is drawn in v. 12 that the Law is in no way to be equated
with sin, but is rather holy, just, and good. For his argument, Paul refers to the
Adam tradition, as he did formerly in Rom. 5:12–21, in such a way that "in the
ego (= I) of Rom. 7:7ff. the Adam from Rom. 5:12ff. (receives) his mouth" (G.
Bornkamm). In this manner, every person, as Adam, can identify him- or herself with the speech of the "I" in Rom. 7:7–24. For as it says in 2 Baruch (54:19),
"[W]e have all become Adam, each one for himself." Paul takes up this confession and consciously avails himself of the first-person form of speech which incorporates every person. This form of speech is known to us biblically from the
Psalms (e.g., Psalms 22; 51; 130), from early Jewish prayers of repentance (see
below), from wisdom texts (e.g., Wisdom 9), and from the writings of Philo of
Alexandria (Som. 1.176f.). Paul also occasionally uses this form of speech elsewhere in his letters (cf. 1 Corinthians 13).

Adam (the "I" in this passage) is the only biblical figure of whom it can be
said that he once lived without the Law, but that the commandment then came
(7:9), and sin took this commandment as an occasion to tempt "me" and to deliver "me" over to death (7:11). Genesis 2 and 3 are thereby in view in this passage in accordance with the way in which they were understood in the early
Jewish interpretation of Scripture, in which Paul himself was educated (cf. Acts
22:3). First of all, the Law, identified with the wisdom at work in creation (Sirach 24; Bar. 4:1; m. Abot 3:14), is considered in this tradition to have been created long (according to Tg. Neof. I to Gen. 3:24, two thousand years) before the
creation of the world. Then, very definite periods of time are again seen to exist
between the creation of Adam, his transfer into the garden of paradise, and the
decree of the commandment in Gen. 2:16f. (Jub. 3:9ff. speaks of forty or eighty
days). Finally, the one commandment given to Adam and Eve is understood to

be the embodiment of the entire Law. Hence, in Tg. Neof. I to Gen. 2:15 it states, "And God the Lord took the man and let him dwell in the Garden of Eden, so that he might serve according to the Law and follow his command-ments." And in the same targum, Gen. 3:22 is commented upon as follows: If Adam had "kept the commandment of the Law and observed its command-ments, he would have lived and, like the tree of life, continued to exist for eter-nity." The Tg. Yer. I to Gen. 2:15; 3:9, 22 represents the same view, and it can be traced back through the Life of Adam and Eve (32 + 37), Josephus (Ant. 1:41–47), and the Apocalypse of Ezra (cf. 4 Ezra 3:7 + 7:11), to allusions in the writings of Philo of Alexandria, an older contemporary of Paul (cf., above all, Leg. All. 1.90–97). In view of all of this, it is very probable that Paul knew this interpretation.

As the ideal example of the commandment (Law) which was given to the first human pair that they might keep it, Paul cites in 7:7 the introduction of the (ninth) and tenth commandment from Exod. 20:17 (Deut. 5:21). In doing so, the last of the Ten Commandments stands as a summary for the entire series. Correspondingly, the "lust" in view in no way refers to sexual desires alone, but to the "beginning of all sin" (Apoc. Mos. 19) and the covetous striving after all of the goods listed by the (ninth and) tenth commandment.

B. From the critical statements of the apostle about the Law thus far in the letter to the Romans, his opponents inferred that [7] for all intents and pur-poses Paul makes the Law and sin one, and thus transforms God's good gift into an instrument of death (v. 13). For a Jew this accusation is especially bitter, since it prevents him from participating in the future world (cf. m. Sanh. 10:1; see above, p. 66). Paul therefore also dismisses the suspicion out of hand. What concerns him, rather, is an entirely different matter. God's Law is good, but it was and is too weak to restrain sin. Indeed, it makes one conscious of sin, but it does not help the person to get free from it. The example of Adam demon-strates this. He would never have become acquainted with sin if the Law, "You shall not covet" (Exod. 20:17 and Deut. 5:21), had not been prescribed for him. The "lust" in view here refers to the desires which are against God as a whole, and not merely inordinate sexual desire (see above). In accord with this, Paul continues by saying that [8] "sin seized its opportunity through the command-ment and worked in me every kind of covetousness." While in the early Jewish interpretation of Genesis 3 the nature and activity of the tempter in the form of the snake are, in part, intensively reflected upon and reported (cf., e.g., Life of Adam and Eve 9ff.; Apoc. Mos. 17ff.), Paul, in contrast, speaks in concise theo-logical abstraction only of the demonic appearance of "the sin" which uses the divine commandment in order to tempt the person to transgress the will of God. Paul's point is that in the beginning, without the commandment or Law (see above), sin had no vital energy of its own. [9] "I," that is, Adam, once lived before God without Law and without sin. At this point Paul is thinking and teaching in accord with the early Jewish tradition surrounding Adam (see

above). Only when the commandment from God came on the scene did sin
spring to life, since, like a parasite, it could make use of the commandment for
its own purposes. [10] The result was that "I" experienced death in that the very
commandment of God which was established to protect life in paradise now
brought about "my" (= Adam's) death. [11] Sin tempted "me," with the help of
the commandment, to transgress the commandment (5:14), so that this commandment can now no longer protect Adam (and Eve) from death, but instead
brands them as law breakers and hence must exclude them from life. [12] From
this there follows the first conclusion that God's Law (in the form of his commandment) is, according to its origin and aim, holy, just, and good. As such, in
contrast to what his opponents maintain, the Law is, for Paul, in no way a sinful
power, but rather the arrangement and gift of God!

2.2.2. 7:13–25a. *The Reign of Sin by Means of the Law*

(13) "Did that which is good thus bring about my death?" By no means!
Rather, sin, in order to appear as sin, worked death in me through that which
is good, so that sin might become wicked beyond measure through the commandment. (14) We know indeed that the Law is spiritual, but I am fleshly,
sold under sin. (15) For what I bring about, I do not know. For I do not carry
out that what I want, but what I hate, I do. (16) But if I do what I do not want
to do, I agree with the Law that it is good. — (17) But now I am not the one
bringing it about, but sin which dwells in me. (18) I know indeed that in me,
that is, in my flesh, nothing good dwells. For the desire is (certainly) at my
disposal, but not the bringing about of that which is good. (19) For I do not do
the good that I desire, but what I do not desire, the evil, that is what I carry
out. (20) But if I do what I do not desire, then I am no longer bringing it
about, but the sin which dwells in me. — (21) I thus discover the Law that,
when I desire to do the good, (only) evil is at my disposal. (22) According to
my inner man, I joyfully concur, namely, with the Law of God. (23) But I see
a different Law in my members which is in conflict with the Law of my reason
and takes me prisoner through the Law of sin which is in my members. (24) I
am a wretched man! Who will deliver me from this body of death? (25) But
thanks be to God through Jesus Christ, our Lord!

A. These verses too still stand under the heading of 7:5. In 7:13–16, in parallel to 7:7–12, the critical question from v. 7 is renewed in view of the "I" which
exists under the Law, is then subsequently once again denied, and finally cor-
rected with the thesis that it is sin which brings about death for the "I" by
means of that which is good (= the commandment). Verses 14 and 15 support
this view, and in v. 16 (as already in v. 12) the fact that the Law is good is confirmed. On this basis, v. 17 begins anew and speaks of the effect of sin in the "I"
which has fallen to it. Verses 18f. support this description, so that in v. 20 what
was maintained in v. 17 can be strengthened. As the inferential particle "thus"

demonstrates, vv. 21–24 outline, in the sense of a concluding deduction from vv. 7–12 and 13–20, the futile situation of the "I" which joyfully concurs with (v. 22) and would like to follow "the Law of God," but is hindered from it by sin. The declaration of thanks in v. 25a marks the turning point characterized by deliverance.

The abandonment of mankind to evil and to the dichotomy between what is desired and what is accomplished, which Paul addresses, is certainly also well known in the Greek and Latin poetry from Euripides (*Hipp.* 358f., 375ff.) to Ovid (*Metam.* 7.17ff.). But only in Jewish texts concerning repentance is it elevated to the point where it is acknowledged to be the result of the radical fallness of mankind to the flesh and its inability over against the will of God. Compare, for example, 1QS 11:9ff.: "I belong to a profligate humanity, to the multitude of wicked flesh. My sins, my transgressions, my mistakes, together with the corruption of my heart, belong to the multitude of the worms and to those who walk in darkness. For no man (determines) his way, no man directs his step; but with God is righteousness and from his hand (comes) perfect conduct . . . "; and 4 Ezra 3:19–22: On Sinai God gave Israel Law and commandments from heaven. "But you did not take the evil heart from them, that your Law might bear fruit in them. For because of his evil heart the first Adam fell into sin and guilt, and likewise all who are born from him. In this way the sickness was continuous: the Law was indeed in the heart of the people, but together with the bad sprout (= evil impulse). Thus, what is good vanished; but the evil remained." Or finally, compare 4 Ezra 9:36f., which directly calls to mind 7:21–24: "[W]e, who received the Law, must disappear because of our sin, together with our hearts, in which it is done; but the Law does not disappear, but remains in its glory." Hence, in this passage Paul articulates experiences with the Law and sin that were completely foreign neither to his former Jewish nor to his Gentile addressees. Moreover, the present-tense style of expression in vv. 14–24, which is characteristic of the lament of repentance, has its model, for example, in Psalms 22, 51, 69, the use of which invites one to repeat the verses for oneself.

The fact that the apostle is striving for intelligibility is also shown by the distinction between the "inner" and "outer" man, the (Spirit-led) "reason" and the weak "flesh" or "body of death," which is known from 2 Cor. 4:16 and taken up anew in Rom. 7:22ff. The contrast between the two is just as sharply worked out by Philo of Alexandria (*Rer. Div. Her.* 267ff.). In so doing, Philo and Paul take up, in a language which was also understandable for their Greek-speaking contemporaries, the early Jewish doctrine that within every person "the good impulse" and "the evil impulse" are struggling for dominance (cf. T. Jud. 20:1ff.; T. Ash. 1:3f.). The evil impulse desires to tempt the person to go the way of evil, while the good impulse desires to protect the person from evil and lead one along the good path, having been instructed concerning it by the wisdom which has become manifest in the Law. In this sense Paul speaks in Rom. 8:6f. of the "aims of the flesh" (= the evil impulse) and the "aims of the Spirit" (= the good impulse, determined by Christ).

Interestingly, in this context Paul also explicitly draws attention to the Jewish "joy in the Law" of which, for example, Psalm 119 speaks. With the characterization of the "I" in Rom. 7:7–25, Paul thus has the Jew in view and not the Gentile. But what the apostle no longer adheres to because of his own bitter experience (cf. Gal. 1:13–17; Phil. 3:4–11) is the early Jewish hope, which he also once shared, that conversion and earnest striving for the good demanded from the Torah could indeed free a person from the power of sin (cf., e.g., Sir. 17:11ff., 25ff.). Paul sees deeper anthropologically than Sir. 15:11–15 and the Pharisaic Psalms of Solomon, which in 9:4f. formulates the principle that "[o]ur actions (take place) according to the choice and will of our hearts, that we do justice and injustice with the work of our hands, and in your righteousness you punish the children of men. Whoever behaves uprightly, gains life with the Lord, and whoever acts falsely, forfeits his life to destruction, for the judgments of the Lord are just regarding man and house." While James 1:13ff. picks up this point of view from a Christian perspective, Paul emphasizes in a substantially more radical fashion that the Adamic "I" without Christ remains inescapably entangled in sin.

B. In order to expound unambiguously the difference between the Law and sin, Paul now once again takes up the question from v. 7. **[13]** Does God's good instruction bring about my death? Again the answer runs, "By no means!" Rather, sin came on the scene, and it is the real power which brings death. Inasmuch as sin procured death for Adam (and Eve) through the misuse of God's commandment, it became manifest in its entirely wicked and demonic nature. Paul develops here anew a concept of sin which, as in 5:13f., extends far beyond the perception (common to Gentiles and Jews alike) that sin is merely a misdeed responsibly committed by an individual. For Paul, sin seized upon the Law (commandment) of God like a parasite; by means of God's instruction it has secured for itself a power contrary to God and in this way rules everything and everyone.

In what follows Paul is concerned only to expose, without illusion, the situation of the "I" as it exists under sin in view of the Law in such a way that his readers (hearers) see themselves addressed by it in their own experience of faith and life. In so doing, the apostle does not lose sight of his main intention to distinguish between sin and the Law. On the contrary, **[14]** as in 7:1, he appeals to the knowledge which the Christians from Rome possess from their instruction in the faith, and then formulates his thought using the contrast between "flesh" and "Spirit" known from 7:5f. According to its origin and intention, the Law belongs to the world of God; it is "spiritual." Even if and where it is misused by sin, it does not lose its holy character as the word of God. But over against it stands the "I," which is fleshly, that is, transitory and open to temptation, and sold into sin as into the power of a slave owner (cf. Gal. 3:22f.). With the statement, the

Law is "spiritual," Paul has once again intensified the conclusion from v. 12 and coined a formulation which finds "no corresponding expression" in early Jewish literature; in other words, it is unique (H. Lichtenberger). In view of v. 14, to accuse Paul of disdain for the Law is thus entirely impossible! But just as important to the apostle is the insight that in its fleshly nature under the rule of sin, the "I," in spite of the Law which was given to protect life (v. 10), is not capable of doing that which could bring about life for itself by its own power. [15] Moreover, the person is not conscious of what the Adamic "I" accomplishes. It does not conform at all, in reality, to his or her desire for the good (the existence of which Paul does not contest!), but carries out what it hates. It is overpowered by lust, transgresses the commandment of God, and as a result kills him- or herself (cf. vv. 8–11). [16] As a result of having fallen under sin (and being driven from paradise; cf. Gen. 3:23f.), the "I" must recognize that, with its actions, it has violated its own life-interests. Hence, although the "I" has fallen under the power of evil, the instruction of the Law was and remains right and good.

[17] Here the apostle begins once again from scratch. The power at work in the state of having come under the reign of death in which the "I" now exists is (not the Law, and also not the will of the "I," but) sin. [18] As the phrase "I know, namely," signals, Paul calls to mind in support of this insights from the Old Testament and Jewish tradition of repentance. But in doing so he exceeds Judaism's horizon of experience in that he no longer even grants to the one who is willing to convert a chance, by virtue of God's mercy, to be able to find the way back to a life of righteousness, not even with the help of the Law, which in the Old Testament and early Judaism is again and again designated as that which preserves life (cf., e.g., Lev. 18:5; Ezek. 20:11; Neh. 9:29; Sir. 17:11; Bar. 4:1; Ps. Sol. 14:2; 2 Bar. 38:2). Paul knows from his own experience that only God's work of redemption in and through Christ offers salvation from the falleness of guilt, and he formulates his thought on the basis of this experience. The Adamic "I" is aware that nothing good dwells in his flesh (cf. Ps. 51:5–7). To be sure, it still has, by all means, the ability to desire that which is good, but it is lacking the power to transform this desire into action. [19] Its lapse shows, rather, that it does not do the very good which it desires, but the evil which is against its will. [20] The subject of this action against the will is thus—as already expounded in v. 17—not the "I" itself, but the sin by which this "I" is possessed. It is sin which determines the endeavors of the "I" and alienates it from its own good intentions.

[21] Therefore, in view of the "I" which is confronted with the Law, but ruled by sin, Paul arrives at the following diagnosis, which is developed by the apostle by means of a rhetorical variation on the concept of the Law: The "I" must discover and concede that, in spite of its desire for that which is good, it is, in fact, only able to do evil. It cannot escape from this "law." [22] According to one's inner man, that is, in his or her good impulse (see above, pp. 109f.), it joyfully concurs with the Law (cf. Pss. 1:2; 19:9; 119:24, 77, 92; Rom. 2:17f.). [23]

But at the same time it must experience that in its own members a different "law" (i.e., the evil impulse, see above, pp. 109f.) conflicts with the "Law" which his reason gives him (i.e., with his good impulse). While the good impulse is equated by Paul with the "inner man" or with the "mind," furnished with the perception of the will of God (cf. 12:2), the evil impulse is concerned with the "members" and with the fleshly body of mankind. The evil impulse conflicts with the good and takes the "I" prisoner through the Law produced by sin, with which sin governs over the person's members. This "Law of sin" is the parasitic reverse of the good commandment (Law) of God. Sin awakens in the person by means of the commandment (Law) all the forbidden lusts and holds one prisoner from this time forward under the judgment of the commandment (Law) (vv. 7, 13, and 14). Paul varies the concept of the Law in vv. 21–23, but he does this so that even those hearers who think from the perspective of Jewish Christians and are versed in the tradition of repentance can and must follow his train of thought. [24] Hence, the only thing which remains for the "I," which, against its better desires, is enslaved to sin and ruled by its "law," is the cry of lament, "I am a wretched man, who will deliver me from this body of death?!" The "body of death" refers to the fleshly existence under the reign of sin, which leads to death.

With this, Paul has described from the perspective of faith the very situation to which he had already referred in 7:5. Before baptism, there are passions at work in "us," that is, in every Christian, which are determined by sin and provoked by the Law, with the result that one is at the service of the judgment of death. The conscious use of the present tense by the apostle since v. 14 shows that he intends to describe an experience which is past to all those who believe (including Paul himself), but at the same time is and should always remain real in the present.

Over against this overwhelming experience stands, of course, the confession in 7:6, introduced with the phrase "but now," that Christians, by virtue of their baptism, have been set free from the Law's declaration of guilt in order to serve God in the newness of the Spirit. In the present context, the thanksgiving which introduces v. 25 makes this same transition from one's prior existence before baptism to a consideration of the new existence in the Spirit. [25a] The existential need of the "I" described in vv. 7–24 is (as in the psalms of thanksgiving, see below, pp. 113f.) placed over against the expression of thanks which expels this need and surpasses it "through our Lord Jesus Christ." The thanksgiving is directed to God through his Son, since he is the one who accomplished the work of salvation, who dwells in the hearts of those who believe by virtue of the Holy Spirit, and who represents them before God (8:26).

2.3. 7:25b–8:1. An Interim Statement

(7:25a: But thanks be to God through Jesus Christ, our Lord!) (25b) (It is) now thus (true) that I for myself serve the Law of God with my mind, but

with the flesh the Law of sin. (8:1) (Moreover it is true that) there is thus no
longer any condemnation for those (who live) in Christ Jesus.

A. The transition from chapter 7 to chapter 8 has always presented the inter-
preter with great difficulties. After all, the thanksgiving abruptly inserted in
7:25a appears to be quite unexpected, while both of the "thus"-statements that
follow this thanksgiving in 7:25b and 8:1 are even more difficult to understand.
Only beginning in 8:2 does the train of thought of the argument again become
clear. But because the thanksgiving in 7:25a fits well with the explanatory statement in 8:2, the exegesis of this passage has attempted to come to terms as well
as possible with the two "disruptive" thus-statements. One group of interpreters
takes as their starting point the supposition that at the copying of the letter to
the Romans, the text fell into disorder beginning with 7:23 and therefore must
be regrouped in the following manner. First, the sentence, "Thus I indeed serve
the Law of God with the mind, but with the flesh the Law of sin" must be made
to follow after 7:23. Next comes 7:24 and the thanksgiving from 7:25a. After
them 8:2 comes first, and then 8:1 is to be read subsequently in connection to
8:2. Yet this (and similar) intrusion(s) into the form of the text has (have) against
it, above all, the fact that the oldest manuscripts of Romans show no uncertainty
at all concerning the transition from chapter 7 to chapter 8. The textual tradition does not justify, therefore, any alteration of the context of the passage. This
holds true also over against those exegetes who maintain that both of the thus-
statements in 7:25b and 8:1 (or also only 7:25b alone) are glosses that a copyist
of Romans originally wrote in the margin of his copy, only to be taken over into
the text itself by later transcribers. The oldest manuscripts necessitate, however,
that the context of the passage be explained as it exists in the wording in which
we have it. Moreover, this is completely possible.

There are only two things to take into consideration. First, in the Old Testament psalms of lament and thanksgiving, the thanksgiving which extols God's
saving activity toward the "I" who is lamenting follows the occasionally extensive
lament in a way that is only apparently abrupt (cf., e.g., the change from Ps.
22:22 to 22:23, or Ps. 69:30 to 69:31). For on the occasion of a religious celebration of thanksgiving, the lament is publicly presented by the one who has been
saved as a remembrance of the need which has been overcome with God's help.
In Romans, the change from the lament in 7:7–24 to gratitude in 7:25a (8:2ff.) is
to be explained in a quite similar way, especially in view of the public reading of
the letter in the gatherings of the churches and the teaching style of the apostle.

Second, it must be taken into consideration that Paul also writes all of his letters, and, above all, the letter to the Romans, in his character as an apostolic
teacher (cf. 1 Cor. 4:17). In addition, it was common in the Jewish (and Hellenistic) school system to summarize or begin lectures with maxims which could
easily be retained. This practice facilitated learning and gave the instruction
terse precision. We have two such summary sentences of instruction before us in

7:25b and 8:1 (cf., in addition, 5:18; 9:18; 10:17; 14:12, etc.). Before he goes on, the apostle thus summarizes what he has already expounded and what he desires to expound further, and he does this in a way that is parallel to 7:5 and 6. If one sees the matter in this way, the (difficult) text needs no rearrangement or corrections.

Hence, the structure of the text is as follows. Romans 7:25a is the thanksgiving (in contrast to the lament of 7:7–24); 7:25b is the first summarizing maxim; 8:1 is the second maxim; and 8:2ff. is a more detailed development of them both.

B. The thanksgiving follows, by way of contrast, the lament of the Adamic "I," which is summarized in v. 24. Such a thanksgiving is appropriate because those who believe have found salvation through the redemption established by God in the sacrifice of Jesus. [7:25b] As far as the situation of the Adamic "I" is concerned, although it recognizes in the Law the good and holy will of God and would also like knowingly to follow it (cf. vv. 22 and 23), it is nevertheless compelled to submit with its flesh (and all its members) to the force which sin exercises over it (cf. vv. 8 and 23). Once again, the apostle intentionally formulates this summarizing maxim from 7:7–24 in the present tense and in so doing brings to expression the fact that every believing Christian bears in him- or herself the unhappy dichotomy of the Adamic "I," whose spirit is indeed willing, but whose flesh is weak (cf. Mk. 14:38 par.). The Christian bears this dichotomy in the sense of a need which is more than something that is simply well remembered, but has been overcome with God's help. [8:1] Yet this need may "now," that is, from the perspective of baptism, also be set over against the principle and maxim of salvation. For those living in and through Christ, there is no longer any fatal condemnation in the coming judgment. Jesus' perfect obedience has destroyed the results of the disobedience of Adam. He has taken upon himself vicariously the judgment of death which applies to the sinner, and every Christian who has been buried together with Christ in death and looks forward to the resurrection may be glad that he or she is set free from the reign of sin and placed under the reign of grace (cf. 5:21 and 7:6).

Excursus 10:
The "I" in Rom. 7:7–25

Ever since the days of the early church, it has been discussed whether *the "I" which speaks in 7:7–25* refers to the person before baptism and without Christ, or to the baptized Christian in his or her lifelong temptations. The church father Augustine first favored the former view and then the latter. Luther and the Reformers followed the later Augustine. In their opinion, in 7:7–25 Paul is speaking of himself and every Christian. Their interpretation is still defended today, although the majority of the interpreters of Paul have in the meantime been convinced that the "I" in 7:7–25 can only refer to the "I" of Adam or of mankind as a whole before baptism and without Christ. The text does not reflect Paul's special temptations with the Law and lust.

When Paul speaks of his own pre-Christian past, the apostle calls himself a blameless and just Pharisee who went forth against the church of Christ and was conquered by God himself through the appearance of Jesus Christ for faith and apostolic service (cf. Phil. 3:4–11; Gal. 1:13ff.; 1 Cor. 15:9f.; 2 Cor. 2:14ff.; 4:5f.). The determinative tone of lament in 7:7ff. has, for sure, impressive Jewish prototypes, but it is only forced upon the apostle from the perspective of Christ, when he looks back at his own past and that of all baptized Christians. Romans 7:7–25 is not a special confession of the apostle concerning his life, but the lament of every baptized Christian, if and when one looks back at his or her pre-Christian past.

There are decisive exegetical grounds for relating Rom. 7:7–25 to the Adamic "I" before baptism and without Christ: (1) The overall structure of 7:7–8:17 is determined by the contrast between Rom. 7:5 and 6, so that 7:5 is commented upon by 7:7–25 and 7:6 by 8:(1)2–17. (2) The apostle's profound conception of baptism (see above, pp. 97ff.) forbids one from characterizing the Christian in 7:14 as still "sold under sin." (3) The present-tense style of the statements in 7:13–25 is to be explained on the basis of the Jewish tradition of repentance, so that there is no necessity of relating the statements of the text first and only to Christians because of it.

Of course, the tradition of the lament and the contrast between the two principal statements in 7:25b ("I for myself serve the Law of God with my mind, but with my flesh the Law of sin") and 8:1 ("There is thus no longer any condemnation for those [who live] in Christ Jesus"), which follow (!) the thanksgiving in 7:25a, also forbid one from relegating Rom. 7:7–25 simply to the past! Paul introduces the thanksgiving in 7:25 with a testimony of a need which the "I" has indeed conquered, but which is and remains always present for it in the form of the cry of repentance. In other words, the "I" which is summoned in 7:25ff. to give thanks knows that it is freed only in and through Christ from the deadly accusation of the Law, and that it is enabled through the gift of the Holy Spirit to follow God's good commandment. Without the Spirit and without Christ the "I" would immediately be thrown back again into the need which Paul portrays in 7:7ff.

With reference to Rom. 7:7–25, Luther continued to emphasize, even into the well-known preface to his translation of Romans in the so-called "September testament" of 1522, that until his or her death even the baptized Christian must be, and must also always remain, "a sinner and righteous at the same time." The text of Rom. 7:7–25 does not correspond exactly to Luther's perspective. But it does move a certain distance toward it. As Paul already emphasized in Gal. 5:16ff., and expounds once again in particular in Rom. 8:5ff., it is precisely the baptized Christian in particular who is and remains threatened by temptation through the power of the "flesh." Moreover, ever since the appearance in his churches of Jewish-Christian preachers of "another gospel" (cf. Gal. 1:8; 2 Cor. 11:4), the apostle had great concern that the Christians which he led into the freedom of faith could again fall out of the grace of God in Christ (cf. Gal. 5:4). The distress of the Adamic "I" under the Law is thus for Paul a danger which has been overcome in faith, but which constantly presents itself anew. According to Paul, therefore, although the Christian is not "a sinner and righteous at the same time," the Christian is nevertheless "righteous and open to temptation at the same time," and will remain this way until he or she is taken up by Christ into eternal glory (cf. Phil. 3:20f.).

2.4. 8:2–17. The New Service in the Spirit as Life in Relation to God as His Child

Just as 7:5 provided the heading for 7:7–25a, the epitome of 8:(1)2–17 is to be seen in 7:6. Against the background of the lament in 7:7–24, Paul now speaks of liberation from the Law of sin and of death and of the new service in the power of the Spirit. He does this in two steps. In 8:(1)2–11 he describes the event which brings about liberation and the resultant structure of the new service; and in 8:12–17 he makes clear that this new service takes place in relation to God as his child and in the expectation of one's future glorification with Christ.

2.4.1. 8:(1)2–11. Liberation from Sin and the New Service in the Spirit

(8:1: [Moreover it is true that] there is thus no longer any condemnation for those [who live] in Christ Jesus.) (2) For the Law of the Spirit of life in (through) Christ Jesus has freed you from the Law of sin and of death. (3) As far as the inability of the Law is concerned, because it was weakened through the flesh, God sent his own Son in the likeness of the flesh of sin, and as an offering for sin, and he condemned sin in the flesh, (4) so that the legal demand of the Law might be fulfilled in us, (we) who walk not according to the flesh, but according to the Spirit. (5) For those who are according to the flesh aspire after that which is of the flesh, but those who (are) according to the Spirit aspire after that which is of the Spirit. (6) For the aspiration of the flesh (is) death, but the aspiration of the Spirit (is) life and peace. (7) For the aspiration of the flesh (is) enmity against God, for it does not obey the Law of God, and it also cannot. (8) But those who are in the flesh cannot please God. (9) But you are not in the flesh, but in the Spirit, if then God's Spirit dwells in you.

But if one does not have the Spirit of Christ, this (person) is not his. (10) But if Christ is in you, then the body is indeed dead on account of sin, but the Spirit (is) life on account of righteousness. (11) But if the Spirit of the one who raised Jesus from the dead dwells in you, then the one who raised Christ from the dead will also make alive your mortal bodies through his Spirit which dwells in you.

Verses 2–4: Jer. 31:31–34; Ezek. 36:27.

A. The structure of the text is clear and simple. Verse 2 explains v. 1, and vv. 3 and 4 connect closely to v. 2 in that they depict how the new enactment of the legal requirement of the Law came into being for Christians. Verses 5–8 continue this explanation and make clear the opposition between life in the Spirit and life according to the flesh. Finally, vv. 9–11 assure the Christians of their endowment with the Spirit and of the hope in the resurrection which is thereby established.

The most important elements of tradition in this paragraph are found in the statement concerning the sending of Jesus in v. 3, in the contrast between the liberating and fatal reality of the Law in vv. 2–7, and in the antithesis between the Spirit and flesh in vv. 4ff. (1) The statements concerning the sending of Jesus in Gal. 4:4f.; Rom. 8:3f.; John 3:16f.; and 1 John 4:9f. are structurally so closely related that one can see in them the variation of an early Christian confessional tradition which speaks of the sending of the Son of God, Jesus Christ, into the world for the purpose of bringing about salvation. In this tradition, elements of early Jewish messianic and wisdom tradition are combined together, based on the person and work of Jesus, into a new Christian whole. According to 2 Sam. 7:14; Ps. 2:7; and Ps. 89:28, the messiah is related to God in the trusting relationship of a "son," and according to Is. 11:2; 61:1f., he is the "sent one" of God, who is endowed with the "Spirit (of wisdom)." The messiah's primordial origins are like those of wisdom (cf. Prov. 8:22; Wis. 9:9 with Mic. 5:1 and 1 Enoch 48:3, 6). As with the messiah, it is also said of wisdom that she is "sent" from God (Wis. 9:10). In the writings of Philo of Alexandria, just as in Wis. 9:1f., wisdom is identified with the creative word of God, which Philo calls the "first born (son) of God" (cf. *Som.* 1.215; *Conf. Ling.* 146). And in view of the fact that in the parable of the wicked vineyard tenants (Mk. 12:1–11 par.) Jesus himself spoke of his messianic sending as the "Son (of God)," taught with an unparalleled wisdom (cf. Mtt. 12:42 par.), and was raised by God, the Greek-speaking witnesses to Jesus coined the formula concerning the sending of Jesus with the help of the traditions outlined above. In turn, Paul then took over their main assertions.

(2) Biblically, the contrast between the fatal and liberating spiritual reality of the Law in vv. 2–7 reminds one most strongly of Jer. 31:31–34. Here an "arrangement" from God and revelation of the Law are promised which surpass the giving of the Law and the enacting of the covenant from Sinai (according to

Exodus 24). In it God will devote himself anew to his people, write his will in the hearts of the people of God, make possible the spontaneous knowledge and fulfillment of this will, and forgive the people of their sins. In Ezek. 36:27 it is also announced that God will grant his Spirit to the people and through it enable them to fulfill his instructions. In Jub. 1:5ff., 23ff., this promise is then taken up and bound together with Nathan's prophecy from 2 Sam. 7:12–14 (cf. on this below, p. 129). Since in 2 Corinthians 3 Paul sees himself placed into the "ministry of the Spirit" in the new covenant (according to Jer. 31:31–34), which cuts off the Mosaic "ministry of death," and since he characterizes Christ as the Spirit of freedom which fulfills this new "arrangement" from God (cf. 2 Cor. 3:6–17), it is natural to interpret Rom. 8:2–7 against the background of Jer. 31:31ff.; Ezek. 36:27; and the early Jewish expectation that the end-times people of God, in fulfillment of the promise of a son from 2 Sam. 7:12–14, will be led into the perfect obedience of the "sons of God."

(3) We have already discussed once before the origins of the Pauline contrast between the Spirit and the flesh (see above, p. 102). At this point, only the following needs to be added. As people of the Hellenistic period, the recipients of the letter to the Romans were no doubt acquainted with the late Greek conception that the person on earth had to bear "the foreign form of the flesh" (Empedokles, *Fr.* 126) and longed to rise up into the imperishable world of the spirit. Paul's manner of expression in 8:3ff. shows, of course, that he is not concerned in this context with this Hellenistic devaluation of the perishable flesh over against the eternal spirit, but with the contrast between sin and righteousness. The (pre-)Pauline expression "flesh of sin" (8:3) corresponds, namely, to the language of the "flesh of wickedness" in 1QS 11:9; while the expression "aspiration of the flesh" in 8:6 has its model in the "striving (or also: impulse) of the flesh" from 1QH 10:23. In the Essene texts from the Dead Sea, the "flesh of sin" stands over against the God of righteousness, who, on the basis of free grace, forgives the sinner his transgressions, fills him with the Holy Spirit, and enables him to praise as well as to walk in perfection (1QS 11:9–18). Paul thinks and argues in a way that is quite analogous.

B. In 8:1 (see above) Paul placed the lament of the Adamic "I" over against the doctrinal statement that [8:1] there is "now" no longer any condemnation which delivers one over to the judgment of death for those who live in and through Christ Jesus. [2] He now begins to develop this principle further. Applied directly to the "I" who is lamenting, the apostle unfolds in v. 2 why it no longer needs to fear condemnation. Through the Law which is determined by the "Spirit of life" in or through Christ, the "I" has been freed from the "Law" of sin and of death which had cursed the Adamic "I" in all of its endeavors in life and which is, in itself, the parasitic inversion of the good will of God (cf. 7:23). The formulation "Spirit of life" is Semitic and, as Ezek. 37:5f. and above all 1 Enoch 61:7 show by way of example, refers to the Spirit of God which fills the eschatological people of God with new life and the knowledge of God.

Already in 1 Cor. 15:45 and 2 Cor. 3:17, the apostle equates this Spirit with Christ, whose destiny and work determine the life of all those who live in him. Romans 8:9f. likewise presents this identification. Verse 2 is therefore to be understood as follows: The Law determined by the Spirit of Christ which makes alive has freed the "I" which laments in 7:24 from the fatal reign of sin. The fact that Paul speaks of the "Law" of the Spirit of life has its ground in the debate with his opponents concerning the Law, sin, and service in the Holy Spirit which he carries on in 7:7–8:17. In 7:7ff., Paul already sharply distinguished the Law of God from sin, and in 7:14 he even honored it with the esteemed predication "spiritual" (which exceeds that of the Jewish tradition!). With this in view, he now once again enhances this positive evaluation of the Law of God as God's goodwill which encounters the Christian in the manner now determined by the Spirit of Christ which makes alive. Jeremiah 31:31ff., together with 1 Enoch 61:7, 11ff.; Jub. 1:15ff., 23ff.; T. Lev. 18:11–14, document the fact that this reading of the text makes the best sense from a biblical standpoint. The new, spiritual order of life, the power of which is Christ, has now taken the place of the Law, which merely stood over against the Adamic "I" and, like a dictator, demanded from it the doing of that which is good, only to condemn it to death in the case of transgression. Conversely, for those who believe the instruction of God is placed within them on the basis of Christ, so that from now on they stand in the knowledge of God and fulfill the will of God spontaneously. Since, in contrast to the situation under Moses, freedom now reigns wherever the Spirit of Christ comes on the scene (2 Cor. 3:17), and since this Spirit of God is a gift of grace to the "godless" who are now justified, the apostle's statement makes good sense when he then declares concerning the new reality of the Law that it has freed the "I" from the spurious law of sin and of death. In the same way, in Gal. 6:2 and 1 Cor. 9:21 Paul calls this spiritual instruction "the Law (or the instruction) of Christ." Moreover, if we understand v. 2 in this manner, the subsequent two verses follow without a hitch and expound further what v. 1 anticipated by way of a thesis. [3] In 7:7–11 and 7:22f. Paul spoke of the weakening of the Law through sin and the flesh. The Law hindered neither the awakening of the lusts, nor the fall into sin, and thus could not accomplish its own fulfillment (cf. thus too Gal. 3:21). As an expression of his own free grace, God has reacted to this inability of the Law in his own way. He sent his own Son "in the likeness of the flesh of sin." This way of speaking, which at first has an artificial effect, makes sense if one traces its intention (within the context of the theology of Old Testament sacrifice). The Son of God became a man like all men, yet in distinction to them he did not sin, but remained obedient to God (until death) (cf. 5:18ff.). This freedom from the guilt of sin qualified the Son of God to become the absolute sacrifice for sin desired by God. Thus, the translation of this text which still appears repeatedly in Bible translations and commentaries, that is, "God . . . sent his Son in the bodily form of sinful flesh and for the sake of sin" (P. Althaus), does not allow one to recognize what the apostle means. In the

Greek translation of Lev. 4:3, 14, 21; 5:6, 7, 8, and so on (which was also used among the Christians in Rome), the phrase "the sin offering to be presented for the sake of sin" is simply given in shortened form as (the sin offering presented) "for the sake of sin." The phrase "for the sake of sin" is thus a technical expression from the language of sacrifice, and is to be understood in this way as well in Rom. 8:3. Paul's statement in 8:3 therefore agrees in terms of content with the theological formulation concerning sacrifice in 3:25 and has its closest parallel in 2 Cor. 5:21. What is meant by it is that, on the basis of his free, elective love toward the godless, God took upon himself the sacrifice which he first required from Abraham according to Gen. 22:9–14, but then in fact spared him. God sent his own Son, who possessed no guilt for sin, so that he might be the offering for sin for the people of God who were being held captive to the Law of sin and of death. With this sin offering, God thus condemned sin in the flesh in the following manner. Sin brought the Son of God to the cross by means of the Law, yet he—although sinless—obediently took upon himself the death of the cross. But God raised him from the dead on the third day and exalted him to his right hand. Hence, sin did not succeed in delivering Jesus over to the eternal judgment of death. Rather, its own reign was broken through the sacrifice of Christ and his resurrection. As a result, with the condemnation of Jesus, sin brought God's judgment upon itself in its most inherent sphere of power, the flesh. However, at this point Paul does not continue along the lines of the theology of atonement in order to speak of the fact that the sinner will be acquitted before the judgment seat of God by virtue of the sacrificial death of Jesus (this is first spoken of in 8:31ff.). [4] Instead, he remains with the theme of the Law, sin, and the new service in the Spirit, and pointedly expounds the purpose of the sending of Jesus in this context. This purpose consists in the fact that the legal demand of the Law is fulfilled by Christians who no longer walk according to the measure of the flesh, but of the Spirit (who is Christ himself; cf. v. 10). Through the sacrifice of Christ, those who believe fulfill the legal demand of the Law, which takes place in the power of the Spirit. On the basis of Jer. 31:31ff. (and Ezek. 36:27), this means that, for the sake of the sacrificial death of Jesus, God no longer considers sinners to belong to those who have deviated from the Law (cf. Jer. 31:32, 34). Rather, they now participate in the obedience of Christ in the power of the Holy Spirit, who indwells them since their baptism, and in the power of Christ (cf. Jer. 31:33f.; Ezek. 36:27) fulfill the will of God which has been given to them anew in their hearts by their resurrected Lord. In other words, Christ has placed those who belong to him in the reality of the Law of the new covenant. By doing so, he has finally, through the overcoming of sin, procured the carrying out of the "spiritual" will of God (7:14) which was imparted to Adam and Eve in paradise for the protection of life, but was misused by sin. Paul and all those who follow his preaching and doctrine are not, accordingly, antinomians, as the opponents of Paul assert, nor are they people who put the Law and sin on the same level (7:7, 13). Instead, they fulfill the will of God by the power of the Holy Spirit, and experience anew this will of God, granted to them from their Lord, as the pathway to life. It is thus not a rhetorical pretense when the apostle maintains in 3:27, 31 that he establishes the Law anew as a mark of faith. Rather, he teaches and shows how the breakthrough of the new revelation and spiritual internalization of the instruction of God promised in Jer. 31:31ff. comes about in and through Christ and how this instruction is then followed by Christians in the power of the Spirit!

In 7:5f. and repeatedly since then, the apostle has already spoken of the far-reaching difference between walking according to the flesh and according to the Spirit. Now, however, since this difference profoundly determines the life of the church, Paul therefore takes it up again in a series of doctrinal statements. [5] "Flesh" and "Spirit" refer to opposing standards and ways of life before God. [6] Those who are determined by the flesh are determined by the "evil impulse" (see above, pp. 109f.). In their thinking and actions they "aspire" after that which is in accordance with the flesh, defined according to Gal. 5:19ff. as the passions, depravity, and worship of idols (cf. thus also 7:8). Conversely, the people determined by the Spirit, by virtue of their "good impulse" (see above), are directed by it toward that which the Spirit desires and helps to accomplish. According to Gal. 5:22f., the desires of the Spirit to be named here would thus include love, generosity, and every behavior which is pleasing to God. Such behavior establishes "peace with God" (5:1) and leads to life.

[7] At this point, the apostle deepens his doctrinal statement further and relates it to the discussion of 7:7–8:17, which is of pressing importance at the present time. Ever since the Fall of Adam and Eve, the "aspiration" of the flesh stands over against God in insubordination and enmity. It is not willing to submit itself to the Law of God (for this expression, cf. 7:22). It is also unable to do so because it is governed by sin and held captive in the condition of being far from God. [8] For this reason, the people determined by the power of the flesh cannot lead a life which is pleasing to God and meets with his approval. The Christians from Rome should keep this clearly in view. [9] With the phrase "but you," Paul again addresses his readers and hearers directly. In contrast to those who lead an existence which is determined by the flesh, the Roman Christians are no longer in the flesh, but already in the Spirit, if the Spirit of God has really taken possession of them (in faith and in baptism) and has taken up residence in them. The flip side of this designation of the Christian life is just as serious as it is clear. Insofar as one does not have the Spirit of Christ, this person does not belong to Christ. With juridical precision, this statement distinguishes between being a Christian and not being a Christian. Paul expresses it because, according to his experience and teaching, the ability to understand Christ, to confess Christ, to believe, and to walk obediently according to God's will all depend on possession of the Spirit (cf. 1 Cor. 2:10ff.; 12:3; Rom. 10:9f.; 14:17f.). Where the confession of Christ, faith, and the obedient life are missing, there can be no talk of belonging to Christ. Only where the Spirit reigns and is at work is the

individual Christian recognizable as such and the church seen to be the body of Christ (1 Cor. 12:12ff.; Rom. 12:4ff.). In vv. 9–11 Paul consequently calls the Spirit, in succession, the "Spirit of God," the "Spirit of Christ," "Christ in us" (cf. Gal. 2:20), and the "Spirit of the one who raised Jesus from the dead." This is easily understood biblically. On the basis of Ezek. 37:5f., God's Spirit is the power of God which creates life from the dead (see above). The messiah Jesus, indwelt by God's Spirit, crucified, and resurrected, is for the apostle (and other early Christian witnesses) the real representative of this Spirit (cf. 1 Cor. 15:45; 2 Cor. 3:17). By the power of the Spirit, he determines the life of those who are his. [10] Correspondingly, Paul continues by saying that if Christ is in you who believe, then you are and will participate in Jesus' death and resurrection (cf. 6:3ff.). As Christ's body was given over unto death (7:4), the body of Christians, together with all of the sinful passions at work in its members, is also given over to death (7:5, 24). But just as Christ was raised by the power of the glory of God, so too God's Spirit is at work toward and in those who believe (cf. 2 Cor. 13:4). The Spirit takes possession of them and leads them to life for the sake of the righteousness brought about by Christ (cf. 1 Cor. 1:30; Rom. 4:25). As those who have been justified, baptized Christians stand in the service of righteousness (6:18ff.) and live before God and unbelievers "in the newness of the Spirit" (7:6). [11] During the time of their earthly witness, the Spirit of God, who raised Jesus from the dead, fills the Christians (from Rome) with the certainty of faith (1 Thess. 4:14; Rom. 6:8) that God will also make alive their mortal bodies by the power of his Spirit and will cause them to partake of the same resurrection glory which has already been granted to the Christ of God in the present (cf. 1 Cor. 15:20–23; Phil. 3:20f.; Rom. 6:4f.). Christians may thus answer the lament of the Adamic "I" in 7:24 as follows: By the power of the Holy Spirit which indwells us, we participate in the righteousness, sanctification, and redemption established by Jesus (1 Cor. 1:30). As a result, we fulfill the instruction of God and, in faith, are certain of our eschatological resurrection.

Excursus 11:
The Pauline Doctrine of the Law

In Paul's dialectic *doctrine of the Law*, as he expounds it in the letter to the Romans, his statements concerning the Law from Galatians and the Corinthian letters, which were already highly controversial during the lifetime of the apostle, are now tied together and become clear. Since in all of these cases it is a matter, above all, of the discussion of the problem of the Law among (Jewish) Christians, the questions concerning the (so-called cultic) Torah which have to do with Jewish worship can for the most part be considered of secondary importance. That is, in all of the mutual polemic and criticism Paul himself is in agreement, even with his most severe Jewish-Christian opponents (cf. 2 Cor. 11:3f.; Phil. 3:2f.; Gal. 1:7ff.; Rom. 3:8), over the fact that Jesus' atoning death brought with it a far-reaching change for the church of Christ in regard to the Jewish sacrificial cult of atonement in the Jerusalem temple. The real conflict concerns to what extent and to what degree baptized Christians are obligated to take upon themselves circumcision, observance of the festivals, the basic purity regulations (cf. Gen. 9:1–7; Leviticus 17–19), and the so-called ethical prescriptions of the Law in order that, in conformity with their baptism in the name of Christ, they might participate in justification at the final judgment.

On the one hand, those opponents of Paul who were still thinking in an entirely ritualistic manner summoned the Gentile Christians in Galatia to keep the food regulations (cf. Gal. 2:12f. with Acts 15:20, 29), to allow themselves to be circumcised according to the example of Abraham (cf. Gal. 5:2; 6:12f.), and also to observe the Jewish feast-calendar (Gal. 4:10). On the other hand, the "liberal" adversaries of the apostle in Corinth and Philippi were satisfied with seeking Christian "perfection" (cf. Phil. 3:15 with James 1:4, 25) by unifying as closely as possible faith in Christ with an orientation of life centered on the Law. In either case, they obviously did not want to let stand the contrast between Moses and Christ, or between justification by works of the Law or by faith alone, which is characteristic for Paul's gospel. Paul too, however, never speaks in his letters of a complete separation between the Law and the gospel (the thought of a "separation of Law and gospel" first appears in the early church around A.D. 150 with Marcion [cf. Tertullian, *Adv. Marc.* 1.19], although his doctrine was rejected as unbearable by the Roman church). Instead, Paul contends for the appropriate relationship between the Law and the gospel. Hence, while his critics, with reference to the example of James, the Lord's brother, in Jerusalem and to Peter (cf. Gal. 2:11ff.; 2 Cor. 11:5), held that the works demanded by the Law are essential in view of the coming judgment of the world (cf. James 2:20–26), Paul represented a more differentiated doctrine of the Law and (final) justification which is very close in content to the preaching of Jesus.

In his teaching, Paul attempted to bring together conceptually, in a dialectical manner, the decisively new aspect of the gospel of Christ with the revelation of the Law before Christ. Hence, already in Galatians (cf. Gal. 2:16ff.; 3:2, 19ff.; 4:21ff. with 5:14; 6:2) and in 1 Corinthians (cf. 1 Cor. 9:19–23) the apostle carefully distinguishes between (1) Jewish obedience to the Law before and without Christ, (2) Gentile lawlessness, and (3) the Christian deed of obedience in fulfillment of the "Law of Christ," in which Christian obedience exists in the "keeping of the commands of God" (1 Cor. 7:19). In the letter to the Romans, Paul maintains this threefold differentiation. Moreover, confronted with the reproach that he nullifies the

Law (3:31) and puts it on the same level with sin (7:7), he presents in 7:7–
8:4 a profound "apology for the Law," with the following result: Through
the sacrifice of Jesus, God has prepared judgment for the reign of sin and
of death (8:3). In addition, through Jesus' death on the cross and resurrection, Christians are also freed from the deadly reign of sin and have died
to the Law as it has been misused by sin ever since the Fall of Adam
(7:4–6; 8:1). But this being dead to the Law does not mean that those who
believe are now transferred into an unbridled freedom, which could be
equated with Gentile lawlessness. Rather, their freedom is realized in service to precisely that righteousness which is God's will (6:13, 18ff.). Indeed, through the end of the reign of sin which God has brought about
through Christ, the commandment or Law of God is also freed from its
misuse by sin and made valid once again. What Paul calls the "Law of
Christ" in Gal. 6:2 and 1 Cor. 9:21 he designates the "Law of the Spirit of
life in (through) Christ Jesus" in Rom. 8:2. Paul bases this formulation on
Jer. 31:31ff. and Ezek. 36:27. As in 1 Cor. 11:25 and 2 Corinthians 3, the
apostle thus views the church as having been placed through Christ into
the time and situation of the new covenant or the new "arrangement" of
God. Hence, through the Spirit who makes alive and liberates, who is
Christ himself (1 Cor. 15:45; 2 Cor. 3:17; Rom. 8:9f.), those Christians
who believe are placed in the new reality of the Law from Jer. 31:33f.
(Rom. 8:2). The Law no longer stands over against them as something foreign and threatening, but moves them from within so that they stand in
the knowledge of God's will and fulfill the legal demand of the Law on the
basis of the power of Christ (Rom. 8:4). In other words, the Christian
church exists for the very purpose (and is also able to accomplish it by the
power of the Holy Spirit) of fulfilling as a testimony the will of God in the
power of Christ (Phil. 2:12–16; Rom. 8:9ff.). The will of God finds paradigmatic expression in the Decalogue (Rom. 13:8ff.) and can be summarized most concisely in the love command (Gal. 5:14; Rom. 13:8). The will
of God will also be the criterion of the final judgment, which God has
given over to his Christ (2 Cor. 5:10; Rom. 2:12–16).

To begin with, however, it is certainly confusing at first when, on the
one hand, the apostle speaks of Christ as the "end of the Law" (Rom.
10:4) and declares that Christians are freed from the reign of the Law
which brings death (Rom. 6:14; 7:6; 8:1ff.), yet, on the other hand, affirms
that he by no means nullifies the Law, but establishes it in faith (Rom.
3:27, 31); when he denies to the Law the quality of being able to create
life (Gal. 3:21; Rom. 8:3), subordinates it by far to the promise given to
the Fathers (Gal. 3:17; Rom. 4:13–15), teaches that it only "came in between" Adam and Christ "in order to increase the trespass" (Rom. 5:20),
and emphasizes that the Law leads only to the knowledge of sin (Rom.
3:20), but then shortly thereafter writes that already in paradise Adam was

entrusted with the commandment or the Law (Rom. 7:9–11), that the
commandment or the Law is from the very beginning holy, just, good, and
indeed, even spiritual (Rom. 7:12, 14), that through Christ the "Law of
the Spirit of life" has come to the fore as liberated, and that those who believe are placed through the Spirit in the position of fulfilling the legal demand of the Law (Rom. 8:2, 14); or when he makes the bold assertion in
Rom. 9:31f. that Israel, in its striving to do justice to the Law on the basis
of works, still did not attain at all to the reality of the Law which is available to faith. But in all of this Paul is merely formulating his position in a
highly dialectical manner and in a way that is by no means absurd! One
must merely keep in mind that he stands in a tradition of understanding
the Law which was previously prescribed to him by early Pharisaism and
the Old Testament and then qualified in a new way messianically by Jesus.

According to the early Pharisaic conception, the Law was created by
God long before the creation of the world. Adam was already entrusted
with it in paradise, and Israel's patriarchs, beginning with Abraham, knew
it and kept it, although it was still unwritten. On Sinai the Torah was then
finally revealed through Moses to Israel as God's people. Its principal part
is the "Ten Words" of the Decalogue (Exod. 20:1–21; Deut. 5:1–22),
which are to be considered equal to the words with which God created
the world. In Sirach 24 and Bar. 4:1, the Law is thus identified with the
primordial, creative wisdom of God, while Sir. 24:10 speaks of wisdom's
installation on Mt. Zion in Jerusalem. Hence, the Torah determines the
temple cult, one's relationship to God, and all of life in Israel; it is the
comprehensive order of life in the true sense of the word. Israel therefore
rejoices in the Law, because it keeps the pious near to God and leads to
life. Conversely, in Sir. 15:15 and Ps. Sol. 9:4f. it is explicitly emphasized
that the person is also free and able to observe the Law. When transgression of the Law does occur, however, repentance and the atonement of
the cult, which has been founded by God out of his goodness, help one to
get over such temporary failures. To be sure, the prophet Ezekiel's recognition that there are also commands in the Torah which "make it impossible" for the people of God "to remain in life" (Ezek. 20:25) is also passed
on in early Pharisaism, but it is not considered further. In addition, the
new "arrangement" of God according to Jer. 31:31ff., which will bring
with it the surpassing of the revelation of the Law on Sinai, is anticipated
as taking place only in the future. In this new covenant the Law no longer
merely stands over against the people of God, but will be written in their
hearts, as a result of which the knowledge of God and the fulfillment of
the will of God take place spontaneously and without instruction from
outside (cf. Jub. 1:15ff., 23ff.; 1 Enoch 61:7, 11ff.). In Jeremiah this new
"arrangement" with Jerusalem is already brought into connection with
Zion (cf. Jer. 31:11ff.), and according to Is. 2:1–4 and Mic. 4:1–4, Zion,

having been elevated in the end-times to the mountain in the center of the world, will then be the place from which the Torah (instruction) goes forth to the nations of the world, which will finally enable them to have peace.

Paul was raised in Jerusalem and instructed in the Scriptures at the feet of Rabbi Gamaliel I (Acts 22:3). In this way he became acquainted with the early Pharisaic and biblical traditions. When, after Pentecost, Stephen and his followers began in their mission for Christ in the synagogues of Jerusalem to criticize the Torah and the temple by appealing to Jesus (Acts 6:11–14), Paul first persecuted them in Jerusalem with all the Jewish means of power available to him. Later, in tracking down their mission, he then persecuted them all the way to Damascus (Acts 8:1–3; Gal. 1:13f.; 1 Cor. 15:9). During this time, the young Pharisee Paul, like the highest Jewish court, most probably saw in Jesus a messianic deceiver of the people and false prophet who was justly handed over to the curse of death on the cross (Deut. 21:22f.), since according to Deut. 13:6 and 17:7 the evil embodied in a deceiver is to be removed, without fail, from Israel's midst. But when the crucified Christ then appeared to him on the road to Damascus in the glory of the Son of God, now exalted to the right hand of God (Gal. 1:15f.), Paul recognized that up until then he had understood Jesus falsely (2 Cor. 5:16) and that he had blindly persecuted the Christian church. In view of the appearance of the glory of God on the face of the resurrected Christ (2 Cor. 4:6), there could be no doubt that in his way and work Jesus was righteous before God, and that in his fanatical "zeal" for the traditions of the Fathers (Gal. 1:14; Phil. 3:6–8) Paul was wrong. The apostle, therefore, had to rethink his views radically with regard to Christ and the Law. In the preaching of Stephen in Jerusalem, Paul had already experienced Jesus' own way of dealing with the Law. Now, after his call to be an apostle, the Christians in Damascus, and later also Peter, reported to him Jesus' teaching on the Law (Gal. 1:18f.). As a result, Jesus' view of the Law appears to become the model for the apostle's own conception of the Law.

According to Mtt. 5:17, Jesus counters the suspicion that he wanted to nullify the Law with the claim that he did not come to abolish the Law, but to fulfill it and through his teaching to complete it (cf., similarly, Paul's point in Rom. 3:31). Jesus appeared as the messianic perfecter of the Torah; that is, expressed in Pauline terms, he preached "the Law (the Torah) of Christ" (Gal. 6:2). In the so-called "antitheses" of the Sermon on the Mount (Mtt. 5:21–48), Jesus contrasted his own messianic interpretation of the will of God to the preaching of the Law as it was given to the "men of old," that is, to the Sinai generation. In doing so, Jesus developed his teaching partly in connection with the Old Testament commandment by means of a deepening of it (cf., e.g., Mtt. 5:21ff., 43ff.), but also partly in sharp contradiction to it (e.g., Mtt. 5:33ff., 38ff.). As far as marriage and divorce are concerned, Jesus even dared to propose that Moses allowed the Israelites the possibility of divorce only in view of their "hardness of heart," but that the inviolable nature of marriage is the original will of God originally established at the creation (cf. Mtt. 19:3–12 par. with reference to Gen. 2:24). Thus, already for Jesus, God's instruction from the beginning of creation could take precedence over the Law from Sinai. Moreover, Jesus himself worked as the messianic "Lord of the Sabbath" (Mk. 2:27f. par.), who establishes the epoch of the new creation. Correspondingly, and for the benefit of his work of love, Jesus sovereignly disregarded the purity regulations which were considered extremely important by the Pharisees (cf. Mk. 7:1–15 par.). Instead, in response to the question of how to best summarize the Law, Jesus answered (in Jerusalem!) in a novel way with the double command to love God and mankind (Mtt. 22:34–40 par.). He also expressly called the one God, who created the world and chose Israel to be the people of his own possession, his "father" (cf. Lk. 11:2–4; Mk. 14:36 par. with Gal. 4:5f.; Rom. 8:15), and, according to the teaching of Jesus, love for mankind is not limited to one's neighbor and partners in the faith, but includes the enemy and persecutor of Jesus' community (Mtt. 5:44 par.). In fulfillment of the command to love one's enemies, Jesus died the death of the cross (cf. Lk. 23:34) on Golgotha before the walls of the Holy City.

Not only the expression (taken over from the Stephen-circle?) "the Law of Christ" (Gal. 6:2; 1 Cor. 9:21), but also, for example, Rom. 12:14–21 makes it possible to recognize how close Paul stands to Jesus' teaching concerning the Law. In the latter text the apostle binds the Christians in Rome to love one's enemy as taught by Jesus, with clear allusion to the corresponding command from the Sermon on the Mount or Sermon on the Plain (cf. Rom. 12:14, 18, 21 with Mtt. 5:44; Lk. 6:27f.). The Pauline teaching concerning the Law, as we have it before us in Romans, thus has its prototype in Jesus' messianic teaching concerning the will of God.

Jesus is crucified and raised in Jerusalem. According to Paul, Good Friday is the great eschatological day of reconciliation for all who believe (Rom. 3:25f.). As a result, Christ brought the ministry of Moses in the old covenant (God's old arrangement) to an end. In contrast to Moses, Paul therefore sees himself called to be a "minister of the new covenant" (God's new arrangement) and to proclaim the gospel of Christ (2 Cor. 3:6). The apostle ascertains his commission to a worldwide mission from (the "Apostolic Council" called together in) Jerusalem (Rom. 15:14–21; Gal. 2:1–10). Yet while the earthly Jerusalem still serves under the Law of sin and of death and seeks its justification in works of the Law, the community of those who believe already belongs to the heavenly Jerusalem (Gal. 4:21–31). The latter live before God in the freedom of love established for them through Jesus' atoning death, that is, in the time and situation of the "new arrangement" in which the Law is fulfilled spontaneously (Gal. 5:14; Rom. 13:8). Yet they too, together with the world, are still moving toward the final judgment according to works in accord with the criterion of the will of God (i.e., of the Law) represented by Jesus, and they too expect reward or punishment for these works (Rom. 2:5–13, 16; 14:10–12, 18, 22–23). But in this process they may remain certain of their final justification, first, because God has chosen them, and second, because the judge of judgment day, Christ, is also the one who continually intercedes at the right hand of God for those who believe, so that even their failures cannot separate them from the love of God (Rom. 8:28–31). At every celebration of the Lord's Supper, the church is assured of its belonging to this new arrangement of God (1 Cor. 11:25), and at that time she thereby implores earnestly for the eschatological arrival of the Lord with her cry, "Maranatha" (= "our Lord, come!") (1 Cor. 11:26; 16:22). This coming of the Lord will take place from Zion and establish the redemption and reality of the new covenant for all Israel (Rom. 11:25–27).

In this way, the Pauline understanding of the Law stands in dialectical continuity to the Old Testament and early Pharisaism. Furthermore, it stands within the movement of God's will within salvation history as it unfolds from Sinai to Zion and is decisively influenced by Jesus' teaching, death on the cross, and resurrection. In the Pauline gospel of the righteousness of God in Christ (Rom. 1:16f.), the grace and instruction of God thus become one, since the Son of God is savior and judge in one person, the redeemer and Lord of the world.

2.4.2. 8:12–17. The Spirit and Life as a Child of God

(12) So then, brothers, we are obligated not, in regard to the flesh, to live according to the flesh! (13) For if you live according to the flesh, you will die. But if, through the Spirit, you put to death the deeds of the body, you will live! (14) For those who are led by the Spirit of God, they are sons of God. (15) For you have not received a Spirit of slavery in order to fear again, but you have received a Spirit of sonship, through which we call, 'Abba, Father!' (16) Precisely this Spirit testifies together with our spirit, that we are children of God. (17) But if children, then also heirs, (and) indeed heirs of God, but as co-heirs with Christ, provided we really suffer with (him), in order that we might also be glorified with (him).

A. With vv. 12–17 Paul brings his discussion in 7:1–8:17 to an end. Verse 12 draws the decisive conclusion from vv. 9–11. This conclusion is then further defined in vv. 13, 14, and 15, each of which connects to the other with "for." Verse 16 continues v. 15, and v. 17 concludes the entire argument in the form of a so-called chain of syllogisms.

In this paragraph as well, Paul again takes up traditions that one must expressly bring to mind in order to be able to replicate the effect of Paul's sentences on his first hearers and readers. When the apostle speaks of the "sons (or children) of God" and of the "Spirit of sonship (being a child)" he is again referring to the biblical and early Jewish traditions which we already mentioned in relation to 8:2, 3. On the basis of 2 Sam. 7:14, the promise that God "(will) be a father for him and he (will) be a son for me" applies to the messiah. Moreover, this promise is an eternally valid covenant arrangement which cannot be broken by God (cf. Ps. 89:20–38). Hence, since Israel, as the people of God, is also called God's only-begotten son in Exod. 4:22f.; Hos. 11:1; Jer. 31:9, 20, and so on, and since the promise which holds true for the house of David is related to all of Israel in Is. 55:3, therefore, within early Judaism, 2 Sam. 7:14, Jer. 31:31ff., and Ezek. 36:27 can already be seen as related to one another. In the so-called book of Jubilees (1:15–18, 23–25) these promises are bound to the expectation that in the end-times Israel will recognize its sins and turn back to God. God will then "create a holy Spirit" for the children of Israel "and make them pure, so that they will no longer turn from me from this day on and into eternity. And their souls will follow me and my entire commandments, and they will act according to my commandments, and I will be a father to them and they will be children to me. And they all will be called children of the living God" (Jub. 1:23–25). As 8:2ff. already demonstrate, Paul regards this promise to be fulfilled in the sending of Jesus, in his sacrifice and resurrection, and in the eschatological gift of the Spirit of Christ to the church.

The call "Abba, Father!" which appears in v. 15, is an appeal to God which repeats the Aramaic vocative "Abba!" (= O, Father!) with the Greek equivalent "Father!" instead of simply replacing the Aramaic word with its translation. The Semitic word "Abba" is so important that the translation is placed beside it without supplanting it (similarly as in Mk. 5:41 par. and 15:34 par.). This striking situation is best explained as follows. The same call, "Abba, Father!" appears in the New Testament in Mk. 14:36; Gal. 4:6; and Rom. 8:15. In Aramaic, Jesus' mother tongue, "Abba" is the address for fathers used in families and is comparable to our current use of "papa!" or also "(dear) Father!" It was precisely this familiar title "Abba" (= "father") which Jesus thus used to praise or to petition God (cf. Mtt. 11:25 par.; Mk. 14:36). As the original form of the Lord's Prayer from Lk. 11:2–4 shows—which begins merely with the address "Father!"— Jesus also taught his disciples to address God as "father," just as he himself did. With the formula "Abba, Father!" Paul may therefore have taken up Jesus' own prayer in such a way that the Christians unacquainted with Aramaic could repeat the call "Abba," but then subsequently reiterate it in the Greek which was familiar to them. Hence, in v. 15 the apostle is reminding the Roman Christians of the prayer that they too speak in their assemblies "in the name of Jesus."

B. Paul now draws the conclusion from what he has presented thus far. But in so doing, the accusation of his opponents, which has been discussed since 6:1,

15 (and 7:7, 13), is still present, namely, that with his preaching of the gospel the apostle is abetting the sinner within the congregation. Beginning in 6:15ff., Paul has attempted to prove his opponents wrong, and in the context of this passage he does so once again. [12] As a matter of holy obligation, baptized Christians must no longer follow the aspiration of the flesh. This obligation proceeds from God's salvific work in the obedient act of Christ (vv. 3f.) and from the gift of the Holy Spirit (vv. 9–11). [13] Hence, if they continue to live according to the measure of the flesh, in spite of the gift of the Spirit which has been allotted to them, the sure result will be death at the day of judgment. But if, instead of this, they bring to death by the power of the Spirit "the machinations" (U. Wilckens) of the body governed by the flesh, they will obtain eternal life before God (cf. 6:22f.). Christians should thus know and bear in mind that they still stand in the midst of the struggle against the temptations of the flesh. Indeed, their own body is the battlefield upon which the fight between the flesh and the Spirit is carried out. [14] God's people may take comfort in this struggle, however, from the fact that they are not dependent upon themselves. Rather, the statement that "those who are led by the Spirit of God, they are God's children" applies to them. This statement is similar in its precision to the legal maxim in 8:9 and belongs with it conceptually. Whoever does not have the Spirit of Christ, does not belong to him; but whoever is led by this Spirit stands in relation to God as his child. The earthly sign of this is the worship service of the church. [15] For in baptism the Christians in Rome have not received a Spirit which would transfer them anew into a state of fear before the power of the slave master that is sin and the Law (cf. 7:14 and Gal. 3:23f.). Rather, they have received the "Spirit of sonship (the relationship of a child)." In this Spirit they participate in Jesus' sonship in relation to God and are members of the end-times people of God (see above). As such, they address God with Jesus' own words. The call "Abba, Father!" may stand alone and can function as a mere "appeal to God" (i.e., as an acclamation). But it can also introduce a prayer of petition (cf. Mk. 14:36). In either case, what is important is that, left to its own power, the spirit of the Christian (cf. 1 Thess. 5:23; 1 Cor. 2:11) is not in the position to pray with the authority of Jesus. [16] But through the Spirit of the resurrected Christ present within them (cf. 8:10), those who believe become capable of such a prayer. Together with the human spirit, the Spirit of Christ who dwells in them invokes God as "Father" and thus makes it possible for fellow members in the church to experience their relationship to God as his child. The apostle is not only concerned, however, with the spiritual experience of the church's common relationship to God as his children which takes place in the earthly gathering of the community. He is also concerned with the fact that this is a promising sign of the coming redemption. [17] Already in Galatians, Paul was moved by the expectation that the salvific community of Jesus Christ would be recipients of that "inheritance" which, beginning with the Fathers, with Abraham at the head, was promised to Israel and now has been acquired for the

church by Christ (cf. Gal. 3:29; 4:7). This same expectation was also previously intimated in Rom. 4:13f. But in our context, the apostle now has in view the promise from 2 Sam. 7:12–14 that one will be brought into the relationship of a child in regard to God. This promise is now made available anew to those who believe through Jesus' sending, death, and resurrection. The crucified and resurrected Christ is its decisive guarantee. Hence, the more clearly Christians presently participate in the conflict of suffering of their Lord, the more certain they may be of their common inheritance of a relationship to God as his child and of their fellowship with God the Father. With the verb "to suffer with" Paul continues the manner of speaking with which in 6:4ff. he expressed the bond between the one being baptized and the destiny of Jesus. As an act which is comparable to the passion of Christ (cf. Phil. 1:29f.; 3:10; 2 Cor. 1:5; Col. 1:24), "to suffer with" means to endure a conflict for the sake of one's testimony and to do so in the certainty of being able to experience the nearness of the Lord, not only in such an earthly fellowship of suffering, but also in the future glory into which Christ has already been taken up by God (cf. 1:4; 6:4–10).

3. 8:18–39. Suffering in the Certainty of Salvation

Paul now brings the section 6:1–8:39 to a close in two steps. In the first step he takes up the Christian's present situation of suffering. The second climaxes in a confession of the unshakable nature of the love of God which has become manifest in Christ Jesus.

3.1. 8:18–30. Suffering in Hope

(18) I am namely of the view that the sufferings of the time which is now present do not carry any weight in comparison to the future glory which will be revealed to us. (19) For the eager longing of the creation awaits the revelation of the sons of God. (20) For the creation has been subjected to futility, not willingly, but on account of the one who subjected it, in hope. (21) For it too, the creation, will be freed from its slavery to corruption, to the freedom of the glory of the children of God. — (22) For we know indeed that the entire creation groans together and is experiencing labor pains together until now. (23) But not only this, even we ourselves also, we who have the first fruits of the Spirit, even we ourselves groan among ourselves in expectation of sonship, (that is) the redemption of our body. (24) We are saved, namely, in hope. A hope which one sees is not hope. For who will (still) hope for what he sees? (25) But if we hope for what we do not see, we wait with patience. — (26) But in the same way the Spirit also assists in our weakness. For we do not know what we should pray in the way that it must be (before God); but he himself, the Spirit, intercedes for us with inexpressible groans. (27) But the one who searches the hearts knows what the striving of the Spirit is, for he intercedes

for the saints as it accords with God. — (28) But we know that everything helps to procure the good for those whom God loves, to those who are called according to his purpose. (29) For those whom he chose in advance he also destined in advance to be conformed to the image of his Son, so that he might be the firstborn among many brothers. (30) But those whom he destined in advance he also called; and those whom he called he also justified; but those whom he justified he also glorified.

A. The text can best be arranged in the following manner. The phrase "I am namely of the view" in v. 18 introduces a thesis which Paul subsequently develops and supports in a threefold way: vv. 19–21, 22–25, 26–27. The concluding vv. 28–30 correspond to v. 18 and flow into a chain of syllogisms which speaks of the glorification of the justified who are now suffering.

Here too the interpretation of these verses confronts the fact that the apostle alludes to traditions and knowledge throughout which were certainly well known to his readers in Rome, but which we today must first painstakingly ascertain. The most important of them are as follows. In v. 20 Paul refers to the consequences which Adam and Eve's Fall into sin had for the creation. The language which the apostle uses is very close to that found in the interpretation of Gen. 3:14–24 in 4 Ezra 7:10–14: "[B]ut when Adam transgressed my commandments, the creation was judged: then the ways in this aeon became narrow and sad and laborious, miserable and bad, full of danger and great impending miseries; but the ways of the great aeon are wide and sure and they bear the fruit of life. If those who are alive thus did not enter into these difficulties and vanities, they could not obtain what is stored up for them." This lament concerning the fallen nature of the creation under judgment corresponds to the experience that the people upon the earth in general, and to an enhanced degree the pious and righteous among them, are exposed to suffering and persecutions. The suffering of the righteous is discussed in the Psalms, in Job, and in the servant songs of so-called Second Isaiah, foremost in Is. 52:13–53:12, but also, for example, in Wisdom 1–5, 1 Enoch 103:9–15, and 2 Bar. 52:5–7. At the same time, these texts also reflect the expectation that the righteous who are overburdened with suffering on the earth shall be glorified by God sometime in the future as a reward, and be vindicated over against their former oppressors (cf., e.g., Is. 53:10–12; Wis. 5:1–7; 1 Enoch 104:1–6). Paul takes up this tradition and with its help explains both in 5:3f. and here in this passage his path in life and the path of all Christians. They are, before God, the "justified who are suffering" (see above, p. 79), as they move toward their heavenly glorification. The expression "to experience labor pains together" in v. 22 is explained by the fact that the time directly before the coming of the messiah to judge will be an epoch full of calamitous events which follow one another in quick succession, that is, the so-called messianic woes. With this perspective as well, Paul is standing on a broad biblical and early Jewish foundation (cf. Mk. 13:8 par.; Is. 24:1–6, 16–23 +

26:16–18; Mic. 4:9f.; 1 Enoch 62:4; 1QH 3:7f.). Inasmuch as the Roman poet Virgil also makes it known in the middle section of his famous Fourth Eclogues (= the Shepherd Poem) that the last period of time before the breaking in of the golden age of peace will be violently shaken by misery, death, and wickedness, we are encountering here a view of the ages which extends far beyond ancient Judaism.

As far as the assistance of the Spirit spoken of in vv. 26f. is concerned, several commentators on Romans have maintained that here Paul intends to allude to the phenomenon of "speaking in tongues" brought about by the Spirit, concerning which 1 Corinthians 14 speaks in detail. But since the apostle does not speak explicitly of "tongues" or "speaking in tongues," it is more probable to call to mind the following two traditions. Beginning with Dan. 12:1, the fact that angels and good spiritual powers, as well as the Fathers and martyred prophets who have already been exalted to God, make intercession before God for the pious who are oppressed on earth is widely attested in early Judaism (cf., e.g., 4Q 400 I 1:16; T. Lev. 3; T. Naph. 8:2; 1 Enoch 40:6f.; Apoc. Zeph. 11:1–6). Yet such intercession in heaven cannot simply be composed in human words, but is presented in the language of the Spirit of "the angels of the countenance of the Lord" (cf. 4Q 400 II 7; 1 Enoch 40:1–10; T. Job 48–50; T. Lev. 3; Rev. 14:3; and 2 Cor. 12:4). This language is closed and forbidden to earthly people, but, according to Paul, the Spirit assists the justified who are still suffering on earth so that their prayers are heard in heaven in the way that corresponds to God (cf. Rev. 8:3).

B. In v. 17 the apostle had indicated briefly that, since their baptism, Christians have not only become the place of struggle between the "flesh" and the "Spirit," but that they must also endure a suffering for the sake of their faith which is comparable to the passion of Christ. He now comes to speak explicitly of this situation of suffering and its place within the history of salvation, that is, in the history of God with humanity. [18] The conviction of faith, introduced by Paul with the rhetorically effective expression "I am of the view," testifies that the suffering laid upon Christians in the present time (before the approaching final judgment) carries no weight over against the glorification promised to them. As 2 Cor. 4:17 and Rom. 5:3f. show, the apostle is not expressing this conviction here for the first time. The justified who are suffering in the present may be certain of their future participation in God's glory because it is guaranteed to them in the person of their crucified and resurrected Lord (cf. Phil. 3:20f.). He is also the one who, by the power of his Spirit now present, makes the afflictions which still must be endured bearable for them.

As indicated above in the text analysis, this doctrine of faith is now supported and expounded by the apostle in a threefold manner. In vv. 19–21, Paul first places the present suffering and hope of the Christian in the context of the fate of guilt that came over the world with Adam's Fall (a theme which was already addressed thematically in 5:12ff. and 7:7ff.). Suffering and the hope of Christians have their place and their meaning in the history of God with humanity! [19] Not only Christians, but the creation as a whole is filled with the eager expectation of experiencing (soon) the revelation of the children of God. This act of the creation's being revealed appears to be conceived of like the act of revealing the Son of Man and the people of the "saints of the Most High" who are embodied in him as declared in Dan. 7:22, 27; 12:1–3. Jesus strengthened this expectation among his disciples (cf. Lk. 12:32; 22:28–30), and it appears in Paul in 1 Cor. 6:2f. and Rom. 5:17, where it is related after Easter to those who are sanctified through Christ's sacrificial death. Moreover, the appearance of the Son of Man and his community in eschatological glory carries the greatest significance for the creation as a whole. [20] For with Adam's Fall, the creation was subjected by God to futility (cf. Gen. 3:14–24 with 4 Ezra 7:10–14, see above), yet not for ever, but "in hope," because the new "man," Christ, shall redeem the world from the consequences of Adam's disobedience (5:15ff.). [21] The future appearance of the salvific community of the (redeemed) "children of God," led by Christ, will complete this redemption in such a way that with the victory of Jesus over the "evil archenemy," death (1 Cor. 15:26), the entire creation as well will be redeemed from its abandonment to decay, in order that from now on it might participate in the glorious nature of the children of God, who have been freed from misery, guilt, and death. What this liberation and participation will look like is vividly described biblically, for example, in Is. 11:1–9 and Revelation 22. As in these passages, so too in our verses, the concept "creation" is not to be limited to humanity, but includes the entire world created by God, which encircles and influences mankind (cf. 1:25). Paul thus teaches one to anticipate a redemption that affects God's entire creation! The destiny of the creation and of the "children of God," whom Jesus gathers around him, belong intrinsically together.

Verses 22–24 also underscore this point, but now in such a way that it is not the future, but the present state of the creation and of Jesus' community of faith which is considered. [22] With the expression "For we know indeed," Paul appeals to the Roman Christians' experience and the insight that they have gained from their faith. Up until this moment, the messianic woes (see above) continue to leave behind their traces in the entire creation; it is afflicted by hunger, epidemics, death, and the chaos of war (cf. Mk. 13:7f.), and therefore it has every reason to groan for redemption (cf. the lament of the earth over the privation of its inhabitants in 4 Ezra 10:9). [23] This longing for redemption also governs the community of faith, so that those who believe represent the entire creation not only in their hope for redemption but also in their "groaning" for redemption (cf. for such groaning, Exod. 2:24; 6:5; Ps. 79:11; Acts 7:34). To be sure, those who believe in the Son of God have received (in baptism) the "firstfruit" of this redemption in the form of the Holy Spirit, who now dwells within them (cf. 2 Cor. 5:5). This firstfruit raises within them the expectation of being able to experience the complete fullness of the "redemption through Christ Jesus" (3:24) already granted to them by God. Nevertheless, the fulfillment of the promise of sonship (cf. Rev. 21:7) is still a matter of hope for them, so that now they still look forward longingly to the redemption of their bodies from decay and death (cf. 1 Cor. 15:42–49, 53–55). God's work of redemption, as the creator, is still incomplete, even toward those who believe. But precisely because it is the redeeming work of the creator God, it must include within it the bodily resurrection of the dead and the salvation of the creation as a whole! [24] Hence, according to Paul, those who have been seized by the Holy Spirit and justified by God through Christ do not yet live in the condition of final perfection, but only in the state of hope in the completion of salvation. Because this salvation has not yet become visible, those who believe still live only in the state of faith and not yet in that of sight (2 Cor. 5:7; cf. with 1 Cor. 13:12). [25] Moreover, because they are not yet able to see redemption, the hope of the Christian church is based on that steadfast patience that Paul mentions in 5:3f., that is, that they will not be ashamed.

[26] Paul explains the reason that they will not be ashamed in vv. 26–27: The "Spirit" comes to help those who believe in the midst of their ongoing weakness. According to vv. 9 and 15, the Spirit refers to the Christ who is at work in Christians and who calls out with them to God. The earthly church of Christ is not capable of speaking the language of the Spirit of the "angels of the countenance of the Lord," which is appropriate before God's throne, nor can they formulate their prayers (of petition) on the basis of the perfect knowledge of God that is granted to these angels (see above). But they may nevertheless take comfort before God in the assistance of the exalted Christ! He, who is the Spirit, intercedes before God on behalf of his own with Spirit-filled petitions for the completion of redemption that are inexpressible for earthly beings. In turn, the heavenly intercession of Christ, also spoken of in 1 John 2:1 and Heb. 7:25; 9:24, strengthens the church on earth. [27] For they may be certain that God, the one who knows the heart (cf. Pss. 7:10; 44:22; Prov. 15:11; Jer. 11:20, among others), understands what the Spirit (= Christ) is all about, for he intercedes for the "saints," that is, for those believers who have been sanctified before God through his sacrificial death (1 Cor. 1:30; 6:11), in the manner that is appropriate before God.

Verses 26 and 27 do not conflict with the certainty Christians have concerning prayer. Rather, the call "Abba, Father!" (v. 15), learned by the church from Jesus, pierces through to God's ear by the power of the intercession of the resurrected one. The church may and can thus pray in the name of Jesus and have confidence of a hearing with God. Nevertheless, the church's insight into God's inscrutable ways (11:33) remains incomplete. Hence, the church must still—like Jesus himself once had to do (cf. Mk. 14:36 par. with Heb. 5:7–10)—learn obedience and accept the fact that her prayers of petition will be answered differently by God than expected (cf. 2 Cor. 12:8f.). But the church may be sure that Christ takes up her prayers and brings them into heaven before God in such a way that they find the hearing which God does desire to give them.

With vv. 28–30 the apostle returns to his introductory thesis (v. 18) and confirms it in the tone of that same certainty of faith which characterized v. 18. The manner of expression which he chooses, especially the triad of "called, justified, redeemed" in v. 30, and the parallel in content in Eph. 2:4–10, make it probable that Paul (once again) depends on baptismal tradition, which [28] he indicates to the Christians in Rome with the introductory phrase "but we know." Yet the tradition concerning which the apostle reminds the Romans extends still further. According to a common Jewish teaching, a person should get in the habit of saying, "Everything which the All-merciful does, he does for the good" (b. Ber. 60b). Paul takes up this tradition and applies it to the matter just discussed. To those whom God loves, that is, to those who believe (cf. 1 Cor. 2:9; James 1:12; 2:5 with Ps. Sol. 4:25; 6:6, among others), all experiences which they (must) undergo—thus also the suffering to be endured in these end-times (v. 18)—help procure the "good," defined in terms of eschatological salvation (cf. 10:15). For they are called by God according to his free decree of grace to precisely this salvation (cf. 1 Cor. 1:26–29 with Rom. 1:5f.). The election according to grace which God has decreed [29] is the deepest and most secure ground of the certainty of salvation for the church of Christ. Paul explains immediately why this is and can be so. Even before they were able to have faith at all (cf. 5:6–8), God had chosen those who believe on the basis of his free grace and determined that they would be conformed to the image of his Son.

It is important to note that the apostle's explicit reference to this determination in v. 29b also interrupts the chain of syllogisms begun in v. 29a and then continued in v. 30. It is obviously important to him to make evident God's election in the form of Jesus. For right from the beginning in 1:4, Paul called the Romans to remember that with the resurrection of the Son of David the eschatological resurrection of the dead as a whole was inaugurated. Moreover, according to 5:12–21, Christ is the new Adam and (Son of) Man, sent from God, whose obedience has overcome the results of Adam's transgression. Then, in 8:3, Jesus is the messianic Son of God, through whose sacrifice the reign of sin was broken and those who live in the Spirit of Jesus are made to partake in eschatological sonship. Hence, inasmuch as, according to Gen. 1:26, Adam was created in the image of God and determines the life of all people, on the one hand, while Christ has come on the scene as the new Adam and life-creating Spirit, on the other, Paul teaches that Christians, as earthly people, must first of all bear the "image" of the first man, and then, after their resurrection, the image of the "last Adam" (1 Cor. 15:44b–49). The apostle presupposes that this teaching is also known by the Christians in Rome. He therefore writes in our context that God has determined that those who love him will participate in the days to come in the same heavenly corporeality which Christ already possesses in the present (cf. Phil. 3:20f.). At that time the messianic Son of God will be—in accordance with the promise of Ps. 89:28–30 (see the comments on 8:3, 12ff.)—the "firstborn" among many brothers (who have been raised like him) (cf. 1 Cor. 15:20; Col. 1:18). In the sending, sacrifice, and resurrection of the messiah, Jesus Christ, God's activity of election not only becomes effective within salvation history, it also becomes evident in a way that brings comfort. With the sending of Jesus and the future of those who believe, which is guaranteed by it, now in view, Paul can continue on with his chain of syllogisms. [30] God has called those who are destined (with their baptism) to partake in Jesus' resurrection glory to be and become his new creation (cf. 1 Cor. 1:26; Rom. 4:17). He has justified them in and through Christ (3:24ff.; 4:25), and he has already given them a share in the glory (righteousness) of the children of God, which was lost to humanity with Adam's Fall (see comments on 3:23). Paul's use of the past tense in vv. 28–30 is at first surprising when one compares it with the way in which the fulfillment of the promise of sonship is viewed in vv. 18–27, where it is still seen as yet to come. But there is an explanation for the contradiction. Verses 28–30, like v. 18, maintain the tone of prophetic certainty. From God's perspective and according to his will, that which can only be developed and completed in the future within salvation history is already accomplished. God has so acted in Christ, once for all, that all time is and remains determined by it. As far as the certainty of their salvation is concerned, those who believe therefore no longer need to express themselves with reservation, since God himself has laid the foundation for this certainty in the sending of Jesus.

3.2. 8:31–39. God's Unshakable Love in Jesus Christ

(31) What then should we say to this? If God (is) for us, who (can then still be) against us? (32) (He,) who did not spare his own Son, but gave him up for us all, how will he not grant us everything together with him? (33) Who will raise a charge against the elect of God? God (is the one) who justifies. (34) Who will condemn? Christ Jesus (is the one) who died, but even more, the one who was raised, who also is at the right hand of God, who also intercedes for us. (35) Who will separate us from the love of Christ? Affliction, or distress, or persecution, or hunger, or nakedness, or danger, or sword? (36) As it is written, "For your sake we are being brought to death the whole day long and we were considered as sheep to be slaughtered." (37) But in all this we overcome victoriously through the one who loved us. (38) For I am convinced that neither death nor life, neither angels nor principalities, neither things present nor things in the future, no authorities, (39) neither height nor depth, nor any other creature will separate us from the love of God, which (is) in Christ Jesus, our Lord.

Verses 31–34: Is. 50:7–9; Verse 36: Ps. 44:23.

A. The structure of the text is disputed. Nevertheless, the verses can best be outlined as follows. Verse 31a introduces with a rhetorical question the solution expressed in v. 31b. Its first half (= "If God is for us") is explained in v. 32; its second half (= "who can then still be against us?") in vv. 33–34. In vv. 35–39 it is further asked, in the style of vv. 33f., who can separate those who believe from the love of Christ (v. 35), whose situation of suffering is then placed in the light of Ps. 44:23. In v. 37 the Christian destiny of victory is set over against the suffering and dangers which vv. 38f. then support more precisely.

The following are the most important of the traditions which the apostle draws upon in these verses. In v. 32 Paul alludes (as in 8:3) to Gen. 22:16. Like Abraham, God sacrificed his own Son for the salvation of the world. But a polemical contrast to the "binding of Isaac" in Paul's statements is not to be ignored, since this tradition was viewed in Judaism, especially after the time of Paul, as a highly meritorious work on Abraham's part which effected atonement for Israel.

Verses 31ff. transfer believing readers into the situation of the (final) judgment. The scene is typified in Is. 50:7–9. There God procures justice for the servant of God who was reviled and tormented by his opponents. Here it is the children of God for whom he establishes justice against all those who accuse them (before the judgment throne of God) and thereby desire to bring about their judgment of condemnation. With this statement the apostle is probably thinking of Satan and the so-called angels of destruction. Their accusation is rejected by the Christ who stands at the right hand of God and intercedes for those who believe (cf. Zech. 3:1ff. and 1 Enoch 40:6f.).

In v. 36 Paul quotes Ps. 44:23 verbatim according to the Greek text of the Septuagint. Psalm 44 is one of the biblical psalms which speak of the destiny of the suffering righteous. As already in 8:18ff., Paul regards the situation of the believers here too as that of the "justified who are now suffering." There is a whole series of early Jewish parallels to the catalog of their sufferings in v. 35 (cf. Ps. Sol. 15:7; 2 Enoch 66:6; and the portrayal of Joseph in T. Jos. 1:3ff.; 2:14ff., who stands against all persecutions and temptations). Paul himself merged this catalog tradition into the enumerations of his own sufferings as an apostle (in 2 Cor. 4:7ff.; 6:4ff.; 11:23ff.) and now aligns himself in Rom. 8:35 with the company of those who must suffer for the sake of their testimony to Christ. Finally, vv. 38f. show that the apostle (together with the early Judaism of his time, from which he indeed originates) sees the world created by God as governed throughout by threatening supernatural and underworldly powers. Ever since the Fall of the angels, which is merely intimated in Gen. 6:1–4, but intensively considered in Jewish texts (such as 1 Enoch 6–11 and 69:2–25), these powers have been working their confusion (cf. also 1 Pet. 3:19). They threaten believers in different ways, but they are nevertheless inferior to the love of God which has been established in Christ Jesus.

B. These verses occupy an important position within the overall outline of the letter to the Romans. They conclude the first main section of the letter (= 1:18–8:39) and make it possible to recognize that God's righteousness in and through Christ really is the central theme of the first part of Romans. Moreover,

vv. 32–34 summarize, in a way that was directive for the ancient church's doc-trine of the Trinity, how in Christ God became and remains "God for us."

Verses 28–30 already express the unshakable certainty of faith. In and with the sending of Jesus, God has chosen, called, justified, and glorified those who believe. The sentences which now follow make it clear how this certainty of sal-vation can be maintained in view of the suffering which still must be endured by Christians. [31] The introductory rhetorical question, "What then should we say to this?" (cf. 9:30), refers back to what has been presented thus far and intro-duces a solution from the perspective of faith formulated by Paul himself: If God in Christ is "God for us" (Immanuel; cf. Is. 7:14) and he has made himself a helper and advocate for believers, then who can still dare to come forward against those who are under the charge of God? The anticipated answer is, "No one!" [32] Verse 32 explains the first part of the solution more closely. As al-ready put forth in 8:3, God did not spare his own Son, but gave him up to the judgment of death for all who believe, as Abraham once gave up Isaac (cf. Gen. 22:16). This took place on the basis of God's free resolve and as an expression of his pure love. As in 4:25, here too Paul has before him Is. 53:12. God made his Son to be the suffering servant of God who vicariously went to death for the many, in order to save them from the threatening judgment of death. With this act, God has, in reality, granted to those who believe everything that they need for (eternal) life. This "everything" includes full participation in the "inheri-tance" of Christ mentioned in 8:17 (cf. moreover 1 Cor. 6:2f.). God's existence for us, that is, his electing grace, comes to complete expression in the gift which he gave mankind when he delivered up Jesus. [33] In the next sentence Paul ex-plains the second part of his solution. In view of this act of grace from God, who can or will still accuse those chosen for salvation, or call into question their share in the inheritance of Christ? At the most, only Satan and his helpers, the so-called angels of destruction, can still attempt this. But they too must fail with their accusation (cf. Zech. 3:1f.), because God himself helps the accused to find justice. It is consistent with Is. 50:8 and 53:11f. that Paul speaks of justification in this context. God desired and continues to desire to help the "many" who are burdened with guilt to find righteousness through the sending of God's servant, Jesus Christ. [34] No accuser can resist this will of God. Although he pleads for the condemnation of the sinner, the accuser encounters the contradiction of the crucified Christ who has been raised by God. This Christ has royal authority at the right hand of God and appears before God in the authority of the Holy Spirit as advocate and intercessor for those who believe in him (cf. 8:26). He as-serts his own vicarious atoning death for the benefit of the sinner; his life pre-sents the ransom for the forfeited life of sinners (1 Cor. 6:20).

Together with 5:8–10, v. 34 thus has the greatest significance for justification. Romans 5:8–10 and 8:33–34 show not only that justification is a forensic act in the forum of the divine court of justice, but, above all, that and in what way Jesus' atoning death really leads once for all to the justification by God of those who believe. Christ was not only the savior once at an earlier time, when God abandoned him on account of the sins of Jews and Gentiles and raised him on account of their justification (4:25), but he remains the intercessor before God for those who believe, beginning with his resurrection and extending into the final judgment. Hence, it is in the continuous work of the crucified one who has been raised that justification is guaranteed to believers, from their baptism to the day of judgment. The Jewish-Christian contramissionaries, with whom Paul had to struggle ever since their appearance in Galatia, repeatedly emphasized that those who would be accepted by God through Christ in the final judgment would only be able to stand if, at that time, they could exhibit faith and works (cf. for this, explicitly, James 2:24). Over against them, Paul remained firm that faith in Christ alone leads to justification (3:28), from the beginning of the Christian life to the boundaries of the final judgment. Christ was, is, and re-mains savior, Lord, and intercessor for those who confess him. For the apostle, there can thus be no other justification than the justification by faith alone in this Christ of God.

[35] As a result, no danger or threat can separate believers from the love of Christ, who gave himself up for sinners in obedience to the will of his Father (Gal. 1:4; 2:20): neither misery and distress, nor persecutions in the frightening times of the "messianic woes" (cf. 1 Thess. 2:2, 14; 2 Cor. 11:23–33; Mk. 13:12f. par.), no hunger, no lack of clothing, no danger, and also not the capital punish-ment which is summoned against the witnesses of Christ (cf. once again 2 Cor. 11:23–33; Phil. 4:11–13; Mk. 13:9 par.). As the quotation from Ps. 44:23 under-scores, the sufferings enumerated all deal with dangers which Christians en-counter as missionary witnesses to their faith in Christ. [36] For the sake of their crucified and resurrected Lord they are considered as sheep to be slaugh-tered, both in their missionary journeys, as well as in the witness to their faith that they give in the cities and villages of Palestine and the Mediterranean world in which they live. Just as it happened to Christ, the servant of God, it also happens in the same way to his followers (cf. Is. 53:7 with Rom. 8:17). [37] But it is precisely this participation in the passion of their Lord which makes the witnesses to faith invincible. By virtue of the assistance of Christ—here the apostle is thinking first of all of the strong and sustaining power of the Holy Spirit (cf. 8:4–17; Mk. 13:11 par.)—the witnesses to faith overcome victoriously all perils and persecutions; they become "conquerors," as described in Rev. 2:7, 11, 17, 26, among other places. In the witnesses to the faith, the love of Christ, by the power of the Holy Spirit, defies the hate of the world. [38] Even the su-pernatural and underworldly principalities can no longer rob them of their sal-vation. In the style of the certainty of faith borne by the Holy Spirit (a style which has already characterized 8:18 and 8:28–30), the apostle now lists ten bearers of supernatural power which rise up in vain against those who believe. The number ten indicates that all conceivable powers in, over, and under the world should be included. In making this list, Paul refers to death as the fiercest

enemy of God (1 Cor. 15:26, 54f.); to the life in which one is separated from God and Christ (cf. 7:24 with 2 Cor. 5:8f.; Phil. 1:23f.); to the fallen angels and principalities, which according to 1 Enoch 6–9 and 69:2ff. are the originators and instructors of all evil in the world; to the present and future, in which one can forfeit faith (cf. 8:18 and Mk. 13:13 par.); to the "authorities," that is, the assemblies around Satan (cf. 1 Enoch 40:7; 53:3; 62:11); [39] to height and depth, that is, the highest and lowest position of the stars, which can influence in a hostile manner the course of life (both expressions appear in Hellenistic texts on magic); and finally, to every other creature in or over the world which, although created by God, is revolting against his ways and purposes. None of them can break the power of the love of God, which appeared in his Son (cf. also 1 John 4:9f.). It is precisely in this love that God chose those who believe (8:28–30) and holds on to them forever. Hence, only those people who have not followed his argument beginning in 7:1, or reject everything which Paul writes, could maintain that with the bold certainty of faith expressed in these sentences Paul is proclaiming "cheap grace."

9:1–11:36. Part Two: The Righteousness of God for Israel

The significance that chapters 9–11 possess within the letter to the Romans will become more evident to the degree that the historical situation within which the apostle is arguing is made clear, and to the extent that the contours of his preaching of justification are kept in mind.

When Paul speaks in his gospel of the righteousness of God for all who believe (1:16f.), he is by no means merely concerned, as we have seen, with the justification of the individual sinner by faith alone for the sake of Christ. Rather, Paul also has in view the eschatological work of salvation of the one God who created the world and chose Israel to be the people of his own possession. This salvific work aims at the redemption of Israel, the Gentiles, and the entire (non-human) creation from sin and the dominion of death. But at this point, Paul now goes beyond the concise remarks from 1:16; 2:9; 4:1, 13 and the short polemical discussion in 3:1–8 by turning thematically to the question of how God's righteousness in Christ becomes effective for the people of God. His main reason for doing so is that the saving work of the one God is incomplete and remains unfinished as long as the majority of the chosen people of God are rejecting the gospel (of Paul) and do not recognize Jesus as the messiah sent from God, in whom God's righteousness, which creates salvation, is embodied (1 Cor. 1:30).

When the apostle wrote Romans, he saw himself and the work of his mission being sharply rejected by large parts of Judaism. In addition, he was not sure for a moment whether and how the early church in Jerusalem would accept his missionary work, together with the collection, which Paul planned to deliver himself (15:30f.). The hostility of the Jews and the distancing of the early church in regard to Paul and his mission did not come about by accident. Ever since the spectacular change in his life, not a few Jews held Paul to be an apostate and traitor to the holy tradition of faith. But even a faction of the Jewish Christians, who with him believed in Jesus as messiah and Lord, could reconcile themselves to the apostle's conception of justification and the Law only with great difficulty, or not at all. To them, the Pauline "gospel to the uncircumcised" (Gal. 2:7) remained foreign and suspicious. This rejection and suspicion would have been much easier to bear as time went on, if Peter and his co-workers had carried out the mission to Israel entrusted to them at the Apostolic

Council (cf. Gal. 2:1–10 with Acts 15:1–35) as consistently as Paul and those who belonged to him carried out their mission work to the Gentiles (Gal. 2:7f.). But this is precisely what did not happen. Instead of going their own separate ways with regard to their mission, Peter paid a visit to the church in Antioch, which was made up of both Jewish and Gentile Christians, shortly after the Apostolic Council. As a result, a public argument came about between Peter and Paul in front of the gathered congregation. The point of dispute was the "truth of the gospel" and its consequences for the ritual behavior of Jewish and Gentile Christians during their common congregational meals (and the celebration of the Lord's Supper!). Evidently, Paul's conception that all those partaking in the meal are freed from, and must remain free of, ritual obligations could not prevail. Hence, from then on, he separated himself from Antioch and carried out the mission to the Gentiles under his own "management" (cf. Gal. 2:11ff. and Acts 15:36ff.). After this separation, the Antiochian mission stood under the influence of the apostle Peter. Furthermore, Peter also became active in the Gentile mission itself, which was originally assigned in Jerusalem to Paul and his assistants in the mission. Under these circumstances, the apostle was forced repeatedly to compare himself (and allow himself to be compared) to Peter. Furthermore, he had to look on as his Jewish-Christian opponents (also) referred to the example of the "rock" and, beginning in Galatia, put into effect in all of the churches which Paul had founded a kind of follow-up and contramission against the Pauline gospel (cf. 1 Cor. 9:3–7; 15:9–11; 2 Cor. 10:12–18; 12:11f.; Rom. 15:18ff.). On the other hand, we have no news of a Jewish mission by Peter and his friends in the faith; it appears to have been interrupted or entirely given up.

In their "repair work" within the Pauline churches, the "contramissionaries" took offense again and again at the fact that the Jews in Ephesus, Thessalonica, Philippi, and Corinth were in each case exceedingly enraged as a result of Paul's previous appearance among them. In their opinion, the newly baptized Christians hung on to the false teaching of a Jewish apostate, whose activities must be stopped. Since Paul, in part, had carried out his mission in buildings which stood right next door to the local synagogue (cf. Acts 18:4–11), and since those who were converted to the faith originated in (large) part from the circle of those "God-fearers" who were accustomed to gathering around the synagogue, the rage of the Jews is easily understandable. Under these circumstances, it is also easy to conceive that the opinion could gain a foothold among Paul's opponents that the apostle's missionary preaching of the gospel does not lead to faith, but to the rejection of the gospel by the majority of Israel. Furthermore, as we have already seen concerning 3:1–8, it did not take much to form the view, on the basis of Paul's own statements (e.g., from 1 Thess. 2:15–16), that the apostle has not only personally given up all of his Jewish privileges, but that he also denies in general the prerogatives of election which belong to the people of God. As a result, at the time that Paul wrote the letter to the Romans, not only had the Jewish mission of Peter perished, but the Pauline gospel as well was under suspicion by its Christian opponents of resulting in the damnation, rather than salvation, of Israel. Naturally, this suspicion did not remain unknown, even in Rome.

Now that Paul has set forth for the Christians in Rome in 1:18–8:39 the way in which his controversial gospel of the righteousness of God for Jews and Gentiles is to be understood, he again takes up "for apparent reasons" the basic question which was only touched upon briefly in 3:1–8, namely, how God's righteousness in Christ also becomes effective for Israel. Only when he has demonstrated this does his message really deserve to be called the power of salvation for *all* who believe, for the Jews first, but also for the Gentiles, as he designated it in 1:16f. And only after the relationship of the Pauline gospel to the Jews, who were especially numerous in Rome, has been clarified could the Christians in Rome dare to comply with Paul's wish for a friendly acceptance and support of his mission, with its goal of reaching Spain, which he expresses in 15:23f. In view of all of this, what Paul has to say in Romans 9–11 is just as decisive for the understanding of his gospel of justification as it is for the realization of his far-reaching mission plans. The following three chapters are thus anything but a mere excursus concerning the problem of Israel, not to mention a merely dogmatic discussion of the question of divine predetermination (predestination), which need not be considered absolutely necessary for the understanding of the doctrine of justification. For in these chapters, Paul is concerned with the very life nerve of his mission and with the question of the faithfulness of God in regard to the promise that he gave to Israel, issues of a far more fundamental concern than the matter of the accompanying salvation and deliverance of the Gentiles. Paul therefore had a very pressing reason for writing Romans 9–11, and in turn these chapters have a very practical meaning for the apostle. As a result, the style in which the chapters are composed is correspondingly personal (cf. 9:1ff.; 10:1ff.; 11:1, 13ff.).

The three chapters comprise a coherent argument. They can be divided into five sections. Romans 9:1–5 forms the introduction; in 9:6–29 Paul expounds the free election of God; in 9:30–10:21 he outlines Israel's encounter with the gospel of the righteousness of God; in 11:1–32 he speaks of the eschatological redemption of all Israel; and 11:33–36 concludes the entire discussion in the form of a doxology concerning the wonderful ways of God.

I. 9:1–5. Lament for Israel

(1) I am speaking truthfully in Christ, I am not lying, and my conscience is a witness for me in the Holy Spirit: (2) (There is) great sorrow for me, and unending pain (pierces) my heart. (3) I wish, namely, to be (under the) curse, indeed, I myself, separated from Christ for the benefit of my brothers, my

kinsmen according to the flesh; (4) they, who are Israelites, to whom belongs
the sonship and the glory and the arrangements (covenant resolutions) and
the giving of the Law and the worship of God and the promises; (5) to them
belong the Fathers and from them the Christ originates, as far as his fleshly
nature is concerned. God, who reigns over all, be praised for all eternity.
Amen.

Verse 3: Exod. 32:32; Verse 4: Gen. 32:28f.; Exod. 4:22; 29:43ff.; Gen. 8:21f. +
    9:17; 17:4; 17:19; 26:3ff.; Exodus 24; Ps. 89:4f. (2 Sam. 7:8–16); Jer. 31:31ff.;
        Ezek. 36:22–32; Verse 5: Sir. 44:1–50:26; Is. 7:14; 9:5ff.; 28:16.

A. The concluding doxology in v. 5 can be related grammatically either to
Christ, or to God, the creator and Lord over all things. The first relationship
would be quite unusual in the Pauline letters, since Paul otherwise never calls
Christ "God," while the second possibility has parallels in 2 Cor. 11:31 and
Rom. 1:25 and agrees with Eph. 4:6. For this reason, the latter is to be preferred.
B. The apostle begins his expositions with a directly emphatic assertion. [1]
He speaks the pure truth, and his conscience, which is filled with the Holy
Spirit—that is, with the present Spirit of Christ (8:9f.)—is a witness before God
and his readers that deep sadness and great pain fill his inner being. [2] For
while Jews and Jewish Christians reproached him for traitorous and frivolous
treatment of Israel's salvific privileges, in truth the situation is quite different.
[3] The apostle would gladly ask God to be under the curse of judgment himself
and far from Christ in exchange for seeing his Jewish kinsmen placed in that
"peace with God" (5:1) into which Paul is now accepted. As Moses once made
intercession for the people of God who had fallen from God and offered himself
as an atonement for their apostasy (cf. Exod. 32:32), so too Paul (whose ministry
on behalf of the gospel corresponds to that of Moses in the old "covenant"; cf. 2
Cor. 3:4ff.) is now willing to offer up his relationship to Christ for the benefit of
the Israelites who stand far from Christ. He knows, however, that this wish will
not be fulfilled for him, and he will show in 10:19 + 11:13ff. that, and how, he as
an apostle of Jesus Christ on behalf of the Gentiles may also work for the deliverance of Israel. So (in the meantime) there remains a discrepancy that tor-
ments Paul within, namely, that those Jews to whom he is related by race stand
(for the most part) far from Christ, although they are provided by God with unparalleled privileges of election. [4] In distinction to the Gentiles, they are descendants of Jacob, and like him bear the name of honor, "Israel" (i.e., "God
prevails"; cf. Gen. 32:28f.); the special relationship to God of "sonship" was dedicated to them (cf. Exod. 4:22 and 2 Sam. 7:14 with Rev. 21:7); God took up residence in his powerful glory in a special way in Israel (Exod. 29:43–46; Ps.
132:8–10, 13–14); he deemed Israel's Fathers, Noah (cf. Gen. 8:21f.; 9:17),
Abraham (cf. Gen. 12:2; 17:4), Isaac and Jacob (cf. Gen. 17:19; 26:3ff.), Moses

(cf. Exodus 24), and the house of David (cf. Ps. 89:4f.; 2 Sam. 7:8–16) worthy of
his gracious arrangements (covenant resolutions); on Sinai God bestowed to the
Israelites through Moses the preferential gift of the Law (cf. Exod. 24:12; Deut.
4:5ff.; 5:22); he took up residence on Zion and by the power of wisdom made
worship possible for Israel (Ps. 74:2; Sir. 24:10); in addition, the promises apply
to Israel, above all the promise to Abraham (Gen. 12:2; 15:4f.; cf. with Gal.
3:16–29 and Rom. 4:13ff.); [5] through the chain of the "Fathers" Israel is bound
to God, to whom, according to the "Praise of the Fathers" (Sir. 44:1–50:26), belong not only the Patriarchs just named, but also David and the prophets; but finally and above all, "the Christ," that is, the messiah from the family of David,
who was promised by God and anointed by the Holy Spirit, originates, as far as
his earthly appearance, from the people of Israel (cf. 2 Sam. 7:12–14; Is. 7:14;
9:5ff.; 11:1–12; Jer. 23:5; 33:14ff.; Mic. 5:1ff.; and Zech. 9:9f.). On the basis of
1:3f., the readers of Romans know that Jesus is this promised son of David.
Nevertheless, Paul does not yet draw a contrast, but sees himself pressed, as the
Jew that he is and remains (11:1), to praise God in view of this overwhelming
series of the "mighty acts of God" (Acts 2:11) on behalf of his people. This
praise of God makes it unmistakably clear to the readers of Romans that the
apostle has not written off Israel. In terms of its content, it points forward to
11:36 and is close to Eph. 4:6. God is praised throughout eternity as the creator
who rules over everything. He is the one to whom Israel owes all her privileges!

II. 9:6–29. The Election and Mercy of God

After this emphatic lament for Israel, the apostle expounds in two sections
(9:6–13 and 9:14–29) God's free election and his free mercy as the power that
creates and upholds Israel, as well as the new people of God now made up of
Gentiles and Jews.

1. 9:6–13. God's Free Election

(6) But it is by no means so, that the word of God could have failed! For not
all who (are descended) from Israel, are (also) Israel. (7) They are also not all
children because they are the seed of Abraham, rather (it is true that) "(Only)
in Isaac shall seed be named to you." (8) That means that it is not the children
of the flesh who are (also) children of God, but the children of the promise
are reckoned as seed. (9) For this word is (a word) of promise: "At this time I
will come, and (then) Sarah will have a son." (10) But (this is so) not only
(with her), but also (with) Rebecca, who was pregnant by one man, by Isaac
our father. (11) For when they were still not yet born and had also not yet
done anything good or evil, so that the purpose of God (which acts) according

to election might endure, (12) not on the basis of works, but on the basis of the one who calls, it states in regard to her, "The older will serve the younger," (13) as it is written, "Jacob I loved, but Esau I hated."

Verse 7: Gen. 21:12; Verse 9: Gen. 18:14;
Verse 12: Gen. 25:23; Verse 13: Mal. 1:2f.

A. In order to understand the argument, one must first of all consider that in the following verses and chapters Paul understands the Holy Scripture to be a living, Spirit-filled utterance of God; he quotes it in accordance with the rules and with all of the artistic skill which he learned in the school of Rabban Gamaliel I in Jerusalem (cf. Acts 22:3). The examples that the apostle adduces for God's free activity of election are not chosen by accident. Rather, 4 Ezra 3:13ff. show that also among the Jews the chain of ancestors, Abraham–Isaac–Jacob–Moses, presented a paradigm for the elective grace with which God had chosen and upheld his people. Romans 9:6ff. thus illustrate what was given to Israel from God in and with the "Fathers" (v. 5). Finally, one should take note of the fact that in v. 8 and vv. 11f. Paul uses the language of justification. In the apostle's view, God's elective grace, as it manifested itself in the history of Israel, and God's work of justification belong intimately together!

B. Paul begins his actual discussions of the problem of Israel with the explicit statement that [6] there can be no talk of the fact that "the word of God" has failed. From the context, that is, on the basis of vv. 4–5 and v. 9, the "word of God" refers to the word of promise with which God, the creator, directs Israel's history. If one thinks of the accusations against the Pauline missionary preaching mentioned above, it is very easy to imagine that in v. 6 Paul is rejecting an opposing insinuation. But for Paul, and according to his gospel of justification, God's word of promise promulgated to Israel remains valid! This assertion has fundamental significance for Romans 9–11 (cf. 11:29). First, it signifies that simple earthly blood ties do not determine membership in the chosen people of God. Israel is constituted by God only through his free elective grace. [7] The first example of this, in accordance with the scriptural witness from Gen. 21:12, is Abraham. Because the ancestral line of the descendants of Abraham, which is desired by God, runs through the promised son Isaac, Israel's forefather had to repudiate his own son Ishmael, together with his mother Hagar, based on God's instruction (cf. Gen. 21:9ff. and Gal. 4:22f.). [8] As a result, only those descendants promised to Abraham in Isaac are the chosen "children of God," and not simply all the fleshly children of Abraham. [9] Hence, the promise given by God in Gen. 18:14 that next year Sarah will have a son is that word of promise and as such is to be respected. [10] But Sarah's pregnancy is only the first example of God's free elective grace in Israel's history. It is no different with Isaac's wife Rebecca. [11] When she became pregnant (by Isaac) and the twins Esau and Jacob were still not yet born, God documented the freedom of his providence,

which acts according to the principle of predestination, in that his creative word
of promise determined that [12] "the older (= Esau) must serve the younger (=
Jacob)" (Gen. 25:23). [13] In the election of Jacob and the setting aside of Esau,
God's word (recorded in Mal. 1:2f.) thus proved to be true: "Jacob I loved, but
Esau I hated." Hence, beginning with Abraham, both Israel's existence, as well
as membership within Israel, are anchored in God's election alone. This accords
with the (well-known) path of justification, namely, justification on the basis of
the free call of God in accordance with his elective grace, and not on the basis
of works (cf. 3:20, 28; 4:2f., 16f.), which Paul unmistakably signals to his readers
through his manner of expression in vv. 8 and 11f. The God who elects and the
God who justifies in and through Christ are one and the same; ever since Abraham, Israel stands and falls based on his action!

2. 9:14–29. God's Free Mercy

(14) What then should we say? Is there some unrighteousness with God? By
no means! (15) For he says to Moses, "I will show mercy on whomever I will
show mercy, and I will be compassionate to whomever I am compassionate."
(16) It is therefore thus true that it is not a matter of the one who wills, or of
the one who runs, but it is of the God who shows mercy. (17) For the Scripture says to pharaoh, "For just this purpose have I caused you to come forward, so that I might show my power in you and so that my name might be
made known in the entire earth." (18) It is therefore thus true that he shows
mercy on whomever he wills, (and) he hardens whomever he wills. (19) You
will then say to me, "Why then does he still find fault? For who is able to
withstand his will?" (20) O man, who are you really, that you raise objections
against God? Does the thing made say to the one who has made it, "Why have
you created me so?" (21) Or does not the potter who works with clay have the
free right to make out of the same lump one vessel for display and the other
for dishonor? (22) But if God, in the desire to show his wrath and to make
known his power, (already) bore in great patience vessels of wrath, which are
created for destruction, (23) (then he did this) also (and above all) in order
that he might make known the riches of his glory concerning vessels of mercy,
which he has prepared in advance for glory; (24) that is, those whom he also
called, namely us, not only from the Jews, but also from the Gentiles, (25) as
he also says in (the book of) Hosea: "I will call those who are not my people,
my people! and those who are not loved, my beloved! (26) And it will happen
that in that place where it was said to them, 'You are not my people,' there
they will be called, 'sons of the living God.' " (27) But Isaiah calls out concerning Israel, "(Even) if the number of the children of Israel is as the sand of the
sea, (still only) the remnant will be saved; (28) for God will be at work with his
speech upon the earth as one who puts into effect and (in doing so) cuts off."

(29) And as Isaiah predicted, "If the Lord Sabaoth had not left behind for us a seed, we would have become like Sodom and we would be just like Gomorrah."

Verse 15: Exod. 33:19; Verse 17: Exod. 9:16; Verse 20: Is. 29:16; Verse 25: Hos. 2:25; Verse 26: Hos. 2:1; Verses 27f.: Is. 10:22f.; Verse 29: Is. 1:9.

A. This paragraph presents several grammatical and historical problems. First, a connecting verb is missing between vv. 22 and 23. Hence, whether and how the verses belong together can only be decided exegetically. Then in its dialogical structure and in the questions which the apostle raises in vv. 14 and 19f., Rom. 9:14–23 recalls 3:1–8. It is thus evident that Paul continues to see himself over against those (Christian) "slanderers" who reproach him with selling out the privileges of Israel and with preaching cheap grace. In response, the apostle again argues with the help of the Scripture, from which he perceives the voice of the living God. The manner in which he handles the Scripture, coordinates the citations from Exodus and the Prophets, and in doing so, in part even changes them somewhat, corresponds to the methods of interpretation which were common in his time and recognized equally by Jews and Christians.

As in 1:18–32, Paul also depends in these verses upon statements and patterns of argumentation that were widespread in the wisdom tradition. The metaphor of the potter (v. 21) is used in a way similar to that in Paul not only in Is. 29:16 and Jer. 18:6, but also in Wis. 15:7. But above all, Wis. 11:23 and 12:3–22 (esp. 12–18) contain the well-known insight that the all-powerful and just God, with whom no one may dispute, does not simply and abruptly destroy even the Gentile peoples who rebel against his ways with Israel, that is, the Egyptians and the unclean dwellers of the Holy Land. Instead, God first of all bears with them in patience and gentleness in order, if still possible, to lead them to repent before their downfall. This magnanimous behavior on God's part should be a lesson to Israel itself, "so that we . . . hope for mercy when we ourselves stand before the judgment" (Wis. 12:22). Paul argues very similarly in vv. 20–23, and it is surely no accident that in v. 17 the Egyptian pharaoh (and not simply Israel) is the biblical paradigm of a "vessel of (the) wrath" of God which is borne with forbearance.

B. The doctrine of God's free elective grace represented by the apostle in vv. 6–13 provokes—quite similarly as in 3:5—[14] the question of whether God's free election does not cause one to conclude that there is injustice with God. Paul rejects this suspicion and once again grounds his teaching explicitly in the Scripture. [15] From the fact that God made no secret to Moses of the freedom of his grace and his mercy (Exod. 33:19) it follows [16] —again Paul formulates a doctrine (cf. above, pp. 113f.)—that what matters before God is not the person's own human exertion of the will or the engagement of all one's own powers as in a run(ning race), but God's mercy; only in God's mercy does Israel's existence have its ground and stability. The Scripture confirms this [17] in that God says to pharaoh in Exod. 9:16 that he was allowed to live in order to become an object for the demonstration of the power of God and to make God known in his activity upon the earth in general, as determined by the character of his name. [18] It it thus true that God shows mercy to whomever he wills, and that he hardens whomever he wills. This doctrine, gathered from the Scripture, should also serve as a warning to Israel. The destiny of the pharaoh could be its own if it resists God's ways. [19] But, as in 3:7f., here too Paul intercepts the objection that as a result of acting in such a way, God no longer has any right to exercise judgment or to find fault (cf. Heb. 8:8). [20] Rebellion against God's judicial freedom is not legitimate for the person created by God. The creature has no right to rebel against his creator (Is. 29:16), [21] but God has the right to create both kinds of creatures, those which he glorifies, and those which he desires to destroy (cf. Jer. 18:6). But it is also to be observed from the Scripture [22] that God's judgments are not an end in themselves. For if God—as can be clearly recognized from the example of pharaoh (and the Egyptians)—has in his magnanimous patience already kept and borne the vessels of wrath which are determined for destruction, [23] then the vessels of mercy, which have been determined by God for glorification, may assume that God desires to make known to them (in the presence of the world) the entire riches of his glory. This mode of argumentation was already indicated in Wis. 11:23f. It thus removes from those who would object the possibility of further critical objections, since Paul's point is anchored in Jewish-Christian doctrine, and leads to the conclusion that although Israel's rejection is indeed a divine possibility, such a rejection is not anticipated in regard to those who are elect (cf. 11:12, 15). The divine proof for this is also already present. [24] It has been given by God in that he has already begun to call "the vessels of mercy" in the form of "us," that is, Paul and the Christians from Rome. The members of the church of Christ therefore originate not only from the line of the Jews, but also from that of the Gentiles, and they all are "called" by God, that is, chosen through Christ for justification and glorification (cf. 8:30). Moreover, the formulations from v. 24 show that Paul is concerned from now on with justification. The transition from Israel to the Christian church that Paul thus carries out at this point is striking, but consistent. Inasmuch as Jesus himself came forth in order to gather from Israel the eschatological people of God, beginning with the twelve disciples chosen by him, the early Christian mission was concerned to continue Jesus' work. Paul too is part of this heritage. From his perspective, the Gentile mission, carried on by him with the consent of the "pillars" in Jerusalem (cf. Gal. 2:7ff.), should not replace, but should supplement the mission to the Jews (entrusted to Peter). As a result, the salvific community of Jesus, which the apostle calls "the Israel of God" in Gal. 6:16, is to consist of both those Jews and Gentiles who are called to faith in Jesus Christ. It is in exactly this sense that Paul speaks of "us" in this verse (cf. also 3:28–30). This "us" does not invalidate the fact that, from the perspective of the history of election, the gospel of Christ applies "to the Jew first, and only then to the Greek" (1:16), but rather confirms it in harmony with God's word as it is attested in the Holy Scripture. [25, 26] God's declaration from the book of Hosea (cf. Hos. 2:25 and 2:1) is verified by the salvific community of Jews and Gentiles which was originally founded in Jerusalem. [27] If in Hosea, of course, the number of the children of Israel is said to be as large "as the sand of the sea," then that is to be evaluated by Isaiah's more critical declaration that [28] from this great number only a remnant will be saved and that God is determined to carry out this word, even with all of its hard consequences. There is thus grace for the children of Israel only at the day of judgment; only the small, predestined "remnant" (and this remnant is identical to the converted Jewish Christians who belong to the church of Christ; cf. 11:5) will come forth from it. This reduction of Israel to a remnant is therefore intended by God, the creator and judge, [29] since it corresponds to the declaration of the prophet Isaiah that only through God's grace are the Israelites preserved from total destruction, as it was once executed on Sodom and Gomorrah (cf. Gen. 19:23ff.). Therefore, just as clearly as the judgment of God is by no means an end in itself, to the same degree the people of God who have been endowed with enormous privileges are not exempted from judgment in view of the appearance of Jesus and the gospel. The apostle explains why this is so in the following discourse.

III. 9:30–10:21. Israel's Rebellion against the Righteousness of God in Christ

There are reasons for the reduction of Israel to a remnant (v. 27), and Paul takes these up in 9:30–10:21. Romans 9:30–33 speaks of the offense which Israel took at the "rock of offense" (= Christ), and 10:1–21 speaks of Israel's disobedience in regard to the righteousness of God for those who believe, that is, the righteousness which became manifest in Christ and is proclaimed in the gospel.

1. 9:30–33. Israel's Offense at the Stone of Stumbling

(30) What do we thus want to say? Namely what follows: Gentiles who are not seeking righteousness have obtained righteousness, that is, the righteousness on the basis of faith, (31) but Israel, which is seeking the Law of righteousness, did not attain to the Law. (32) For what reason? Because (it is not sought) on the basis of faith, but on the basis of works. They took offense at the stumbling stone, (33) as it is written, "Behold, I place in Zion a stone of stumbling and a rock which causes offense, and the one who depends on him will not be put to shame."

Verse 33: Is. 28:16 + 8:14.

A. Romans 9:30–33 is a decisive turning point in the Pauline argument. It summarizes the discussion up until this point and in doing so introduces the most important catchwords for the discussion of Israel's misunderstanding of the righteousness of God which comprises all of the following chapter. Verse 30 summarizes the Gentiles' position before God according to vv. 24–29. In v. 31 this is contrasted to the situation of Israel, and vv. 32f. support this in view of the Scripture as a living word from God. Hence, when in vv. 32f. Paul refers to Is. 28:16 and 8:14 and interweaves both passages together, he is again proceeding as an early Christian scribe. Both verses were already being interpreted in the synagogues at the time of Paul as referring to the messiah, and Paul is simply following this custom. Moreover, 1 Pet. 2:6–8 and Barn. 6:2–4 show that it was a fixed style of early Christian doctrine to argue for faith in Christ with the help of Is. 28:16 and 8:14 (and Ps. 118:22).

B. From the discussions beginning in v. 24 we may infer that which the mission experience of the churches in Rome confirms, namely, [30] that Gentiles, who by nature did not strive to follow the "way of righteousness" (Mtt. 21:32) before God, in order to be able to stand before the judgment throne of God (cf. also Gal. 2:15 for this negative evaluation concerning the Gentiles), have nevertheless obtained righteousness. Specifically, they obtained the righteousness which God promises to those who live on the basis of faith (in Jesus Christ as savior and Lord) (cf. 3:26, 30). [31] Israel's situation, in contrast, is different. Israel strives with all its powers after the Law which prescribes righteousness, but does not attain to the Law (ahead of the Gentiles). This statement by the apostle, which at first seems unusually strange (and also presents a serious enigma for the interpretation of this passage), can be explained, however, on the basis of (3:27, 31 and) 8:3f. Although Israel is concerned with the fulfillment of the Law and, with it, for righteousness before God, it did not attain to the fulfillment of the Law into which Christ places those who believe. Correspondingly, the reality of the Law is also closed to Israel, that is, that reality which, in accordance with 2 Sam. 7:12–14, was opened up through the sacrifice of Jesus to those who believe (see above, pp. 117ff.). For Israel, the Law is not yet written in their heart, and Israel lacks the power of the Spirit of Christ. As a result, Israel still stands over against the Law, and up until now has not obtained the righteousness of faith. The decisive reason for this resides in Israel's disposition in life. [32] Instead of living before God on the basis of faith, Israel stands before the Law and attempts to follow the path which is—as Paul already indicated in 3:20 (cf. Gal. 2:16)—condemned by God to fail, namely, to be justified on the basis of works. The Jews have therefore taken offense at the stone of stumbling, [33] which, according to the words of Isaiah, God himself has laid in Zion (= Jerusalem). Moreover, they have not accepted the invitation, expressed by God in the same context, that the one who places his believing trust upon this rock will not be put to shame. Simply put, Israel has not recognized the messiah sent from God, Jesus Christ, who completed his commission on the cross in

Jerusalem. Instead, the crucified messiah has become an offense to the Jews (cf. 1 Cor. 1:23f.). The very fact that Paul says this in such a general way and also maintains the same manner of speaking in chapter 10 shows that at the time of the composition of the letter to the Romans the vast majority of Israel stood distant from the gospel of Christ. Israel did not follow the pathway of faith.

2. 10:1–13. Israel's Failure to Recognize the Righteousness of God

(1) Brothers, the desire of my heart and my prayer for them before God (is directed) toward (their) salvation. (2) For I bear witness concerning them that they have zeal for God, but not according to (proper) knowledge. (3) For they are obstructed from the knowledge of the righteousness of God, and in striving to establish their own righteousness, they have not submitted to the righteousness of God. (4) For Christ is the end of the Law in regard to righteousness for everyone who believes. — (5) Moses writes, namely, of the righteousness (which is obtained) on the basis of the Law that, "The person who did them (= the commandments) will live through them." (6) But the righteousness, (which is obtained) on the basis of faith speaks thus: "Do not say in your heart, 'Who will climb up into heaven?' " — that means, to bring Christ down; (7) or, "Who will climb down into the abyss?" — that means, to bring Christ up from the dead. (8) But what does it say? "The word is near you in your mouth and in your heart" — that means, the word of faith which we preach. (9) For if you confess with your mouth, "Jesus is Lord!" and believe in your heart that God raised him from the dead, you will be saved. (10) For with the heart one believes unto righteousness, but with the mouth one confesses unto salvation. (11) For the Scripture says, "Everyone who trusts in him will not be put to shame." (12) There exists, namely, no distinction between Jew and Greek, but there is the same Lord over all, who distributes his riches to all who call upon him. (13) For, "Everyone who calls upon the name of the Lord will be saved."

Verse 5: Lev. 18:5; Verse 6: Deut. 9:4 + 30:12; Verse 7: Ps. 107:26 (Deut. 30:13); Verse 8: Deut. 30:14; Verse 11: Is. 28:16; Verse 13: Joel 3:5.

A. Paul begins in v. 1 with a personal affirmation (comparable to 9:1–5), supports it in vv. 2f., and then in v. 4 formulates the Christian antithesis to the Jewish disposition. As support for this, he then contrasts Moses and the righteousness of faith with one another in vv. 5–13 in view of the witness of the Holy Scripture and the confession of Christians.

Once again the apostle understands Holy Scripture as the living word of God and argues with its help. Especially striking is the fact that in doing so Deut. 30:12–14 appears as a speech given by the righteousness of faith. For not only in Deuteronomy itself, but also in the Jewish interpretation of the Scripture, these very verses are related to the Torah (the Law). For example, in Bar. 3:29f. they are brought into connection with the wisdom that in Bar. 4:1ff. is identified with the Law. Over against this interpretation, the righteousness of faith recognizes in the "word which is near" (from Deut. 30:14) the gospel of Christ and follows its voice.

In vv. 9f. Paul refers to the confession of Christ. This confession is known to us in a twofold form, that is, as a short invocation of Christ, "Jesus is Lord," which is spoken in the power of the Holy Spirit within the gathering of the church (cf. 1 Cor. 12:3), and as a fully developed doctrinal confession (= a creed) that is used in the instruction associated with missions and baptism (cf. 1 Cor. 15:3–5). The latter summarizes the decisive content of faith in memorable brevity. In Rom. 6:17 Paul has already referred to the creed known in Rome and now comes to speak of both forms of the confession.

B. With a personal affirmation that in tone recalls 9:1ff., the apostle now refers to the decisive point which separates Jews and Christians. [1] That his Jewish kinsmen would find (eschatological) salvation is the personal wish of his heart and at the same time the subject of his prayers before God. [2] For Paul testifies concerning them that they really are zealous for God. In doing so, he is able to recognize himself as a prime example, since before his call he was a "zealot" for the traditions of the Law from the Fathers (Gal. 1:14; cf. with Num. 25:11, 13). His readers probably also saw in Paul an example of his own statement, especially since Paul's spectacular change of life was a part of the general Christian narrative (cf. Gal. 1:23 and Acts 9:1–29; 22:3–21; 26:9–20). But as the apostle had experienced in his own life, this Jewish zeal for God is characterized by a deficient knowledge of God. As lamented in various ways in the Pauline letters, what is meant by this is that the Jews do not grasp what God has done for them and for the world in Christ. Instead, they live in the state of delusion (cf. 1 Cor. 2:7f.; 2 Cor. 3:14f.). For them, the same Christ who is made by God to be wisdom for those who believe (i.e., he leads them to the true knowledge of God) and procures for them righteousness, sanctification, and redemption (1 Cor. 1:30), is a hindrance to faith. [3] They are thus lacking the knowledge of the righteousness of God. The expression "the righteousness of God" is meant here as comprehensively as possible. Rather than submitting to God's activity of election, which originally made Israel into the people of God and determined that they would come to righteousness through Christ (cf. 9:11, 16, 23f.), the revelation of the righteousness which creates salvation through the atoning death and resurrection of Christ (Rom. 3:24–26; 4:25) remains closed to them. In v. 3, however, the apostle is not speaking of a conscious rejection of God's righteousness, but of a delusion under which Israel unknowingly stands and which can be taken away from God's people only with God's help (cf., likewise, Acts 3:17). In their delusion, the Jews are still concerned about their own righteousness before God. But in their opinion, it is not Christ, but the Law, which assists one to stand before the judgment throne of God, and it appears to them to be completely possible to lead a blameless life in righteousness according to the criterion of the Law. Here too Paul can and must think first of all of himself (cf. Phil. 3:6). Yet he is no exception. Indeed, it says in the early Pharisaic Psalms of Solomon, "Our action takes place according to the choice and will of our heart, that we do righteousness and injustice with the work of our hands, and in your righteousness you regard the children of men. — The one who practices righteousness gathers for himself life with the Lord, and the one who does injustice forfeits his own life to corruption, for the judgments of the Lord are promulgated in righteousness against person and house" (Ps. Sol. 9:4–5; cf., similarly, Sir. 15:14f.). But since this (Pharisaic) conception fails to recognize the ways of God in and with Christ, Paul himself experienced in his own life on the road to Damascus what he now expresses as the Christian advantage in knowledge over against Israel, which persists in unbelief. [4] Specifically, what Paul experienced is that, by virtue of the will and the grace of God, Christ is the end of the Law unto righteousness for every person who believes. Christ, not the Law, decides who is justified in the judgment. That is to say, it is not those who, without Christ, are striving to practice righteousness on the basis of their own power who will be justified, but those from Israel and the Gentiles who believe, that is, who recognize in Christ the one who atones for them and the one who is their eschatological advocate before God's throne (8:31–34). Hence, Rom. 10:4, which is hotly contested among interpreters of Paul, is intended to be read from the perspective of (final) justification. Here the decisive question is whether the Law's verdict of guilt, which is pronounced on every sinner, has a fatal effect before the judgment throne of God or not. From Paul's perspective, it is only in view of Christ being at the right hand of God, and in view of the atonement accomplished by him, that this guilty verdict does not lead to death. The crucified and resurrected Christ is the savior and Lord sent by God, who alone brings an end to the death-producing verdict of the Law. In this context, Paul is therefore not speaking of the fact that the commandments of God were or would be annulled in Christ. Indeed, in 8:2ff. the apostle showed with desirable clarity that, through his sacrifice, Christ did not set aside the holy will of God, which had fallen under the reign of sin, but confirmed it and established it anew in power! He does not rescind these statements in 10:4. But in the confrontation with Israel's unbelief, it is now a matter of whether the Law or Christ assists one to righteousness, and in view of this alternative Paul expresses himself unambiguously against the Law and for the Christ of God. Nevertheless, if one thinks in terms of the history of salvation, it can be said with good reason, based on Paul, that the salvation brought forth through Christ came about precisely through the obedient fulfillment of the will of God by the Son of God (5:18ff.). In addition, 8:2ff. presents the possibility of saying that Christ has brought forth the new, eschatological reality of the Law of Jer. 31:31ff. But these considerations do not necessitate translating the Greek word τέλος (= telos) in v. 4 with "goal" or "final goal," instead of with "end." In our context, everything depends for Paul on the fact that in the final judgment it is not the Law, but the messiah,

Jesus, that is, the one who was given over to death by God for the sake of our transgressions, and raised for the purpose of the justification which grants life, who has the decisive word before God (cf. Rom. 4:25). Therefore, Paul does not call Christ the goal, but the end of the Law, which in turn opens up the righteousness of faith for every one (Jews and Greeks) who believes.

[5] In order to fortify the thesis of v. 4, Paul now contrasts Moses and the voice of the righteousness of faith. On the one hand, Moses writes concerning the righteousness which is based on the Law that those who have fulfilled the commandments of God will obtain life through this fulfillment of the Law (Lev. 18:5). Moses thus places one before the demand of the Law. [6] On the other hand, the righteousness of faith fulfills the Law (written in the heart) through Christ (Rom. 8:3f.), and its eyes are also opened through the Holy Spirit to Christ as the wisdom of God (1 Cor. 1:30; 2:10). By virtue of this insight, it discerns that God's word of command in Deut. 30:12–14 is not to be related to the wisdom of God revealed in the Mosaic Law, following Bar. 3:29–38, but to the wisdom of God revealed in Christ. According to its insight, therefore, the scriptural word is to be read as the wisdom of God from the perspective of Christ. The righteousness of faith thus follows this word and does not ask, being perplexed, "Who will climb up into heaven?" for that would mean still having to bring down from heaven the Christ whom God has already sent. [7] It also does not ask, "Who will climb down into the abyss?"—that is, the place from which the dead look forward to the resurrection. (Together with the Jewish exegesis of his time, Paul sees in the sea, concerning which in Deut. 30:13 it is said, "Who will go over the sea for us?" the depth of chaos of the underworld and therefore reads Deut. 30:13 and Ps. 107:26 with and into one another.) To pose this question means still wanting to lead Christ up from the dead, whom God has already raised from the dead. In contrast, the righteousness of faith recognizes that God has already sent the messiah and that Christ has already completed the descent into the world of the dead (cf. 1 Pet. 3:19), so that throughout the entire world he is proclaimed as the resurrected Lord and messiah (cf. Acts 2:36). [8] Therefore it confesses with Deut. 30:14 that God's word of command already fills the mouth and heart. In other words, it is near to those who believe in the form of the apostle's (or apostles') preaching of faith. This preaching, viewed correctly, is God's word (1 Thess. 2:13), and from it the hearers receive the Holy Spirit (Gal. 3:2), who enables them to believe and teaches them to say the confession. As the scriptural word puts it, mouth and heart participate in this confession. [9, 10] With the mouth one calls out within the gathering of the church, "Jesus is Lord" (1 Cor. 12:3), and with the heart, that is, from the very center of the human person, one believes that God raised Jesus from the dead. It is precisely this confession of faith, expressed by mouth and heart, which completely adjoins those who speak it to their crucified and resurrected Lord and leads them to salvation, namely, the salvation through the righteousness promised by God to everyone who believes in Jesus. [11] In this salvation, God's promise from Is. 28:16,

which Israel ignores (cf. 9:33), finds its confirmation, that is, that the one who places his trust of faith in the messianic rock, Christ, will not be put to shame before God. [12] Moreover, justification applies without distinction to Jews and Greeks. God is one and the same for them both (cf. 3:30), and he shares his riches of forgiveness by grace to all those who "call upon" him. The Eighteen Benedictions spoken by every Jew (even until today) speaks at the end of the sixth benediction of God's riches of forgiveness in a paradigmatic way: "Praise be to you, Lord, who forgives much." Paul expresses this same praise in view of God's salvific work in Christ. "To call upon the (name of the) Lord" has the meaning in the Old Testament of "to confess (recognize) God" (Jer. 10:25), "to call upon God for help" (Ps. 116:4), and "to acknowledge and proclaim God with praise" (Ps. 80:19; 116:13, 17). In this context what is meant is that confession in which God's power and gift are thankfully acknowledged. [13] Paul then continues with reference to Joel 3:5, in which the eschatological salvation reaches "the one who calls upon the name of the Lord." In the New Testament that has a double ring. It no longer means merely the confession of God, the creator and judge, but also, and above all, the confession of Christ (1 Cor. 1:2), who, after his exaltation to the right hand of God, was designated with the name of God, "Lord," and now reigns until he can lay everything, pacified, at the feet of God (Phil. 2:9–11; 1 Cor. 15:25f.). Salvation is thus allotted to the one who confesses Christ as Lord. For it is the one who confesses Christ that recognizes and speaks the righteousness of faith, while it remains hidden to Israel (v. 3). In vv. 14ff. Paul will expand this still further. The fact that in doing so he calls attention to Joel 3:5 has special significance. As Acts 2:16–21 shows, the promise of the eschatological pouring out of the Spirit from Joel 3:1–5 was fulfilled for the early Christian church on Pentecost. Since then, the gospel is preached by order of the exalted Christ among Jews (and Gentiles). In the Greek Bible, Joel 3:5 runs, "And it will take place, that everyone who calls upon the name of the Lord will be saved. For the one (who) is saved will be on Mount Zion and in Jerusalem, and people who proclaim the good news (the gospel), those whom the Lord has called in." The apostles called into mission by the resurrected Christ have come to know themselves as those who proclaim the good news (of the gospel) from Joel 3:5, and Paul finds himself to be the last (and most important) of them (1 Cor. 15:5–11). The citation from Scripture in v. 13 thus invites the Christians (from Rome) who are versed in the Scriptures to remember the early Christian mission of the apostles, which had its beginning in Jerusalem, and which is now also served by Paul.

3. 10:14–21. Israel's Disobedience to the Gospel

(14) How then shall they, of course, call upon (the one) in whom they have not believed? But how shall they believe (in the one) of whom they have not heard? But how shall they hear without one who preaches? (15) But how shall

they preach, if they are not sent? As it is written, "How greatly welcome are the feet of those who preach good tidings!" (16) But not all have obeyed the gospel. For Isaiah says, "Lord, who has believed our message?" (17) Thus (it is true that) faith (comes) from the message, but the message through Christ's word of command. (18) But I say, have they not heard? Certainly! "Their sound penetrated throughout the entire earth and their words to the ends of the (inhabited) world." (19) But I say, did Israel not know? As the first, Moses says, "I will make you jealous of those who are not a people, I will make you angry over a people who do not understand." (20) But Isaiah is daring and says, "I have allowed myself to be found by those who did not seek me, I became manifest to those who did not ask after me." (21) But to Israel he says, "I have stretched out my hands the whole day toward a people who are disobedient and contradictory."

Verse 15: Is. 52:7 (Nah. 2:1); Verse 16: Is. 53:1; Verse 18: Ps. 19:5; Verse 19: Deut. 32:21; Verse 20: Is. 65:1; Verse 21: Is. 65:2.

A. Although in v. 14 Paul introduces a new discourse with "then, of course," he nevertheless continues in it the argument with Israel which he conducted in 10:1–13. Verses 14–21 thus stand in a direct relationship with vv. 1–13 and form the concluding section of the discussion begun in 9:30 concerning Israel's rebellion against the righteousness of God in Christ. The structure of the passage is as follows: The chain of syllogisms in vv. 14f. provide the presupposition for the negative statement in v. 16. Verse 17 then offers a summarizing doctrinal thesis. On this basis, two questions are raised in vv. 18 and 19 in order to exonerate Israel, to which in vv. 18, 19, 20, and 21 statements from the Scripture are contrasted which accuse Israel. Once more the Holy Scripture, as God's word, determines everything that the apostle has to contribute to the argument. Finally, since the textual tradition in no way casts suspicion on v. 17, it is not advisable to attempt to see the doctrine consciously formed by Paul in this verse (see above, pp. 113ff.) to be a subsequent gloss from the hand of a later transcriber of the letter to the Romans.

With the quotation from Joel 3:5 in v. 13 Paul had reminded his readers of the early Christian mission that went out from Jerusalem, in which he himself participates. The two most important traditions from which the apostle proceeds in vv. 14–21 also point to the same mission context. First, to the careful reader of the Bible, it is striking that in the citation from Is. 52:7 in v. 15 Paul speaks of a plurality of those who preach good tidings, although both the Hebrew, as well as the Greek text which the apostle had before him, speak only of a single messenger of salvation. Paul arrives at his version of the text because he (in accordance with Rabbinic and early Christian custom) combines, by way of interpretation, the Greek version of Joel 3:5, which speaks of several people who preach the good news (see above, p. 157), with Is. 52:7. Both scriptural passages are thus seen to explain one another and to speak of the appearance of the apostle as a messenger of the good news of the gospel. With this understanding, Paul is probably proceeding on the basis of the early Jewish exegesis of Isaiah. This exegesis notes concerning both Is. 40:9, as well as Is. 52:7, that at the inauguration of the royal reign of God there will be a great number of people who hail God and spread abroad the news of the commencement of his reign (cf. Tg. Is. 40:9; Midr. Teh. to Ps. 147:1 § 2; and Ps. 68:12 in the Septuagint). For Paul and the apostles as a whole, who are entrusted by the resurrected Christ with the preaching of the gospel, this eschatological hour has already been inaugurated with Jesus' exaltation to the position of being Lord. They are therefore those end-time "evangelists" who were announced by the prophets Joel and Isaiah.

In v. 16 Paul speaks of the fact that only a very few Israelites have been granted faith in the gospel and then supports this failure of the Jewish mission with Isaiah 53:1. The message which is spoken of in Isaiah 53 is the unbelievable news of the suffering fate and exaltation of the servant of God, through which God provides justification for his people. There is solid justification for the fact that the apostle equates this message with the gospel of Christ. According to Mk. 10:45 par. and 14:24 par., Jesus interpreted his own way of suffering on the basis of Isaiah 53. Moreover, from 1 Cor. 15:3–5, Rom. 4:25, and 2 Cor. 5:21, we can see that the interpretation of the atoning death of Jesus from the perspective of Is. 53:11f. was the heart of the gospel which went out from Jerusalem. With the quotation from Is. 53:1 Paul is thus again lining himself up with all the apostles and, in the midst of his acute situation of dialogue (see above, pp. 142ff.), is consequently causing the Christians in Rome to consider that the rejection of the gospel by the majority of Israel is not caused in some special way by the Pauline gospel, so that better missionary results could be reached with another gospel (Gal. 1:6; 2 Cor. 11:4). Rather, Paul's point is that Israel's rejection is an event which has been announced by God in the Scripture and which therefore equally affects the message of all the apostles.

B. At this point, the apostle begins to draw his conclusions from what has been said in vv. 1–13. In order to do so, [14] he makes use of a rhetorical chain of syllogisms, a rhetorical form which was well known in his day. To begin with, it is impossible to invoke Christ as Lord, that is, to speak the Christian confession, where faith is lacking. But in turn, faith will be lacking where one does not hear Christ (preached), and hearing will be lacking where there is no preacher available. [15] But only the one who (at the right time) is "sent out" (i.e., appointed to be an apostle) can be a preacher, just as Isaiah announces when he speaks of the longed-for, and therefore highly welcomed, appearance of those messengers who declare the good news of the beginning of the reign of God, the gospel of Christ (Is. 52:7). Of course, the apostles, with Peter at the head, did go out from Jerusalem and, as Jews, first preached the gospel to the Jews (and only later to the Greeks or Gentiles as well). And what was the result? [16] Paul formulates his answer to this question in a way that is cautious rhetorically, but nevertheless clear for those who know the situation. "Not all" have demonstrated the

obedience of faith to the gospel, in other words, only a very few Jews have followed the call of the gospel. This formulation shows that at the time of the composition of the letter to the Romans, the mission to the Jews entrusted to Peter
(cf. Gal. 2:7f.) was a failure. Certainly the apostle is putting the blame for this
failure neither on the "man of rock" (1 Cor. 15:5; Gal. 2:9; Mk. 3:16 par.), nor
on one of the other apostles. The refusal of the gospel by the majority of the
Jews is an event foreseen by God. For Isaiah speaks of the fact that no faith is
being granted in the message of the salvific destiny of the servant of God (Jesus
Christ) (Is. 53:1). It lacks and literally remains without a favorable hearing. [17]
And it is indeed desired by God that faith be awakened by the message which
the apostles preach, but this message is based on Christ's word of command. In
v. 8 Paul already spoke of this word of command taken from Deut. 30:14, and
there too he equated it with the apostles' preaching of faith. He now once again
makes that which he has previously said more precise. Paul's point is that the
apostolic preaching which awakens faith is itself indebted to and serves the
gospel of Christ. This gospel presents a power of revelation and salvation (1
Cor. 9:16f.; Rom. 1:16f.) which, through the appearance of the resurrected
Christ (1 Cor. 15:5–10; Gal. 1:15f.), has been opened up and entrusted to the
apostles (including Paul). In the doctrinal statement from v. 17 the source from
which and the purpose for which Paul and all the apostles live are thus summarized. They have the gospel, which has been entrusted to them, by commission
of the resurrected Christ and, with it, they must preach faith in Christ as the
saving way of salvation. This preaching is an activity of the Spirit and awakens
faith in those who open themselves up to it in obedience (Gal. 3:2). The Israelites, however, have not opened themselves up to the gospel in obedience (v.
16). [18] Paul therefore asks, in order to exonerate them, whether they have not
by chance heard. But the answer to this question has been indicated previously
by the Spirit of God in the Scripture. According to Ps. 19:5, the problem for the
Israelites cannot be attributed to a lack of hearing, since the message of the
apostles has resounded over the entire earth, so that Israel too has become
aware of it. [19] But if Israel has become aware of it, the further question is
then raised concerning whether Israel perhaps did not recognize the significance of what it was hearing. The answer is that Israel had indeed recognized it,
but not acknowledged it. Israel's knowledge of the ways of God is obstructed
and restricted. As Moses, the first witness, testifies, Israel stands under the
judgment (of purification) announced in Deut. 32:21. The one God, whose
salvific work in Christ Israel does not want to become effective on her behalf,
replies to this disobedience by making his chosen people jealous and angry over
those who are not a people, that is, those who, according to Israel's understanding, are entirely unwise in regard to God, that is, the Gentiles. God turns to the
Gentiles and, on the basis of his free decree of grace, enables them to participate
in the salvation through the messiah which is promised to Israel. The Gentiles
partake of the good which Israel expected for itself, and it is precisely this

experience which stirs up and should stir up the jealousy and anger of the people of God who are (apparently) cheated out of their special rights. Both Peter
and Paul had more than enough experience of the way in which this anger and
jealousy actually worked itself out. In Jerusalem, Peter barely escaped Jewish
ambushes (Acts 12:1–17), and in the synagogues in which Paul appeared as an
apostle of Jesus Christ, he was inflicted five times with the life-threatening punishment of flogging, and once was even stoned (2 Cor. 11:24f.). Moreover, Paul
and his co-workers had experienced that the Jews who were resident in the various places in which they ministered also attempted to hinder and prevent the
preaching of the gospel in regard to the Gentiles whenever possible (1 Thess.
2:16; cf. with Acts 17:5; 18:12ff.). This conduct is evidence of the fact that Israel
is distant from God and under God's wrath (cf. 1 Thess. 2:16 with Deut.
32:19f.). But this wrath of God concerning Israel will one day pass away and
yield to God's mercy (cf. Deut. 32:35–36). God has not turned away forever
from his people. [20] Isaiah is the second witness to this fact, and in his
prophetic authority he dares to speak God's own word for this hour: God has allowed himself to be found and was revealed to those who neither sought nor
asked after him, that is, to the Gentiles. [21] But in regard to Israel, although
God stands there with outstretched hands in order to accept and receive his
people to himself, they are disobedient, they contradict their God, and they ig-
nore his call. This is the point of Is. 65:1–2, and this is also the way that it is actually taking place among Israel and the Gentiles up until this very moment.

With this, Paul has now expressed the manner in which Israel's situation is to
be understood in the light of the Holy Scriptures. For to Paul, the Scriptures
are filled with God's Spirit and continue to speak into the present. Hence, as
predicted, Israel stands opposed to God's ways in and through Jesus. The
knowledge of God's righteousness is blocked to them, and in their delusion they
offer resistance to the gospel instead of opening themselves up to it. Such disobedience in regard to God's call places Israel in the situation of the judgment
announced in Deut. 32:21: Israel must and will be angry and jealous over the
apparent loss of its privileges. But God desires to turn this angry jealousy to Israel's benefit, and he will do so, for even in the hour of wrath God remains sympathetic toward his disobedient people because of his faithfulness and mercy.
On the basis of this insight, which Paul gains from the perspective of faith, the
apostle now goes on in chapter 11 to a prophecy concerning history, by which
he shows how Israel will be led to its promised redemption by its God and the
God of all people.

IV. 11:1–32. The Way of God's Mercy

In 9:6 Paul established programmatically that God's elective word of promise
for Israel is inviolable, and from 9:30–10:21 it followed that God remains near

to his people, although he has placed them in the condition of anger and jealousy over the Gentiles' obtaining of salvation. In 11:1–32 the apostle now draws the necessary conclusion from both of these statements. With a prophetic insight concerning history, he also sets forth the way of mercy which God will follow in order to lead all Israel to its promised redemption. Paul does this in three steps. In 11:1–10 he shows that initially only a "remnant" from Israel has attained the promised salvation, while the rest of Israel stands under the hardening ordained by God. Romans 11:11–24 then makes clear, however, that the majority of Israel has been hardened only temporarily for the benefit of the salvation of the Gentiles. Finally, in 11:25–32, the apostle reveals the secret of faith which has been disclosed to him concerning the salvation of all Israel through the messianic redeemer who comes from Zion.

1. 11:1–10. The Chosen Remnant

(1) Now I say, has God by chance rejected his people? By no means! For I also am indeed an Israelite, from the seed of Abraham, (from the) tribe of Benjamin. (2) "God has not rejected his people, whom he foreknew!" Or do you not know what the Scripture says in the passage about Elijah, as he appeared before God against Israel: (3) "Lord, they have killed your prophets, torn down your altars, and I alone am left remaining, and they are trying to take my life!" (4) Yet what does the oracle of God say to him? "I have left behind for myself seven thousand men who have not bowed their knee before Baal." (5) In exactly the same way, at the present point in time a remnant is now also at hand in accordance with the election of grace. (6) But if from grace, then no longer from works; otherwise grace would no longer be grace. — (7) What then? Israel did not attain what it is striving for, yet the elect attained it; but the rest were hardened, (8) as it is written, "God gave them a spirit of stupor, eyes in order not to see, and ears in order not to hear, until this very day;" (9) and David says, "Let their offering table become for them a snare and a trap and an offense and a recompense, (10) let their eyes become darkened in order not to see, and bend their backs everywhere!"

Verse 2: 1 Sam. 12:22; Verse 3: 1 Kings 19:10, 14; Verse 4:
1 Kings 19:18; Verse 8: Deut. 29:3 (Is. 29:10); Verses 9f.: Ps. 69:23f.

A. The paragraph breaks down clearly into two parts: vv. 1–6 and vv. 7–10. The question posed by Paul in v. 1, whether God has rejected the people of his possession, is immediately also denied in v. 1 with reference to the election of Paul himself. Verse 2 strengthens the denial with words from 1 Sam. 12:22. The Scripture's refusal of the notion that God has rejected his people is then subsequently supported typologically. Just as God left behind seven thousand Israelites who were true to the faith at the time of Elijah, in the present time he has chosen a small remnant from Israel to be obedient to the gospel. Only this remnant, chosen to believe, has already attained salvation (v. 7), while all the rest of Israel stands under the judgment of hardening announced not only by Moses (v. 8), but also by David (vv. 9f.). Again the Holy Scripture gives the apostle and his readers in advance the way in which Israel's situation is to be understood in view of the gospel.

Already in 9:27, 29 the apostle had quoted Is. 10:22f. and Is. 1:9 and drawn attention to the fact that in the judgment only a remnant from Israel will be saved and preserved. Now he takes up this thought again and makes clear who this remnant is that is being separated out from Israel by God. According to the Essenes from Qumran, the chosen remnant refers to the (remnant) community which is established with God's help by the priestly Teacher of Righteousness and consists of those who are truly faithful to the Law. This remnant separates itself from the godless Israelites and with their perfect obedience provides atonement for Israel (cf. 4QpPs. 37 III 15f.; 1QS 5:5ff.; 1QH 6:8f.). Paul's view is totally different! For Paul the remnant is the small band of Jewish Christians, who have already been chosen to believe and precede the redemption of all Israel. Instead of the remnant "damning all who transgress the commandment" (1QS 5:7), as the Essenes did, according to Paul they are a sign of hope which God has established for all Israel.

B. The declarations of judgment in 9:27–29 and 10:19 suggest the question which Paul now poses explicitly: [1] Has God rejected his people? If one recalls the apostle's hard words of judgment concerning the Jews from 1 Thess. 2:15f., which were also certainly known to his Jewish-Christian opponents, then one can surmise that behind the question posed by Paul resonates a reproach against his preaching which was being made by his adversaries. It is thus all the more important to the apostle to deny the question emphatically. This clear negation is surprising, since thus far in the letter it has only been intimated (indirectly) in 2:4 and 9:6. But for precisely this reason it may also have caught the special attention of Paul's readers.

In support of his negation, the apostle first refers to himself. He is an Israelite chosen by God to believe. He is part of Abraham's seed, from the tribe of Benjamin, and he bears the Jewish name "Saul" after the first king of Israel, who had been elected by God from the tribe of Benjamin (cf. 1 Sam. 10:1). This reference to the apostle's Jewish descent is also astonishing. For in Phil. 3:5ff. he calls the very privileges which he here names as evidence of God's faithfulness a "loss" and "rubbish," inasmuch as in view of the saving knowledge of Christ they are of no value. Yet now he sees in them the unmistakable mark of the elective grace of God. In v. 1 the apostle is obviously concerned, therefore, to clear up misunderstandings which his highly dialectical and also misleading statements concerning Israel up until now could have caused and perhaps have already brought about (among the Christians from Rome and elsewhere). But Paul intends to do more than merely clarify his own conception. [2] He thus now repeats the fact, with words from 1 Sam. 12:22, that God has not rejected his people, and adds to them himself the phrase, ". . . the people *whom he foreknew.*" This elective grace, the significance of which for the existence and history of Israel the apostle has referred to again and again since 9:6, is the ground of hope for the salvation of all Israel! In order to underscore the promise to the chosen people declared in 1 Sam. 12:22 still further, Paul now reminds his readers in Rome of what the Scripture reports "in the Elijah (passage)"—we would say today, in the Elijah stories. [3] On Mt. Horeb, Elijah raised accusations against Israel and perceived himself to be the last of God's faithful. Moreover, the godless were still attempting to take his life (in 1 Thess. 2:15f. Paul spoke in a similar way). [4] But God's answer to the lament (accusation) of his prophet was surprising. God had kept for himself—without Elijah knowing about it—a community of seven thousand who still confessed the Lord; his providence thus gives the lie to the prophet in his insistence that he is the last of the faithful in Israel. Hence, the scriptural narrative concerning Elijah allows the following application to the present: [5] In addition to Paul alone (from v. 1), there is also at the present point in time (already) a remnant of Israelites who have been chosen by God by virtue of his elective grace. This remnant is that band of Jews who believe in Christ, that is, who are circumcised not only in the flesh, but also in the Spirit (2:29). In Rome, for example, Prisca and Aquila, and Andronicus and Junia are considered among them (16:3, 7). They are a sign of the fact that God has not abandoned his people, but rather has chosen from this people a community of believers for himself. As in the days of Elijah, the history of God with Israel thus also continues to go on today and points, full of hope, into the future. (Under these circumstances, Paul does not need to repeat his accusations from 1 Thess. 2:15f.) [6] Moreover, this history is determined entirely by the free elective grace of the one who justifies the ungodly (4:5). This grace has nothing in common (cf. 9:16) with the attempt to establish one's own righteousness on the basis of works of the Law (9:33; 10:3). Under these circumstances, it would consequently be a fundamental offense against one's own election if the Jewish-Christian community insisted in a renewed way upon the principle of righteousness "on the basis of faith and works of the Law," and then desired to attack Paul's preaching from this perspective (but cf. James 2:24 for precisely this view).

[7] Of course, this now raises an enormous problem. By virtue of God's elective grace only a small remnant community of Jewish Christians have thus far attained to the righteousness for which Israel as a whole has strived (10:3f.), while the rest of the Jews have not attained it. They have been, as Paul writes, hardened by God. [8] Hence, by referring to Deut. 29:3 the apostle now clearly and explicitly expounds what he had only intimated in 10:3 and 10:18f. God has struck the vast majority of Israel with a spirit of stupor and given them eyes and ears which cannot see and hear what he has done for them in Christ. This hardening is still at work; and is testified to not only by Moses, [9] but also by David, the Spirit-filled author and speaker of the Psalms (cf. Sir. 47:8–10). In Ps.

69:23f. he even pronounces a curse on Israel: Instead of being the place of the divine goodwill, their "offering table" (i.e., according to Rabbinic understanding, the sacrificial altar of atonement in the temple) shall become for them a snare and a hindrance to faith. This formulation must have reminded Paul's reader of the fact that, in spite of the atoning death of Jesus on Golgotha, which God had enacted (3:25f.), the sacrifice of atonement was still being offered as before in the Jerusalem temple. Such acts declared that Israel did not want anything to do with God's work of reconciliation through Jesus' death on the cross. [10] (Also) according to David, Israel will be struck with blindness (cf. v. 8) and—as it states in the Greek text of the Psalms, which Paul cites—"their back bent"; that is, Israel will be robbed of its freedom. As in Gal. 3:23f. and 4:25, Paul is thereby alluding to Israel's service as a slave under the Law. According to the witness of Moses and David, therefore, the numerical majority of God's people stand under the hardening ordained by God. While a small "remnant" of Israelites have already been chosen for faith, the others have all been confined by God to unbelief and disobedience in regard to the gospel of Christ (10:16; 11:32). They take offense at Christ (9:32) and stir themselves up against God's will, being full of anger and jealousy over the righteousness of God which has been opened up to the Gentiles, but which is seemingly taken away from them (10:19).

2. 11:11–24. The Temporal Hardening of Israel

(11) Now I say, have they by chance taken offense in order that they might fall? By no means! But through their fall salvation (has been allotted) to the Gentiles, in order to provoke them to jealousy. (12) But if their fall (means) riches for the world and their diminution riches for the Gentiles, how much more (will then) their full number (mean)! — (13) But to you, the Gentiles, I say, that inasmuch as I am now an apostle to the Gentiles, I glorify my ministry, (14) so that I might perhaps provoke my flesh to jealousy and save some of them. (15) For if their rejection (already means) reconciliation for the world, what (then can) their acceptance (mean) other than life from the dead? — (16) For if the first fruits of the dough (is) holy, (then) the (entire) dough (is) also; and if the root (is) holy, (then) the branches (are) also. (17) But if some of the branches were broken off, but you, you who are a shoot of a wild olive tree, were grafted in among them and became a sharer of the oil-dispensing root of the olive tree, (18) then do not boast in regard to the branches. But if you do boast (know that) you do not bear the root, but the root bears you! (19) You then will say, "Branches were (indeed) broken off so that I might be grafted in." (20) True! They were broken off on the basis of unbelief, but you stand (only) on the basis of faith. Do not be arrogant, but fear (before God). (21) For if God did not spare the natural branches, then he will quite certainly also not spare you. (22) Behold now the kindness and the

severity of God: in regard to those who have fallen, severity; but in regard to you, the kindness of God, if you remain in his goodness, for otherwise you will be cut off. (23) But those will be grafted in (again), if they do not remain in unbelief, for God has the power to graft them in again. (24) For if you were cut out of the olive tree which is by nature wild and, contrary to nature, were grafted into the cultivated olive tree, then how much more will they, who are according to nature, be grafted in again into their own olive tree.

Verse 16: Num. 15:17–21.

A. The structure of the paragraph is easy to recognize. Verses 11–12 and vv. 13–15 are parallel in construction. With their intensified and precise content, these verses expound the fact that Israel's partial hardening remains encompassed by God's intention to provoke his people to jealousy over those Gentiles who have already attained salvation (cf. 10:19). Both groups of sentences lead to identically formulated statements (= vv. 12 and 15). In each case, by employing an argument from the lesser to the greater they make clear that an acceptance of the full number of all the Israelites by God may be expected as an eschatological event of redemption. Verse 16 is dependent upon v. 15, but introduces a new metaphor and provides the foundational thesis from which Paul proceeds in his rhetorical dialogue with "the" Gentile Christian, a dialogue which he conducts until the end of v. 24.

In order to understand Paul's argument one must be familiar with the concepts and metaphors used by the apostle in these verses. In v. 12 he speaks of the "full number" of Israel (and then in v. 25 of the "full number of the Gentiles"). Both times what is meant is that number of all Israelites and Gentiles, determined by God from the very beginning, who will attain salvation. (Only) when in each case this "full number" is reached, does God bring about the final events (cf. 2 Bar. 23:4 and *b*. Yeb. 62a; 63b). The comparison in v. 16 of the first fruits of the dough with the rest of the dough is based on Num. 15:17–21. It is used by the apostle in a transferred sense (to refer to people) in the same way as it is in Rabbinic texts, which, for example, call Adam, who according to Gen. 2:7 was created out of earth, "the first fruits of the world." In early Jewish literature, the "root" (of Israel) is, above all, Abraham. He is called the chosen root from which the people of God grow (cf. T. Jud. 24:5; Jub. 16:26; 1 Enoch 93:5, 8; Philo, *Rer. Div. Her.* 279). The olive tree is a metaphor for Israel (cf. Jer. 11:16), and in Jub. 1:16 the future people of God are called "the plant of righteousness."

B. Using the same rhetorical sentence as in v. 1, Paul now poses the difficult question which grows out of vv. 8–10, namely, [11] whether the majority of Israel has taken offense (at Christ) so that, as a consequence, they have come to fall once and for all. In 1 Thess. 2:16 Paul himself had intimated this possibility. Therefore, v. 11 may again reflect something of the critical debate in which the apostle is entangled and which has now followed him all the way to Rome. But

Paul rejects the fact that Israel should suffer the fate of the Egyptian pharaoh (cf. 9:17). Israel is not being subjected to the judgment of destruction, but to the judgment of purification. Its fall is for the benefit of the salvation of the Gentiles. But the fact that the nations have unexpectedly obtained salvation should, according to God's will (cf. the quotation from Deut. 32:21 in 10:19), move the hardened majority of Israel to angry jealousy. We have already made clear what this looks like and what its ramifications are (see above, pp. 160f.). [12] Because Israel's hardening remains within the purview of God's work of purification on behalf of his people, Paul can look beyond the time of Israel's present delusion. He thus states that if the fall of the majority of Israelites, that is, their diminution to a very few who have become obedient to the gospel (cf. 10:16; 11:5), has already enabled the Gentile world to attain the riches of salvation, then how much more will the reacceptance and salvation of the full number of Israel mean someday for the world! In other words, on that day when God will lead all Israel (11:26) to salvation, his reign will begin conclusively. [13] Paul now turns quite emphatically to his readers in Rome, the majority of whom come from the Gentiles, and once again goes through the insights just expressed (in vv. 11–12) with his addressees. He explicitly assures those who come from the ranks of the Gentiles that he, the Jewish missionary to the Gentiles (Gal. 1:16; 2:7ff.; Rom. 1:5), thankfully glorifies the ministry entrusted to him by God through Christ. He specifically does so [14] because this ministry takes part in the work of purification which God is accomplishing toward his people. The apostle is being allowed and desires to be an apostle to the Gentiles for Israel's sake! Hence, the anger and jealousy over the Gentiles and personal persecution that he encounters in his missionary journeys from the side of the majority of Israel do not speak against the preaching of the apostle, as some maintained even as far as Rome, but for it. Paul is being allowed and desires to bring about God's word of judgment from Deut. 32:21, and precisely by doing so to prepare his earthly kinsmen for the salvation which has been promised to them. Moreover, if in doing so he is also successful in leading a few Jews to reflection and to faith in the gospel through his ministry already in the present (cf., e.g., the conversion of Crispus according to Acts 18:8 and 1 Cor. 1:14), then Paul can bring to light for the Gentiles that small, chosen "remnant" which is a sign of hope for all Israel (cf. v. 5). [15] If, namely, the rejection of the majority of Israel has already lead to the reconciliation of the Gentile world (cf. 2 Cor. 5:18–20), then the reacceptance of those who have been temporarily rejected must bring with it nothing other than "life from the dead," that is, victory over the "ancient foe," death, once and for all and the coming of the reign of God (cf. 1 Cor. 15:26). The resurrection of the dead and the redemption of all creation now being hoped for (cf. 8:18–24) are, for Paul, essentially bound together with God's reacceptance of all Israel. The redemption of the entire world depends on God's way with Israel; it is the decisive component of the history of election and salvation! Paul expounds this point so emphatically not only because he must defend his gospel in Rome against the reproach that with his ministry he is leading Israel into hardening instead of to salvation. Paul does so because he also sees himself up against a group of Gentile Christians who look down upon Israel in its hardened state and maintain that God has turned himself away from Israel once and for all, and that the salvation of the Gentiles through the gospel is the crown of all his works. Paul himself furthered this way of thinking with his statements in 1 Thess. 2:14–16, and such a view even stands out at the conclusion of the book of Acts as a Pauline legacy (cf. Acts 28:23–28). It is thus all the more important to take exact cognizance of what Paul himself maintains in the following verses concerning such tendencies.

[16] The thesis with which Paul opens the dialogue with "the" Gentile Christian is determined by the conviction of faith that God is not revoking his word of promise toward Israel (9:6). The double comparison of the first piece of the dough, which sanctifies the entire dough, and the root, which also sanctifies the branches, is therefore best interpreted on the basis of 9:5 (and 4:1ff.). On the basis of the Fathers, and, above all, on the basis of Abraham, Israel is and remains chosen. But Israel is chosen for salvation precisely by the God who has made it clear in the election of "our father" Abraham and with the promise declared to him, that he will justify the ungodly through Christ alone (cf. 4:5, 17, 24f. with 9:11f., 16, 32; 10:12; 11:6). The salvific community of all those who take part in the promise to Abraham thus grows out of Abraham. But equally important is the fact that not only the small remnant (v. 5), but all Israel is determined to belong to this community (vv. 25ff.). [17] Behind the metaphors which now follow stands the equation from Jer. 11:16 of Israel with the olive tree. The cultivated olive tree which Paul refers to is thus the salvific community rooted in Abraham, that is, "the Israel of God" (Gal. 6:16). In contrast, the wild olive tree with its shoots symbolizes the Gentiles. But ever since the church father Origen, it has been repeatedly maintained that in speaking of the grafting in of a wild olive branch into a cultivated olive tree Paul is ignoring all gardening experience, as though he deviates from all botanical reality because of his apostolic viewpoint. However, from the handbook of a Roman agricultural expert living in the first century A.D. it becomes apparent that in Paul's day one actually did bring old olive trees to new, fruitful growth through the grafting in of wild olive branches (cf. Pseudo-Columella, Arb. 5.9.16). Throughout vv. 17ff. the apostle thus appeals to experiences familiar to his readers.

From the root of Abraham grows the good olive tree sanctified by God. If a Gentile, as a wild olive shoot, was grafted in in the place of some of the branches that were broken off from the olive tree by God, and thereby partakes of the root of Abraham which gives forth the oil, then [18] he or she should not boast or look down upon the branches that were broken off. Rather, the Gentile should be aware of the fact, and remain so, that it is the root which bears and causes him or her to grow, and not somehow the other way around. Without the promise to Abraham, in which he or she is allowed to partake, the Gentile

Christian would be nothing. [19] The objection that the olive branches were therefore broken off for the very reason of making the grafting in of the wild branches possible (and of rejuvenating the stunted olive tree) is thus indeed accurate, but it does not justify any arrogance on the part of the believing Gentiles concerning those Israelites who have been blinded. [20] They were broken off and hardened on the basis of their unbelief, and the Gentile Christian, newly grafted in and chosen by God to believe, stands and falls before God only by faith (according to Abraham's example; cf. 4:18–22). The faith which, following Abraham's footsteps, justifies, has nothing to do with pride, but instead has everything to do with the fear of God. [21] For if God did not spare the Israelites, who by nature sprouted from the root of Abraham, he has even less reason to spare the grafted-in Gentile, if he or she forgets the basis upon which one lives before God. Peace with God, justification, and reconciliation stand and fall with faith (Rom. 5:1–11). But unbelief causes Jews and Gentiles alike to fall under God's judgment. On the one hand, Paul thus speaks of the disobedience (11:20, 23), the fall (11:11f.), and the unbelief of Israel (11:20, 23), which have in the course of time yielded a hardening and rejection of the majority of God's people. Yet, on the other hand, he emphasizes at the same time that in its delusion Israel has no idea of God's righteousness (10:3) and at the moment has been struck with blindness by God (11:8–10). This naturally raises in and of itself the critical question (of Paul's opponents) concerning why God can then still find fault. How can Israel be held accountable for a trespass which it indeed cannot avoid? Paul already pursued this question in 5:12ff. In turning to answer it again, he now also depends on that aspect of the biblical understanding of sin which comes to the fore by way of example in Leviticus 4. According to the biblical understanding, sin is not only the conscious offense of a freely responsible person against God's will, it is also the involuntary transgression of this will, both of which cause an individual or a group of people to be guilty. It is in precisely this involuntary condition of guilt in regard to the revelation of the righteousness of God in Christ that Israel now finds itself. For Israel's present unbelief is ordained by God; Israel cannot and may not yet come to a full understanding of Christ. [22] For the (Gentile) Christians who grasp these connections, God's kindness and severity become clear as they are exemplified in God's way with Israel. God is kind and remains kind to those who acknowledge this kindness. At the moment, those who do so are primarily Gentiles. God is severe and remains severe, however, toward those who reject this kindness. [23] Yet as the creator, God has the power to graft the Israelites once again into the cultivated olive tree which grows out of the root of Abraham, if they do not willfully persist in their unbelief. And he is willing to do so. [24] For if God was able to graft shoots deriving from the wild olive tree into the cultivated olive tree, how much more can he reinsert the olive branches which were broken off by God himself into the tree which grows from the root of Abraham once they are freed from their unbelief. In vv. 25ff. Paul will continue this view of salvation history and bring it to its crowning conclusion. But at this point, in a way that cannot be misunderstood, he has already declared in regard to the arrogance of the Gentile Christian concerning the unbelieving Jews that the ultimate goal of all of God's works is not the deliverance of the Gentiles from their sin and separation from God, but the deliverance of the people of God's own possession. To be sure, God also desires to save Gentiles (through Christ), not in place of the Israelites, but rather in addition to them. For God's word of promise given to Israel remains valid for the future and cannot be broken (cf. 9:6 with 11:29). Hence, the Gentile Christians in Rome can and should no longer appeal to the perspective, earlier (co-)represented by Paul himself, that Israel was totally overtaken by God's judgment of wrath (1 Thess. 2:16). By virtue of an insight granted through revelation, Paul himself has been led beyond this former viewpoint, and in the following verses he now lets his addressees share in his new insight, so that their constricted horizon of thought might also be enlarged.

3. 11:25–32. The Mystery of the Salvation of All Israel

(25) I do not want, namely, to leave you in ignorance, brothers, with regard to this mystery, in order that you might not be wise among yourselves: A partial hardening has come upon Israel until (that point in time) when the full number of the Gentiles will have entered in. (26) And consequently all Israel will then be saved, as it is written, "The redeemer will come from Zion, he will take away ungodliness from Jacob. (27) And this will be the covenant-arrangement which is (issued) from me for them, that I will then take away their sins." (28) As far as the gospel is concerned, (they are) enemies (of God) for your sake, but as far as election is concerned, (they are) beloved (by God) on account of the Fathers. (29) For the gifts of grace and the call of God are irrevocable. (30) For just as you were disobedient toward God, but have now found mercy on the basis of their disobedience, (31) so too they have now become disobedient on the basis of the mercy rendered to you, in order that they also might now find mercy. (32) For God has shut up all in disobedience, in order to show mercy to all.

Verses 26f.: Is. 59:20f. (+ Ps. 50:2); Verse 27: Is. 27:9.

A. The structure of this paragraph is as follows. Verse 25a introduces the announcement of the "mystery," which is then imparted in vv. 25b–27 (and at the same time supported by the Holy Scripture as the voice of God). In vv. 28–29 and vv. 30–32, the theology of election and soteriological significance of this mystery are then expounded.

Once again, these verses can be understood only if one first knows the traditions to which Paul is referring. When Paul speaks of the "entrance" of the "full number of the Gentiles" which has been determined by God (see above, p. 166), he has in view the Old Testament and early Jewish expectation that in the end-times the Gentile nations will make a pilgrimage to Zion, view the glory of Jerusalem, and in their own way participate in the salvation which God has made possible for Israel (cf. Is. 2:2ff.; Mic. 4:1ff.; Tob. 13:13; Ps. Sol. 17:30f.; T. Benj. 9:2). But for Paul, in contrast, the pilgrimage of the Gentiles and their participation in salvation precede the salvation of Israel, without replacing it.

By way of suggestion, there is already a reference to the salvation of "all Israel" in the Hebrew text of Is. 59:20 when it says, "He comes indeed for Zion as redeemer and for all in Jacob, who turn back from their sin. . . . " Then in T. Benj. 10:11 it is explicitly stated that (after the resurrection of the dead) "all Israel will be gathered to the Lord," just as it also says in *m*. Sanh. 10:1 that "all Israel has a share in the coming world." Thus, in a way which is typical for Paul, he once again makes use of the Holy Scriptures in vv. 26f. in the same manner that a scribe would. Paul hears the Scripture as the voice of God and allows Is. 59:20f. and 27:9, both of which speak of the removal of sin from Israel, to interpret one another. What is striking in this is the way in which the apostle speaks of the coming of the redeemer. Unless he had a different (Greek) text of the book of Isaiah before him than the one we possess today, there is a conscious exegetical allusion to Ps. 50:2 in v. 26. In Paul's version, the redeemer will not only come, as the Hebrew text of Isaiah says, "for Zion," or as in the Greek text, "for the sake of Zion," but "from Zion." According to Is. 2:2ff. and Mic. 4:1ff., Mt. Zion will be elevated in the end-times to the central mountain of the world, and, according to 4Qflor. 1:12 and 4 Ezra 13:35, the messiah from David's lineage will appear there and complete his eschatological work of carrying out the reign of God. Besides the victory over ungodliness, this work consists of the salvation and ingathering of all Israel from all the regions of the world (cf. Is. 43:5ff. with 4Qflor. 1:12f.; 4 Ezra 13:39–49). It is on this basis that the apostle formulates in Rom. 11:25–32 his highly emphatic prophecy concerning Israel's future history.

B. The expression [25] "I would not like to leave you ignorant of the fact, (dear) brothers," is already known to the readers of the letter from 1:13 (cf. thus too 1 Cor. 10:1; 2 Cor. 1:8; 1 Thess. 4:13). With it Paul is letting the Christians from Rome share in the insight which God gave him concerning the divine direction in history. As indicated in vv. 13ff., the apostle does so in order to prevent the (Gentile) Christians in Rome from perceiving themselves as, in reality, the main recipients of the grace of God and, correspondingly, from despising Israel, which allegedly has thus become totally ruined in God's sight. Paul wants to keep those in Rome from indulging in such an illusory overestimation of themselves! We have already made it clear that Paul thereby backs away from his own statements in 1 Thess. 2:14–16 and to what great degree he does so.

That which the apostle now imparts to the Romans he calls a "mystery." A "mystery" is an event which has been prepared by God and hidden from the world and its wisdom, but disclosed, as a matter of grace, to the apostle. In turn, now the apostle not only may, but also should share it with his fellow Christians

(cf., similarly, 1 Cor. 2:7). And the first part of the mystery is this: The hardening, which Paul spoke of in 10:2f. and 11:8–10, is ordained to remain over the
majority of Israel only until the "full number" of the Gentiles who have been
destined to salvation through the gospel (Mk. 13:10) have "entered in." In his
preaching, Jesus too speaks of "entrance" into the (future) reign of God (Mtt.
5:20; 7:21), while the letter to the Hebrews speaks of the "entrance" of those
who believe in Christ into the heavenly place of rest (Heb. 3:18f.; 4:3), and the
Revelation of John praises the one who is blessed to be able to enter into the
heavenly city of God, which is the new Jerusalem (Rev. 22:14). Paul thinks similarly. When the dead have been raised and all of the Gentiles who are destined
by God for salvation have entered into the salvific community, for whom the eschatological city of God is prepared on Zion (cf. Is. 26:2; 4 Ezra 7:36, 123f.;
13:36), then the partial blinding of Israel will also be taken away. Although this
means that the Gentiles may still enter into the community of salvation before
the large part of Israel and rejoice in the presence of God and his Son, [26]
their incorporation nevertheless becomes a signal for the salvation of "all Israel." For this is the second part of the mystery announced by Paul. As already
indicated in the (Hebrew) text of Is. 59:20 (cf., moreover, Is. 45:17, 25), and anticipated in the early Jewish literature (T. Benj. 10:11; *m.* Sanh. 10:1), the people of God as a whole (and not merely the small remnant from 11:5, who have
already now been chosen to believe in Christ) will participate in salvation. God
remains faithful to his elective promise and will not bring it to fulfillment only
partially, but fully. But the Scripture not only says that all Israel will be saved, it
also indicates in what way this will take place. As declared in (Ps. 50:2 and) Is.
59:20f., the redeemer will appear from Zion, the mountain of God, and remove
ungodliness from Jacob (= Israel). On the basis of 1 Thess. 1:10 (cf. with Rom.
5:9), there is no doubt that the redeemer in view is Christ. The messiah, Jesus
Christ, sent by God and descended as a man from the people of God (1:3f.; 9:5),
will redeem the people of God from their sin at his arrival in glory, the so-called
parousia from Zion (cf. 1 Thess. 2:19; 3:13; 4:15; 5:23; 1 Cor. 15:23 with Mtt.
24:3, 27, 37–39). [27] After the acceptance of the Gentiles, his atoning death
also comes to benefit the very people of God who have opposed Jesus and the
gospel in an unknowing delusion (cf. 1 Cor. 2:8 with Rom. 10:3; 11:8–10). But
now they will recognize that Jesus was and is not only the savior and Lord of the
Gentiles, but also, and above all, was and is the shoot of the root of Jesse sent by
God as a confirmation of his promises to the people of God (Is. 11:10), that is,
that Jesus is the promised messiah (cf. Rom. 15:8, 12). He is the one who frees
Israel from the guilt of its sin! For God promised to the Fathers of Israel, beginning with Abraham (9:4f.; Gal. 3:15–18), and repeatedly confirmed through the
prophets Isaiah (cf. Is. 59:21) and Jeremiah (Jer. 31:31ff.), who according to Sir.
48:22ff. and 49:7 likewise belong to the Fathers of Israel, that the final valid
covenant arrangement to proceed from God will be composed of the fact that
Israel's guilt will be forgiven (cf. Is. 27:9 with Jer. 31:34), and that the Spirit of

God will enable God's people to come to a genuine knowledge of God (cf. Is. 59:21 with Jer. 31:33f.).

The mystery of revelation which Paul made known in Rome thus runs as follows: When the full number of the Gentiles have entered into the city of God and have been led into the community of salvation, the partial hardening of Israel will be taken away. In accordance with the biblical promise, Israel too, in its entirety, will thus be redeemed from its sins through the Christ who appears from Zion and likewise be led into the community of salvation. It is primarily this salvation of all Israel from the hardening of unbelief that is the goal of salvation history, and not the fact that the Gentiles are already obtaining salvation. This understanding of the goal of redemptive history, which Paul here announces as special knowledge gained from revelation, God had imparted to him before through the Scriptures, since Paul hears and reads them in the Spirit of faith as the word of the living God (cf. the constant reference to the speaking and acting of God as "I" in 9:9, 13, 15, 17, 25, 33; 10:19–21; 11:27). The Pauline prophecy concerning history thus corresponds to his spiritual interpretation of Scripture.

[28] From what has been said thus far, the following can therefore be maintained with regard to the relationship between Israel and the Gentiles. As far as the gospel of Christ and faith are concerned, most Israelites are still being compelled into the situation of enmity for the sake of the Gentiles' gaining of salvation, the latter of which is now being accomplished. It is this condition of enmity that characterizes sinners and the flesh as they stand over against God (in the judgment) (cf. 5:10; 8:7). The majority of Israel thus still find themselves in the condition of sinful rebellion against God's act of revelation in Christ. But—and this distinguishes them from the Gentiles!—for the sake of the word of promise which was given to the Fathers, Israel is and remains, from God's perspective, the object of God's elective love (and with it, of his future mercy) (cf. Hos. 11:8ff.; Is. 43:3f.). [29] For God does not regret the gifts of grace which Israel has experienced (and which Paul listed in 9:4f.). Furthermore, his call of election which went out to the people of God in Abraham (cf. Gen. 12:1f.; Is. 51:2 with Gal. 3:8; Rom. 4:13ff.) is inviolable (cf. 9:6). On the basis of Rom. 4:5 and 9:12, it can be determined that this "call" is the call of God which justifies the ungodly. Justification is the work of his mercy, and it is precisely this mercy which determines Israel's history from beginning to end (cf. 9:15f. with 11:30–32). [30] The following analogy between the salvation of the Gentiles and the redemption of all Israel can consequently now be ascertained: Just as the Gentiles (even as far as Rome) once lived in disobedience toward God, but have now found God's mercy because the majority of Israel still remain captive in disobedience in regard to the gospel, [31] the converse also holds true for the majority of Israel. They were and continue to be disobedient to God because his mercy is still at work for the benefit of (the full number of) the Gentiles. But this present, ongoing disobedience also has the purpose and goal of

causing the (majority of the) Israelites to partake of God's mercy, and to do so "now." For Paul, the final events are imminent, and the full number of the Gentiles, whose salvation his own mission work serves to bring about, has almost been reached. Therefore, in prophetic certainty, he can speak of the fact that the time of mercy for all Israel is also imminent. Indeed, from God's perspective, it is already inaugurated. [32] For the fundamental principle of the history of election is at the same time the characteristic of the righteousness of God which determines this history, orders the world for the sake of its own benefit, and establishes it aright (a righteousness concerning which the majority of Israel still has no idea; 10:3). This principle is that God has shut up Gentiles and Jews in the sin of disobedience, in order that he might show mercy on them all for their salvation in and through Christ (cf. Gal. 3:22).

A small, chosen remnant from Israel, with Paul as a prime example (11:1–5), together with many of the Gentiles whom God has ordained to this end, have already opened themselves up to the call of the gospel and are confessing Christ as their savior and Lord. The mission "to all the Gentile nations" (Mk. 13:10) is nearly completed. But with it the hour of the salvation of "all Israel" has also come. When the missionaries to the Gentiles have reached the goal of their work, then Israel will also finally recognize Jesus Christ, the messianic redeemer who comes from Zion, to be its savior and Lord. As a result of faith in him, they will then receive justification and the forgiveness of their sins. The fact that in the future Christ and justification will not bypass Israel is just as certain as the fact that the Gentile mission continues to provoke the majority of God's people to anger and to stir them up to jealousy (10:19; 11:13f.). Just as Paul was once conquered for the obedience of faith on the road to Damascus through the appearance from heaven of the resurrected Christ, so too will the same thing take place for the majority of Israel at the parousia of Christ. For God has chosen Israel to experience justification and redemption through Christ. This promise of election will be fulfilled when the people of God, who are still burdened by the sin of unbelief, will be accepted by the returning Christ on the basis of pure grace and mercy and led into the salvific community made up of Gentiles and Jews. The gospel declared on earth by all the apostles, including Paul (1 Cor. 15:1–11), thus has its designated time limit. But Christ Jesus, who is declared in this gospel and who authorizes the preaching of the apostles, is and remains the one and only savior, Lord, and judge of all Gentiles and Jews. Apart from confessing Christ there is therefore no salvation for Israel before God.

V. 11:33–36. Praise for the Way of God

The apostle concludes his prophecy concerning salvation history with an artistically formulated hymn of praise to the salvific work of God:

33 O the depth of the riches and wisdom and knowledge of God!
How unfathomable are his judgments
and untraceable his ways!

34 For who has known the mind of the Lord?
Or who has been his counselor?

35 Or who has extended (something) to him,
so that it must be repaid to him in kind?

36 For from him and through him and to him are all things.
His is the glory forever. Amen.

Verse 34: Is. 40:13; Verse 35: Job 41:3.

A. By way of composition, the hymn to God at the conclusion of Romans 9–11 corresponds to the short declaration of praise which Paul attached in 9:5 to his enumeration of Israel's special privileges of election.

The artistic structure of the hymn documents that the apostle was not only a great theologian, but also a spiritual poet of stature. The hymn is framed by a threefold introductory line on the one hand (v. 33a), and by a corresponding three-member concluding line on the other hand, which then flows into a so-called doxology, that is, into praise of the power and glory of God (v. 36). The middle section consists of three double lines, each of which contains a parallelism in regard to its clauses, which in succession describe the depth of the knowledge of God (v. 33b), the wisdom of God (v. 34), and the riches of God (v. 35) praised in the introductory line. The poetry in the hymns of early (Hellenistic) Judaism provides the model for Paul's descriptive praise of the greatness of God both in terms of its style and content. A particularly impressive parallel to Romans 11:33–36 is found in 2 Bar. 14:8f., where we read, "[W]ho, O Lord, my God, understands your judgment, or who fathoms the depth of your way, or who contemplates the difficult burden of your paths, or who is able to contemplate your inscrutable decree, or who from those who have been born (of dust) has ever found the beginning and end of your wisdom?"

B. By virtue of the spiritual insight granted to him into the ways which God has followed and will follow with the chosen people of his own possession, Paul has developed in Romans 9–11 a comprehensive view of salvation history. The words of God from the Holy Scripture are its inner guide, and its determinative principle is the mercy of God (9:15f.; 11:32). The apostle has explained to the Christians from Rome his spiritual perspectives on history, which are open to those people who can hear and understand them in the Spirit of faith (cf. 1 Cor. 2:13). Under these circumstances, it is appropriate that his concluding statements provide a transition to worship. Paul himself obviously wrote the hymn which follows. But inasmuch as his manner of expression does not correspond verbatim with Romans 9–11, but only in terms of content, it is possible that Paul

did not initially compose this praise of God for the letter to the Romans, but
had already taught and prayed it earlier and in another situation. Nevertheless,
this portion of the text fits very well into the overall composition of the three
chapters. [33] Paul and his readers do stand, in fact, in an attitude of worship
before the unreachable depths of the riches of the wealth, wisdom, and knowledge of God. On the basis of Dan. 2:22; 1QS 11:19; and 2 Bar. 14:8f., as well as
1 Cor. 2:9, the "depths" refers to the unfathomable dimensions of the works of
God within salvation history. Only those who are taught by the Holy Spirit can
therefore fathom and praise them (cf. 1QM 10:11 with 1 Cor. 2:10).

The "knowledge of God" in this context does not mean, as in 2 Cor. 10:5, the
knowledge which has God as its object, but the knowledge which God himself
exercises. It determines and governs everything (cf. 1 Sam. 2:3; Additions to Esther 4:17; and the Greek translation of Pss. 19:3; 94:11 with 1 Cor. 3:20; 13:12;
Gal. 4:9). The forensic decisions and the ways in which God directs the destiny
of Israel and the nations (cf. Ps. 9:26 in the Greek translation = 10:5 in the Hebrew text, and Pss. 36:7; 97:8 with Ps. 25:4ff.; Ps. 145:7) are unfathomably well
planned. Those who believe are allowed to know and have already heard from
Paul in chapters 9–11 that they are being sustained by God's unshakable faithfulness and mercy (cf. 11:29, 32). For those chosen by God, everything which
God has foreseen for them works for the good (cf. 8:28ff.).

[34] The "wisdom of God" creates and upholds all things (cf. Prov. 8:22ff.;
Wis. 9:9ff.), without God needing any instruction concerning it (Is. 40:13; Wis.
9:16). But God's wisdom is only recognizable to those with whom God shares it
by the power of the Holy Spirit. For Paul, these are above all Christians, since
they are the ones who recognize Jesus as the wisdom of God (1 Cor. 1:30; 2:6ff.).

[35] The "riches of God" regarding knowledge, wisdom, glory, and so on are
immeasurable (cf. Philo, *Leg. All.* 1.34); God is indebted to no one for them.
The apostle expresses this truth with words from an ancient Greek translation of
Job 41:3, only the vestiges of which are still known to us. The divine riches
which Paul praises are primarily God's riches of kindness (cf. Rom. 2:4), grace,
and mercy (Eph. 1:7; 2:4, 7). The Gentiles have already experienced these
riches (11:12), and all Israel is still to partake of them (11:26ff.).

[36] The immeasurable depths of the riches, wisdom, and knowledge of God
identify him as the God who is the creator and sustainer of all things. Everything comes from him, everything has its existence and order through his Spirit,
word, and wisdom, and everything is directed toward him, that is, accomplished
for the sake of his glorification (cf. Philo, *Spec. Leg.* 1.208). In God everything
has its ground and goal (Sir. 43:27), and in Jesus, Christians see the mediator of
the old and new creation (cf. 1 Cor. 8:6; Col. 1:15–20). Therefore, as a direct result of their insight gained from faith, praise and glorification for all eternity are
due to the God who (through Christ) has created all things, sustains all things,
and not only desires, but will also save all things from death and the dominion
of evil!

Looking back, there can no longer be any doubt whatsoever concerning the significance of Romans 9–11 within the letter to the Romans as a whole. Paul has shown the Christians from Rome that, and in what way, his mission work as the apostle to the Gentiles is integrated into God's ways with Israel. The history of salvation, which is determined by God's decree of election, is the comprehensive horizon within which God's righteousness is brought to bear. This history finds its goal in the salvation of all Israel through the return of the messiah, Jesus Christ, and documents that, even before the Gentiles, God had chosen the people of his own possession for justification through Christ. In view of this perspective, that criticism of the Pauline gospel which raises the accusation against the apostle that his preaching of Christ does not lead to the conversion of Israel, but to its hardening, must collapse.

In these three chapters Paul has clearly designated himself to be an apostle to the Gentiles for the sake of Israel (11:13ff.). Furthermore, his statements concerning God's ways with Israel just as clearly transcend and correct his prior invective concerning the Jews from 1 Thess. 2:14–16. In view of these developments, a comprehensive overview of the relationship between Paul and Israel is now in order.

Excursus 12:
Paul and Israel

Four separate phases can be recognized in *the relationship of the apostle Paul to Israel:* (1) The first phase is the period of Paul, the Jew, before his call to be an apostle. The time after his conversion can then be divided into three subsequent periods, namely, into (2) the years before his appointment by Antioch as a missionary (to the Gentiles); (3) the Antiochean years; and (4) the time of the mission to the Gentiles which was freely planned and carried out by Paul and his association of co-workers. All of the letters of Paul handed down to us in the New Testament originate from this last phase. Hence, we must reconstruct what the apostle experienced and thought in the earlier phases from Paul's own letters, as well as from the reports in the book of Acts, which were first written down after Paul.

(1) In his youth Paul lived entirely as a testimony to the privileges of election (listed by him in Rom. 3:1f. and 9:4f.) and dedicated his life to the service of the Torah. Saul, born in Tarsus in Cilicia and descended from a pious Jewish family (Phil. 3:5; Acts 23:6) from the tribe of Benjamin (Phil. 3:5; Rom. 11:1), apparently had a mastery not only of Greek, but also of Hebrew (that is, of the language of the Bible and of the Jewish worship service) (Phil. 3:5). He then studied at the schoolhouse of Rabbi Gamaliel I in Jerusalem (Acts 22:2f.) and joined the Pharisees. In Gal.

1:14 he designates himself to be a "zealot for the traditions (of the Law) of my Fathers," who stood out in particular among his contemporaries and fellow students for his earnestness. During this time he lived a life of blameless righteousness according to the criterion of the Law (Phil. 3:6) and possibly had the responsibility of instructing the foreign Jewish pilgrims who streamed to Jerusalem for the pilgrimage feasts concerning the Law and the significance of circumcision (Gal. 5:11) (M. Hengel). Over against apostate Jews, he rigorously stood up for the keeping of the Torah. As a result, Paul persecuted Stephen and his fellow Christians in Jerusalem itself, and then as far as Damascus, with all the means of power available to him, that is, with the consent of the high priest and the Jewish court (cf. Acts 8:1–3; 9:1ff.; 22:4; Gal. 1:13; 1 Cor. 15:9). What offended Paul in Stephen's preaching of Christ and of those who followed him was (according to Acts 6:13f.) the preaching of a crucified pseudo-messiah, the scorning of the temple, and the disregard of the Law. In other words, Paul was offended by the deceptive misinterpretation of the messianic promises as applied to Jesus and by the devaluation of precisely that "giving of the Law" and "worship of God" by which Israel was distinguished by God from the Gentiles (Rom. 9:4f.). Naturally, as a pious Jew, Paul had repeatedly prayed (along with others) prayers of repentance such as Psalm 51 or Neh. 9:6ff. But there is no evidence of an inner crisis, not to mention a mental breakdown in the life of Paul, the Jew, in response to the Law. Romans 7:7–25 does not represent a confession concerning the life of the apostle (see above, pp. 114ff.).

(2) In A.D. 32 or 33 Paul encountered the resurrected Christ, now exalted to the right hand of God, on the road to Damascus (cf. Gal. 1:15f.; 2 Cor. 4:5f.; Acts 9:1–29; 22:3–21; 26:9–20). This experience compelled him to the insight that the Christians whom he was persecuting were right and that he himself, with his militant zeal for Israel's inherited tradition of faith, was wrong. Indeed, he was wrong before God! It was precisely this reevaluation of all of his previous criteria concerning what it meant to be pious and ungodly, which was forced upon him by his Damascus Road experience, which caused Paul to become a missionary to the Gentiles (Gal. 1:16). He was thus no longer a sinner and part of the wicked who were combating God's ways in Christ as a result of his fight for the Jewish privileges of salvation. Instead, he was now chosen by God on the basis of his free grace and mercy, accepted through Christ, and appointed as a messenger of the gospel. Hence, under these circumstances, which Paul himself had experienced, the Jewish conception of the exemplary sinfulness of the Gentiles (cf., e.g., Gal. 2:15) could no longer be a principled hindrance to the fact that the "godless" Gentiles could also be accepted through Christ and placed into the state of having peace with God! This was true even though the Gentiles, unlike Israel, did not possess any

divine privileges of election. We do not know, however, whether at the time of his call to be an apostle Paul had already been confronted with Philip's revolutionary resolution to preach Christ not only in the Jewish synagogues, but also among the Samaritans, who were hated in Israel as heretics (Acts 8:5). The only thing that is clear is that immediately after his call Paul preached Jesus as Israel's messiah, who was crucified and raised from the dead "for us" (1 Cor. 15:3–5), and faith in him as the only way to be saved for Jews (and Gentiles). Moreover, he did so both in Damascus and in Arabia (cf. Gal. 1:16, 23). That in doing so he encountered fierce opposition from Judaism is quite understandable. Just as Paul had earlier punished the apostate Christians, the Jews now also took measures against the apostle who had fallen apostate to the Christians. They caused him to be whipped for his disregard for the Law and turned him over to the local police officials as a disturber of the peace who ought to be flogged with lashes (cf. 2 Cor. 11:24f. with Acts 26:11). When he subsequently moved to Jerusalem two or three years after his call and then dared to appear there in the synagogues, as Stephen had done before him, his life was put in danger and he had to be brought by the apostles to Tarsus for safety (Acts 9:28–30).

In spite of these life-threatening disputes, Paul had neither denied nor rejected Israel's privileges of election in general in his ministry as an apostle of Jesus Christ. His statements from Phil. 3:4–10 only appear to point in this direction. Of course, as far as justification in and through Christ is concerned, neither circumcision, faithfulness to the Law, nor Israelite ancestry can transform a Jewish evildoer into someone who is righteous before God. Not only Gentiles, but Jews as well attain the righteousness of faith solely and only from Christ and for his sake. Nevertheless, Paul did not mean that God's promises to Israel, together with the Law, had come to nothing. Had he been of this opinion, he would never have begun his missionary preaching in the Jewish synagogues. Nor would he have consciously sought contact with the early church in Jerusalem, which was persisting in its missionary efforts (among the Jews) within Jerusalem, the most important city of the world from the perspective of the history of salvation (cf. Gal. 1:18ff.; Acts 9:26ff.). Undoubtedly, the report already mentioned from 2 Cor. 11:24f., that is, that in the early period of his missionary work Paul was sentenced five times (!) by the synagogue courts to be punished by whipping (with thirty-nine blows on the chest and back), refers to the beginning of the Pauline mission in the synagogues of the Diaspora. In these synagogues Paul sought contact with Jews and (God-fearing, but still uncircumcised) Gentiles, and desired to preach to them Christ as Israel's messiah and as the Lord of the world. That the gospel of the righteousness of God in Christ applies first to the Jews, and then also to the Greeks (Gentiles) (Rom. 1:16f.), is thus not merely a belated

Pauline insight, but the conviction which determined his life as an apostle of Christ from the very beginning.

(3) When the mission church in Antioch resolved to begin preaching the gospel programmatically among the Greek-speaking Gentiles (Acts 11:19–21), it was Barnabas from Jerusalem (Acts 4:36) who brought Paul from Tarsus to Antioch and, as a result, placed him on the path of the mission to the Gentiles (Acts 11:19–26). Together with Paul, Barnabas undertook the first major missionary journey, which led them from Cyprus, Barnabas's home, as far as Iconium, and then back again to Antioch (Acts 13–14). It goes without saying that both of them began their missionary activity in the synagogues. There they found lodging, and also, when necessary, work (cf. 1 Cor. 9:6). On the Sabbath they then had the possibility of speaking, at the same time, to both Jews and Gentiles concerning the mission of Jesus and of salvation. It was only during this first missionary journey that the problem therefore arose of whether the Gentiles who had converted to faith in Christ must, like Jewish proselytes, be circumcised and placed under the Law of Moses in order to participate in salvation through the messiah Jesus (cf. Gal. 2:4; Acts 15:1ff.). This shows that previously Paul had not yet essentially gone beyond the framework of the Jewish expectation regarding salvation. Nor were these Jewish perspectives given up at the "Apostolic Council," which was called in Jerusalem to deal with the disputed question of the converted Gentiles' responsibility in regard to circumcision and their obligation to the Law (Gal. 2:1–10; Acts 15:1–29). At this time, the "pillars" of the church, James, Peter, and John, agreed with Barnabas and Paul that the latter should go to the Gentiles, and Peter to the Jews. Moreover, it was determined that neither circumcision nor the entire Jewish observance of the Law should be required of the Gentiles. Rather, they should merely make a financial contribution to the needs of the poor Christians in Jerusalem (Gal. 2:6–10). As a result of this agreement, the entire mission to the Gentiles remained tied to the mission to the Jews and oriented toward Jerusalem. Paul willingly accepted and esteemed the Jerusalem settlement as long as he could conduct his own missionary work in freedom (cf. Rom. 15:19, 25ff.). The period of Paul's activity as a missionary to the Gentiles in Antioch is thus characterized by the transition to an organized Gentile mission. But there is no evidence that the apostle consciously gave up his conviction concerning Israel's privileges of election. Hence, the fact that the gospel first pertains to the Jews, and (only) subsequently also to the Gentiles, was not a matter of dispute between Paul, Barnabas, and the pillar apostles in Jerusalem. The only ones who did not go along with the Jerusalem agreement were those Jewish Christians who in Antioch and Jerusalem pressed for the circumcision of all the Gentiles who had converted to faith in Christ (Acts 15:1f.). They rejected it because it appeared to mollify the exclusive Jewish privileges of salvation.

(4) Hence, during the fourth phase of Paul's activity the differences came to the fore in a way that could not be overlooked. When Peter and Paul appeared before the gathered church in Antioch, an incident to which Paul refers only briefly in Gal. 2:11ff., they could not agree concerning to what degree the Jewish food and purity regulations ought to be required of Gentile Christians during their common meals with those Jewish Christians who were still living and thinking ritually. (This question affected the fellowship of the Lord's Supper and was therefore highly explosive). On the one hand, Paul pleaded for the freedom of the Gentiles from all legal obligations. On the other hand, Peter, Barnabas, and the majority of the Jewish Christians from Antioch, under pressure to do so from those having been sent out by James in Jerusalem, the Lord's brother, decided that the Gentile Christians could by all means be expected to keep the so-called minimum Noahic commandments (cf. Acts 15:20, 29 with Gen. 9:1–7 and Leviticus 17–18). Paul, however, considered this to be an offense against the "truth of the gospel" and thus decided from then on to continue the mission to the Gentiles entrusted to him with his co-workers alone (and without these obligations). The paths of Paul and Barnabas were now divided. But Silas (Silvanus) from Jerusalem continued to side with Paul in this controversial issue and therefore participated in Paul's new independent mission (cf. Acts 15:27, 38–41; 16:25; 17:14; 18:5 with 1 Thess. 1:1; 2 Thess. 1:1; 2 Cor. 1:19).

The majority decision in Antioch, reached against the advice of Paul, now also gave new impetus to the Jewish Christians who had been defeated at the Apostolic Council (and in their train, to Paul's opponents in general). As a result, from this point on Paul saw himself persecuted and criticized from two sides. From the one side, he was attacked by those Jews who stood against him in their rejection of his preaching of Christ *per se*. From the other side, he was persecuted by Jewish-Christian critics and contramissionaries who were led by the so-called Judaizers who had appeared against Paul in Galatia. Against Paul, they appealed to the model of James, the Lord's brother, and also to that of Peter (cf. 2 Cor. 11:5). But as if this double front were not enough, Paul now also had to experience firsthand that his successful mission to the Gentiles aroused tendencies of disdain among the Gentile-Christians for those Jewish Christians who still thought and lived ritually, and with it, even contempt for Israel. He was therefore forced (in addition) to put the Gentile-Christian "Paulinists" who were boasting of themselves in their place (cf. Rom. 11:13ff.; 14:1ff., 13ff.).

The fact that Paul had to address this threefold constellation explains the occasionally highly dialectical statements of the apostle that are found in all of the extant Pauline letters. It repeatedly forced Paul to take conceptual steps that are of almost incomprehensible breadth in order to

straddle apparently diverse ideas. Take, for example, the dispute with the
Jewish-Christian contramissionaries over justification that occurs in the
letter to the Philippians. There the apostle explains that the privileges
which pertain to Israelite ancestry which he once so highly esteemed, that
is, circumcision, being a member of the Pharisees, and the blameless
righteousness of the Law which he enjoyed, are now worth only "dung" in
comparison to the righteousness of faith which God grants in and through
Christ (Phil. 3:4–11). But then in Rom. 3:1f. and 9:4f. the same apostle
boasts of the salvific privileges which stand as a mark of the continuing
election of Israel. Or to give another example, in Galatians Paul narrates
that the Gentile (Christian) Titus (whom he had specifically taken to the
Apostolic Council as a "test person") was not compelled to be circumcised
in Jerusalem (Gal. 2:1–3). He consequently warns the Gentile Christians
against being circumcised subsequent to their faith, because, if they are,
Christ will no longer be of any value to them (Gal. 5:2ff.). But then, "in
deference to the Jews," Paul himself determines to circumcise Timothy
personally, who was his assistant in the mission and who came from a Jewish mother (Acts 16:3). Yet in Romans he finally writes that the circumcision that takes place outwardly in the flesh is of some value only if it
corresponds to the circumcision of the heart in faith (Rom. 2:25, 29), or
if—as in the case of Abraham—it is received as a seal of faith (in Christ)
(Rom. 4:11). This apparent vacillation can only be understood when one
considers that Paul cherishes, without compromise, the gospel of justification. Nevertheless, he does not see all religious customs in Israel as having
come to an end with this gospel. Nor would he have ever been able to
gain an entrance into the synagogues in the Diaspora with his proclamation of Christ if there had been a Jewish Christian in his staff of co-workers who had intentionally remained uncircumcised.

Today we probably perceive the contrast between 1 Thess. 2:14–16 and
Romans 9–11, with which we were confronted in our interpretation (cf.
above, pp. 143, 164, 169f.), as being stronger than Paul himself would have
been inclined to evaluate it. Nevertheless, it is not to be undervalued.
Within the situation of struggle in which Paul was (also) involved in Thessalonica, the apostle wrote in 1 Thess. 2:14–16 that he had suffered persecutions from the Jews, "who killed both the Lord Jesus as well as the Prophets,
and persecute us, and do not please God, and oppose all men, who hinder
us from speaking to the Gentiles in order that they might be saved so that
they fill up the measure of their sins. But the judgment of wrath has come
upon them totally!" The language of these Pauline statements is essentially
supplied from early Jewish sources (cf. Neh. 9:26 with Josephus, *Ant.* 9.265,
281; 10.38), although it also picks up Gentile criticism of the Jews as well
(cf. additions to Esther 3:13e with Josephus, *Contr. Ap.* 1.310; 2.125, 148).
But Paul increased the traditional reproach of the Jews by adding the

statement that the Jews have killed Jesus (cf., for the same point, Acts. 2:23, 36; 3:15; 4:10; 7:52; 10:39). The apostle also held to this view in 1 Cor. 2:8 (cf. with Acts 3:17; 13:27). It is true, of course, that the death penalty of crucifixion was finally carried out against Jesus by the Romans. But, from the perspective of legal history, in view of the fact that Jesus was tried before the High Council, Paul's point cannot simply be dismissed out of hand (cf. A. Strobel, *Die Stunde der Wahrheit*, Tübingen, 1980, 81ff.). And as unfortunate as the effects of Paul's statements from 1 Thess. 2:14–16 may have been, it is just as important to consider, first of all, that in these statements Paul is speaking not as a Gentile but (as the prophets of Israel before him) as a Jew. Second, in them he is raising an apostolic accusation only against those Jews who are continuously hindering his preaching of the gospel in the synagogues of the Diaspora. It is thus highly doubtful that with these statements he intended a general renunciation of his people. For a little while later he emphasizes in 1 Cor. 2:8 that the crucifixion of Jesus was carried out by the Jewish "rulers" as a result of an unknowing delusion. Furthermore, within the Jewish-Christian horizon of thought, the very fact that it was an *unknowing* transgression signals that it is *not* a matter of an unforgivable sin, but rather of a sin which (by virtue of the atoning death of Jesus) can be forgiven by God if the Jews turn back and exercise faith in the gospel (cf. Leviticus 4 and Acts 2:38f.; 3:17ff.; 10:42f.; 13:38f.). Hence, 1 Cor. 2:8 already lays the groundwork for the conception of Israel's delusion found in Rom. 10:2f. and 11:8–10, 25ff., a delusion which does not place Israel under the judgment of wrath definitively and thus exclude it from justification and forgiveness through Christ, but rather one day passes away. This point is formulated explicitly for the first time in 2 Cor. 3:14–16, where we read that since the days of Moses Israel stands under a hardening ordained by God, which does not allow it to come either to the true knowledge of the Torah, or to an understanding of the gospel. Only when Israel turns to Christ, the Lord, is "the veil" of delusion taken away from its mind (v. 16). The only aspect of his prior thinking that Paul thus corrects absolutely in Romans 11, on the basis of a deeper spiritual insight (as also indicated previously in the Holy Scripture) into God's ways with Israel as the people of his own possession, is his supposition from 1 Thess. 2:16 that the people of God were overcome by God's judgment of wrath "totally" or "forever." The delusion that has been ordained by God now appears to him as a judgment of purification, which is preparing Israel for the saving recognition of Christ. As such, it will one day pass away. Romans 9–11, together with the relationship to Jerusalem, which Paul never gave up, therefore show irrefutably that a Gentile-Christian anti-Semitism can never legitimately be derived from Paul, not to mention supported from the perspective of his theology of justification (cf. for this issue also Eph. 2:11–22).

As far as the relation of Paul to Israel is concerned, it is important to make clear in conclusion that the apostle first lost his freedom, and then as a consequence, also his life over his preaching of Christ, which, by virtue of God's will, incited the Jews to "jealousy" and "wrath" (Rom. 10:19; 11:14), as well as over his ministry (in regard to the collection) to "the poor among the saints in Jerusalem" (Rom. 15:26). For Paul personally brought the monies to Jerusalem which had been collected by him from the Gentile church. But when, following the advice of James, the Lord's brother, Paul wanted to register in the temple (in order to assume the costs for) the offering of redemption on behalf of four poor Jewish Christians, who had taken upon themselves a Nazirite vow (Num. 6:1–21), he was recognized by Jews (from Ephesus). They accused him of criticizing Israel, the Law, and the temple, and reproached Paul for taking an uncircumcised Gentile with him into the area of the temple which was reserved exclusively for Jews. In their view, Paul had thus intentionally desecrated the temple. This aroused the Jewish crowd and they seized the apostle. When they threatened to strike him (dead), he was taken into custody by the Roman temple security and shortly thereafter escorted to Caesarea because of Jewish death threats. After a two-year period of imprisonment in Caesarea, Paul was transferred by the Romans, at his own request, to Rome in order to be able to defend himself before an imperial court (cf. Acts 21:15–34; 23:12–35; 25:1–12). In Rome, Paul was martyred during the reign of Nero. In the end, the "wrath" that he kindled among the Jews and their "jealousy" over the Gentiles cost Paul his life. Hence, he was not only an apostle to the Gentiles, but also became a martyr of the faith for the sake of Israel.

12:1–15:13. Part Three:
The Testimony of the Righteousness of God in the Life of the Community

Paul has now answered the question concerning the relationship of Israel to the (Pauline) gospel, a question of equal significance for the Christians in Rome and for Paul personally. Having done so, he turns to the question, which is no less significant, of how the life of the church can and should appear as a sign of the righteousness of God. From Galatia on, his critics have reproached him with the fact that he cheapens the gospel in an entirely unacceptable manner and that his preaching causes one to miss the necessary earnestness of God's judgment, thus creating a capricious freedom among the (Gentile) Christians. In the letter to the Romans, beginning in 2:16, Paul has resisted these accusations. Already in 6:1ff., 15ff., and then once again in 8:3–11, the apostle pointed to the fact, in no uncertain terms, that with their justification those who believe are placed into the "service of righteousness" (6:18). Hence, their liberation from the power of sin is anything but a license to live from now on according to one's own discretion or to sin. At this point Paul now returns to these statements and links them to an exhortation to the church which is of fundamental significance.

Viewed from this perspective, 12:1–15:13 is anything but a mere appendix to the theological expositions of chapters 1–11. Rather, it deals with the verification of justification in the life of the church. Nevertheless, the sequence of placing chapters 1–11 before 12–15 is intentionally planned by Paul. This is confirmed by the fact that this arrangement is also found in the other Pauline letters as well. First, salvation is addressed, and then follows the exhortation to the church which results from this encouragement (cf., e.g., Gal. 1:1–5:12 and 5:13–6:10, or Col. 1:1–2:23 and 3:1–4:6). This organizational structure presumably derives from the preaching associated with baptism. It makes clear that God accepts sinners unconditionally in Christ, but as a result places them under the reign of Christ and enlists them in service. Moreover, those who believe receive the power for such service through the gift of the Holy Spirit. Hence, it makes good theological sense that Rom. 12:1–15:13 does not come in the letter to the Romans until now, since Christians have been and are enlisted in the service of Christ only as a result of their prior justification, which in turn is grounded in God's merciful election. In their conduct, therefore, it becomes clear, and ought to be visible before the eyes of the unbelieving world, just what God, the creator, can fashion out of the lives of the ungodly in and through Christ. Paul thus does not know, and has also never approved, of a justification which does not introduce and lead to a life of righteousness.

The letter to the Romans has become for Christianity not only Paul's theological "testament" (G. Bornkamm), but also a textbook on the gospel of justification. This evaluation of the letter has led to the fact that again and again the apostle's concrete manner of argument, which was directed first and foremost to the Christians from Rome, is overlooked in reading it, or at least viewed as less important. As far as the exhortation to the church in 12:1–15:13 is concerned, when viewed from this angle it is emphasized that the expositions of the apostle in 12:1–13:14 were determined from the very beginning for use by the (early) Christians in general. In contrast, the specific questions of the Roman church were dealt with beginning only in 14:1. This view correctly observes that in 12:1–13:14 Paul does make statements and arrangements which he had prepared much in advance and in part has already expressed in other contexts (cf., e.g., Rom. 12:3–8 with 1 Cor. 12:4–31, or Rom. 13:11–14 with 1 Thess. 5:4ff.). Furthermore, there is such a close relationship between Rom. 12:1f. and 1 Pet. 1:14; 2:5, between Rom. 12:6f. and 1 Pet. 4:10, and between Rom. 13:1–7 and 1 Pet. 2:13–17, that one can trace the instructions in both apostolic letters back to a common apostolic teaching in which not only faith was discussed, but also the life of faith which is to be led by baptized Christians. For example, 1 Thess. 4:1 and 1 Cor. 4:17 show that Paul had actually expounded such generally accepted teaching. In Romans 12 and 13 (but also in 14:1–15:13, cf. with 1 Cor. 8:7ff.) we thus encounter doctrinal statements which, in part, Paul had already represented before the composition of Romans. Of course, Paul does not call attention to this fact on his own, and for precisely this reason we must first endeavor to understand what the apostle hoped to accomplish in Rome with his discourses, and only then pursue the general significance of his teaching.

The arrangement of Paul's exhortations as a whole is loose. After a programmatic introduction (12:1–2) there follows in 12:3–13:14 instructions for living together and for the service of the church, both toward those within and toward those outside of it. In 14:1–15:13 suggestions are then attached concerning the question of how the "strong" and the "weak" who are quarreling with one another in Rome can mutually "accept" each other under the gaze of Christ. This loose succession of themes and statements shows that in 12:1–15:13 the apostle does not desire to give an exhaustive presentation of how justified Christians must live and what actions they must permit in others. Rather, Paul summons the members of the church to contemplate what he writes and then, on the basis of the insights gained, to reflect further on their own in order to decide for themselves. Paul thus unambiguously places his addressees under obligation, but he just as clearly establishes for them the freedom of their own responsibility before God.

I. 12:1–2. Worship as the Testimony of One's Life

(1) I now exhort you, brothers, by virtue of the mercy of God, to present your bodies as a living and holy sacrifice, pleasing to God, (which is) your reasonable worship of God. (2) Do not be conformed also to this age of the world, but be transformed through the renewal of your thinking, so that you can verify what the will of God is, that which is good and pleasing and complete.

A. The language of these two verses is worthy of note in several respects. As Ps. 51:3 or Dan. 9:9, 18 show, the mercy of God refers to that divine conduct in which God turns to sinners and forgives them of their sins. For the apostle, therefore, grace, compassion, and mercy belong very closely together, since the God who justifies the ungodly (4:5) is the same God who shows compassion on whomever he desires (9:18). He is the one who has shut up Gentiles and Jews in unbelief in order to show compassion on them all (11:32).

At the time of Paul, the catchword "reasonable worship of God" had a special nuance and significance. In the Hellenistic period, the educated pious turned away from the coarse and bloody sacrifices in the temples, considering it to be more appropriate to honor in the Spirit the invisible, spiritual deity. Their prayers were thus the "spiritual" or "reasonable" sacrifice which truly corresponded to the nature of God (cf., e.g., Corp. Herm. 13:18, 21). Philo and Hellenistic Judaism also incorporated this way of thinking. Since with their heavenly praise the angels present to God a bloodless "reasonable" sacrifice (T. Lev. 3:6), in the same way the Spirit-filled hymns and thanksgivings of the pious on the earth are also the most perfect offering that can be presented to God (Philo, *Spec. Leg.* 1.272, 277). The writings of Paul and 1 Peter (cf. 1 Pet. 2:5) make it clear that this Hellenistic-Jewish way of thinking and expression was then taken over into the New Testament as well.

The three concluding words from v. 2 can be understood in the sense of qualifications of the will of God, as if Paul wanted to say that one should test what the good, pleasing, and complete will of God is. But it is more likely linguistically to understand the three adjectives, which are all governed by a definite article, as more precise definitions of what the will of God is in terms of its content; that is, the will of God is that which is good, that which is pleasing (to him), and that which is complete.

B. Paul exhorts the Christians from Rome by virtue of the mercy of God. [1] He himself, together with his addressees, are indebted for their very life of faith to this mercy. They all live only on the basis of the gift of God, who justifies them in and through Christ and has established them in a relationship in which they have peace with himself. His righteous and merciful work in Christ has therefore laid the foundation for the service which those who believe now owe him. It is to this service which Paul is programmatically summoning his readers. Paul's authority for doing so is derived from the fact that he is the one who has been permitted to exhort, advise, and request others in the name of God to do that which is necessary for them as believers. In making this admonition, the apostle uses the same word in the phrase, "I now exhort you," that he used to describe his work of preaching in 2 Cor. 5:20. Preaching the gospel and exhorting the church (*Paraklesis*) belong together for Paul. Both are done by him in an admonishing tone which implores and invites the hearers to gain insight and to join Paul in contemplating the message.

What distinguishes Israel from the Gentiles, and continues to do so, is that God makes it possible for them to worship God (aright) through his dwelling on Zion (cf. 9:4). But as this text makes clear, the Christian church also stands in the service of God, and Paul therefore summons it to its own form of the same "reasonable" worship of God as practiced in the Jewish synagogues (in which God is served in a way that corresponds to his spiritual nature, a nature which is accessible to human reason). This worship of God has a remarkable breadth. It encompasses hymns, prayers, and spiritual exhortation, all of which Paul valued and explicitly advised to be cultivated (cf. 1 Cor. 14:26; Col. 1:11ff.; 3:16f.; Rom. 11:33ff.; 15:6, etc.).

But the living, holy, and God-pleasing sacrifice offered by Christians consists not only of prayer, praise, and admonition, but at the same time, and beyond this, it also consists of the giving of one's body and life in the service of righteousness (6:18, 22). According to Paul, the worship of God which truly corresponds to God's nature and will includes the bodily act of obedience. Only when they really serve God with their soul, understanding, heart and hands, in other words, always and everywhere, will the Christians do justice to their creator and the merciful God who saves them. According to Paul, the "body" is the existence bestowed upon mankind by God, in which the creatures of God live with and for one another. Even if the flesh passes away, the body will be resurrected (1 Cor. 15:44 ff.). The creatures' acts with and for one another will thus endure beyond death and the day of judgment. The worship of God will also remain, while the adoration of God will fill the entire being of those who have been resurrected (1 Cor. 15:28). Those who believe, having been chosen by God for justification, already belong completely to him here on earth. Hence, their earthly worship of God cannot remain limited to special times of devotion, but must encompass the believers' entire life, including even one's daily acts of charity and manner of conduct. The apostle thus does not mention a single word about a piety which is merely spiritual. It is precisely this aspect which gives his admonition its pointed nature. It is through their service to righteousness that Christians belong entirely to their Lord. In turn, their Lord has the right to demand from them this all-encompassing service.

[2] The next sentence explains this further. According to Gal. 1:4, Christ gave himself up to death for Christians in order to deliver them from this present evil age. Viewed from this perspective, it is improper for them to continue to conform to this age in their behavior. Rather, those who believe should be

transformed by the renewal of their (evaluative) thinking. Conversely, God has given the unbelieving Gentiles over to an understanding which is incapable of perceiving the will of God (1:28), while without Christ the understanding of the repentant (Jewish) sinner is also unable to do in actuality that which he or she recognizes to be good (7:22f.). Only liberation from the power of sin, an orientation toward Christ, and the gift of the Holy Spirit can enable those who believe to recognize and to do what pleases God. At this point Paul is consequently reminding the Christians in Rome of their baptism, summoning them to leave behind, in faith, the state of affairs described in 1:28 and 7:22f., and calling them to yield to Christ in their thinking (cf., quite similarly, Col. 3:10 and Eph. 4:23). In this way they can and should become those in this world who are contemplating the will of God in advance of its full realization. For in Jesus the criteria for that which is the will of God have been given in advance to those who believe. Indeed, already in early Judaism the point had been firmly established that the pious must do only what is good and pleasing in God's eyes (cf., e.g., 1QS 1:2). The wisdom granted by God therefore assists one to a perfect way of life in that it instructs one to do that which is righteous and well-pleasing according to God's commandments (Wis. 9:6, 9; cf. with James 1:17; 3:17). In addition, "the good" continued to be the guiding concept of popular Greek philosophy, which instructed its adherents in a way of life characterized by righteousness and the fear of God. Hence, in the same way as the apostle's formulations in Phil. 4:8f., the manner of expression in Rom. 12:2 has a familiar, and yet again a special ring for the Gentiles and Jews in Rome who have converted to Christ. In contrast to early Judaism and Greek philosophy, they fulfill the will of God (only) through Christ (8:4), and only from him do they finally obtain the criteria for that which in the world can be called good, well-pleasing, and perfect. It is no longer that which every person says and thinks which determines the Christian life. Rather, those who believe test, with the help of their reason, now oriented to Christ, what is really good and what is reprehensible from among all that is thought and desired. As a result, they are zealous for that which is good in God's opinion (cf. 1 Thess. 5:15; Gal. 6:10; Rom. 2:10; 12:9; 13:3).

Romans 12:1–2 thus offers a normative program for the Pauline exhortation to the church (*Paraklesis*). It concerns the worship of those who have been justified, which is to be conducted in the everyday affairs of the world according to the criteria established by Christ for what is good and what is reprehensible. In the following passage, Paul now presents paradigmatic instructions for what this (all-encompassing) worship of God should look like (in Rome).

II. 12:3–8. Community according to the Measure of Faith

(3) For by virtue of the grace which has been granted to me, I say to each (individual) among you not to strive for anything beyond that for which one must

strive, but to strive to be prudent, each one, as God has apportioned to him the standard of faith. (4) For just as in one body we have many members, but all the members do not have the same function, (5) thus we, the many, are one body in Christ, but each one in relationship to one another as members. (6) Indeed, we have different gifts of grace according to the grace which has been bestowed on us; perhaps prophecy, (but then) in the right relationship to faith, (7) or perhaps service, (but then) in (the Spirit) of service, or perhaps the teacher, (but then) in (the Spirit) of teaching, (8) or perhaps the preacher, (but then) in (the Spirit) of preaching, the benefactor, (but then) in (the Spirit) of sincerity, the administrator, (but then) in (the Spirit) of being ready to take initiative, the one who bestows care, (but then) in (the Spirit) of friendliness.

A. The structure of the text is simple. In v. 3 Paul formulates an exhortation aimed at every individual member of the Christian house churches in Rome, which is then supported in vv. 4 + 5. This support is subsequently specified more specifically in vv. 6–8. As a whole, the apostle is concerned to call to mind the standard according to which the church of Jesus Christ lives together and by which she can perform her service of testimony effectively.

Already in 1 Cor. 12:12ff. Paul had spoken of the Christian community as the "body of Christ." In Rom. 12:4f. he picks this up again, and this way of speaking is then continued in Col. 1:18ff.; 2:17ff; 3:15; Eph. 1:23; 2:16; 4:4ff., 12ff.; 5:30. It is still not definitively clear just how the apostle came to his designation of the church as the "body of Christ," a designation which is characteristic of his letters. Nevertheless, as F. Lang (*Die Briefe an die Korinther*, NTD 7, 1986, 178ff.) has already established, a threefold root for this concept can be detected. For the apostle this new way of speaking about the church as Christ's body came about from a combination of the tradition of the Lord's Supper, the so-called Adam-Christ typology (in 1 Cor. 15:44–49; Rom. 5:12–21), and the tradition taken up by the apostle concerning Jesus as the Son of Man-messiah who was given up to death and resurrected for us (cf. the use of Psalm 8 concerning the Son of Man in 1 Cor. 15:27 and Rom. 5:12ff. with Mk. 10:45 par.). According to biblical and early Jewish tradition, the heavenly Son of Man represents the people of the saints of the Most High, that is Israel as the people of God. In that one Son of Man all Israel stands embodied before God (cf. Dan. 7:13f., 22, 27). Linguistically, in the Semitic languages "Son of Man" simply means a "person." This points us, in turn, to the early Jewish speculation concerning Adam, the first person. According to 4 Ezra 6:54 and Pseudo-Philo, *Lib. Ant.* 32.15, the people of God came forth from the body of Adam, whereas elsewhere Adam's body is said to be as large as all humanity (cf. T. Ab., Rez. B, 8:13; cf. with Rez. A, 11:9). Since Paul sees in Christ not only the Son of Man and new Adam, but also views the eschatological "Israel of God" to be the church of Christ (cf. Gal. 6:16), it is natural for him, as a converted Jew, to see the Israel of God, that is, the Christian church, as represented before God in Jesus. For Jesus' death stands vicariously for the death of all, while his resurrection guarantees for all the resurrection from the dead (1 Cor. 15:20–22; Rom. 5:18f.; 6:3–5). Or expressed differently, the surrender of the body of Christ to death on the cross liberates all those who believe from the Law's declaration of guilt (Rom. 7:6). Furthermore, by their common participation in the one bread of the Lord's Supper, which materially symbolizes Jesus' body of death, "the many," that is, all who belong to the community, are incorporated into the fellowship of the one body of Christ (1 Cor. 10:16f.). Their unity with Christ and Christ's unity with them in one body are as strong as the marital fellowship of husband and wife, in which the two form one flesh (cf. 1 Cor. 6:13, 16f.; Gal. 3:27f.; Eph. 5:29–33 with Gen. 2:21–24).

The one body of Christ is thus for Paul not merely a metaphor, but a reality which has been established for believing Christians by the crucified and resurrected Christ. By virtue of their baptism they are therefore "baptized into" Christ's body (1 Cor. 12:13; Gal. 3:27). Moreover, at every celebration of the Lord's Supper they are reassured anew of their participation and fellowship in the body of Christ (1 Cor. 10:16f.; 11:20, 23–24). Hence, the obligation to a new and common way of life, which Paul impresses upon the Corinthians in 1 Corinthians 12 and the Christians from Rome in Rom. 12:3–21, proceeds at the same time both from his addressees' experience of baptism and from their participation in the Lord's Supper. The special point of this obligation is that, through the embodied worship of God by the members of the body of Christ, the fact that Christ is really present in the world in a bodily manner is and should become visible for all those who still do not believe. In other words, the love of Christ for all people is embodied in the obedience of Christians, which functions as a testimony to its reality.

But in order to appreciate the apostle's statements in Rom. 12:13ff. appropriately, not only must these connections from the history of tradition be made clear, but the difficult situation in which the Christian house churches in Rome were living, to which Paul writes, must also be kept in mind. As already noted in more detail in the introduction (see above, pp. 6–8), after the decree of the so-called Edict of Claudius the Christian house churches could no longer attach themselves to the synagogues, which enjoyed legal privileges, but had to form their own organizations. Moreover, they had to determine their form of organization in accord with valid Roman law. As a result, the only possibility which was available for the Christians was to organize themselves as an association of indigenous or immigrant citizens. But ever since the time of Caesar (murdered in 44 B.C.), it was strictly forbidden in Rome for such associations to become politically active. Even the faintest suspicion of conspiratorial activity led to their dissolution. Under these circumstances, the Christian house churches were open to the public and had to exist separate from the Jewish synagogues. But as such, they were exposed to constant supervision by the imperial secret agents and police institutions. Paul had surely heard of these circumstances through his friends and acquaintances mentioned in Romans 16. His statements of advice to the Roman Christians in chapters 12–15 are therefore determined by the desire to maintain the continuing existence and mission possibilities of the house churches in Rome for as long as they could be justified from a Christian perspective.

B. Hence, beginning in v. 3, the apostle is not simply stringing together statements of principle, [3] but already in v. 3 is directly addressing each Christian within the house churches in Rome. Although in this exhortation he makes use of a popular rhetorical play on words with the verb "to strive," he nevertheless has very concrete things in mind. In 8:5ff., Paul distinguished between a way and manner of striving against God which was determined by the flesh, and a manner of striving which was pleasing to God and determined by the Holy Spirit. Then in 11:13ff. he summoned the Gentile Christians in Rome not to exalt themselves over the Jews as a result of self-deception. Finally, in 16:17f. he will warn the Christians from Rome against those people who deviate from the doctrine of faith which was familiar in Rome and thus sow discord in the house churches. Under these circumstances it makes complete and practical sense when Paul urges every member of the church not to engage in autocratic ways of thinking, but to endeavor to gain that prudence which is measured by the standard of faith which has been established for all. In Paul's day, the catchword "prudence" occupied a highly ethical place of value. In the philosophies of the time, prudence belonged to the (four) main virtues to which a reasonable person should devote oneself. In the same way, Hellenistic Judaism saw prudence to be a gift of excellence with which the wisdom of God equips those who open themselves up to it (cf. Wis. 9:11). For Paul, prudence finds its standard and plumb line in the doctrine of faith which has been previously given to the church. As he already made clear in 6:17, this doctrine or standard is a highly esteemed blessing. In terms of content, it is identical with the "gospel" which the apostle cites in 1 Cor. 15:3–5. All the members of the church in Rome should therefore orient themselves by means of this gospel, and for the benefit of this common orientation renounce all striving which could rupture the fellowship of the believers.

The interpretation of v. 3 in terms of a measure or quantity of faith which is established individually by God for every member of the church, although it has been popular in the history of the church, is thus difficult to maintain from the Pauline letters. Paul does know of a strong and weak faith (cf. 14:1ff.), and he can speak of deficits in faith (1 Thess. 3:10), of its growth (2 Cor. 10:15), and of its intimate connection with love, without which even the faith which moves mountains is nothing (Gal. 5:6; 1 Cor. 13:2). Nevertheless, the criterion of faith given previously by God to every member of the church is not an individual criterion, but the gospel of Jesus' atoning death and resurrection, which is equally valid for all who believe. It is from this common basis of orientation that Paul draws his exhortation. [4] In support of his exhortation, he refers to the example of the many different members which together form one body and are assigned to one another, an example which was used throughout the ancient world (cf. Liv. 2.32; Dio Chrys., *Or.* 33.16). [5] The body to which the apostle refers, of course, is not just any fellowship in which people live together, but the fellowship of "the many" (for this expression, see above, p. 87) who, by virtue of the sacrificial death of Jesus, have been called to be the community of Jesus Christ (1 Cor. 10:16f.). In their individual diversity they are still all members of the one body of Christ and, as such, are obligated to unity. No one can or ought to endeavor to follow one's own ways of thinking and life at the cost of the other person. The apostle's following statements explain what this means more precisely. [6] The grace of God, on the basis of which they, as Christians, all live together, is imparted differently to every individual member of the church and makes it possible for each one to be active with his or her special gifts for the good of the body of Christ (cf. Eph. 4:7). The following list of the gifts of grace, which are indispensable for the building up and preservation of the church of Christ, is led off with that of prophecy and service. In regard to Spirit-led prophecy, one must pay careful attention that the prophetic statements correspond to the standard of faith which has been given previously to all. In chapter 11 Paul himself presented what this means, practically speaking. Arbitrary or, even worse, illusory prophecy is detrimental to the church (cf. 11:13ff.). [7] It is no different in regard to service. It may not be conducted simply according to partisan opinions, but must keep itself to the standard of what is useful for all. The spheres of prophetic activity and of service are then outlined by the apostle even more precisely. To prophecy belongs the duties of the teacher and of the preacher (on the basis of 2 Cor. 1:3ff., one could also translate it: of the minister who comforts). The teacher must adhere to the doctrine which has been prescribed to him and pass it on without falsifying it (cf. 6:17). [8] The preacher who is called to exhort and comfort the church must say and do that which serves the building up of the church (cf. 1 Cor. 14:1ff.). Even for those who are active in the service of the church there are therefore criteria from which, for the sake of the good of the church, they may not deviate. For example, the one who does good, who supports others from his or her own means, should do this sincerely and without secondary intentions. The one who presides over the church and must care for the ordered unity of the church's members should not dedicate himself to this task on the side, but with the requisite supply of strength and time. The one who is entrusted with the care of those members of the church who are suffering need should do this in a friendly manner and not with an air of repulsion or of superiority.

Taken as a whole, the following thus applies: The fellowship and testimony of the (house) church(es) in Rome, which together form the body of Christ, can flourish only when every individual member and group within the church remains mindful of the good of all, and thus sets aside individual interests for the sake of the common life and witness.

III. 12:9–21. The Way of Life in Love

(9) Let love be genuine. Abhor evil, hang on to that which is good, (10) be devoted from the heart to one another in brotherly love, seek to outdo one another in showing respect. (11) Do not be negligent in taking initiative, be aglow with the Spirit, serve the Lord, (12) rejoice in hope, be steadfast in affliction, persevere in prayer. (13) Contribute to the needs of the saints, be mindful of hospitality. (14) Bless those who persecute you; bless and curse not. (15) Rejoice with those who rejoice, weep with those who are weeping. (16) Be mindful among one another of unanimity. Do not strive after high things, but adapt oneself to humble things. Do not consider yourself to be wise. (17) Do not requite evil with evil to anyone. Be mindful of that which is good before (the eyes of) all people. (18) When possible (and) as far as it depends on you, maintain peace with all people. (19) Do not avenge yourselves, beloved, but make room for the wrath (of God), for it is written, "Vengeance is mine, I will repay, says the Lord." (20) Rather, "If your enemy is hungry, give him something to eat; if he is thirsty, give him something to drink. For if you do that, you will heap burning coals on his head." (21) Do not let yourself be overcome by evil, but overcome evil through the good.

Verse 15: Sir. 7:34; Verse 16: Prov. 3:7; Verse 17: Prov. 17:13; Verse 19: Deut. 32:35; Verse 20: Prov. 25:21f.

A. The instructions which are given here by the apostle in a loose series revolve around two poles, the love for one's neighbor which is to be exercised above all within the church, and the love for one's enemy which is to be exercised outwardly toward those who are not Christians. The (house) churches of the early Christians (and ancient church) could not have endured (for centuries) within a non-Christian environment without this twofold attitude.

What Paul demands here has its parallels in other apostolic letters (see below). Viewed as a whole, his exhortations are fed from a threefold source: from the Old Testament, from early Jewish instruction, and from the Jesus tradition. Beyond the explicit quotations in vv. 19 and 20, words from the Scriptures also resonate in vv. 15, 16, and 17. On the other hand, the early Jewish interpretation of the will of God provides the best parallels to v. 21. In T. Gad 6:1–3; T. Jos. 18:2; and T. Benj. 4:2–3 the renunciation of retribution and the need to extend forgiveness to one's (personal) enemy are already enjoined just as clearly as in Paul's writings. Finally, the Jesus tradition clearly stands behind v. 14 (cf. with Lk. 6:28 and Mtt. 5:44), while the relationship between v. 18 and Mtt. 5:9 can hardly be overlooked. The interweaving of these three strands of tradition can be explained when one considers that in all three cases it is a matter of the interpretation of the one will of God as it manifests itself in the Ten Commandments. The early Christian missionaries, including Paul, made use of the Old Testament and early Jewish interpretation of the divine commandments.

They then combined them with the Jesus tradition in order to instruct the missionary churches concerning the "way of righteousness" (Mtt. 21:32) which they are obligated to follow in obedience to their crucified and resurrected Lord. Hence, although the early Christian instructions concerning correct behavior exhibit manifold contacts with the popular philosophical ethics of the time, the distance between them also remains unmistakable. While Epictetus (*Diss.* 3.24.54–56) and Josephus (*Bell.* 4.494) both warn one of the dangers of humility and equate it with subservient shabbiness, Paul does not hesitate not only to summon his readers to precisely this humility, but also to present Jesus as the very model of humility (cf. Phil. 2:8).

Before one evaluates this section merely to be an exemplary list of traditional, albeit valid and foundational rules for Christian conduct, one should keep in mind the circumstances of the day. According to the report of the Roman historian Tacitus (*Annals* 13.32.2), in the year A.D. 58, that is, two years after the composition of the letter to the Romans, a Senate trial was brought against a prominent Roman woman, Pomponia Graecina, because she had been charged with "the exercise of a religion from a foreign land." Although the aristocratic woman was set free by the Roman court of honor, the incident documents how easily the house churches in Rome could incur enmity and be held under suspicion. For they no longer belonged to the synagogues and (according to Roman judgment) really were part of a foreign, oriental religion. At the time of the letter to the Romans, the Neronian persecution of Christians was thus already casting its shadow in advance over the Christian congregations.

B. The first group of exhortations in vv. 9–13 concern behavior within the community. [9] The instruction to live without hypocrisy in love and from love heads the entire list. The love of God in and through Jesus Christ is the ground of the Christian life of faith (8:35, 39). On this basis, in the Pauline letters (just as with Jesus and in the Johannine writings, cf. Mk. 12:31 par.; 1 John 4:7–14; John 13:34) love is the royal way for all who believe in Jesus Christ (cf. 1 Cor. 13). As the first concrete expression of this, the dual exhortation to abhor evil and to do what is good with all one's strength now follows. The path of the Christian is not to be determined by hate and a lack of love, but by love in accordance with Jesus' example (cf. Gal. 2:20 and Rom. 15:3). [10] In explicitly summoning his readers to brotherly love the apostle now develops further what has just been said (cf. in the same way already 1 Thess. 4:9 and, moreover, 1 Pet. 1:22; 2:17; 3:8; Heb. 13:1). Then, as previously done in Phil. 2:3, he advises the church to outdo one another in showing mutual respect (for a criticism of the opposing attitude, cf. the clear presentation in James 2:1ff.). In chapter 14 this exhortation will be developed further in more detail. But already at this point it is clear that the interactions of the members of the congregation with one another are to be determined by the the gift of love which all members of the community experience from Jesus. Moreover, this gift should go beyond and change the criteria and rules of behavior which are in effect for them as

Gentiles and Jews. [11] A threefold group of instructions now concern the life of the church as a whole. Just as the book of Revelation summoned the churches in Asia Minor (cf. Rev. 2:4; 3:15f.), so too the apostle summons the Christians from Rome not to be negligent in taking initiative, in their spiritual engagement, and in their service for Christ. The church is in need of the Spirit and the courage "of the first witnesses," not only in the beginning, but also throughout the years of its common witness. [12] A second threefold group of exhortations now supplement the first. By the power of the hope which inspires them, the members of the church should endure what they encounter in unshakable joy (cf. similarly 1 Thess. 5:16; Phil. 3:1). They can and ought to remain patient in the midst of afflictions (cf. thus already 5:3) and practice prayer unceasingly, which through Christ's mediation binds them with God and God with them (cf. 8:26f.; 1 Thess. 5:17; Col. 4:2; Eph. 6:18 and Acts 1:14; 2:42; 6:4). [13] Next to the spiritual obligations stand the practical. Here Paul first names the obligation to care for those fellow members of the church who are in need, whom Paul designates as the "saints" who have been made holy through Jesus' sacrificial death (cf. 1 Cor. 1:2; 6:11). The Pauline exhortation points (together with 12:8) to the fact that in the Christian churches of Rome—as in the Jewish synagogues—regular collections were also taken for the poor of the church and that those who were poor were then cared for by specially commissioned members of the church from the proceeds of the collection. In addition to showing care for fellow Christians who are suffering need in one's own churches, Paul also exhorts them to show hospitality (cf. to this theme also 1 Tim. 3:2; Tit. 1:8; 1 Pet. 4:9 and Heb. 13:2). Without Christian hospitality, fellow Christians and the missionaries who were traveling through were in difficult straits in the ancient cities.

[14] Beginning in v. 14, Paul deals in a second group of instructions with obligations which grow for the members of the church (predominantly) out of their encounter with non-Christians. In doing so, the summons to love one's enemy stands at the head of the list, now given in the sharpened form of the exhortation to bless those who persecute the Christians and to renounce the practice of cursing one's persecutor, a command which is also known from the Jesus tradition (cf. Lk. 6:27ff. par.; 9:52ff.). Paul and the early Christian missionaries were constantly exposed to persecutions (cf. 1 Cor. 4:11; 2 Cor. 11:24ff.). The Christians in Judea and Thessalonica also knew them, and the contours of coming persecutions were already becoming visible in Rome at that time (see above). In this situation, Paul asks the Romans to behave in the way which was not only taught by Jesus himself, but also proved true by him (cf. Lk. 23:33f. with 1 Pet. 2:23 and Is. 53:12). According to 1 Cor. 4:12f., the apostle himself also endeavored to maintain this attitude. Loving one's enemy offers the classic example of what it means for a Christian to be no longer conformed to the criteria of the age of this world (cf. v. 2 and for this theme also 1 Cor. 13:5–7). Indeed, until Christianity became a state religion in the fourth century A.D., the

practice of loving one's enemy remained one of the main characteristics of the Christian church within its non-Christian environment! [15] While the Stoic Epictetus summoned his disciples to persuade others through being immovable in joy and suffering (cf. *Diss.* 2.5.23), Paul summons the Christians in Rome to identify themselves with their fellow men and women in a shared joy and shared suffering. This applies not only within the church (cf. 1 Cor. 12:26), but also toward one's fellow men and women overall (cf. Sir. 7:34). Christians do not comprise a self-enclosed fellowship, but are openly sympathetic toward the joys and sufferings of their fellow citizens. [16] Of course—as Paul enjoins in again taking up the instructions from v. 3—they can attempt such an openness only if they are mindful of their commonality and if they, in accordance with Prov. 3:7, give up all wise self-conceit so that they are prepared to accept the inconspicuous cares and problems of the simple members of the church. Instead of warning one of the dangers of a fawning and servile humility, as Epictetus did (cf. *Diss.* 3.24.54–56), Paul comes to the opposite conclusion based on the biblical picture of God (cf. Pss. 113:5–7; 138:6; Sir. 11:12; Lk. 1:48) and on Jesus' way of sacrifice (cf. Phil. 2:8; 1 Cor. 1:26–31). Hence, it is precisely this turning to the "lowly and the insulted" and their needs which comports well with the members of the church of Jesus Christ and makes visible before the world that the crucified and resurrected Christ is and remains truly present in this world. [17] The next exhortation is also formulated in view of the church's witness before the eyes of all people (cf. Prov. 3:4; Phil. 4:5). It is based on Prov. 17:13; 20:22; Jer. 18:20, and in terms of content stands in close accord with Jesus' prohibition concerning retaliation (Lk. 6:29f. par.). Ever since Paul wrote 1 Thess. 5:15, it has been part of the rules of conduct taught by Paul in all of his churches. Moreover, 1 Pet. 3:9 stands in this same tradition. The common nature of the apostolic exhortation to the churches is obvious here. As already seen in v. 14, the concern of this exhortation, in terms of content, is the testimony of that love which remains true to Jesus' way and commandment while itself still in the situation of being treated wrongly. Only where the demonic circle of "as you do to me—so will I do to you" is broken can life flourish in peace. [18] The Christians' testimony of love is their contribution to peace, to which they, together with all people whom the church encounters, strive (cf. Mtt. 5:5, 9). Through their Lord, Christians are placed into a position of peace with God (5:1), who is himself the God of love and peace (2 Cor. 13:11). On this basis it is their task to live as witnesses and keepers of the common peace, wherever and however this is possible. From the side of the church of Christ, whether or not to work for peace is therefore not a matter of debate, although, as a worst-case scenario, the opposing side can disrupt it or even reject it. The next verses deal with what should happen in such cases.

[19] Because God is the judge and he has reserved for himself the right to judge those who lie in wait for the community (Deut. 32:35), it is not for Christians themselves to punish those who do evil. Rather, they should patiently

make room for God's coming judgment of wrath. [20] In the meantime, it is their task, as Paul expounds it with words from the Greek Bible (Prov. 25:21f.), to stir up their adversaries to repentance through the doing of good in view of the approaching wrathful judgment. "Standing with burning coals on one's head is attested in an . . . Egyptian text as a ritual of penitence" and is therefore to be understood in Prov. 25:21f. as "a picture of remorse" (H. Ringgren). This same interpretation also commends itself for Rom. 12:20. Even in a situation of opposition and persecution, Christians should still endeavor to keep their opponents from the consequences of their evil deeds. [21] Paul then closes this section with a striking instruction reminiscent of Jewish instructions to the community. In T. Benj. 4:2–3 it states, "The upright man . . . has mercy on all, even when they are sinners. And even when they plan evil concerning him, he overcomes evil through the doing of good, for he is kept by God." Moreover, in early Judaism, Joseph was taken to be a prime example of such an attitude (cf., e.g., T. Jos. 17). In T. Jos. 18:3 he is thus praised for his generosity (toward his brothers). Instead of Joseph, however, the apostolic exhortation is based on the conduct and example of Jesus (cf. Rom. 15:3; Phil. 2:1–11; 1 Pet. 2:21–25).

IV. 13:1–7. The Christian's Relationship to the Institutions of the State

The paragraph which now follows has persistently determined the political ethic of Christianity. Yet in the course of the history of the church and its interpretation of Scripture it has undergone very different evaluations. It is thus all the more important to portray clearly its original meaning as carefully as possible.

(1) Every person should submit to the governing authorities. For there is no authority except from God; but those which exist are established by God. (2) Therefore (it is true) that the one who opposes the governing authority is resisting the ordinance of God. But those who offer such resistance will bring upon themselves the judgment (of God). (3) For those who rule are not (a ground for) fear for work which is good, but for that which is evil. Do you desire not (to have) fear the governing authority? (Then) do good and you will experience commendation from it. (4) For it is God's servant for you for good. But if you do evil, be afraid! For it does not carry the sword to no avail. For it is (also) God's servant as an avenger who brings wrath on the one who does evil. (5) Therefore, to submit is necessary, not only on account of the judgment of wrath, but also on account of one's conscience. (6) Therefore, indeed, you also pay the taxes that are due. For those who permanently concern themselves with this are God's employed servants. (7) Give to every one what you owe them: to the one (to whom you owe) taxes, taxes; to the one (to whom you owe) dues, dues; to the one (to whom you owe) fear, fear; to the one (to whom you owe) honor, honor.

A. Verses 1–7 form a self-enclosed unit thematically. But the textual tradition does not suggest, either for the paragraph as a whole or for v. 5, that either one be considered a subsequent interpolation. On the one hand, important catch-words used by Paul in 12:1–21 once again appear in 13:1–7. Thus, for example, the language of "that which is good" and "that which is evil" appears in 12:2, 9, 17, 21 and 13:3, 4; of the "wrath (of God's judgment)" in 12:19 and 13:4, 5; and of God's "vengeance" and "avenger" in 12:19 and 13:4. On the other hand, the statements concerning "being indebted" in 13:7 prepare for the manner of ex-pression and argumentation in 13:8. Hence, from the standpoint of its language, Rom. 13:1–7 is firmly embedded in the present context of the letter.

The text receives its structure through the three instructions given in vv. 1, 5, and 7. The instructions from vv. 1 and 5 correspond to one another. And in each case they are further explained by Paul. The foundational instruction from v. 1 is explained by four sentences, each of which is linked to what proceeds by "for" (= vv. 1b–4), while its repetition in v. 5 is explained further by v. 6. Verse 7 then not only gives a four-part instruction; it also functions at the same time as a summary of what has been said in this section.

Within the New Testament, this paragraph has close parallels to 1 Pet. 2:13–17 (and to 1 Tim. 2:1f.; Tit. 3:1f.). In it three strands of tradition are inex-tricably intertwined. (1) These verses employ the technical language of the of-fice of the Roman magistrates to an astounding degree, and at the same time conform to the pattern of the state which was common in the Hellenistic-Roman period. The "governing authorities" (v. 1), "rulers" (v. 3), and "employed servants" (v. 6) designate the numerous offices and office bearers of the exten-sive bureaucracy of the Roman state. The language in v. 3 of "commendation" by the power of the state can be beautifully illustrated by the custom of the Roman emperor sending letters of commendation to deserving officials and in-dividual cities in the Roman empire in the event that they had manifested espe-cially good conduct politically. On the basis of its use as a (technical) expression, the "sword" concerning which Paul speaks in v. 4 refers not to the sword of judgment, but to the state police and judicial authority. The police soldiers who accompanied the Roman tax collectors (in Egypt) were called "sword bearers." Moreover, the designation of the imperial (finance) officials as "employed ser-vants" (v. 6) was also customary.

(2) But these verses are also unmistakably based on Old Testament and Jew-ish tradition. Already in the letter of the prophet Jeremiah to the Jewish exiles in Babylon from Jer. 29:1–23 the people are summoned to the greatest possible loyalty toward the power of Babylon as a foreign government. Moreover, this biblical instruction persistently influenced Pharisaism and early Judaism. Thus, until the outbreak of the (first) Jewish war of resistance against Rome in A.D. 66, offerings "for the Caesar and the Roman people" were presented twice a day in the Jerusalem temple (Josephus, *Bell.* 2.197). Furthermore, in the Sayings of the Fathers 3:2 the following saying by Hanina, the last Jewish head official of

the temple, is transmitted: "Pray for the well-being of the government; for if there had been no fear before it, we would already have swallowed one another alive." In Prov. 8:15f. it states that the kings and rulers on earth judge and decide rightly by virtue of the wisdom granted to them by God. In Sir. 17:17 we read that God "orders a ruler for every people," while in Wis. 6:3–4 it is emphasized that the power of the earthly rulers is granted to them only by God, so that they are "servants of his kingdom" and stand under the judgment of God if they misuse their power. Conversely, beginning with Prov. 24:21 and extending on to Philo (cf., above all, *Leg. Gai.* 140), the constant Jewish conviction is that fear and the giving of honor are due to those who rule.

(3) The question is disputed, however, whether in vv. 1–7 reference is also being made to the narrative concerning Jesus' position in regard to taxes owed to Caesar (Mk. 12:13–17; Mtt. 22:15–22; Lk. 20:20–26). If one compares the three accounts of the report which we have in the Gospels with Rom. 13:1–7, the Lukan text clearly stands the closest. Only in Luke, as in Rom. 13:1f., is there reference to the authority (of the state) (cf. Lk. 20:20), and only in Lk. 20:22 is "giving taxes" mentioned, as in Rom. 13:6f. Inasmuch as Paul also betrays a special acquaintance with the Lukan tradition elsewhere in his letters (cf., e.g., 1 Cor. 2:6, 8 with Lk. 23:13, 35; 24:20; Acts 3:17; 13:27; or 1 Cor. 11:23–26 with Lk. 22:19–20 and 1 Cor. 15:4–5 with Lk. 24:34), it is quite possible that the (Lukan form of the) narrative about Jesus was present in the apostle's mind during his dictation of this text as well. Of course, it is striking that for Paul the question concerning the paying of taxes takes precedence in v. 7, while he handles the command which was of more importance for Jesus, that is, to give to God what is God's, only by way of suggestion.

But interestingly, it can easily be explained historically why the apostle accented his discussion in this way. The Roman historian Tacitus reports in his *Annals* (13.50–51) that in A.D. 57 or 58 the Roman people submitted a grievance to Caesar concerning the shameless and extortionary practices of the tax and duty collectors. In response to this protest, Caesar considered for a short time relinquishing the paying of taxes altogether, but was hindered by his advisors from this plan, since it would have been ruinous for the state finances. Overall, therefore, only a limited reform of the nature of taxes and duty came about. But Tacitus also speaks in his report of the concern on the part of those responsible that, without a curbing of the greed of those who held the state lease for collecting taxes among the people, "the burden of the tax carried throughout so many years without complaint could change suddenly into embitterment." Suetonius confirms this entire occurrence in his biography of Nero (10:1). From Tacitus and Suetonius we thus encounter the situation that at the time of the composition of the letter to the Romans one had to suffer in an extraordinary way under high taxes and duties (both) in Rome (and throughout the entire Roman empire). This pressure was somewhat relieved for the citizens of Rome in that, besides duty, they had only to pay certain taxes such as sales tax, inheritance tax, and taxes for emancipation (of slaves), but did not have to pay any income tax. But unfortunately we do not know to what degree these tax privileges were also enjoyed by traveling Jewish entrepreneurs like Prisca and Aquila (16:3), Jewish-Christian missionaries like Andronicus and Junia (16:7), or the members of the house churches in the city of Rome, who by no means came only from Rome. Hence, the paragraph of Rom. 13:1–7, which at first appears to be formulated in an entirely general fashion, is in fact aimed in verses 6 + 7 at a Roman situation which is both contemporary and pressing. On the basis of a comparison of Rom. 13:1–7 and 1 Pet. 2:13–17, one could also say, therefore, that the basic apostolic exhortation to loyalty toward the institutions of the state, which underlies both texts, is thus actualized and sharpened by Paul specifically in regard to the question of paying duty and taxes, since this question was especially important at the time of the writing of Romans. Consequently, in these verses the apostle is not simply concerned only with foundational instruction concerning the relationship of Christians to the state. Rather, and more importantly still, he is concerned with the practical question of how the small Roman house churches should conduct themselves toward the state institutions and toward those who hold the state leases for tax collection, who are attempting to exact duty and other (indirect) taxes from them in an entirely arbitrary manner. Paul's concern is all the more crucial in that these house churches are excluded from every direct, political possibility of influence and as an association stand under a strict prohibition against political activity (see above, pp. 191f.).

B. Romans 13:1–7 stands under the thematic heading of 12:1–2, as do all of the instructions in chapters 12:1–15:13. At this point, Paul's goal is to elucidate, by means of a contemporary and pressing example, what the all-encompassing worship of God, which Paul demands from Christians, looks like in the midst of the everyday occurrences of the world. Specifically, the "good" which they must emulate in all situations, and therefore also as citizens of Rome, is love. Moreover, vv. 1–7 are framed by statements which point to the imminent day of God's judgment and the eschatological coming of Jesus Christ (cf. Rom. 12:19–21 and 13:11–14). In this eschatological situation, therefore, the Christians from Rome are to endeavor to exercise peace and love toward every person (12:18, 21). This applies to the state institutions as well.

[1] In harmony not only with the Old Testament, but also with early Jewish tradition and the tradition concerning Jesus, Paul emphasizes at the beginning of his instruction the obligation of "every person," that is, of both non-Christians and Christians, to submit themselves to the existing political authorities. The reason for this is that these authorities do not possess their power as a result of bypassing God. Instead, they possess and exercise it according to divine arrangement (cf. Jer. 29:7; Dan. 2:21; Prov. 8:15; Sir. 17:17; Wis. 6:3f.; Letter of Aristeas 196, 219, 224; Lk. 20:25). The apostle establishes this basic point without erecting a more profound theological theory concerning the nature of the state

or even of God's gracious act of provision in the government. He is satisfied with the statement that the institutions of the state exercise their power according to the will of God, the creator and sustainer of the world. [2] Since this is true, the one who rebels against the power of the state is resisting the arrangement, and with it, the will of God. The Greek word which the apostle uses here was still translated by Luther with the word "order," although today it is usually rendered "ordinance." It does not mean an institution of creation, but a legally valid notification or even an announcement of the will of God (Gal. 3:19). Correspondingly, the state is not an order of life directly instituted by God, but a (human) form of life which exists from and according to God's directive (cf. 1 Pet. 2:13). Whoever obstructs this ordinance, brings God's judgment of condemnation upon him- or herself (cf. 2:2f.; 3:8). From the remarks of Paul (which in today's terms are astoundingly one-sided) it is apparent that he expressly dissuades the Christians in Rome from all opposition against the authority of the state. We do not know exactly whether among the Christians in Rome there were those who were inclined toward such opposition. Josephus reports that in the first years after the inauguration of the reign of Nero as Caesar the movement in Judea and Jerusalem of the zealots who were fighting against the rule of Rome was strengthened (*Ant.* 20.160ff.). But historically it is more than risky to transfer this report concerning Judea and Jerusalem to the Jewish synagogues in Rome, and then from them on to the Christian churches! For by the middle of the 50s A.D. the house churches in Rome had already formed their own associations, which were distinct from the synagogues. Moreover, their problem was not political opposition, but rather the question of the degree to which the church, which has been redeemed from the rule of sin through Christ's sacrificial death, should and may still have dealings with unbelievers at all (cf. 1 Cor. 5:9ff.; 6:1–11). It is in this context that Paul exhorts one to have respect for the state institutions and dissuades the Roman Christians from all manner of behavior which could be interpreted as political protest. [3] He sees no cause for such a protest, since only those who do evil have any cause to fear those who rule according to God's will, while those who take great pains to do the good are benefited and commended by them—and for Paul Christians also certainly belong to this group (cf. 12:2)! Surely the Christians in Rome also knew about the imperial commendations which were given for especially deserving officials and even entire cities within the empire. The "good" for which they were commended consisted in their faithfulness to the emperor, and Paul does not hesitate to urge the Roman Christians to continue just such a faithfulness. For him such faithfulness is in harmony with the will of God, and it is precisely those who believe who are able to recognize this and should observe it. [4] The power of the state is God's servant (cf. Wis. 6:4), if and when it maintains justice and order for the benefit of every citizen. The person who dares to violate either one experiences the state's police and judicial authority. In this case, as well, the power of the state serves God and assists in dispensing the divine judgment of wrath over every evildoer (cf. 2:9). In spite of the mistrust now dawning in Rome in regard to the Christian house churches (see above, p. 195) and the burdensome pressure of the taxes (cf. vv. 6f.), Paul (still) sees no cause to doubt that the power of the Roman state serves God's intention to preserve the world rather than allowing it to sink into chaos. (But in view of the persecutions against Christians in A.D. 64, together with the blasphemous demands of the Roman cult surrounding Caesar, the character of Rome is then evaluated differently in Rev. 13:1–8.) [5] Because, however, the apostle does not yet know of any persecution of Christians being directed by the state, the following exhortation is consistent. Paul formulates it without having any models to follow in his tradition, and it is precisely this unique character of Paul's exhortation which gives these verses their special significance within the whole of 13:1–7. Paul's point is that for Christians there is a double motive for loyal submission to the power of the state. The first reason is the reality of God's judgment of wrath upon evildoers as representatively carried out by the state courts. But fear of the power of punishment alone can and should not settle the matter. It is important to Paul, in addition, that the Christians from Rome submit "for the sake of conscience" to that which the state demands from them. According to 2:15, the conscience is a general human phenomenon, namely the consciousness of good and evil. One could also say that the conscience is every individual person's critical consciousness of responsibility. But 13:5 is concerned with more than this. According to 12:2, it is precisely the Christians who are called to recognize and adhere to the good in the world, which is God's will. Their conscience is thus oriented to the goodwill of God recognized by them. They should submit to the institutions of the state, therefore, because they recognize to what degree these institutions serve the good which God intends, and at the same time restrain the evil, which God does not intend. In other words, Christians should submit because of the responsibility which derives from their insight into that which the state performs for them and for all citizens in accordance with God's ordinance. Although Paul does not intend to make the Christians from Rome into patriots who are faithful to Caesar, he nevertheless expects them to fulfill their obligations as citizens on the basis of their Christian insight into God's will and way with the world. [6] The fact that up until now they have paid the taxes which have been demanded from them (and will continue to do so in the future) is a confirmation for the apostle that the Roman Christians accept and understand what he expects from them. Paul welcomes the fact that the Christians from Rome pay their dues as an example of the complaint-free patience mentioned by Tacitus. He does not consider them to be the kind of people who boycott their taxes, but regards them to be exemplary taxpayers. But in his discussion he also takes into consideration the state-licensed tax collectors and officials. In performing their occupation they too stand not only in the service of Rome, but also of God. Here Paul is certainly thinking of the fact that, with the help of the monies collected by those authorized to deal with the finances, the state is doing that which contributes to the welfare of all and is necessary. For example, the safety of the avenues of traffic and commerce guaranteed by Rome was a great advantage for the traveling early Christian missionaries, Paul included. [7] On this basis Paul concludes his entire exhortation with the instruction that the Christians from Rome should give to every person his or her due (as one who stands directly in the service of the state, but indirectly in the service of God): to the tax collector, taxes; to the one given the lease to collect dues, dues; to the police soldiers who punish the evildoers and (for this purpose) bear the sword, fear (cf. vv. 3f.); and to the various occupants of the power of the state, honor (cf. Sir. 10:23–24; Philo, *Leg. Gai.* 140; Josephus, *Ant.* 6.80; 9.153 with 1 Pet. 2:17). If the text is interpreted in this way, 13:1–7 takes on a clear thematic coherence, while at the same time providing the best transition to v. 8 in terms of content.

The apostle's general manner of expression also makes it possible, of course, to posit that at the end of v. 7 Paul is once again taking up Jesus' word from Lk. 20:25 and on this basis intends to recall the fear which is due God himself above all others (cf. 1 Pet. 2:17 with Sir. 1:1ff.; 2 Cor. 5:11; 7:1; Rom. 3:18). On the other hand, on the basis of 12:10 (and 1 Pet. 2:17: "Honor all people!"), the honor owed could also be thought to refer to the fact that Christians owe such honor to every person. In this case as well such a reading would provide a possible transition to 13:8, though not as clear as in the previous possibility. The common doctrinal tradition from which Rom. 13:1–7 and 1 Pet. 2:17 both proceed can thus obviously lead to conclusions that are accented differently. Hence, although 1 Pet. 2:17 is formulated more precisely than Rom 13:7, this does not imply a contrast to Paul.

Romans 13:1–7, taken as a whole, presents an apostolic instruction from Paul's perspective concerning the way in which, in their specific time and situation, the Christians from Rome should conduct themselves toward the ruling authority of the state and its demands in regard to taxes. The Christian house churches already belong to Christ, the eschatological Lord of the world, and as his witnesses they are approaching God's impending day of judgment. As they do so they should respect the existing power of the government and its demand for money, since they recognize that by means of the state authorities God is promoting the good and holding evil in check not only for the benefit of all people in general, but also for the churches. The intention which Paul pursues with his statements thus gives these verses an undeniable one-sidedness. Yet this one-sidedness also makes it apparent and advisable that the fundamental question of how Christians should relate to the power of the state *per se* should not to be decided from Rom. 13:1–7 alone, but on the basis of all of the pertinent texts of the Old and New Testaments.

Excursus 13:
Christian Life under the Power of the State

Romans 13:1–7 is indeed a very important passage. But it is not the only text which must be taken into consideration in order to observe the way in which Paul desired to see *the life of Christians* regulated *under the power of the state.*

1. The apostle's own life shows that he had already developed an attitude toward the state authorities of his time of both distance and tolerance at the same time. From birth Paul had already possessed the coveted Roman right of citizenship (cf. Acts 22:28). This right bestowed on him the position of a privileged citizen of the state, to whom applied not only the respective indigenous legal rights, but also and above all the overarching Roman rights of the Roman empire. As a Jew who grew up and was educated in Jerusalem (Acts 22:3), Paul thus recognized the jurisdiction of the Jewish court, and as an apostle on his missionary journeys he continued for a long time to submit himself as well to the synagogue communities in the Diaspora, which were legally independent (cf. 2 Cor. 11:24). Three times Paul even patiently endured the Roman punishment of whipping for publicly disturbing the peace (cf. 2 Cor. 11:25 with Acts 16:20ff.). But after his arrest in Jerusalem, when it became apparent that he was to answer to the highest Jewish court for being an alleged desecrater of the temple and when it was equally apparent that his conviction was very probable, Paul made use of his rights as a Roman citizen and had his case transferred to the imperial court in Rome (cf. Acts 25:9–12).

2. In the same way, it is also possible to understand the Pauline instructions concerning the life of Christians under the state courts under the rubric of "distance and tolerance."

2.1. In 1 Cor. 6:1–11 the apostle summons the Christians from Corinth to a way of acting in which the church of Christ literally renounces the public legal institution available in the city and attempts to settle (in a way that is legally binding) budding conflicts between Christians within their own ranks. For Paul the independent jurisdiction of the Jewish communities of the Diaspora may have served as a model for this arrangement. But according to 1 Cor. 6:2, 9ff. and 2 Cor. 6:14–7:1, the theological basis for the distancing of the Christians from prescribed state administration of justice is found for Paul in the fact that the "saints" (= Christians), who have been sanctified through Jesus' atoning death and called to be co-judges with Christ in the future, may no longer take part in earthly legal affairs on the same level with those over whom they will one day hold court. In his emphasis on the distance between the community of the disciples and the unbelieving world, the apostle finds himself in complete

harmony with Jesus (cf. Mk. 10:42ff. par.). It is therefore quite understandable (and on the basis of the Pauline texts can also not be criticized
in principle) that an independent canon law came to be developed within
the church with reference to 1 Cor. 6:1–11.

2.2. In Rom. 13:1–7 Paul summons the Christians from Rome to the
greatest possible loyalty toward the existing power of the state and sees in
it an ordinance of God. In harmony with the will of God, which created
and graciously sustains the world, the state institutions are to promote the
good and restrain evil (with the power of the police). Christians should be
the first to recognize this with gratitude. They should also not refuse the
state demands for dues and taxes. But before one concludes on the basis of
Rom. 13:1–7 that "[n]obody before has so understood and expressed the
dignity and significance of the state the way Paul has," and then concludes
as far as the preservation of the existing world from chaos is concerned
that, for the apostle, "the government plainly (belongs) together with the
gospel" (so P. Althaus in the excursus "Christianity and the State" in the
previous edition of this commentary), the following must be kept in mind.
In Rom. 13:1–7 Paul equally forgoes a comprehensive presentation of the
hierarchy of the Roman offices of the state, such as that reported by the
Hellenistic rhetorician Aristides in his praise of Rome (cf. *Or.* 26.31f.). He
also does not present a fundamental discussion concerning the legitimate
and illegitimate exercise of one's ruling power, like that presented in detail
in the Letter of Aristeas (187–224). In spite of the undeniably idealistic
tone in which Paul writes, he is not intending to speak timelessly "of the divinely established nature and mandate of the government," as Althaus
maintains. Rather, he is merely calling for an appropriate respect before
those who bear the power of the Roman state and who exercise their governing authority according to God's ordinance. Moreover, like all powers
on the earth, they too must answer before God's throne in the final judgment. Furthermore, submission to the state institutions and a willingness
to pay dues and taxes are constituent elements of that embodied worship
of God in the midst of the everyday affairs of the world to which Paul calls
Christians in Rom. 12:1f. It is precisely this calling which shows that, according to the letter to the Romans as well, Christians stand and live at a
distance from the present world-age and its thought norms. In contrast to
the world, it is the love of God which determines their lives in their service
of witness. As a result, they have been given the mandate to maintain
peace with all the people whom they encounter to the degree that it is hu-
manly possible for them to do so (Rom. 12:9, 14, 17–18, 21; 13:8–10).

3. Finally, if one attempts to push through to a theological evaluation of
Paul's perspective, several circumstances must be considered.

3.1. Romans 13:1–7 is by no means the only New Testament text that
deals with the relationship of Christians to the state, but only one of several

equally important passages: Mk. 12:13–17 par.; Acts 5:29; (Rom. 13:1–7) 1 Pet. 2:13–17; Revelation 13. According to all of these texts, Christians must regard the state as a form of government which, in accordance with God's ordinance and his will, restrains chaos. For Christians, there can be no question of toying with the idea of anarchy. But Christians must also continue to expect that the power of the state will take on demonic features. These impulses can confront them with the decisive question of whether they desire to confess Christ or give their allegiance to the bearers of political power who claim for themselves divine dignity and authority. In this, and in all other cases in which the testimony of the gospel is prohibited or essentially limited, Acts 5:29 thus applies: "One must obey God more than men!" Nevertheless, all of the New Testament texts dissuade one from violent opposition against the power of the state. Furthermore, the possibility that the Christians, who were completely without influence politically, could one day successfully insist upon a humane form of government which corresponds to the claims of the gospel, and then go on to bring it about, did not yet even exist within the field of vision of the New Testament texts.

3.2. It is therefore demanding too much from the biblical statements concerning the state, and at the same time overloads them, if one attempts to extract from them a theological theory concerning the "order of creation and preservation" of the state. God ordains that the state can and should exercise authority. But the state is a "human institution" (1 Pet. 2:13), that is, a form of government created by mankind for mankind. It is consequently to be respected and promoted by Christians. But the state is not to be exaggerated theologically so that the government itself is viewed as an expression of God's grace!

3.3. While during the biblical period Christians could not exert any substantial influence on the state and its exercise of power, today Christian citizens have the possibility of influencing the state institutions directly and indirectly in many countries and of taking upon themselves the responsibility of governing. Under these circumstances Christians need principles which can be discussed and which will make it possible for them to combine their Christian faith with their responsibility as citizens of the state. Measured by the biblical texts and presuppositions, such principles are to be evaluated on the basis of whether they maintain the difference between the church (as the body of Christ) and the civil community, whether they adequately bring to bear God's will in Christ on both forms of life, and whether they relate church and state positively to one another.

In the Protestant tradition, two such paradigms, above all, have been put forward for consideration. The first is Luther's traditional doctrine that the Christian, although a citizen of the kingdom of heaven (cf. Phil. 3:20), must nevertheless still live together with unbelievers within the so-called worldly regime. It is this reality which must be taken into consideration in all of one's political decisions and activities. This so-called two-kingdom (or better, two-regime) doctrine found its classical expression in Articles 16 and 28 of the Augsburg Confession. The second model is found in the (fifth thesis of the) Barmen "Theological Declaration" of 1934 (which was outlined above all by Karl Barth). Here the way in which church and state are to relate to one another in accordance with modern political experience is taught even more clearly than in Luther's paradigm. The declaration picks up Rom. 13:1–7 and 1 Pet. 2:13–17 directly and teaches that "[t]he Scripture tells us that according to a divine ordinance the State has the task of caring for justice and peace in a world which is not yet redeemed and in which the Church also exists. It is to do this according to the measure of human insight and ability granted to it and by employing the threat and exercise of force. The Church acknowledges with gratitude and awe toward God the blessing of this, his ordinance. It also calls attention to God's Kingdom, to God's commandment and righteousness, and consequently to the responsibility of those who govern and of those who are governed. The Church thus trusts in and obeys the power of the Word, through which God upholds all things. . . ." In this thesis, the quintessence of Luther's two-regime doctrine is taken into account. This, together with its closeness to the aforementioned biblical texts, makes it advisable today to orient oneself concerning the question of the Christian's conduct toward (and within the) state authorities, above all, on the basis of Barmen fifth thesis.

V. 13:8–10. Love for One's Neighbor as Fulfillment of the Law

(8) Owe no one anything—apart from the (word) to love one another. For the person who loves one's neighbor has fulfilled the Law. (9) For the (well-known commandment), "You shall not commit adultery," "You shall not murder," "You shall not steal," "You shall not covet," and any other commandment that there is besides, is summarized in this one word, "You shall love your neighbor as yourself." (10) Love does nothing evil to one's neighbor; (thus) love (is) now the fulfillment of the Law.

Verse 8: Lev. 19:18; Verse 9: Exod. 20:13–15, 17; Deut. 5:17–19, 21; Lev. 19:18.

A. In terms of content, these verses summarize the exhortation to the church (*Paraklesis*) up until this point. Verse 8 is linked to 13:7 and at the same time once again picks up the catchword and theme of love which has already been a matter of debate since 12:9. Verse 9 explains v. 8. Verse 10 then draws the conclusion from vv. 8 and 9 that the church of Christ is fulfilling the Law by means of the love which it is to show.

In vv. 8 and 9 Paul refers to the commandment to love one's neighbor from Lev. 19:18. This commandment already occupied a definite and special position within Leviticus 19, and it later took on great significance for early Judaism. In Leviticus 19 the "neighbor" is clearly one's fellow Israelite and Jewish country-man. The command to love one's fellow Israelite, and even to continue to do so when he does evil and is full of hate, is subsequently then clearly enjoined in a pointed fashion in T. Gad 4 and 6. For Rabbi Akiba (born ca. A.D. 50), Lev. 19:18 is one of the great central rules in the Torah (cf. Sifra 89b). On the basis of Lev. 19:34 and in connection with it, the love command is then also extended to the foreigner, that is, to the non-Israelite (cf. Sifra 91a). Finally, for Hillel the Elder, who taught between 30 B.C. and A.D. 10, the so-called Golden Rule (cf. Mtt. 7:12; Tob. 4:15; Sir. 31:15), which closely approximates Lev. 19:18, 34, is a summary and bridge by which a Gentile who desires to cross over to Judaism can enter into the entire Torah (cf. b. Sabb. 31a, Bar.). Hence, only with Jesus, and then, based on him, with Paul and John, does the love command transcend the 613 individual commandments (= 248 commands and 365 prohibitions), which according to early Jewish reckoning constitute the entirety of the Torah.

In v. 9 Paul quotes from the Ten Commandments. As one can imagine, the significance of the Decalogue for the early Judaism of Paul's day was great. Al-ready in Deut. 5:22 the Decalogue functioned as the center of the Torah. God had imparted the "Ten Words" directly to the people, while all the rest of the commandments were transmitted to Israel only through the mediation of Moses (Deut. 5:23–31). Philo of Alexandria thus emphasizes the same situation in his writing concerning the Decalogue; for him all of the individual commandments can be traced back to the Decalogue, which was given to the people without a mediator (Decal. 18 + 19). Hence, the Decalogue is identical with the Law of the cosmos. Josephus too underscores the fact that the people learned the words of the Decalogue directly from God (Ant. 3.89, 93). Moreover, the Jew-ish phylacteries and doorpost boxes found in Qumran contained for the most part the Decalogue, thus documenting its significance for the Essenes as well. According to m. Tamid 5:1 it was recited daily in the temple during the morning prayer. For early Judaism, therefore, the Decalogue is "the shortened form of the Law of faith and life, the essence of the Jewish religion" (G. Stemberger). It is not until the period after A.D. 70 that several Rabbis come to emphasize that the Decalogue does not occupy a special place within the Torah. They did this, however, in order to restrain the exclusive esteem granted to the Ten Commandments among Jewish heretics and Christians (cf. y. Ber 1:8f., 3c and b. Ber. 12a). But this Rabbinic dogma did not destroy the esteem for the Deca-logue completely. Rather, according to the Sayings of the Fathers 5:5 the tablets of the Law, upon which the Ten Commandments were written, are considered to have been fashioned on the eve of the Sabbath at the time of creation. And in Pesiq. R. 21:19 it states that "[t]he Ten Commandments were said in corre-spondence to ten words with which the world was created." Paul appears to have already been thinking in a similar way when in Rom. 7:7ff. he illustrates the one commandment that had been given to Adam in paradise (cf. Gen. 2:16f.) with the (ninth and) tenth commandment and then equates it with the Torah as a whole.

B. Immediately after v. 7 (v. 8 is adjoined to v. 7), the apostle brings the first part of his exhortation to the church to a climax. [8] While the Christians in Rome can satisfy their individual "creditors" (so designated in v. 7) by paying taxes and dues and showing respect and honor, they remain obligated all their life to the love command, a command which is well known to them. The paying of taxes and dues, as well as paying respect to those in authority on earth, will all pass away, but the love commanded by God remains (cf. 1 Cor. 13:13). With it the Law is continually fulfilled (cf. Gal. 5:14; Col. 3:14). [9] The individual commandments (from the second half of the Decalogue) concerning adultery, murder, theft, and covetousness are enumerated here by Paul by way of example in the order followed in Deut. 5:17ff. according to the Greek Bible. These commandments, which are also familiar to Paul's addressees, together with every other commandment of the Torah, can be summarized in the one word (= command) which is to be read in Lev. 19:18: "You shall love your neighbor as yourself!" [10] Love for one's neighbor is the essence and summation of the entire Torah; it does nothing evil to one's neighbor (cf. 12:17, 21), and it is—as Paul, in conclusion, once again underscores with a recapitulation of v. 8—the fulfillment of the Law.

As clear as these statements of the apostle are, they appear to be just as difficult theologically. The reason for this is not merely that in this text Paul makes it clear that he presupposes among the house churches in Rome a knowledge of the Decalogue and of Lev. 19:18 (cf. so too in 7:1). The difficulty also derives from the fact that he proceeds on the assumption that they are valid for Christians as well and thus summons them to fulfill the Law through love. Moreover, he does this in spite of the fact that in 7:6, 8:2, and 10:4 he has unambiguously declared that Christians have died to the Law of Moses and that Christ is the end of the Law. Is the apostle contradicting himself? Or is he quoting here—as though by mistake—Jewish-Christian tradition, which in reality is far from his own thinking? Neither possibility is correct. Already in 6:18ff. Paul had spoken of the service to the righteousness (of God) in which those Christians who have been baptized now stand. Then in 8:3ff. he emphasized that those who believe in Christ do not somehow exist in a state of lawless capriciousness, but in the freedom of fulfilling (the legal demand) of the Law by virtue of the sacrificial death of Jesus and the Holy Spirit which has been allotted to them. Paul means by this the fulfillment of the will of God, which through Jesus has been freed from the misuse to which sin drove it, and now for the first time in history since the Fall of Adam has really been put into effect. As that which is written by the Holy Spirit in the hearts of Christians, this will of God transcends the form in which the Torah from Sinai appeared (cf. Jer. 31:31ff.). Nevertheless, it is identical with itself, so that the will of God determines the entire history of revelation from Adam, through Moses, to Christ and the day of judgment.

From this perspective, Rom. 13:8–10 is by no means unintelligible or theologically inappropriate. Together with the Jesus tradition (cf. Mk. 10:17–22 par. and 12:28–34 par.), and strengthened by Jesus' death and resurrection, Paul takes as his starting point the fact that the love command (from Lev. 19:18) not only summarizes the Torah of Moses, but also transcends it in the sense of Jer. 31:31ff. In taking this point of departure, the Decalogue functions for Paul as the principal part of the Torah. In it the content of the will of God, which has been valid since Adam, can be perceived by way of example. The so-called second tablet of the Decalogue thus also offers the best introduction to the practical performance of love, an introduction which the Christians in particular also need. If, therefore, they keep in mind the second tablet of the Decalogue in the various situations of life which they will encounter, and know, moreover, that Jesus extended the command to love one's neighbor to include even the persecutors and enemies of the church (cf. 12:14), then they will have the best conceivable guide for their own testimony of love, which is to be brought forth in the power of the Spirit. But this also places them in the position of having to fulfill the Law on an ongoing basis (cf. 8:4 with 13:8, 10). It is precisely this point which Paul intends to expound in the Roman context. Hence, no longer will it be possible or permissible to say about the Pauline gospel in Rome that, according to the gospel of the apostle, (Gentile) Christians are being placed in a state of freedom which is, in reality, only a coverup for wickedness (cf. Rom. 3:8; 6:1, 15 with 1 Pet. 2:16). Seen in this light, this section has its place within the debate forced upon Paul by his critics concerning the (alleged) Pauline antinomianism, a debate which extended even as far as the letter to the Romans. Within this context this passage is intended and written to be just as practical (and not only foundational) as Rom. 13:6f. This is best confirmed by the fact that in Rom. 13:8–10 Paul is once again merely repeating and making more precise what he already presented in Gal. 5:14 and 6:2. In a word, Paul does not teach lawlessness, but the fulfillment of the Law (of Christ) in love by the power of the Holy Spirit.

VI. 13:11–14. Christian Conduct in View of the Coming Salvation

(11) And take this to heart in the knowledge of the present point in time, that the hour is already here for you to rise up from sleep; for salvation is now already nearer for us than at the time when you came to faith! (12) The night is advanced, but the day has come near. Therefore, let us lay aside the works of darkness, but put on the weapons of light. (13) Let us walk with propriety as in the day, not in feasting and bouts of drunkenness, not in visiting brothels and orgies, not in strife and angry passion, (14) but put on the Lord Jesus Christ and have no concern for the flesh (to satisfy its) lusts.

A. Romans 13:11–14 provides the eschatological foundation for the exhortation to the church (*Paraklesis*) which Paul has expounded thus far. In terms of the composition of the letter, these verses present the counterpart to the introduction in 12:1–2. Verse 11 follows from vv. 8–10 and, together with v. 12a, supports the Pauline exhortation by pointing to the nearness of the day of judgment, a day which is directly imminent and which brings the completion of salvation for Christians. Paul derives three challenges from this point in vv. 12b and 13a. These challenges are then contrasted with a short catalog of vices in 13b, which is arranged in three pairs. Verse 14 then offers a concluding exhortation. It contrasts the conduct which Paul desires over against that which he does not desire and in so doing provides the transition to 14:1ff.

The close relationship between 13:11–14 and 1 Thess. 5:1–11, Col. 3:1–11, and Eph. 5:8–20, both linguistically and in terms of content, shows that in this section Paul is taking up in part hymnically formulated elements of the baptismal liturgy (cf. Eph. 5:14) and traditional motifs from the early Christian speeches of exhortation which were delivered to the baptized members of the church of Christ. Therefore, much of what Paul writes may have already been familiar to the Roman Christians. But whether or not in vv. 11–14 the apostle is actually strictly quoting a portion of the baptism liturgy and commenting on it (so H. Schlier) can no longer be determined with surety.

B. In 12:1f. Paul summoned the Roman Christians to an embodied form of worship, to a distancing from this age, which is coming to an end, and to a renewal of their thinking and conduct. [11] He now urges them to lead their lives in the knowledge of what is about to take place. For the Roman Christians it is time to prepare themselves for the coming of the Lord! At the time of their baptism they were summoned to arise from the sleep of neglecting God and to turn to Christ in order to be enlightened by him with a new understanding (cf. Eph. 5:14 with Ps. Sol. 16:1–4). At this point, Paul renews this summons and gives it an eschatological foundation. Now, even as he is writing the letter to the Romans, the eschatological salvation has already come closer for him and his addressees than at the hour of their conversion to faith in Christ. In the opinion of the apostle, the months and years which have passed since then can be subtracted from the set period of time which still remains until the day of judgment arrives. Together with 1 Thess. 4:13–5:11, this verse is thus a clear testimony to the expectation of the imminent return of Christ which Paul carried ever since the very beginning of his apostolic work. This expectation has already come to expression in the twofold "now" of 11:31, and at this juncture in Paul's argument gives an eschatological perspective to his entire exhortation to the church. With their justification Christians have already obtained a share in the redemption established by God in and through Christ (Rom. 3:24–26). Nevertheless, its consummation within the history of salvation in the form of the eschatological deliverance has still not yet come about (cf. Rom. 5:9; 8:23ff.). It will only arrive when Christ returns from Zion, all Israel is saved, and the dead are raised (cf. 1

Cor. 15:20–28; Rom. 8:29ff.; 11:15, 25–32). [12] It is precisely this consummation which has now been brought into immediate proximity. In the Old Testament, the dawn referred to here is the time of the rising of the "sun of
righteousness," whose appearance brings deliverance and salvation (Mal. 3:20).
Against this background, the metaphorical language of v. 12 can thus be easily
understood. Christians now stand in the early twilight of the day of judgment,
which for them will not be a day of terror, but "the day of our Lord Jesus
Christ" (1 Cor. 1:8; 2 Cor. 1:14), "the day of redemption" (Eph. 4:30). At the
final judgment, God's love and mercy will prevail for those who believe (Rom.
8:31–39; 11:32), and they will be granted to participate in the heavenly glory of
Christ (Phil. 3:20f.). On the basis of this (imminent) expectation, it follows that
the Christians (as they once did at their baptism, so too now and ever anew in
the future) must lay aside "the works of darkness," that is, those works which
prompt them to spread the darkness (as an adversary of God) (cf. Rom. 6:20f.,
23 with 1 John 3:8 and 1QS 3:21–26). Instead of these, they should put on the
"weapons of light" which have been created by God and made available like
armor for those who faithfully trust in him (cf. 1 Thess. 5:8; Eph. 6:11, 13ff.
with Is. 59:17; Wis. 5:17–19; T. Lev. 5:3; T. Jos. 6:2). For Christians are still engaged—like their Lord himself (cf. 1 Cor. 15:25)—in the battle against the powers and influences of darkness. Indeed, they are on the side of the light which
characterizes God and his Christ and proceeds from them (cf. Ps. 104:2; Col.
1:12f.; John 1:4f.; 1 John 1:5–7). The weapons of which they should make use in
this battle are faith, love, righteousness, and truth (Eph. 5:8f.; 6:13ff.). [13]
Those who look forward to the impending day of the Lord should therefore act
with propriety, that is, in such a way that no reproach (from those outside) falls
upon the church through the behavior of Christians (cf. 1 Thess. 4:12 and 1 Pet.
2:12). This is underscored by a "catalog of vices" which, just as in 1:26ff., is
aimed at Gentile lapses and which is intended (as always in the Pauline letters)
to be placard-like in its description. Gluttony and drunkenness carried on at
night, touring from brothel to brothel or more fashionable orgies, not to mention
the activity and feuds which grow out of such undertakings, form no part of the
identity of Christians. This small catalog also takes on a certain poignancy in that,
according to Suetonius's biography of Nero (26:1f.), Nero personally was in
the habit of disguising himself at night and indulging in licentious adventures
in the taverns and alleyways of Rome. But even without the example of Caesar in
their city, the Christians from Rome had no trouble conceptualizing what it was
that Paul was exhorting them to avoid. [14] Hence, instead of being concerned
with how the fleshly nature can best satisfy its lusts, it is their duty "to put on"
the Lord Jesus Christ. Paul hereby once again draws attention to their baptism
and in so doing summons them to maintain that which was granted them at that
time and to confirm it anew. As sinners from among the Gentiles and unbelieving Jews, the Roman Christians had formerly been baptized into the body of
Christ and as a result became members of Christ's body (cf. 1 Cor. 12:12f.;

Rom. 12:4f.). The body of Christ is the salvific community (see above, pp. 190f.). Moreover, in early Jewish texts, among others, the human body is also described as a garment with which a person is clothed (cf., e.g., 2 Bar. 49:3; 2 Enoch 22:8). Paul shares this concept (cf. 2 Cor. 5:2f.) and transfers it to the body of Christ. Therefore he can already say in Galatians that to be baptized into the body of Christ means to put on Christ (Gal. 3:27). Paul is now also reminding the Christians in Rome of precisely this "putting on." As those who formerly became members of the body of Christ, they too should thus now live with a special determination as the new persons whom Christ has made (cf. 1 Cor. 8:6; Col. 1:15–20; 3:9–10). This means, in other words, that they should live in the praxis of an embodied worship of God (12:1f.). Christians ought to encounter not only one another, but also those who do not belong to the church with precisely that love with which Christ himself has already encountered them and in the near future will encounter them anew (cf. 12:9, 14; 13:8–10 with 15:7 and Col. 3:13).

With this, the apostle has brought the first part of his exhortation to the community to an end. But at the same time, he has also prepared his readers for what follows, where the mutual acceptance of the members within the church is once again explicitly treated thematically.

Excursus 14:
The Nature of the Pauline Exhortation to the Church (*Paraklesis*)

If one surveys the letters of Paul which have been handed down to us, it quickly becomes evident that at least half of what the apostle wrote consists of words of advice and exhortation concerning correct behavior. Obviously, *exhorting the church* is not merely an appendix or addition to the gospel entrusted to Paul, but a decisive part of it.

1. This is already evident from the apostle's manner of expression. Paul uses the same verb for the exhortation of the church as he does for the preaching of the gospel, namely, παρακαλεῖν = *Parakalein* (cf. 2 Cor. 5:20 and 6:1 with Rom. 12:1, or 1 Thess. 2:12 with 4:1). According to the context, its meaning is "to call in," "to invite," "to summon," "to exhort," "to request," "to encourage," or "to comfort." In the same way, the noun which belongs to it, παράκλησις = *Paraklesis*, is used in the Pauline letters both for preaching and proclamation and for exhortation (cf. 1 Thess. 2:3 with 1 Cor. 14:3 and Phil. 2:1). It means "exhortation," "request," or "comfort." In contrast, the verb frequently used in Greek rhetoric for exhortative speech, παραινέω = *Paraineo*, together with the noun belonging to it, παραίνεσις = *Parainesis*, from which the loanword "paraenesis" is derived, often used in research for the Pauline exhortation of the church, as well as for that of the New Testament as a whole, is missing in

the Pauline letters. If one really wants to do justice to the apostle, therefore, Paul's kind of exhortation to the church must thus be called *Paraklesis*. It is both a request and an exhortation, an invitation to a new obedience and summons at the same time, and, for Paul, it belongs to the gospel.

2. The reason for this can be quickly recognized. The Christ, whom Paul is to proclaim among the Gentiles by God's mandate (Gal. 1:16), is, in one person, both the servant of God who went to death "for us" and the "Son of God in power" who has been appointed to God's right hand as "Lord" (cf. 1 Cor. 15:3–5; Rom. 4:25; 8:3 with Phil. 2:6–11; Rom. 1:3f.). The one who saves and the one who rules, i.e., the Christ who both offered himself up for us out of love and who reigns, cannot be separated. In his gospel Paul must consequently not only speak of the crucified Christ, whom God has established for our righteousness, sanctification, and redemption (1 Cor. 1:23, 30; 2:2), but also of the reign of Christ, of his intercession before God's throne, and of the judgment of the world which, as a mandate from God, he must carry out in the future (cf. 2 Cor. 4:4; 5:10; Rom. 1:1–5; 2:16; 8:34). The apostle's *Paraklesis* thus follows the dimension of his Christology, and for precisely this reason therefore includes the promise of grace, comfort, encouragement, and exhortation at the same time.

3. Nowhere in his letters does the apostle allow any doubt to arise concerning the fact that God's work of salvation in and through Christ precedes every human act, including faith (cf. Rom. 5:6–11, to name just one passage). Moreover, he makes it equally clear that justification (at baptism as well as at the final judgment!) is obtained not on the basis of the works of the Law, but on the basis of faith alone for the sake of Christ (cf. Gal. 2:16; Rom. 3:20, 30; 8:33f., 38f.; 11:32). In exact correspondence to this, Paul makes it clear that at the final judgment before God someone's personhood is considered to consist of more than the bad or good works which he or she has accomplished (cf. 1 Cor. 3:14f.; 5:5). Nevertheless, the apostle never tires of summoning the Christians entrusted to him to correct conduct and of reminding them that love for God, for one's neighbor, and even for one's enemy is the real dimension which faith takes on in life (Gal. 5:6; 1 Cor. 13; Rom. 13:8–10). The apostle's extensive *Paraklesis* documents the fact, to be sure, that for him faith in Christ has its criterion, that is, its touchstone, in the confession brought about by the Spirit (cf. Rom. 10:9f. and 1 Cor. 12:3). Nevertheless, correct conduct, and with it the doing of good, is the signature, that is, the characteristic of faith before others, just as it is before God and the judgment seat of Christ (cf. 1 Thess. 4:9–12; 1 Cor. 10:31–33; Rom. 12:9–21 and 1 Thess. 5:23f.; 2 Cor. 5:10; Phil. 2:12–16; and Rom. 14:10–12).

4. The *Paraklesis* of the apostle does not present a self-enclosed ethical

system, but rather follows programmatic principles which it then explains in direct application to the apostle's respective addressees in Thessalonica, Galatia, Corinth, and also Rome. The first part of Paul's *Paraklesis* in Rom. 12:1–13:14 gave us an example of this. Here the apostle's principle is that Christians are to dedicate their entire bodily existence to the "reasonable" worship of God, that is, to that worship of God which corresponds to the Spirit and mind of Christ (1 Cor. 2:16). Furthermore, they are no longer to conform to the criteria and modes of behavior of this world, which is coming to an end, but rather should actively follow the knowledge gained through their reason, now oriented to Christ. The good which is given to them to do and to promote in the various situations of life in which they find themselves is thus the love to which they are called according to Jesus' command. In Gal. 6:2 Paul calls it "the Law of Christ"; in 1 Cor. 12:31, as the way which Christians must go, it is called the way which surpasses all other Christian ways of behaving. The apostle then describes what this way looks like in 1 Corinthians 13. The power for such a new way of life lies in the Holy Spirit (Gal. 5:25), which Paul understands and experiences as the Spirit of the resurrected Christ in the present (cf. Gal. 2:20 with Rom. 8:15f., 26f.). Moreover, the love for one's neighbor and one's enemy which is lived out by Christians places those who believe in a position of fulfilling the Law (Gal. 5:14; Rom. 8:4; 13:8–10). At the same time this love transcends (in the sense of Jer. 31:33f.) the casuistry of the (according to Rabbinic enumeration) 613 individual commandments of the Mosaic Torah. It is therefore no contradiction when the apostle emphasizes that Christians may and should serve in that freedom (from the Law) into which they have been brought through the gospel (Gal. 5:1, 13; Rom. 6:18), but then simultaneously characterizes Christian freedom as fulfillment of the love taught by the Law (Gal. 5:13f.), or as service to that righteousness which God himself exercises and loves (Rom. 6:18ff.). Luther understood this dialectic classically when he begins his tractate from the year 1520, "The Freedom of a Christian," with the statement, "A Christian is a perfectly free lord of all, subject to none. A Christian is a perfectly dutiful servant, subject to all" (*Luther's Works*, vol. 31, 1957, p. 344) and then supports this on the basis of 1 Cor. 9:19 and Rom. 13:8. Inasmuch as the apostle gives only exemplary instructions in his *Paraklesis*, he thus challenges his addressees to think further on their own in accord with their own Christian freedom and to decide for themselves what all must still take place in regard to what is good. On the other hand, since Paul emphasizes the continuing lordship of Christ (Rom. 14:7–9) and stresses that what matters in Christ is the observance of the commandments (1 Cor. 7:19 compared with Gal. 5:6), he also shows them that their "reasonable" and embodied worship of God is a liturgy which does not end.

5. Whenever the Pauline *Paraklesis* is surveyed in detail it is repeatedly

confirmed that linguistically and in terms of content it runs parallel to exhortations being given in contemporary popular philosophy and in the
synagogues in which Greek-speaking Jews came together. When the apostle, for example, summons one to consider and to do "that which is good"
(Rom. 12:2, 17, 21), or when he admonishes his reader to consider "what
is true, honorable, just, pure, and worthy of love, and that which is pleasing, is called virtue, and is worthy of praise" (Phil. 4:8), or when he advises
one to behave "with propriety" (1 Thess. 4:12; Rom. 13:13), any person of
his time who had been raised in the Greek environment could agree with
him. On the other hand, when Paul encourages the Christian community
(in Philippi) to an exemplary and, in the true sense of the word, enlightening conduct in the midst of a depraved and disconcerted generation of
people (Phil. 2:15), this corresponds to the exhortation from T. Lev. 14:3
that the children of Levi should be "lights of Israel" before and in distinction to the Gentiles (cf. Is. 49:6). On the basis of such parallels scholars
have repeatedly concluded that apart from the love command there is
hardly anything specifically Christian in the (Pauline) *Paraklesis*. Even the
love command itself, in reality, is seen to be nothing more than just good
Jewish tradition (cf. Lev. 19:18 and T. Gad. 6:1: "And now, my children,
let every one love his brother and root out the hate from your hearts, so
that you love one another in work and word and in the disposition of your
souls!"). As correct as these observations are, the conclusion drawn from
them is just as wrong! Although Paul clearly and strictly distinguishes the
community of Christians, who have been sanctified through Jesus' sacrificial death, from both unbelieving Jews and sinful Gentiles (cf. 1 Cor. 6:1–8;
2 Cor. 6:14–7:1), nevertheless his ethical interest is not aimed at now suddenly imparting to this community nothing but new, "specifically Christian," instructions. Rather, Paul is concerned to urge Christians to observe
the will of God, which was not annulled by the mission of Jesus, but established anew in power (Rom. 8:3f.). Like Jesus, Paul too ascertains this divine will, paradigmatically, on the basis of the (Ten) Commandments (see
above, pp. 208–210). For this reason he can adopt without qualification
content and expressions from the interpretation of the (Ten) Commandments being expounded in the Greek synagogues of his day and which
Paul himself, under certain circumstances, had also used for a period of
time (in Jerusalem) (cf. Gal. 5:11 and for this same point, above p. 178).
What this interpretation of the Law looked like can be seen beautifully
from Philo's writing on the Decalogue (esp. 50–153 and 154–78), from
Josephus (*Contr. Ap.* 2.190–219), or from the speeches of exhortation in
the so-called Testaments of the Twelve Patriarchs. In each case one encounters the endeavor to keep the content of God's commandments pure,
but at the same time to speak a language which was understandable to interested visitors of the synagogues during the Hellenistic period. It is

precisely this endeavor which also characterizes the style of the Pauline *Paraklesis*. Moreover, we have already mentioned that in terms of content Paul's *Paraklesis* derives not only from the synagogue interpretation of the Law, but also from the Jesus tradition (cf. 1 Thess. 4:13–5:11; 1 Cor. 7:8–16; 9:13f.; Rom. 12:9–21, etc.). We have also already been struck by the fact that the apostle is engaged with other missionaries in the passing on of a "catechism" concerning modes of behavior, which they all expounded alike, or at least very similarly (cf. 1 Thess. 4:1f.; 1 Cor. 11:2; [14:33–36] 15:11, and see above, p. 186). The criterion for the instructions which Paul takes over and passes on, as well as for those he formulates himself, is thus to walk worthy of the gospel (Phil. 1:27), or to do justice to the "will of God in Christ Jesus" (1 Thess. 5:18).

6. On the basis of 1 Thess. 5:1–11; 1 Cor. 7:29–31; and Rom. 13:11–14, one can (and must) come to the conclusion that the Pauline *Paraklesis* is framed within the horizon of the imminent expectation of the day of judgment. The apostle desires to prepare the churches entrusted to him to meet Christ, their Lord and judge, in the near future. For by virtue of his atoning death, Christ has rescued them from the present, evil age of this world (Gal. 1:4). Therefore they need not conform any longer to the criteria of this age, which is quickly coming to an end (Rom. 12:2), but should lead an existence within the community which pleases their Lord, who is coming soon (1 Cor. 7:32ff.). Hence, for the church of Christ, the impending judgment of the world is not an event of unequaled terror, as it will be for all unbelievers. Instead, it will bring the establishment of God's righteousness in and through Christ for the Gentiles, as well as for "all Israel" (Rom. 11:25ff.) and the (nonhuman) creation as a whole, which until now stands under the power of futility and death (cf. 1 Cor. 15:25f., 50–57; Rom. 8:20f.). Thus, the good and creative will of God will be completely established through Christ at the final judgment, and for this reason, those Christians who still live under persecution and suffering look forward, full of expectation, to the "day of the Lord." Paul expected it to come still during his own life (1 Thess. 4:17; 1 Cor. 15:51). This expectation was not fulfilled, so that Christians today must think beyond Paul in regard to many essential questions. But it is also true for Christians today—as it was for the apostle and his time—that they too take their starting point from Jesus' mission in the world, his death on the cross, and his resurrection. Moreover, they too stand under his lordship, and experience the support of the exalted Christ, who is still in the process of subjecting all things to his Father. And finally, in view of the world which is still unredeemed, they too anticipate in hope and longing the coming of the Lord for the establishment of God's righteousness.

7. For Jesus, the will of God can be summarized in the double command to love God and one's neighbor unreservedly (cf. Mk. 12:28–34

par.). The Pauline *Paraklesis* also lives in this double dimension. This becomes immediately evident when one considers the following three aspects. First, it goes entirely without saying that the questions concerning
worship belong, as 1 Cor. 11:17–34, 14:1–40, and Col. 3:16–17 demonstrate, to the Pauline *Paraklesis*. With his instructions, Paul thus also intends to order his churches' relationship to God. Second, Paul often
speaks of Christians as the "saints" that they have become through Jesus'
atoning death (cf. 1 Cor. 6:1f.; 2 Cor. 1:1; Phil. 1:1; Rom. 1:7; 8:27;
15:25f., etc.). In addition, he explicitly refers to the "sanctification" which
they have experienced through Jesus' sacrifice (1 Cor. 1:2, 30; 6:11; Rom.
8:29f.). Hence, just as commanded in the Holiness Code, "Be holy, for I,
the Lord your God, am holy!" (Lev. 19:2), so too the obligation for Christians to sanctify their way of life before God, which they lead in the power
of the Holy Spirit (cf. 1 Thess. 4:3–7; 1 Cor. 6:19f.; Rom. 6:19, 22), also
grows out of the sanctification which they have experienced in Christ. And
finally, Paul repeatedly shows that the final meaning of the mission of
Christ is the glorification of God (Phil. 2:11; 1 Cor. 15:28; Rom. 15:7).
Therefore, because the Pauline *Paraklesis* follows his Christology, it is
consequently consistent that Paul would also see the goal of the life of all
those who may call Jesus Christ their Lord to be the glorification of the
one God, who created the world and chose Israel to be the people of his
own possession, and who, as such, is the Father of Jesus Christ (cf. 1 Cor.
6:19f.; 10:31; Col. 3:17).

VII. 14:1–15:13. Mutual Acceptance within the Community

In this, the last section of his (paradigmatic) exhortation to the church
(*Paraklesis*), the apostle now addresses a dissension which is burdening down
the Roman house churches and concerning which he was probably informed by
his friends (named in chapter 16). For in the churches of the city of Rome two
groups now stood over against one another, which the apostle (similarly as in 1
Cor. 8:1–11:1) here refers to as those who are "weak" in faith (14:1; 15:1) and
those who are "strong" in faith (15:1). Moreover, there were disputes between
the two groups (14:1). And only from today's point of view does the cause of the
strife appear insignificant. At the center of the dispute was the fact that the
group of the so-called "strong" did not maintain any definite food regulations.
They partook—as they could pay for it—of wine and meat from the public mar-
kets, and they also saw no reason for the setting aside of special days of celebration. The "strong" thus lived in the midst of their surroundings, which on the
one hand were Jewish and on the other hand Gentile, in the freedom of faith.
Paul consequently considers them to be essentially right in their position and attitude (cf. 14:14; 15:1f.). In contrast, the attitude of the "weak" was characterized

by definite prescriptions and considerations. They avoided meat and wine and distinguished certain days from others (14:5, 21). The strong disdained this conduct and in reaction were condemned by the weak because of their free lifestyle (14:3). In Rome, therefore, adherents of a free-Pauline and of a legal-ascetic perspective were opposing one another. Most likely this opposition concerned the question of how ritually thinking and living Jewish Christians could live together (and maintain table fellowship) with Gentile Christians who knew and observed no such regulations, a question which was still extremely pressing in Paul's day. Moreover, the fact that in this dispute there were also those among the converted Gentiles who were of like mind with the Jewish Christians is to be presupposed just as much as the fact that Prisca and Aquila (16:3) belonged to the camp of the "Paulinists." The rival positions cannot, therefore, be divided strictly according to ethnicity, although Jewish-Christian and Gentile-Christian interests respectively were at the core of the two groups.

Within the letter to the Romans itself, 11:13ff. (cf. with 12:3, 16) and 15:7–13, above all, point to the existence of two groups which were opposed to one another in this way. In 11:13ff. Paul rebukes Gentile Christians who as a matter of self-deception overestimate their own position before God over against the Jews. In 15:7ff. the apostle then summons the strong and the weak to a mutual acceptance of one another and then, in direct connection with this, declares that Christ has confirmed God's faithfulness to his promise in regard to "the circumcision" (that is, to the Jews), while for their part "the Gentiles" should recognize and boast in the mercy of God that has come about for them in and through Christ. Hence, Rom. 14:1–15:13 is concerned with the question of how (Christian) Jews and (Christian) Gentiles, with their different styles of faith and life, can live together as partners in the church.

This problem, as such, was not new. At the so-called Apostolic Council (according to the Pauline presentation in Gal. 2:1–11), the concrete questions concerning the common life and table fellowship of Jewish and Gentile Christians were not discussed. A confrontation between Peter and Paul consequently came about over the subsequent attempt of James and his emissaries to impose the instructions of the so-called Apostolic Decree (from Acts 15:20, 28f.). While Peter and the majority of the Jewish Christians from Antioch agreed with James's suggestion, Paul had rejected it and ultimately initiated, together with Silvanus, their own independent missionary journeys (see above, p. 143). As a subsequent movement, Jewish-Christian contramissionaries then attempted to convince the Pauline churches in Galatia that in order really to participate in the blessings of the Abrahamic covenant in Christ they must take upon themselves, in addition, circumcision, the Jewish calendar of festivals, and certain legal duties (Gal. 3:1ff.; 4:9ff.; 5:2ff.). Not satisfied with that, Jewish-Christian contramissionaries had also unsettled the church in Philippi with certain demands for perfection, which caused Paul to respond bitterly in retaliation (Phil. 3:2ff., 15, 17ff.). In Corinth as well the opposition between the strong and the weak had also broken out over the question of whether and under what circumstances Christians may participate in Gentile sacrificial meals or may eat meat offered for sale in the meat market, even though the animals had not been ritually slaughtered and drained of blood (cf. Lev. 17:12ff.) and, moreover, had been dedicated before their slaughter to the Gentile gods. In the arbitration of this disputed question, Paul had indeed considered the strong to be right, who, on the basis of their Christian freedom, considered both practices to be permissible. But at the same time he made it unmistakably clear that, for the sake of the troubled conscience of the weak members of the church, they must relinquish the right to exercise their own freedom (1 Cor. 8:7ff.; 10:23ff.). The questions which the Apostolic Decree attempted to answer with reference to the minimal commandments of the Torah (Genesis 9; Leviticus 17–18) were thus decided by the apostle on the basis of the obligation of the conscience of the strong to love their neighbor. Furthermore, Paul offered himself as the prime example of such conduct (cf. 1 Cor. 9:19ff.). The problem complex which we catch sight of in Romans 14 is therefore analogous to the situation in Galatia and Corinth. It probably even has something directly to do with it.

As already stated in the introduction (see above, pp. 6–8), the decree of expulsion issued against the Jews by the Roman emperor Claudius in A.D. 49 was rendered invalid at the beginning of the reign of Nero (in A.D. 54). As a result, those expelled, among whom were found not only Jews, but also Jewish Christians like Prisca and Aquila (cf. Acts 18:2f. with Rom. 16:3), could gradually return to the city. Hence, for five years (or longer) the Gentile Christians, who did not fall under the Edict of Claudius, had been able to perceive themselves as the real occupants and witnesses of the Christian faith within the world capital. Now, along with the Jews who had been formerly expelled, came also those Jewish Christians back to Rome who had earlier been forced to withdraw to Corinth, Ephesus, Philippi, and so on. But during the years of the expulsion they had not only maintained and cultivated their ancestral Jewish customs, but had also experienced *nolens volens* the debate concerning the Pauline gospel and its consequences that was being conducted during those years in all these cities. Thus, with their Jewish customs alone those who returned already embarrassed the Gentile Christians in the Roman house churches, who in the meantime had become established. But, in addition, they also reacted differently to the criticism of the apostle's preaching of the gospel, which had hurried on ahead of him to Rome. In their house church, therefore, Prisca and Aquila presumably stood up for the Pauline position, while others were against it. Under these circumstances, the apostle had to mediate the dissension between the strong and weak very cautiously in order neither to repel his friends, nor to unintentionally support his opponents. He does this on the basis of the same position which he had already taken up in 1 Corinthians 8–10 and which his gospel prescribed for him.

1. 14:1–12. One Lord and Judge for Both the Weak and the Strong

(1) But accept the one who is weak in faith, without lapsing into disputes over scruples! (2) The one believes that he is able to eat everything, but the other is weak and accepts only vegetables. (3) The one who eats should not disdain the one who does not eat; but the one who does not eat should not condemn the one who eats, for God has accepted him. (4) Who are you, you who judges a strange (house) slave? He stands or falls (indeed) before his own lord; but he will endure, for the Lord has the power to establish (him) firmly. (5) The one, namely, judges one day differently than the other, but the other judges every day (the same). Each (of them) ought to be completely convinced in his own view. (6) The one who is mindful of the (particular) day is mindful of it for the Lord; and the one who eats (everything), eats for the Lord, for he says the prayer of thanksgiving to God; and the one who does not eat (everything), does not eat for the Lord and (also) says the prayer of thanksgiving to God. (7) None of us lives, namely, for himself, and none of us dies for himself. (8) For if we live, we live for the Lord, and if we die, we die for the Lord; if we then live and if we die, we are (the possession) of the Lord. (9) For to this purpose Christ died and became alive, in order that he might be Lord over both the dead and the living. (10) But you, why do you condemn your brother? Or you also, why do you disdain your brother? We all (must) indeed stand before the judgment seat of God, (11) for it is written, "I live, says the Lord, for to me will every knee bow, and every tongue will confess God with praise." (12) Thus (it is) now (true) that every one of us will have to account for himself (before) God.

Verse 11: Is. 45:23.

A. The arrangement and structure of this carefully formulated paragraph are easy to detect. In v. 1 the apostle begins with a foundational instruction (which already points forward to 15:7). Verses 2–4 and 5–6 are then constructed in parallel fashion in order to present each of the two positions which are competing with one another in Rome side by side in such a way that both remain equally related to Christ. In vv. 7–9 this same relationship is then expounded thematically. Verses 10–11 refer back to v. 3a and provide eschatological perspective for Paul's exhortation. This perspective is then summarized, by way of conclusion, in the doctrine of v. 12.

In regard to the tradition and conceptual world of the paragraph the following is worthy of note. We are familiar with the fact that the practice of abstinence from meat and wine existed among various ancient communities. It was practiced by the Pythagoreans just as it was by the followers of Hellenistic cults. Philo ascribes it to the "Therapeutae" (otherwise unknown to us) (*Vit. Cont.* 37), and Eusebius of Caesarea is even able to report that James, the brother of the Lord, abstained from the eating of meat and all alcoholic beverages (*Ecclesiastical*

History 2.23.5). In our context, the report of Josephus (*Vit.* 13–15) concerning a group of Jewish priests who at the time of Nero were sent captive to Rome by the Roman procurator Felix is of special interest. Josephus reports that out of respect for the ritual Law they nourished themselves only from figs and nuts which they had taken with them from the Holy Land. Moreover, if vv. 5f. are compared with Philo's interpretation of the commandment concerning the sanctifying of the Sabbath in *Decal.* 96–105, it becomes evident that when Paul speaks of the special estimation of a particular day in all likelihood this concerns the Sabbath (and with it the question of whether and to what degree the biblical commandment concerning the setting apart of the Sabbath from Exod. 20:8–11 and Deut. 5:12–15 is also valid for Christians). Moreover, Roman authors like Tacitus deride and disdain the Jews because of their idleness on every seventh day (cf. *Hist.* 5.4). For in spite of the numerous festival days kept by the Romans, a religiously motivated renunciation of work by all classes of people was unknown to them.

B. Paul continues his exhortations from chapter 13 in that [1] he now summons the "strong" in Rome (cf. 15:1) to accept in brotherly love the fellow brother or sister in the church who is weak in faith and in doing so to renounce reproaching him because of his scrupulous considerations. The designation "weak in faith" is based on the presupposition that strength of faith is the attitude which is really to be desired. In terms of content, being weak in faith means being unsure concerning what breadth and significance faith in Christ has for the religious form of life (cf., similarly, Mtt. 16:8). The mutual acceptance which Paul here commends thus has its model in Jesus' own conduct toward sinners (15:7), and was especially applicable in regard to those Jewish Christians who, as stated above (p. 221), came back after years of banishment into the house churches in Rome which in the meantime had become oriented toward the Gentile Christians. [2] The issue which separates the weak and the strong is the highly significant question for Jewish Christians concerning which food may be accepted and which not in order to keep oneself from being rendered ritually unclean. The strong are unencumbered in regard to this question and eat everything, while the weak limit themselves to vegetarian nourishment, thus avoiding the meat which was dedicated to the gods and could possibly still contain blood, the consumption of which was strictly forbidden to Israel (cf. Lev. 17:10ff.). [3] But the strong, who eat everything, as well as the weak, who renounce the consumption of meat, should both abstain from reacting toward one another with disdain or condemnation. For God has accepted the brother who is still weak in faith. [4] As far as this brother is concerned, he is considered to be a valuable (house) slave who has been purchased from the power of sin (1 Cor. 6:20; Gal. 4:5) and now belongs to Christ personally. The strong must therefore not criticize this person, because he is responsible to his own lord, for better or for worse. But this lord is both strong enough and willing to grant stability to his slave and to stand by him in the judgment.

[5] Parallel to what has just been said, Paul now discusses a second point of difference between the strong and the weak. It concerns taking cognizance of a particular holy day (in the week). This problem presents itself not only in Rome, but also, as Gal. 4:10 and Col. 2:16 show, in other churches of Paul as well. But more clearly than in these other texts, in Rom. 14:5ff. the apostle also grants legitimacy to the Jewish-Christian segment of the church. If in his thinking, now oriented to Christ (12:2), the Jewish Christian has reached the conclusion that his setting apart of the (Sabbath) day is good and right before God, then this standpoint is just as acceptable before God as that of the Gentile Christian who does not know or keep the Sabbath. This text thus does not give any trace of a Christian setting apart of a day of rest oriented on Exod. 20:8ff. and Deut. 5:12ff. (but cf. Acts 20:7). Accordingly, as far as Paul is concerned, there can be no talk of a systematic adoption of all of the commandments of the Decalogue! [6] Instead, Paul merely respects the fact that the one who considers the (Sabbath) day special, does so in the interest and service of the Lord. (Only later textual traditions add to our text the parallel thought that the exact same situation pertains to the one who does not set apart any special day of rest during the week.) Unfortunately, we do not know whether the advocates in Rome of a Christian keeping of the Sabbath were thinking on the Sabbath specifically of Christ's deliverance of those who believe. Paul passes over this question and turns directly to the problem of eating. In doing so he emphasizes that the one who accepts all food does so in the interest of the Lord just as much as the one who avoids meat, because both of them say the prayer of thanksgiving over that which they enjoy. Hence, while the apostle remains silent concerning the questions of a special Christian hallowing of days of rest, this text nevertheless shows very clearly that he not only knew the custom of saying prayers of thanksgiving over food (and drink), but also considered them to be essential. The custom of saying prayers of thanksgiving (before and) after the meal, here approved of by Paul and taken over by early Christianity from the Jewish tradition, has its roots in Deut. 8:10. The prayer is directed toward God and follows (at least) the following form:

> Praise be to you, Lord, our God, King of the world, who feeds the entire world through his goodness! In grace, love, and mercy he gives bread to all flesh, for his grace endures for ever. According to his great, everlasting goodness, he has not left us wanting and may he not leave us wanting food in eternity for the sake of his great name. For he feeds and cares for all and renders good to all and prepares food for all his creatures, which he has created. Praise be to you, Lord, who feeds all (P. Billerbeck, *Kommentar zum Neuen Testament aus Talmud und Midrasch*, 4/2, 1928, p. 631).

The first Christian version of a prayer of thanksgiving to be said at the table is handed down in the Didache (Did. 10:1–6). Here too—exactly as Paul presupposes in v. 6—the thanksgiving is directed to God. The thanksgiving sanctifies the food which has been eaten (1 Tim. 4:4–5) and in this way removes from the opponents the occasion to accuse one another before God on account of their food.

[7] Inasmuch as Christ went to death for "the many" and was raised, there is no longer any reason, nor any possibility, for Christians to live and to die without regard for their fellow brothers and sisters in the faith. [8] In life and in death those who believe are and remain allied to their Lord and are his (valuable, hard-earned) possession (cf. v. 4). [9] The sending of Jesus to death, together with his resurrection, which climaxed in his exaltation to the right hand of God, have made him, in accordance with God's will, "Lord" over the living and the dead (cf. Phil. 2:6–11; Rom. 10:6–10). In 1 Thess. 4:14ff. it is precisely this understanding of faith which makes it possible for the apostle to comfort the Christians from Thessalonica who are concerned about the premature death of fellow Christians. In our context, Paul resists with its help the mutual alienation of the disputing parties within the Roman house churches. [10] With an emphatic address to each person who is embroiled in the dispute, the apostle now forbids (the weak from) judging and (the strong from) disdaining one another respectively. Because both must appear forthwith (cf. 13:11) before the judgment seat of God and there receive their sentence, they have no ground for prematurely disqualifying one another. Whereas Paul speaks of the "judgment seat of Christ" in 2 Cor. 5:10 and writes of the judgment of God through Christ Jesus in Rom. 2:16, here in v. 10 mention is made only of the "judgment seat of God." This has a parallel in Rev. 20:11ff., though the prophecy concerning judgment from Rev. 20:4–15 cannot easily be brought into harmony with the Pauline statements concerning final judgment (in spite of an undeniable relationship!) (see above, pp. 45f.). But since in Rom. 8:33f. the apostle speaks of God as the judge and of Christ as the intercessor and defender of those who believe, who sits at his right hand, this verse may also be interpreted in this same sense. [11] The following quotation from Is. 45:23 also speaks in favor of this interpretation. Paul prefaces it with the introductory formula that repeatedly appears in the Old Testament, "I live, says the Lord . . ." (cf., e.g., Is. 49:18; Jer. 22:24; Ezek. 5:11). This is a typical indication of the fact that in dictating his letters the apostle speaks from memory, that is, that he quotes in the way which was typical among Jewish teachers of the Holy Scripture. In Phil. 2:10f. the same quotation is related to the work of the exalted Christ. This makes it probable that here in vv. 10f. Paul is also thinking of the final judgment, at which, under the mandate of God, Christ is active. Christ has the mandate to subject all things to God, his Father, and to bring everything to the praise of the one God, who shall be all in all (1 Cor. 15:25–28). The goal of the final judgment is thus a positive one, namely, the carrying out and establishment of the completed reign of God. In accord with what has been said, it is therefore true that [12] every individual believer will have to give an account of his or her actions and omissions before the judgment seat of God. This renders all premature judgment within the church superfluous (cf. 12:19f.), but increases the importance of the church's mutual

responsibility before the Christ who as the redeemer is at the same time also
the heavenly Lord, advocate, and judge of the members of the congregation.

2. 14:13–23. The Edification of the Community through Respect

(13) Let us therefore no longer condemn one another! But rather direct your
judgment toward this, namely, not to give any reason for offense or scandal to
one's brother. (14) I know and I am convinced in the Lord Jesus that nothing
in and of itself is unclean; only to the one who considers something to be unclean, for that person it is unclean. (15) For if your brother suffers grief for
the sake of (your) food, you are no longer walking in accordance with love. Do
not ruin through your food the one for whom Christ died. (16) Your good
should not, indeed, be defamed! (17) For the reign of God does not consist in
eating and drinking, but in righteousness, and peace, and joy in the Holy
Spirit. (18) For the one who serves the Christ in this is pleasing to God and
esteemed by men. — (19) We are therefore now pursuing that which serves
peace and mutual edification. (20) Do not destroy the work of God on account of food! Indeed, all things are clean. But it is bad for the person who
eats (it) while being offended. (21) It is good not to eat meat or to drink wine,
or anything at all at which your brother takes offense. (22) The faith, which
you have, have for yourself before God. Blessed is the one who must not condemn himself for that which he approves. (23) But the one who has scruples,
if he eats, has already brought condemnation upon himself, because (he) does
not (act) on the basis of faith. But everything that (is) not (done) on the basis
of faith is sin.

A. In accordance with the oldest and best Greek text, we have translated the
verb in v. 19 as an indicative, although the majority of the later textual witnesses
read the hortatory subjunctive, "Let us therefore now pursue . . . ," which appears easier to integrate into the flow of the Pauline argument. But it is precisely this ease of interpretation that makes it possible to recognize that the later
text presents a variant which recasts the indicative, which appears unusual, in
conformity with the passage as a whole.

In this passage Paul argues in two parallel paragraphs: vv. 13–18 and vv.
19–23. Verse 13 connects to 14:10–12 and gives the instruction which holds the
two paragraphs together, namely, that one is not to cause a brother any offense
to his faith. This instruction is then supported and further developed in vv.
14–18. Verse 19 summarizes what has been said and, beginning in v. 20, this is
then divided into a further series of exhortations as a recapitulation of the conviction expressed in v. 14. This is finally then rounded off by v. 23, whose manner of expression consciously refers back to 14:1–2.

B. From what Paul has said in 14:10–12, it follows convincingly that [13] the
members of the church have no business at all condemning one another (in the

imminent final judgment). On the basis of vv. 5 and 10, this exhortation is directed not only to the weak, who have begun the practice of judging, but to the weak and strong alike. In a way that is rhetorically very effective, the apostle then continues, however, with an exhortation that is directed specifically toward the strong. Instead of judging one another, one's critical gaze is to be aimed at offending the faith or causing a scandal through one's own conduct to the (weak) fellow brother or sister in the church, which could bring one to fall in his or her faith. [14] But Paul does not demand from the strong that they give up their insight into the faith. Rather, he confirms them once again in their position. For just as boldly as Jesus, and certainly also dependent upon the Jesus tradition from Mk. 7:15, he makes clear that according to his own apostolic conviction (which for a former Pharisee is revolutionary!) nothing in itself is unclean. This conviction is valid "in the Lord Jesus," that is, everywhere where Jesus is confessed as Lord and faith is found. In the church of Christ the old, Jewish distinctions between clean and unclean, which were so deep-seated, are therefore abolished (cf. 13:14 and Gal. 3:27f.). Certain foods are thus now unclean only for those who consider them (on the basis of custom and upbringing) to be so. This view, however, makes the weak person vulnerable in his or her convictions concerning faith, and it is precisely this fact which the strong must thoughtfully take into consideration. [15] Hence, if the eating practices of one who is strong in faith plunge the weak member into grief, so that the weak brother or sister goes astray in his or her faith, the person who is strong in faith is not walking in accordance with the love that does no evil to one's neighbor (13:10). Through the choice of his food the strong ought not to ruin the conscience of the one for whom Christ went to death. [16] The good which the church has obtained through Christ, that is, concerning salvation and the knowledge of God, ought not to be given up to slander! On the basis of 1 Cor. 10:30 and Rom. 3:8, this could be referring to the criticism within the church of the behavior of the strong by the weak. But the use of this same language in Rom. 2:24 leads one to think rather of a warning from the apostle not to discredit the church and the salvation obtained by it before the eyes and ears of unbelievers through an offensive dispute between the strong and weak. If one understands the text in this way, then it fits especially well with what Paul writes in vv. 17f. [17] The catchword "God's reign," or the "kingdom of God," which is found here and which characterized the preaching of Jesus, is used by the apostle relatively seldom. Yet Paul too states that through the redemptive act of God in and through Christ those who believe are saved from the power of darkness, placed under the reign of the crucified and resurrected Son of God (Col. 1:13), and look forward to their participation in God's coming kingdom. Conversely, evildoers will not inherit the reign of God (Gal. 5:21; Eph. 5:5), but only those who are sanctified through Christ (1 Cor. 6:9ff.). Moreover, this way of speaking belongs within the context of the early Christian exhortation associated with baptism. Read against this backdrop, this text's refined statement makes good sense as well. In its formulation it calls to mind 1 Cor. 4:20 and signifies that demonstratively candid eating and drinking are not the distinguishing characteristics of the Christian expectation of God's reign, not to mention the proleptic appearance of this reign in the reality of the life of Christ's church. Instead, these characteristics are righteousness, peace, and joy in the Holy Spirit. In this context, "righteousness" refers to that "faithfulness to the community" which is lived out by the members of the congregation, "peace" refers to that mutual behavior which is averse to all dissension, while "joy" refers to the joyful cheerfulness with which afflictions are endured together within the church and with which the imminent coming of the Lord is anticipated (cf. Phil. 2:17f.; 3:1; 4:4f.). As "fruits of the Spirit" (Gal. 5:22), all three ways of behaving make it clear that the almighty God is already present within the (gathering of the) congregation (cf. 1 Cor. 14:25). [18] As a result, the one who serves "the Christ" (cf. 15:3, 7) of God in the power of the Holy Spirit and lives in righteousness, peace, and joy, is found acceptable before (the judgment throne of) God and receives recognition among the people who surround the church. The apostle is thus very concerned that with its lifestyle the church provide an example which does not repulse unbelievers, but is inviting and enlightening to them (cf. Phil. 2:15; 2 Cor. 8:21).

[19] Paul now continues accordingly. As already stated in 12:(3–8) 9–21 and once again expounded in the previous text, Christians should see in this mutual peace a good which corresponds to their stand in faith (cf. 5:1) and which is worth striving for. It is this "good" which they are "pursuing," that is, which they are endeavoring to achieve according to their abilities (cf. for the expression, Ps. 34:15; 1 Pet. 3:11; and Heb. 12:14). To the same degree, they should be concerned with the mutual "edification" of the church. The apostle occasionally designates the church of Christ as the "building of God" (erected through the preaching of the apostle) (cf. 1 Cor. 3:5–15). Correspondingly, he calls an activity which is concerned with the furtherance of the life of the church and the strengthening of faith, "edification" (or "building up") of the church (cf. 1 Thess. 5:11; 1 Cor. 8:1; 14:3–5; Eph. 4:12). [20] The opposite of "edification" is "tearing down" or "destruction." With the repetition of the exhortation already expressed in vv. 14f., the apostle now once again warns (the strong) not to ruin "the (construction) work of God" for the sake of (his) food, that is, the church as a whole (1 Cor. 9:1) as well as the individual believer within it who has become new in and through Christ (cf. 2 Cor. 5:17; Col. 3:10f.). The freedom of the strong to eat whatever they want can confuse the weak concerning faith in Christ, and this is precisely what ought not to happen in the body of Christ. [21] In order not to offend one's (weak) fellow believers, it is thus imperative to renounce meat, wine (which has been dedicated to foreign gods either at a sacrificial feast or through a donation of the beverage), and every other form of nourishment which to the weak can become a hindrance to their faith (cf., e.g., Exod. 23:19; 34:26; Deut. 14:21). [22] The strong can and should live in accordance with his or her own faith, as far as it concerns one's standing before God,

and the person who is strong in faith is well situated if one is not aware of any transgressions in his or her conduct or eating customs. At the meal times of the church, however, the strong must show consideration for the weak, although in one's own house he or she is free (cf. 1 Cor. 10:27; 11:22). [23] Conversely, the person who partakes of what is considered to be ostensibly unclean food according to his or her scruples, takes upon him- or herself the condemnation of God's judgment, because that person has not acted on the basis of faith. For every action that does not take place from faith or is not based on it is sin, because and inasmuch as it is determined by other circumstances, regulations, or requisites than those which ought to be decisive on the basis of one's confession of Christ, the Lord (cf. 1 Cor. 12:3; Rom. 10:9f.). For Paul, this statement has a fundamental significance. The weak are, of course, primarily in view. If, in spite of his or her scruples of conscience, the weak person eats what is considered to be unclean, that person transgresses what is deemed by him or her to be the valid will of God, and this is precisely what constitutes sin. But the one who is strong is also being addressed as well. For the strong it would be and is sin to compel the brother who is still unsettled in the faith to follow his or her own example, or, indeed, to demonstrate his or her (Gentile-Christian) freedom in order to expose the narrow-minded cowardliness of the weak (Jewish Christian). Such behavior violates the love taught and lived by Christ.

3. 15:1–6. Self-Denial in Accordance with the Model of Christ

(1) But we, the strong, are obligated to bear the weaknesses of the weak and not to please ourselves. (2) Each of us should please his neighbor for the good, that is, for the edification (of the church). (3) For the Christ also did not please himself, but as is written, "The reproaches of those who are reproaching you fell on me." (4) For what was written previously was all written for our instruction, so that we might maintain hope in patience through the comfort of the Scriptures. (5) But may the God of patience and of comfort grant to you to be intent on one and the same thing among one another, as it corresponds to Jesus Christ, (6) so that unanimously with one mouth you might praise God, the Father of our Lord Jesus Christ.

Verse 3: Ps. 69:10.

A. In vv. 1 and 2 Paul summarizes his exhortation to the strong and supports it in v. 3 through a reference to the conduct of Christ, a way of life which was designated previously in the Scripture. The quotation from Scripture brings him to an axiomatic remark in v. 4 concerning the value of the Scripture for the Christian community. Verses 5f. then offer a benediction that applies to the entire congregation (made up of strong and weak) and asks God for the Spirit of harmony.

What Paul writes in v. 4 concerning the significance of the Old Testament for the church of Jesus Christ was not only his own conviction and that of his school (cf. 1 Cor. 10:11; 2 Tim. 3:14–16), but also that of early Christianity as a whole (cf. Lk. 24:44f.; John 5:39; Heb. 1:1f.). Moreover, a very interesting analogy to it is found in the use of the Scriptures by the Essenes from the Dead Sea. Here too, in this Jewish religious community, the writings of the Prophets and the Psalms, as well as texts from the five books of Moses, were all related directly and specifically to the life and teaching of the "congregation" based on a special consciousness of their election and endowment with the Holy Spirit (cf., e.g., the Habakkuk Commentary from Cave 1, or the Commentary on Ps. 37 from Cave 4 of Qumran by the Dead Sea). Since texts from the Prophets, Psalms, and Torah likewise occupy the middle point of the early Christian and Pauline interpretation of the Scriptures, the parallel between the Essene and early Christian interpretation of the Old Testament is evident. The crucial difference, however, consists in the relationship of the "Scriptures" to God's salvific work through Christ, which is decisive for Christians, but which is not followed by the Essenes.

B. Paul now places himself unambiguously on the side of the "strong," with whom he had previously already ostensively agreed in 14:14. [1] As one of them and together with them, he now emphasizes their common obligation to tolerate and bear the weaknesses and limitations of the weak. The strong have no business in the church living only to please themselves, but rather must fulfill the "Law of Christ" (cf. Gal. 6:2) in regard to the weak. The same thing that Paul had often experienced himself and written to the Corinthians (cf. 1 Cor. 9:19ff.; 10:33) is also true here, namely, [2] that every one who is strong is obligated by Christ to live in such a way that is beneficial for one's neighbor and builds him or her up, even as it does the church as a whole. Such behavior is based on Jesus' instruction and model. [3] The apostle refers to Jesus here (as in 9:5 and 14:18) as "the Christ," and in so doing calls attention to the messianic mandate imparted by God to Jesus to bring salvation to Israel and the Gentiles through his mission and by virtue of his sacrifice (cf. 1 Cor. 15:3–5; Rom. 1:3f.; 15:7ff.). On his way into the depths of suffering, the Son of God was not too good to undergo the humiliation which, according to Ps. 69:10, the righteous one must take upon him- or herself. The reproaches of the godless who reproach God have befallen the Son of God (cf. Mk. 15:32). This great model of self-denial and renunciation can and must cause the strong, on their part, to practice self-denial in their relations with their weak Christian brothers. Elsewhere the apostle also refers to the example of the Christ who himself gave up his privileges (cf. 2 Cor. 8:9; Phil. 2:5ff.). Moreover, Psalm 69 (together with Psalm 22) is the psalm with whose help early Christianity explained Jesus' path of suffering (cf. Mtt. 27:34; John 2:17; Heb. 13:12f.). Paul also stands in this tradition and therefore attaches to the quotation from Psalm 69 a remark which expounds in a fundamental way the significance "of the Scriptures" (i.e., of what the Christians later called the "Old Testament") for the Christian community.

[4] That which God has proclaimed and written beforehand in the Holy Scriptures through the working of his Spirit (cf. 1:2; 16:26; 2 Tim. 3:15f.) is to be read by the Christian church, which itself is made alive by the Holy Spirit (cf. 1 Cor. 2:10ff.), as a valid instruction for those who believe in Christ. For them, the voice of the living God, which points to Jesus, to his work, and to the "Israel of God" which is led by him (Gal. 6:16), is perceptible in the Old Testament "Scriptures." Accordingly, the church of Christ may and can relate the Holy Scriptures, read from the perspective of Jesus, to themselves, to their path in life, and to God's future with the world. For Christians, interpreting Scripture thus means gaining an orientation to the present in the light of what God allows them to perceive through the written, prophetic word of his witnesses. The comforting exhortation of the Scripture therefore enables those who are patiently taking upon themselves whatever it is that they must bear to hold firmly to the hope of redemption and of the eschatological arrival (parousia) of Christ (cf. 5:3–5; 8:23–25). In the concrete case concerning which the apostle writes in 14:1–15:3, this means that the consideration of Christ's path of suffering, which first led Jesus from glory into weakness, and then from weakness to a life based on the power of God (2 Cor. 13:4; Phil. 2:6–11), and all of this in the light of the Scriptures, can fortify the (strong) Christians in their hope of being accepted by God themselves as they go along their own way of patient self-renunciation. Moreover, it can also strengthen their hope of then being able to join in with the grateful rejoicing of the righteous who have been saved, a rejoicing which has already been indicated in Ps. 69:30ff. But praising God is not a matter only for the individual within the congregation. [5] Rather, Paul expresses the prayerful wish that the God who bestows patience (cf. the Greek translation of Pss. 62:6 and 71:5) and grants comforting encouragement to those who hope in him (cf. 2 Cor. 1:3) will give the Christians from Rome the ability to be intent on one and the same thing among one another, and to do so in a way that corresponds to Christ's example and will (cf. Phil. 2:2ff.). [6] In this way, unanimous praise of the one God who, for the community of Christians, is the Father of their Lord Jesus Christ, will come about among them (cf. for this designation of God, 2 Cor. 1:3; Col. 1:3; Eph. 1:3; 1 Pet. 1:3, etc.). The following verses then make clear the goal to which the praise of God should be directed and how it is supported.

4. 15:7–13. Mutual Acceptance of Those Who Have Been Accepted

(7) Therefore, accept one another, just as the Christ has also accepted you, to the glory of God. (8) I am saying, namely, that Christ became a servant to the circumcision for the sake of the trustworthiness of God, in order to confirm the promises of the Fathers; (9) but the Gentiles should praise God for the sake of (his) mercy, as it is written, "Therefore I will confess you with praise among the peoples and sing praises to your name," (10) and again it says,

"Rejoice, you peoples, together with his people," (11) and again, "Praise the Lord, all Gentiles, and let all the peoples bring him praise," (12) and again Isaiah says, "The root of Jesse will arise and the one who rises in order to rule over the peoples, in him will the peoples hope." (13) But may the God of hope fill you with all joy and peace in believing, so that you will abound in hope in the power of the Holy Spirit.

Verse 9: Ps. 18:50; 2 Sam. 22:50; Verse 10: Deut. 32:43; Verse 11: Ps. 117:1;
Verse 12: Is. 11:10.

A. Verse 7 again takes up the exhortation from 14:1 and combines it with the soteriological foundation already adduced in 14:3, 7–9, 15. The foundation for the apostle's instruction is then given in vv. 8–12 from the perspective of salvation history. Paul does so by making use of a chain of Scripture quotations from the Psalms, the Torah, and the prophet Isaiah, which are bound together by the catchword "(the) Gentiles." Verse 13 then concludes this *Paraklesis* with a benediction that continues the one found in vv. 5f.

Inasmuch as Paul extensively quotes "the Scriptures" in vv. 9–12, and does so, above all, according to the Greek translation of the Old Testament, he documents (just as clearly as in Romans 9–11) what the Old Testament means to him. For Paul it is the living word of God, which determines and enlightens the church's present experience (cf. 15:4).

B. Finally, Paul once again summons both the strong and the weak mutually "to accept" one another. [7] He had already expressed this exhortation in 14:1, making the basis for this exhortation clear in 14:3, 7–9, 15, and 15:3. Now he joins this exhortation directly together with its support. Christ, the messiah, has already "accepted" all of the Roman Christians, whether they count themselves part of the strong or the weak. This means that he has enabled them all to attain justification and "peace with God" through his atoning death (cf. 5:1). Therefore they too are now also obligated to accept and esteem one another as brothers and sisters in the faith (cf. Mk. 10:42–45 par.). Indeed, the earthly Jesus was reproached by his Pharisaic opponents with the accusation that "[t]his man accepts sinners and eats together with them!" (Lk. 15:2, cf. with Mtt. 9:11). Now, however, the former Pharisee Paul considers this same accusation to be positive, and even designates the essence of Jesus' work of reconciliation in these terms. The apostle, of course, does not doubt that Jesus accomplished his work on earth to the glory of God and that he will continue to serve the glorification of God to the end of his messianic mission (cf. Phil. 2:11; 1 Cor. 15:25–28). But in our context the expression "to the glory of God" probably refers to the mutual acceptance of the Roman Christians. Verses 5f. make this more likely, as do vv. 9, 11, and 13. For the mutuality required from them is a part of the embodied worship of God to which they are called (12:1f.), and should thus serve to glorify God (cf. Col. 3:16f.). [8] In order to bring together Jewish and Gentile Christians completely, Paul now places Jesus' work of reconciliation within the

broad sphere of salvation history. Jesus was and is, first and foremost, the messiah and redeemer of Israel. He therefore served "the circumcision" through his
mission and the giving up of his life (cf. Mk. 10:45), and precisely in so doing
documents that God remained unswervingly faithful to his (messianic)
promises. On this basis the gospel applies first to the Jews (1:16), and all Israel
will attain salvation through Christ in accordance with the promise (11:25ff.).
The Jewish Christians from Rome are to recognize this and thank and praise
God for it. [9] But the Gentiles (who are Christians) should also join in this
praise, and may do so, since God, in Christ, has proven his mercy to them as
well on the basis of his free grace. As a result, they too have participated together with the Jews in the salvation which was and remains promised to Israel.
This praise from the Gentiles for the undeserved and unexpected mercy of God
bestowed upon them in Christ corresponds to the [10, 11] summons to all Gentiles to join together with the people of God, Israel, in praising the Lord, a summons which was written down beforehand by the psalmists in Ps. 18:50 (2 Sam.
22:50) and Ps. 117:1 and supported by the Torah in Deut. 32:43. [12] But of
equal importance is the fact that the Gentiles' praise of God also corresponds to
the messianic promise expressed by Isaiah (in Is. 11:10). The coming "root" (cf.
Sir. 47:22) from the tribe of David, founded by David's father, Jesse (cf. 1 Sam.
16:6ff.), will not merely be the salvific king for Israel alone, but will also be the
ruler of all the Gentile peoples, for whom the Gentiles have hoped as well. This
promise has found its fulfillment in Jesus' mission, sacrifice, and exaltation to
the right hand of God (cf. 1:3f.; 9:32f.), and it will find its consummation in
Christ's parousia from Zion (cf. 11:26f.). The mutual acceptance between Jewish and Gentile Christians in Rome, together with their common praise of God,
thanking God for the sending and sacrifice of his Son, anticipate in a certain
sense the song of praise of the eschatological, salvific community made up of
Jews and Gentiles and redeemed by Christ. [13] Accordingly, Paul concludes
his *Paraklesis* with the benediction that the God who has awakened the hope of
the church for redemption in and through Christ, and who will also fulfill this
hope completely, might fill the Christians from Rome totally with spiritual joy
and harmony in their common faith. Paul prays this so that, by the power of the
Holy Spirit, they might be brimming over with hope in the imminent inbreaking
of the definitive reign of God initiated by Christ, the messiah of Israel and Lord
of the world (cf. 14:17).

In this section of his *Paraklesis*, which has now been brought to a close, the
apostle has not said what his partisans in Rome would have expected from him,
nor has he contradicted the Jewish Christians in a way which would have confirmed his opponents in their criticism of Paul. Rather, within the context of the
concrete, problematic situation in which the Christians from Rome are cur-
rently standing, Paul has given an exhortation on the basis of the freedom of the
gospel which expects several things from both groups and requires from those
who are strong in their faith the greater act of self-denial. Such an expectation,

however, merely corresponds to the model of Christ and to the apostle's own conduct during his missionary journeys (cf. 1 Cor. 9:19ff.). The apostle has thus not compromised anything.

The third section of the letter, as a whole, has therefore maintained both a principled and at the same time practical focus. Moreover, the *Paraklesis* within it, which is developed by way of example, is an essential element of the Pauline gospel. The detailed conclusion to the letter which is still to follow is thus determined by the question of how, with the help of the Christians from Rome, Paul can bring to a conclusion the preaching of the gospel among the Gentiles to which he has been commissioned.

15:14–16:27. Conclusion

Paul now brings his letter to a conclusion. In doing so, he first returns yet again to the question already raised at the beginning of his writing concerning his apostolic mission (15:14–21) and the intention of his visit to Rome. In response, he formally expresses at this point his wish to carry the gospel as far as Spain by proceeding out from the Roman Christians and with their help (15:22–24). Following this he then reports concerning his impending visit to Jerusalem, and asks the Romans for their intercession on his behalf so that he can bring the work of the collection, which has been taken from the Gentile Christians for Jerusalem and with which he was commissioned at the Apostolic Council (15:25–32), happily to an end. He then closes with his first benediction (15:33). After this follows the recommendation for Phoebe, who (most likely) delivered the letter to the Romans, and a detailed list of greetings to all those whom Paul knows in Rome (16:1–16). Finally, Paul once again explicitly warns the Roman Christians concerning the false teachers who are pushing forward toward Rome (16:17–20), appends the greetings of his co-workers (16:21–23), and ends his writing with an artistically formulated eulogy of praise which corresponds exactly to the preface of his letter (16:25–27).

The conclusion of the letter is thus of marked interest for our understanding of the apostle and his mission. But it also presents a whole series of interpretive problems that must be handled case by case. Moreover, the conclusion of the letter makes it clear, without a doubt, that the epistle to the Romans is a writing in which the apostle intends to move the Christians from Rome to agree with him concerning the subject matter of his gospel and to grant him the support he needs to accomplish the goal of his apostolic commission to the Gentiles. Just as he has missionized the eastern region of the Mediterranean world "from Jerusalem" (15:19), he now desires to push through to the west from Rome. It is this second phase of his work as an apostle of Jesus Christ that the letter to the Romans introduces. Hence, the letter to the Romans only became the "Testament of Paul" (G. Bornkamm) in that in delivering the collection to Jerusalem the apostle lost his freedom, and as a consequence, also his life. As a result, the mission to Spain that had been planned did not occur.

I. 15:14–21. The Ministry of the Apostle to the Gentiles

(14) Even I myself am convinced, my brothers, concerning you, that you also are full of goodness, filled with all knowledge and in a position to show one another the way. (15) Nevertheless, I have written to you at times quite boldly by way of reminder as one who does so because of the grace which has been granted to me from God (16) to be a servant of Christ Jesus to the Gentiles and as one who administers the gospel of God in a priestly manner so that the offering of the Gentiles might be acceptable, sanctified through the Holy Spirit. (17) Hence, I have a ground for boasting before God in Christ Jesus. (18) For I will not venture to say anything except that which Christ has worked through me in regard to the obedience of the Gentiles, in word and deed, (19) in the power of signs and wonders, in the power of the Spirit of God. Accordingly, beginning from Jerusalem and in the surrounding region and as far as Illyricum I have brought the gospel of Christ to fulfillment, (20) but in such a way that I have seen my honor to consist in preaching the gospel where the name of Christ has not yet been named, so that I do not build on a foreign foundation, (21) but just as it is written, "Those to whom it has not yet been proclaimed concerning him, they shall see; and those who have not yet heard shall obtain insight."

Verse 21: Is. 52:15.

A. In vv. 14 and 15 Paul expounds why he has written the spiritually independent Christians from Rome as candidly as he has done, and points as support to the grace of the apostolic commission which has been granted to him by God. As he then amplifies further in vv. 16–19, the commission to preach the gospel of God from Jerusalem into the entire eastern region of the Mediterranean world, a task worthy of boasting about before God, was allotted to him through Christ. Its purpose was to lead the Gentiles to the obedience of faith. In vv. 20f. the apostle then adds that in doing so he had, in each case, conducted a pioneer mission and that he had not missionized where others had gone before.

This remark alone, not to mention the manner of expression already used in vv. 17ff., makes it clear that Paul is separating himself from the opinion of those who do not concede him any ground for boasting before God and who conduct their missionary endeavors differently than he does. Against this backdrop, the highly astounding statement from Gal. 1:15–20 that Paul has preached the gospel entrusted to him "beginning from Jerusalem" can also be explained, since the spheres of duty and the boundaries of the Jewish and Gentile mission were formerly staked out in Jerusalem at the so-called Apostolic Council (cf. Gal. 2:6–10). The apostle is thus claiming to have kept precisely this agreement, including its provision concerning the collection "for the poor among the saints in Jerusalem" (cf. below to v. 26). Rather than Paul, it is therefore those who are disputing his position and, beginning in Galatia, are constantly appearing in his churches (cf. 2 Cor. 10:14f.) with the desire to correct and supplement the Pauline preaching, that is to say, the contramissionaries (see above, pp. 142 f.), who have illegitimately behaved differently in regard to the mission. In this section we will thus once again catch sight of the front against which Paul is defending himself so thoroughly. Hence, the statement concerning the Pauline apostolate and mission in vv. 15ff., which at first appears to have the character of a general principle, (again) takes on an entirely practical meaning from the perspective of the compositional intention of the letter.

B. After having brought his *Paraklesis* to an end, Paul takes one more bow before the Christians from Rome. [14] Already in 1:8 he had praised their good standing in the faith, which was known throughout the whole world. At this point, he now assures them anew that, according to his conviction, they are, by virtue of the goodness which enlivens their lives and their spiritual knowledge, by all means in the situation of finding their way themselves and (in the case of conflicts also) of showing others the way. In reality, they therefore do not need the apostle's exhortation. [15] The fact that he nevertheless "at times quite boldly" exhorts them (cf. merely 3:8; 6:19; 11:13ff.; 12:3; and especially 14:1–15:13) and calls attention to that which they, as baptized Christians, could already know concerning God, Christ, the gospel, the Law, judgment, and so on (cf., e.g., 2:2; 3:19, 29f.; 6:3ff.; 7:1, 14; 8:22, 28f.; 13:11ff.; 15:4), is based on the divine commission of grace which Paul received through Christ (cf. 1:5). [16] Consequently, he may and is obligated to be a "servant of Christ Jesus to the Gentiles." For "servant" the apostle employs the same word here as in 13:6. Both in the Greek translation of the Old Testament as well as in the New Testament it can designate the servant of a person (Josh. 1:1 [variant reading]; 2 Sam. 13:18; 1 Kgs. 10:5; Phil. 2:25), but in particular also the priest who performs service in the temple (Neh. 10:40; Sir. 7:30; Heb. 8:2). In Is. 61:6 it is then said, in a transferred sense, that all members of the eschatological people of God will be called "priests of the Lord," a concept which the New Testament subsequently took over (cf. Rev. 1:6; 20:6; Heb. 13:15f.; Rom. 12:1f.; 1 Pet. 2:5). Moreover, the following words in our text, "to administer in a priestly manner," and "the (sacrificial) offering of the Gentiles" leave no doubt that Paul describes the special commission which he received as an apostle of Jesus Christ as the spiritual service of a priest within the eschatological people of God, which is made up of those who have been sanctified by Jesus' sacrificial death and called into the priesthood of all believers (cf. likewise in 1:9 and Phil. 2:17). But unlike the Levites and Priests who do service in the Jerusalem temple, Paul need no longer be concerned about the orderly offering of material sacrifices (cf., e.g., Exod. 30:20; Num. 8:22; 16:9; 18:6ff.). Instead, the liturgy which he must follow is prescribed for him by the gospel. The sacrificial offering with which he is charged consists of the offering of those Gentiles who have been converted to faith in Christ and sanctified through the sacrificial death of Christ and reception

of the Holy Spirit, and are thus acceptable to God. [17] Paul therefore has a
special office before God from the Lord who has commissioned him, concerning which he may boast. Moreover, he need not let anything or anyone dispute
this ground for boasting (cf. 1 Cor. 9:15–18). [18] The administration of his office was and is irreproachable as well. For whatever he has accomplished up
until now in word and deed in order to bring the Gentiles into obedience to
Christ, their Lord, is a result of the power of the resurrected Christ which determines Paul's life (cf. Gal. 2:20). [19] Furthermore, he has testified to the
gospel and done the deeds and wonders which are characteristic of an apostle of
Jesus Christ; that is, he has brought about faith, founded churches, and performed healings (cf. 1 Cor. 2:4f.; 2 Cor. 12:12; Acts 5:12; 14:3; 15:12). But there
is even more. Paul has observed the commission to bring the gospel to complete
fulfillment (cf. Col. 1:25) which was conferred upon him as part of God's eschatological plan of salvation for the world and which corresponds to the common
apostolic agreement in Jerusalem between the "pillars" of James, Peter, and
John, on the one hand, and Barnabas and Paul, on the other (Gal. 2:6–10). In
other words, Paul had agreed to take the gospel out from what was considered
to be the headquarters (as well) of the Christian salvific community, when
viewed from the perspective of the history of salvation, to as far away as Illyricum. Illyricum (Dalmatia) borders on Macedonia, which was missionized by
Paul in his missionary journeys to Philippi and Thessalonica. Even if one takes
into account that the apostle himself had conducted missions "only" in the
Roman colony of Philippi and in the provincial capitals of Ephesus, Thessalonica, and Corinth, but had left the mission in the surrounding regions and
outlying areas in each case to his co-workers and to the newly founded
churches, this fulfillment of his commission to go out with the gospel, which
Paul very briefly outlines here geographically, represents an enormous achievement. And it appears all the greater the more one takes into consideration ancient travel conditions and living circumstances. Moreover, the apostle
conceived of his mission within the context of the worldwide dimensions of
God's plan for the Gentiles and Jews as understood from the perspective of salvation history. Hence, in actuality he did exert himself more than all of the
other apostles (1 Cor. 15:10) in order to lead the "full number of the Gentiles,"
which was predetermined by God, into the eschatological community of salvation before the redemption of all Israel takes place (cf. 11:25). [20] But Paul
does not give an account of the range and significance of his apostolic commission without explicitly adding by way of clarification that in all of his missionary
work he has always seen his badge of honor to consist in preaching the gospel
only where the name of Christ has not yet been named. To build upon a foundation which other missionaries have already laid before him was (and is) not
the apostle's style! [21] Rather, he was granted the commission to extend the
message of God's servant, Jesus Christ, among those "to whom one had never
before preached concerning him" (Is. 52:15). Here, once again, the apostle's

global conception of his mission rings through and, at the same time, a clear dividing line is drawn over against all those who continually travel after him, thinking that they must improve Paul's preaching (cf. 2 Cor. 10:13ff., and above, pp. 6, 142f.). In 16:17–18, the apostle will once again explicitly warn the Christians in Rome against this type of person. But at this point he first fixes his eyes upon his next strategic mission goal, namely, to push forward to Spain through and with the help of Rome.

II. 15:22–24. Through Rome to Spain

(22) Therefore I have also been hindered these many times from coming to you. (23) But now I no longer have any more room in these regions, but for many years I have already had a longing to come to you, (24) as soon as I travel to Spain. I hope, namely, to see you while passing through and to be sent on my way there by you, after I have first been able to enjoy myself with you to some extent.

A. Verse 22 is attached to vv. 14–21 with "therefore," and introduces afresh the theme of the apostle's journey to Rome which was initially raised in 1:13ff. Paul then deals with this theme in vv. 23f. and "almost incidentally" (U. Wilckens) familiarizes his addressees with the real reason for his impending visit to Rome.

These verses are therefore of special significance for the controversial question concerning the purpose for the writing of Romans (see above, pp. 8ff.). They make clear, once and for all, that the apostle is not, in some way, desiring in Rome to go against his solemn principle, which he declared in vv. 20f., of only preaching Christ where no one has yet missionized before him, that is to say, of only conducting pioneer missions with the gospel. Instead, Paul's real desire is only to cultivate spiritual fellowship with the Roman Christians in order, having been sustained by this fellowship, to journey further on to Spain. Already in 1:12f. Paul had expressed himself in this direction. There he also stated that although originally he had envisioned more far-reaching plans, and had even desired earlier to be the first to preach the gospel in Rome, he was nevertheless hindered from doing so by God (1:13–15). He now repeats what he had said at the beginning. Moreover, what he has presented to the Roman Christians in the letter to the Romans is only a "reminder" of that which they have already experienced from other missionaries (v. 15). In turn, what he hopes for from them is an escort to Spain, after he and they have come to terms completely concerning the gospel. Hence, the letter to the Romans is intended to create a solid basis for this fellowship, and with it, at the same time, to prepare for Paul's pioneer mission in the western region of the Mediterranean world.

B. Paul's many and various tasks have hindered him up until now from pushing through to Rome via Macedonia and Achaia. [22] He thus endeavors once again to make his continuing absence clear to the Romans. As he did before in 1:13, here too he again employs a passive formulation, which indicates that the hindrance has come about from God and not from the apostle himself. [23] Indeed, Paul has wanted for a long time to come to Rome, and now he finally sees the opportunity to do so before him, since he does not perceive there to be any more room in the regions between Jerusalem and Illyricum (cf. v. 19) for the initial mission among the Gentiles with which he has been entrusted. He has done what he was commissioned to do in those regions. [24] He now desires, therefore, to press on further to Spain. At the time of Paul, the Straits of Gibraltar functioned as the border of the (Mediterranean) world (1 Clem. 5:7). Hence, since his missionary tasks in the eastern region of this world are fulfilled, the apostle is pushing further to the west, that is, "to the end of the world" (cf. 10:18). If this statement is taken together with v. 19, the concept of the Pauline mission to the world comes fully into view. As the one who has been called by God through Christ to be the apostle to the Gentiles, Paul desires to forge ahead to Spain in order, by so doing, to prepare the way for the redemption of all Israel and the parousia of Christ from Zion (cf. 11:13ff.). His mission is thus sustained by the apocalyptic hope of being able to be one of the missionary forerunners of the redemption of the Gentiles and Jews (E. Käsemann). Rome will thus only be a way station for the apostle, albeit a very significant one. After he has come to a spiritual understanding with the Roman Christians, has shared with them what he can, and has received from them sufficient encouragement and edification (cf. this verse with 1:12), he hopes to be escorted by them on his journey to Spain. If one takes into consideration the enormous costs that the Pauline mission to the world has incurred, with its huge travel program and the staff of co-workers employed in it by the apostle (even with the modest personal expense and endeavor of the apostle to defray his living costs as much as possible by his own manual labor, cf. 1 Cor. 9:6; 2 Cor. 11:7; Phil. 4:10–18), one recognizes what is meant concretely by "escorting him on his travels" (cf. for this also 16:23). The Christians from Rome are to help Paul go on to Spain with their connections, their money, and also, circumstances permitting, by the dispatching of helpers in the mission who will work together with Paul. Although at first Paul only intimates this, he is nevertheless already working up the courage to express his wishes and more thoroughgoing intentions in regard to his announced trip to Rome. Rome is to be the location for Paul from which he will bring his mission to the Gentiles to a close.

III. 15:25–33. The Trip to Jerusalem with the Collection

(25) But now I am setting out to travel to Jerusalem in order to serve the saints. (26) For Macedonia and Achaia have determined to make a common

contribution for the poor among the saints in Jerusalem. (27) They have namely made this resolution and are (indeed) indebted to them. For if the Gentile peoples have come to share in their spiritual things, then they are also obligated to serve them with fleshly things. (28) When I have therefore brought this to a conclusion and have given over to them the proceeds, sealed, I will travel further to Spain by way of you. (29) But I know that when I come to you I will come in the fullness of the blessing of Christ. (30) But I ask you, brothers, (sustained) by our Lord Jesus Christ and through the love of the Spirit, to fight together with me in your intercessory prayers on my behalf, (31) that I will be delivered from those who are disobedient in Judea, and (that) my service for Jerusalem is acceptable to the saints (there), (32) so that I then, according to the will of God, can come to you in peace and can rest together with you. — (33) But the God of peace (be) with you all. Amen.

A. This passage is connected directly to vv. 22–24. In the introductory sentence, which is formulated parallel to v. 23, Paul informs the Roman Christians of his immediately impending departure to Jerusalem and then supports this in terms of content in vv. 26f. In vv. 28f. he returns to the theme of his trip to Spain and his announced visit in Rome. In vv. 30–32, in a form which recalls 12:1, he then asks his addressees for their spiritual assistance and intercession for his impending visit to Jerusalem and for a blessed conclusion to the work of the collection. Verse 33 closes Paul's exposition with a benediction.

The early church in Jerusalem had fallen into economic distress (Acts 11:27–29) due to the lack of a continuing income of its own and because of the famine that hit Palestine between A.D. 46 and 48 (cf. Josephus, *Ant.* 20.101). In response, at the Jerusalem Apostolic Council in the year A.D. 48, Barnabas and Paul had taken on the obligation "to remember the poor" during the mission to the Gentiles which had been assigned to them (Gal. 2:10). In other words, they were to help the mother church through a collection of money from among the Gentile Christians that would then benefit the poor of the church in Jerusalem. Already in Galatians Paul added that he was passionately interested in this collection. The extent of this interest is documented in 2 Corinthians 8 and 9. In these chapters we have before us two appeals for contributions in which Paul asks the church in Corinth (chapter 8) and the churches in Achaia as a whole (chapter 9), to whom 2 Corinthians is co-addressed (2 Cor. 1:1), to carry out fully and bring to completion at this time the collection which had already been announced to them. In making these appeals, Paul refers to the collection of donations in Macedonia (i.e., above all in Philippi and Thessalonica), which had already been conducted with an astoundingly good result. In Rom. 15:26f., he now makes it known that the collection has also come to a conclusion in Achaia. For the sake of the Romans, he then establishes the proper sacred significance of the collection, a significance which it (probably) had for Paul from the beginning. The gospel went out from Jerusalem (cf. 15:19) and in doing so opened up eschatological salvation for the Gentile Christians. This spiritual gift of grace thus obligates its recipients to stand by those Christians in Jerusalem who are now suffering distress. For Jerusalem, with its original church, is not only the city of the crucifixion and resurrection of Jesus, but will also be the place of his parousia from Zion (cf. 11:26). The obligation of the Gentile Christians toward the original church is consequently of a spiritual nature and for precisely this reason is binding before God. Moreover, its fulfillment is more than merely a matter of mercy and love for one's neighbor. For in and with the collection, the (hearts of the) Gentiles (who are Christians) turn visibly toward Zion, as promised in Is. 2:3 and Mic. 4:2, and with it the treasures of the nations also stream back into the city of God (cf. Is. 60:5ff.). But there is still more! According to 2 Cor. 9:12–14, Paul anticipates the thanksgiving of the Christians in Jerusalem that will take place at the hour in which the contribution is received there, and in which the spiritual fellowship of Jewish and Gentile Christians before God will be expressed. Since for the apostle the work of the collection will thereby finally demonstrate the fellowship of faith that exists between the Gentile and Jewish Christians, he is concerned to hand over the money that has been collected, personally and properly sealed, to Jerusalem. Only then will he depart for his mission to the western regions.

Verses 30–32 betray the fact, however, that Paul looks upon his trip to Jerusalem with a certain apprehension. The opposition against his person and work by a broad section of Judaism was well known to Paul (cf. Acts 9:23–30; 2 Cor. 11:24; and Rom. 10:16; 11:13f.), and in Jerusalem special persecution now threatened Paul as the former ideal Pharisee who had defected to Christ. In addition, after all the disputes that have taken place between him and Jewish-Christian opponents since the Apostolic Council (see above, pp. 142f.), Paul was obviously no longer sure to what degree "his" collection would be welcomed by the Christians in Jerusalem. Acts 21:18ff. show that there really were problems in this respect. For precisely this reason, Paul asks the Christians from Rome to intercede in their prayers as much as they could for the success of his endeavor. Moreover, if the addressees, who were well respected throughout all of Christianity, having been convinced after the reading of the letter to the Romans of the good character of the apostle's ministry, would use their influence on Paul's behalf with their Christian friends in Jerusalem, he would certainly be thankful for this as well. The actual outcome of the trip to Jerusalem, which is reported on beginning with Acts 21:27, shows how justified Paul's apprehensions were.

The concrete constellation within which the letter to the Romans stands has often been underestimated in research on Romans. As a result, at various times v. 31 has been taken as grounds for seeing in Romans the outline of an apology for the Pauline gospel which has as its real addressees the Jewish Christians in Jerusalem. As such, Paul is only making it known to the Roman Christians secondarily, almost as an aside (J. Jervell, among others). Surely there is little dispute that during the dictation of his letter in Corinth the apostle would also have thought again and again of the arguments with which he could confront his Jewish-Christian critics in Jerusalem. But to the same degree, the fundamental idea that the letter to the Romans is to be seen, in reality, as a letter to Jerusalem is overdrawn. Inasmuch as the apostle never broke with James or distanced himself from the Jewish Christians in Jerusalem, if need be it would have been thoroughly possible for him to write directly to Jerusalem, without having to take the unusual detour of sending an indirect communication of his apology to Rome (on this question, cf. also above, pp. 3ff.).

B. Paul now also informs the Christians from Rome that [25] he is about to depart to Jerusalem in order to carry out, in his opinion, an important service there on behalf of the saints. [26] The Christians in Macedonia and Achaia have, at the instigation of the apostle, made a resolution to collect a contribution for the poor among the church in Jerusalem. [27] This resolve is grounded in the fact that, as Gentile Christians, they are deeply and firmly obligated spiritually to the original church from Jerusalem. For they have obtained a share in the spiritual treasures of the mother church through the gospel which has gone out from Jerusalem. Accordingly, they are obligated before God at least to serve the brothers and sisters in Jerusalem with the earthly means that they need. The contribution which has come together is to be a visible documentation of the spiritual fellowship which exists between Jerusalem and the Gentile-Christian congregations. Moreover, such a fellowship must continue to exist if they do not want to sever their roots within the history of salvation, which are found in their common filial relationship to Abraham (cf. 11:16ff.). [28] When Paul has personally brought the work of the collection to a good conclusion in Jerusalem, with which he (and Barnabas) were commissioned at the Apostolic Council (cf. Gal. 2:10), and properly given over the monies which have been entrusted to him, the circle will be closed symbolically. Paul went out with the gospel from Jerusalem, and with this revenue he is returning to the city of God (cf. v. 19). Following this he can then also consider moving on further to Spain, using Rome as a way station (so above, v. 24). [29] The apostle is thus convinced of the fact that at that time he will come to Rome in the fullness of the blessing that derives from the unity of the salvific community comprised of Gentile and Jewish Christians, all of whom worship one and the same God, a unity which is now being visibly demonstrated in the collection (cf. 2 Cor. 9:12–14). [30] In order that all this might come about, the apostle has a concrete request for his addressees. He expresses it no less urgently than his programmatic *Paraklesis* as a whole, which he initiated in 12:1. That is, he expresses it as that which is supported by the authority of the resurrected Lord who determines his life, and by the spiritual love for God and for all of his brothers and sisters in the faith which fills him (Gal. 2:20; 1 Corinthians 13; Rom. 5:5). [31] Specifically, Paul's request is that, together with him, the Christians from Rome are to fight in their intercessions before God on behalf of Paul and his affairs, so that in his journey he might be spared from the snares of the Jews in Judea and Jerusalem who are not obeying the gospel and so that the collection might also be acceptable to the saints (i.e., Christians) there. Both prayer concerns betray the fact that Paul is fearing persecutions at the hands of certain Jews and that he knows of opposition against his work in the ranks of the original church in Jerusalem. Because the relations of the Roman Christians to the mother church in Jerusalem were probably already good at the time of Paul, he assigns great significance to their intercessions (and perhaps also to their practical intervention in Jerusalem on Paul's behalf). [32] Hence, Paul would very much like to bring his commission concerning the collection from the Gentiles, which he had earlier taken over, to a spiritually good conclusion. Then, in his joy over the completed work, he would like to come to Rome in order to refresh himself among the Romans (from the exertion which by that time will lie behind him). Paul then explicitly adds to this, as he did before in 1:10, that such an outcome will only be granted to him by virtue of the good will of God (cf. James 4:15).

With this, Paul comes to the end of his epistolary discussions. [33] As in his other letters, he therefore closes with a benediction, which then provides a transition to his concluding greetings (cf. 1 Thess. 5:23; 2 Cor. 13:11; Phil. 4:9; and 2 Thess. 3:16). In these closings the apostle gladly uses the Jewish designation, the "God of peace" (T. Dan 5:2; cf. 16:20; 1 Cor. 14:33; 2 Cor. 13:11; Phil. 4:9; 1 Thess. 5:23). It is also found in Heb. 13:20. In our context this designation has the following meaning: May the God who is the ground and source of all peace for those who believe, because he has reconciled them to himself (5:1, 11), be with all the members of the (house) church(es) and accompany them. Paul then strengthens this benediction with his "amen," that is, with his believing affirmation: So may it be and remain true!

Excursus 15:
Does Chapter 16 Belong to the Letter to the Romans?

The sixteenth chapter of Romans presents a special problem in view of the question concerning whether the apostle could extend greetings to so many fellow Christians in a letter to a Christian congregation in Rome with which he was still unacquainted personally, together with the fact that various long versions of Romans are attested to in the beginning centuries of the church. It must therefore be clarified whether chapter 16 is an original element of the letter to the Romans, or whether we have before us a later supplement to the letter. In this context, it has been conjectured that chapter 16 dealt with a letter of recommendation (addressed to Ephesus) on behalf of the patroness Phoebe (16:1f.), and that only later was it made a component of Romans by subsequent transcribers of the Greek text. For inasmuch as Paul had missionized for years in Ephesus, it is very easy to imagine that he would extend greetings to an entire series of fellow Christians in Ephesus, while it is precisely these very greetings which at first glance appear strange within the letter to the Romans.

When one summarizes the complicated evidence of the Greek textual tradition, three versions of Romans can be recognized: First, the best textual witnesses, which, above all, are preserved for us from Egypt (the so-called Sinaiticus, Vaticanus, Codex Ephraemi Syri Rescriptus, and Codex Claromontanus manuscripts, etc.), represent the long version familiar to us from all present ecumenical editions of the Bible (= Romans 1–16). Second, the church father Origen traced a short version of Romans, which contained only chapters 1–14, back to the ship owner from Asia Minor, Marcion, and his separatist church (cf. Origen's *Commentary on Romans* 7.453 in the Lommatzsch edition), although this version was not disseminated merely among Marcion's followers. Finally, papyrus 46, to be dated around A.D. 200, offers a version of Romans which initially encompassed only Romans 1–15. In this version the concluding "amen" in 15:33 was then subsequently omitted and the statement of praise from Rom. 16:25–27 (with the "amen") was attached in its place. Only then does Rom. 16:1–23 follow, so that in this position it obviously functions as an addendum to the letter.

An attempt to relate these three versions to one another in a way that makes sense within the history of the transmission of the text leads to the following solution. The long version of the letter, which encompasses Romans 1–16, existed in the beginning. This version was then subsequently shortened by two chapters by Marcion for material reasons, so that a version of Romans is produced which consists of only chapters 1–14. Little by little this short version is then again supplemented, first by the addition of chapter 15. Papyrus 46 reflects this state of affairs, without having significantly influenced the later transmission of the text. Finally, the entire length of the letter is reconstituted, except that now the statement of praise which concludes chapter 16 (= 16:25–27) either appears twice, that is, after chapters 14 and 16 (so, e.g., in Codex Alexandrinus), or only after chapter 14, with a different benediction following 16:23, "May the grace of our Lord Jesus Christ (be) with you all. Amen" (16:24), as attested in the great majority of the manuscripts being used by the ancient church.

The result of these reflections is that the long text which includes 1:1–16:27 represents the oldest and historically authentic version of Romans. If we take this as our starting point, all the complicated hypotheses concerning a later supplement to Romans, which, in any case, can only be supported with difficulty, become superfluous. In Romans 16 we then have a list of recommendations and greetings which really were originally addressed to Rome. This also best explains the fact, which can hardly be explained as part of a writing to Ephesus, that Paul does not express his recommendations and greetings directly (as his co-workers do in

16:21–23), but extends his greetings to those concerned only by means of the recipients of the letter (cf. so too Col. 4:15 and for this point, below, pp. 249f.).

IV. 16:1–2. A Recommendation for Phoebe

(1) But I recommend to you Phoebe, our sister, who performs the service (of provision) in the church of Cenchreae, (2) so that you might receive her in the Lord, as is fitting for the saints, and stand by her in every matter in which she needs you. For she has also become a patroness for many, and of myself as well.

A. Already at the time of Paul there was, besides apostles, prophets, teachers, and administrators (1 Cor. 12:28), also an office of deacon in the mission churches, which above all was responsible for provision and care (cf. Rom. 12:7f.; Phil. 1:1; 1 Tim. 3:8ff.). It was occupied by men and women alike. Phoebe performed this office in the church of Cenchreae, and did so in such a comprehensive manner that Paul gives her the unusual title of "patroness." Phoebe's office was thus of more importance in Cenchreae than what we designate today with the concepts of "deaconess" or "sister." She was a benefactress financially, someone who exercised care socially, and a confidant (a "mother of the church") in such a way that it gave her authority in the church and made the members of the church responsible to her. As this example already indicates, in Romans 16 we will encounter the fact repeatedly that women played a role in the work of the early Christian mission churches which was in no way merely subordinate, but rather fundamental. Phoebe is merely the first of these women whom Paul calls by name (cf. further to vv. 3, 6, 7, 12, and 15).

B. [1] Paul recommends Phoebe, his sister in the faith, to the Christians from Rome. She held the office of deacon in the church of Cenchreae, that is, of the eastern harbor city of Corinth on the Saronic Gulf. Presumably, she is the one who brought to Rome the original writing of the letter to the Romans, which Paul had written or dictated in Corinth (cf. below to vv. 22f.) during his last three-month stay in Greece (Acts 20:3). [2] Paul therefore asks that Phoebe find a hospitable reception in Rome and support in all the "matters" which she brings to Rome. The Greek word used by Paul for "matters" can designate every kind of business, including legal affairs (cf. 1 Thess. 4:6). Moreover, in receiving Phoebe the Roman Christians should keep in mind that Phoebe is still the patroness of the church of Cenchreae and that many Christians, among whom is Paul as well, are indebted to her. Hence, since the word "patroness" had in Rome a special nuance, it was probably consciously inserted by the apostle in order to secure for Phoebe respect in Rome and a willingness to help.

V. 16:3–16. A List of Greetings

(3) Greet Prisca and Aquila, my co-workers in Christ Jesus. (4) They risked
their own necks for my life; not only I alone have them to thank, but also all
the churches of the Gentiles. (5) (Greet) also the church in their house. Greet
my beloved Epaenetus, who is the first fruit of the province of Asia for Christ.
(6) Greet Maria, who has exerted herself in various ways for you. (7) Greet
Andronicus and Junia, my kinsmen and my fellow prisoners, who are highly
regarded among the apostles, and who were also in Christ before me. (8)
Greet Ampliatus, my beloved in the Lord. (9) Greet Urbanus, our co-worker
in Christ, and my beloved Stachys. (10) Greet Apelles, approved in Christ.
Greet the (Christians) from the household of Aristobulus. (11) Greet Herodion, my kinsman. Greet those from the household of Narcissus, who are in
the Lord. (12) Greet Tryphaena and Tryphosa, who have toiled in the Lord.
Greet the beloved Persis, who has exerted herself in various ways in the Lord.
(13) Greet Rufus, the chosen in the Lord, and his mother, (who) at the same
time (is) mine. (14) Greet Asyncritus, Phlegon, Hermes, Patrobas, Hermas,
and the brothers with them. (15) Greet Philologus and Julia, Nereus and his
sister, and Olympas, and all the saints with them. (16) Greet one another with
a holy kiss. All the churches of Christ greet you.

A. The list of greetings is constructed in a staggered manner. First Paul has
greetings extended to those in Rome with whom he is especially bound together
on the basis of his mission (vv. 3–7). Then follow greetings to other friends and
acquaintances, including entire house churches (vv. 8–15). Finally, v. 16 forms
the conclusion with a call for a holy kiss and a greeting to the Christians in
Rome from all of the churches in the East represented by Paul.

There are many interesting and informative features to be found in this list
of greetings, the following of which should especially be emphasized in our context. The first thing to note is that Paul extends greetings to several women and
men who, like himself, were born as Jews and are now Jewish Christians (cf. vv.
3, 7, and 11). The apostle had already come to know and value Prisca and
Aquila, and Andronicus and Junia during his mission in the eastern regions. A
similar thing is true with Rufus and his mother (v. 13). The fact that they all
(again) now find themselves in Rome documents two things. It demonstrates
the mobility of people who move from the East to Rome and then again away
from Rome, a fact which is otherwise also attested historically (cf. James 4:13ff.
for a critical evaluation of this pattern). However, it also shows that after the
invalidation of the Edict of Claudius (see above, pp. 6–8) Jewish Christians as
well actually did come (back) again to Rome. This is a confirmation of the situation which we had presupposed for the interpretation of chapter 14 (see above,
pp. 219ff.). When Paul wrote the letter to the Romans, Jewish Christians were

not only once again living in Rome, but they could also once again travel unhindered into the capital of the world and take up residence there.

Of no less interest is the fact that in vv. 5, 14, and 15 Paul extends greetings to those who belong to three Christian house churches. Just as the Jews in Rome (and elsewhere) assembled, in part, in house synagogues which were spread out individually throughout the city, and Gentiles met in domestic cultic fellowships, the Christians also met in various house churches. They came together, for example, in the house of Prisca and Aquila, and also in the houses of the women and men listed in vv. 14f. Since public buildings or large halls which belonged to the church itself were not yet at their disposal, the Christians met in the homes which those members of the church who were well-off could make available, and there they celebrated their worship services, held common meals, and lived as Christians. According to archaeological excavations in Rome and elsewhere, the size of a house church was thus (at the most) the seventy or eighty people who could find a place to sit in such a dwelling. The letter to the Romans was thus read aloud and discussed in these kinds of individual, domestic gatherings of the church.

Naturally, this list of greetings cannot provide a representative glance into the social composition of the house churches in the city of Rome. However, it is interesting to note that the friends and acquaintances of the apostle come from different social strata. While in Prisca and Aquila we are dealing with free (small) entrepreneurs who moved from city to city, in the Christians from the household of Aristobulus and Narcissus (vv. 10f.) we encounter slaves or freedmen of the two patrons under whose charge they work. Also Urbanus, who was a co-worker of Paul (v. 9), and Rufus, whose mother had also cared for Paul (v. 13), appear, judging from their names, to be men of a free background. In contrast, on the basis of their status-related names, other persons appear to be slaves or freedmen, that is, people from a background which was not originally free. Among them belong, for sure, Persis (v. 12), Hermes (v. 14), and Nereus (v. 15), and very probably also Ampliatus (v. 8), Herodion (v. 11), Tryphaena and Tryphosa (v. 12), and Julia (v. 15).

The name Junia (v. 7) also indicates that this woman belongs to the social class of the freedmen or to the descendants of a freedman of the Roman line of nobility Iunius. From this line, for example, came the murderer of Caesar, Brutus, and numerous high Roman officials, some of whom were also engaged in the eastern regions of the empire. But there are more than just historical circumstances attached to this name. In the editions of the Bible commonly used today, the accusative form of the Greek name which stands in Paul's text, Ἰουνιᾶν (= Jounian) is rendered with the man's name "Junias." "Junias" is, of course, a shortened form of the name Iunianus (a name which is attested often in ancient sources). But the shortened form is not found anywhere in the entire corpus of ancient literature. To speak of a "Junias" in Rom. 16:7 is thus pure conjecture. On the other hand, the woman's name "Junia" is repeatedly attested in ancient inscriptions. Since the accusative form of Junia is also Ἰουνιᾶν (= *Jounian*), it is best linguistically to view Rom. 16:7 as a greeting from Paul to Andronicus and (his wife?) Junia. The Greek church fathers also always understood Rom. 16:7 in this sense, while there is no reason in the text to replace the woman's name with a man's name (which itself is only hypothetically demonstrable).

Andronicus and Junia were Jews by birth and had already become Christians before Paul. They were highly respected within the circle of those apostles who were called to their missionary office earlier than Paul (cf. Gal. 1:17; 1 Cor. 15:7) and probably belonged to this circle themselves. Only to the person who wants to limit the apostles to the circle of the Twelve which Jesus himself had gathered (cf. Mk. 3:13ff.) will the fact that women as well were counted as part of the circle of the apostles appear strange. But in 1 Cor. 15:5 this circle is consciously distinguished from the larger group of "all the apostles" which Paul mentions in 15:7. Moreover, given the ancient societal roles and relationships, it would have been difficult to reach and address women from a missionary standpoint without the active collaboration of women. The membership of (Andronicus and) Junia among the apostles can thus also be very easily understood on the basis of the circumstances surrounding the early missionary endeavor.

B. In the following verses Paul does not simply greet his friends and acquaintances himself, but extends his greetings to them by means of the Roman Christians. This request that they pass on his greetings makes good sense within the letter to the Romans in particular. For in making this request Paul avoids every possibility of putting them off as a result of prematurely assuming familiarity with the Roman house churches. Instead, he maintains a polite distance. Moreover, by doing so he also avoids isolating his circle of friends. Rather, he counts on the fact that his special friends will be "accepted" by the other Christians as they extend to them his greetings, just as he had advised them all to accept one another in 15:7ff. If and when they deliver Paul's greetings, the Roman Christians could also make it clear that they were in agreement with the wishes of the apostle, who was, indeed, a controversial figure in Rome. The indirect delivery of these greetings was thus carefully considered by Paul and was part and parcel of his overall intention in writing. [3, 4] At the head of Paul's friends stands Prisca (a shortened form of Priscilla) and her husband Aquila. The placing of the name of the woman first signals her significance for the mission. Paul had come to know the Jewish-Christian couple in Corinth, and had found work and accommodation with them. Driven out of Rome by the Edict of Claudius (see above, pp. 6–8), they had transferred their leather-working business—we would say today their saddlery—to Corinth (cf. Acts 18:2f.). After they had already energetically promoted the apostle during his mission in Corinth, they then traveled further on to Ephesus together with him and for years were his patrons and helpers there as well (cf. Acts 18:18f.; 19:8–10). Now they have traveled on ahead of Paul and returned again to Rome. Here too—as they did before in Ephesus, cf. 1 Cor. 16:19—they have gathered around them a Christian house church. Most probably, therefore, it was in Ephesus that they had brought the apostle, who had fallen into great affliction, to safety by risking their own lives (cf. Acts 19:23–20:1 and 1 Cor. 15:32; 2 Cor. 1:8ff.). Paul is consequently indebted to them for his deliverance and for their decisive assistance with the mission in Corinth and Ephesus. And this also obligates all Gentile-Christian churches to be thankful toward both of them. [5] Epaenetus, to whom Paul extends greetings next, is the first one in Ephesus, the capital of the Roman province of Asia, to have come to faith. Perhaps he moved to Rome together with Prisca and Aquila. [6] The name Maria corresponds to the Hebrew name Miriam (cf. Exod. 15:20f.), but in Latin inscriptions is also attested as a name for a Gentile woman. But since Paul extends greetings to a woman of this name in the first group of his friends and then adds that she has endeavored much on behalf of the Romans as a missionary, it is certainly a reference to a Jewish-Christian woman who was known to him from his work and deserving in regard to the mission in Rome. [7] We have already seen above that with Andronicus and Junia we are dealing with two outstanding missionaries within the circle of those apostles who were called before Paul (see above, p. 249). Paul had come to know the married couple (?) when he lay in prison together with them (cf. 2 Cor. 11:23). Like Paul himself, they too were therefore evidently engaged in the mission to the Gentiles. From the fact that they are now resident in Rome the conclusion can thus be drawn that they too, like Maria, have also missionized there. [8, 9] We know nothing more about those named in vv. 8 and 9 than what Paul writes. [10] Since Aristobulus is a name borne by aristocratic Jews, the man mentioned here could also be a Jew of means who had moved to Rome. He was evidently not a Christian himself. But among the slaves or freedmen who belonged to his household there was indeed a group of Christians about whom Paul had heard and to whom he now extends greetings. As Christians they formed a kind of trade guild. [11] Judging from the name, the Jewish-Christian Herodion was a slave or freedman of the royal house of Herod. We do not know whether Paul already knew him from the East, or whether he first belonged to the Roman "Synagogue of the Herodians" which is attested there and from there found faith. The Christians who come from the estate of the non-Christian Narcissus also represent a common guild, as did the people from the house of Aristobulus. [12] According to Paul, the two women, Tryphaena and Tryphosa, who are certainly related to one another, have also proven themselves in the mission. Just like Persis, who is mentioned immediately following them, they have helped to spread the gospel. For in the early Christian period, missions was not merely a matter for men. In this list of greetings alone, Paul names eight women who were active in missions! [13] Rufus, who was chosen by God to believe (cf. 8:33; Col. 3:12), is the son of a woman who had also already cared for Paul (somewhere during his missionary journeys). Once again we are thus dealing with two people who moved to Rome from the eastern regions. [14] The relationship between the five men named in v. 14 cannot be discerned. Together with several other Christian brothers, they form either a house church or a Christian brotherhood. [15] From Paul's following greetings we can observe that a married couple (Philologus and Julia) and a pair of siblings (Nereus and his sister), together with Olympas, form the core of an additional house church, concerning which Paul had received positive information. He surely would not have extended special greetings to the persons called by name in vv. 14 and 15, together with their house churches, if they had distanced themselves from his gospel. Rather, all of the women and men named, beginning in v. 3, ought to be considered Christians who belonged not to the critics, but to the advocates of the Pauline doctrine. [16] The apostle then concludes his list of greetings with a call for a holy kiss, which functions to seal the fellowship between brothers and sisters in the faith which exists among all members of the churches in Rome (cf. likewise in 1 Thess. 5:26; 1 Cor. 16:20; 2 Cor. 13:12; and 1 Pet. 5:14). In early Christianity the holy kiss was the sign of mutual acceptance and forgiveness. It appears to have preceded each celebration of the Lord's Supper within the churches (cf. 1 Cor. 16:20–22 with Did. 9:5; 10:6; Justin, *Apol.* 1.65.2; and Hippolytus, *The Apostolic Tradition* 46.8).

The special nature of this preceding list of greetings becomes abundantly clear in that at this point Paul now switches over to a direct form of greeting in order to pass on to the Christians from Rome the greetings of "all the churches of Christ." Practically speaking, this can only refer to all of those churches that Paul himself had founded and that had taken an active part in the work of the collection, which itself was designed to serve the unity of the church as a whole (cf. 15:25ff.). Hence, inasmuch as he is about to bring the collection to Jerusalem in order to document the connection of the Gentile Christians to the mother church on Zion, he now extends greetings to the Christians from Rome from these same churches. In this way, he desires to promote the unity under the gospel of all members of the body of Christ and to incorporate the Roman Christians into the fruit of his missionary work, now coming to an end in the East. When all is said and done, therefore, the apostle is concerned in his letter with the unity of Gentile and Jewish Christians in the faith, and with this, in serving the church as a whole.

VI. 16:17–20. A Warning against False Teachers

(17) But I admonish you, brothers, to take heed of those who are instigating dissensions and scandals against the teaching which you have learned; turn away indeed from them! (18) For such people are not serving our Lord Christ, but their own stomach, and through eloquence and blessings they are deceiving the hearts of the unsuspecting. (19) Your obedience (of faith) has

indeed become known to all. So I rejoice then concerning you, but would like
you to be wise with regard to the good, but unspoiled with regard to evil. (20)
But the God of peace will soon crush Satan under your feet. — The grace of
our Lord Jesus be with you!

A. This passage has occasionally appeared strange to interpreters of Romans
for two reasons. First is the fact itself that Paul inserts such a sharp warning into
his concluding greetings. Second, it has seemed strange that in it expressions
and concepts are used which otherwise seldom appear in Paul's writings or do
not appear at all. Nowhere else does the apostle ever speak of "eloquence," of
"formulas of blessing" in a contemptible sense, of "those who are unsuspecting,"
or of the "crushing of Satan." Under these circumstances, some have taken this
section to be an addendum by another hand, while others have accounted for it
as merely an expression of Paul's literary custom in which he desires at the end
of his letters to warn his readers against people who could be dangerous to the
church (cf. Gal. 6:12f.; 1 Cor. 16:22; 2 Thess. 3:14). But on the basis of the
transmission of the text there is no reason to consider this section to be a subsequent insertion into the Pauline text. Moreover, if one takes into consideration
that, from 2:16 on, Paul is constantly taking up and refuting arguments which
his Jewish-Christian opponents have brought up against him, this warning
against false teachers no longer in any way appears unmotivated. Rather, in it
Paul summarizes the criticism of his opponents, which the apostle has already
had in mind up until now and which he has already previously expressed in 3:8.
In v. 17 Paul first presents his warning formally and then in v. 18 supports it. In
v. 19 he then continues his warning, adding to it an eschatological promise in v.
20a. Verse 20b offers the usual concluding greeting found in the Pauline letters
(cf. 1 Cor. 16:23; 1 Thess. 5:28; 2 Thess. 3:18). Moreover, because the best
Greek manuscripts contain this greeting, the fact that it belongs to the text is
not to be doubted.

B. As in 12:1 and 15:30, here too Paul begins once again with an explicit request: [17] The Christians in Rome are to be wary of persons who engage in
critical disputes concerning the faith and deviate from the doctrine relied upon
in Rome (cf. 6:17 with 1 Cor. 15:3–5) in ways that cause a scandal. The Romans
should turn away from such people as far as possible. In making this request
Paul is thus now warning explicitly against those agitators who are causing unrest within the house churches and assailing the gospel which has taken root in
Rome. According to Gal. 5:20, the stirring up of dissensions is a fleshly act
which excludes one from God's coming reign as king. Moreover, scandals to the
faith come about when, in addition to the obedience of faith, Jewish Christians
demand from the Gentile Christians circumcision and other forms of observing
the Law (cf. Gal. 1:7; 5:7–12), or when the question concerning which foods are
and are not allowed is played up in those churches in which Gentile and Jewish

Christians live together (cf. Gal. 2:11–14; 1 Cor. 8:13; Rom. 14:13, 21). The one who incites scandals in Rome is thus to be identified with those who "slander" the apostle's preaching of the gospel as a message of cheap grace (3:8). Just like the churches in the East, which he himself founded, Paul therefore also sees the Roman house churches being threatened by traveling Jewish Christians who are conducting missions after and against Paul (cf. 15:20f.). So he formally advises the Romans to maintain their distance from these false apostles, whenever and wherever they appear in Rome.

[18] There can be no fellowship between Paul and the Christians from Rome on the one hand, and "such people" on the other hand, nor should any be allowed, since in reality they are disguised servants of Satan. Instead of serving Christ, they live for their own stomach, that is, they are intent on revenue and the gaining of provisions from the churches into which they come (cf. Phil. 3:18f.; 2 Cor. 11:7–11, 20; 12:14). Hence, just as the snake once "deceived" Eve in paradise (Gen. 3:13), they too "deceive" the hearts of the unsuspecting to follow "another Christ" and "another gospel" other than what the Romans have learned and Paul has taught (cf. 2 Cor. 11:2–4, 13–15; Gal. 1:6–9). In order to accomplish this, they devote themselves to a preaching which is easily accessible and garnished with promises of blessing. With this description Paul could be referring to the way and manner which, for example, the Judaizers who are missionizing in Galatia spoke of the blessings of the Abrahamic covenant, which they maintained are allotted first and only to those who are circumcised (cf. Gal. 3:8f., 14). Paul thus sees the gospel and the faith being threatened in Rome (as well). In his warning he is concerned with nothing less than salvation and the loss of it. (However, this does not simply excuse the placard-like, degrading, and slanderous style of his polemic against the heretics! Paul also sounds this tone in his other letters, and in doing so he is unfortunately by no means alone; cf., e.g., 2 John 7f.; Jude 4ff.; 2 Pet. 2, etc. Nevertheless, he is violating the instructions of Jesus and the behavior to which Paul himself had enjoined the Romans, cf. 12:14ff. with Mtt. 5:44; 7:1!)

[19] Paul now praises the standing in faith of the Christians from Rome one last time (cf. 1:8; 15:14) and takes pains to distinguish between them and the false teachers now infiltrating among them. Indeed, Paul derives spiritual joy from the Roman Christians, whose obedience of faith is known worldwide. It is his wish, therefore, that they remain mindful of the good, but that they also show themselves to be pure and unapproachable in regard to the influences of evil (i.e., of the servants of Satan). Matthew 10:16 thus appears to stand in the background of the apostle's instruction. [20] Moreover, the Roman Christians should know and depend on the fact that there will soon be an end to Satan's helpers. The eschatological fulfillment of the so-called "Protoevangelium" from Gen. 3:15 is at the door. The God of peace (cf. 15:33) will soon "crush under your feet" the snake, that is, Satan, who is at work in the deceptive words of the

false teachers. As in the parallel early Jewish texts (cf. T. Lev. 18:12 and T. Sim. 6:6), this refers to an eschatological promise, whose content can be clarified beautifully on the basis of Rev. 20:1–4 (cf. with 1 Cor. 6:2f.; 15:23ff.). With God's aid, the Christians will triumph in the near future over Satan and his helpers, in order that they may dwell and reign together with the living Christ. With this promise, the apostle has finally arrived at the end of his writing and closes, as he also does elsewhere in his letters, with a concluding blessing. This picks up the benediction from 15:33 by imploring God on behalf of his addressees for the support of the power of grace which belongs to the crucified and resurrected Christ.

VII. 16:21–23(24). Greetings from Paul's Co-Workers

(21) Timothy, my co-worker, greets you, and Lucius and Jason and Sosipater, my kinsmen. (22) I, Tertius, greet you, the one who has written this letter in the Lord. (23) Gaius, my host and the host of the whole church, greets you. Erastus, the city treasurer, greets you, and brother Quartus. [(24) The grace of our Lord Jesus Christ (be) with you all. Amen.]

A. First, in v. 21 Paul's co-workers extend their greetings. Then in v. 22 Paul's secretary gives his greeting. Finally, in v. 23 the greetings of several Corinthian members of the church, who are close to Paul, are appended. Verse 24 is found only in those Greek manuscripts which do not contain vv. 25–27. Verse 24 is thus a secondary supplement to the text; for its history, see above, p. 245.

The most interesting remark in this section of the text historically is found in v. 22. In a move which is quite unusual in the Pauline letters, the writer of the letter, Tertius, takes the opportunity of giving a personal greeting. We discover at the same time that he was the one who "has written" the letter to the Romans. There are therefore three possibilities concerning the completion of the letter. The first possibility is that Tertius had drafted and composed the entire letter himself, based on a few fundamental instructions from the apostle (something which was very common in the ancient world!). But the highly complicated content of the letter, which in part also has a very personal accent (cf., e.g., 1:8–17; 2:16; 3:8; 6:19; 9:1–5; 11:13; etc.), excludes this possibility. On the other hand, Tertius could have taken dictation from the apostle in stages in Greek shorthand and then subsequently expanded it and presented it to Paul for his additions and corrections. This process is easier to imagine, although the fact that there are sentences in the letter which remain incomplete (so-called anacoluthons), as in 2:20; 5:6, 12; 9:22f., rather speaks against it. The most probable scenario, therefore, is that Paul dictated the letter to the Romans to

Tertius word for word in laborious detail and, for the sake of his enormous achievement, gave his faithful secretary the opportunity to furnish his Christian work with a greeting of his own to the Christians in Rome. In no way, therefore, does v. 22 provide grounds for declaring Romans not to be genuine because it was not composed by Paul, but by Tertius!

B. The greetings from Paul's co-workers are opened up by Timothy. [21] Ever since Paul encountered him in Lystra and won him for the faith (Acts 16:1ff.; 1 Cor. 4:17), Timothy was *the* assistant to Paul in the mission. According to 1 Thess. 1:1; 2 Cor. 1:1; Phil. 1:1; Col. 1:1; and Philemon 1, he was even co-responsible for these important letters from the apostle. In Phil. 2:20, Paul publicly vouches for Timothy's like-mindedness. Indeed, Timothy was Paul's "right hand" (W. H. Ollrog). Together with him, three Jewish Christians then send their greetings, Lucius and Jason and Sosipater. Since Luke is the familiar form of Lucius, there is the possibility of equating Lucius with the Luke mentioned in Col. 4:14 and 2 Tim. 4:11. As a result, Paul would be more closely acquainted with Lucius/Luke than with the others and was accompanied by him on his journey to Jerusalem with the collection (see below). In this way the affinity of Paul to the Lukan tradition, which in part is striking (see above, pp. 19, 200, 232), could be explained, as well as confirming the eyewitness nature of Luke's report of Paul's trip to Jerusalem (Acts 20ff.). For his part, Jason is certainly the man who received Paul in Thessalonica and as a result experienced affliction (cf. Acts 17:5–7). Sosipater may be identical with the Sopater mentioned in Acts 20:4 who came from Beroea. All three men evidently belong to the church delegation which is accompanying Paul to Jerusalem and will complete the work of the collection there. Their greetings to Rome fortify the fellowship within the Church toward which the apostle is working (cf. 15:25–33; 16:16). [22] For the sake of his prodigious labor in writing down the letter, which he carried out in the Lord, the apostle's secretary, Tertius (which means, "the third"), is now allowed to greet the Christians from Rome with his own hand. [23] In addition, Paul also allows Gaius from Corinth to have a word, in whose house he was put up during his last visit in Greece, mentioned in Acts 20:3, and in which he could have dictated the letter to the Romans. Paul himself had previously baptized Gaius in Corinth (cf. 1 Cor. 1:14). Gaius also extends his hospitality to the "whole church"; that is, Christians who are traveling through are received by him, and the church in Corinth is probably also being allowed to gather at his house. In his case, therefore, we are not talking about a man without means. Together with him, Erastus, the city treasurer from Corinth, gives his greeting, who likewise is also a member of the Corinthian upper class. If the names of Phoebe (16:1), Prisca and Aquila (16:3), and Gaius and Erastus are considered as a whole, the nature of the circle of people who had helped Paul to raise the considerable costs for his missionary journeys becomes clear; it was those who were well-to-do financially. But in emergencies, the apostle had also received

collections for support from his churches (cf. Phil. 4:10ff.). Last of all, the
Christian brother Quartus (which means, "the fourth") sends his greetings. His
simple name, derived from a number, shows him, as well as Tertius, to be a man
from a background which was not free. Perhaps he was responsible for caring
for the apostle in the house of Gaius.

Verse 24 does not belong to the original text of Romans. It contains a benediction which is modeled according to 1 Cor. 16:23; Gal. 6:18; Phil. 4:23; and 1
Thess. 5:28.

VIII. 16:25–27. A Concluding Doxology

(25) But to him who is mighty to strengthen you according to my gospel and
the preaching of Jesus Christ, according to the revelation of the mystery,
which was hidden for eternal ages, (26) but is now revealed and made known
through prophetic writings according to the order of the eternal God for the
(inauguration of) the obedience of faith among all peoples, (27) to the only
wise God, through Jesus Christ, to him (is due) the glory for evermore.
Amen.

A. Just as Romans begins in 1:1–7 with a stylized prescript (= introduction to
the letter), according to the best Greek manuscripts preserved for us it also
closes with an extensive praise of God. This section thus corresponds to 1:1–7
and is likewise formulated with great care. Hence, this praise of God, which
consciously recalls the prescript, is not a secondary ornamentation to the text, as
some commentators repeatedly maintain, but from the very beginning was an
original element of the letter to the Romans (see above, pp. 244f.).

In regard to its structure, an originally short statement of praise, "But to him
who is mighty to strengthen you . . . to the only wise God, to him (is due) the
glory for evermore!" (vv. 25a + 27), was then expanded by a series of more precise definitions which consciously recall the manner of expression found in the
prescript of the letter and have the same liturgical character. In vv. 25 and 26a,
the subject matter of the gospel which has been entrusted to Paul and on the
basis of which he preaches Christ is once again emphasized by the parallel formulation (cf. the double, "according to . . ."). In v. 26b, the purpose for which
this gospel was made known to the peoples of the world is once again expressed.
The conclusion from v. 27 is then formulated in such a way that the (house)
church, which up until this time has followed along with the person who is reading aloud, can itself repeat after and join in with him or her: " ⁚ . . . to him (is due)
the glory for evermore. Amen."

The prescript signaled the readers that in the following letter to the Romans
the subject matter would be the gospel of Christ which had been entrusted to
Paul. The concluding doxology thus makes it clear to them that throughout the

entire letter the subject matter has been nothing other than precisely this gospel.

B. In 1:11 Paul had emphasized that he would very much like to come to Rome in order to strengthen his fellow believers there on the basis of the grace of God with which he is inspired. [25] In his letter he then gave them an insight into his message concerning Christ. It is based on the gospel of God's righteousness, which was entrusted to him. This righteousness became a reality within the history of salvation, prior to anyone's faith, in the mission, atoning death, and resurrection of Jesus (3:21–26; 5:6–8). In and through Christ, the almighty God, who created the world and made Israel into the people of his own possession, has chosen Jews and Gentiles to obtain salvation through justification by faith alone (8:29f.; 11:32). The apostle now closes his letter, therefore, with a doxology that applies to the God who, on the basis of his free grace, can and will strengthen the Romans along their path of faith in accordance with the Pauline gospel and the apostle's preaching of Christ (cf., similarly, 2 Thess. 2:17; 3:3; 1 Pet. 5:10). Hence, Paul's gospel is not concerned with just any message of revelation, but with the revelation of the salvific decree of God in and through Christ, which has been preserved from the very beginning of time but remained hidden to all earlier epochs of history (cf. 1 Cor. 2:6ff.).

[26] But what previously lay in divine silence has now been revealed by God. Christ has appeared as the "Lord of glory" (1 Cor. 2:8). Moreover, for those who believe and are filled with the Holy Spirit, the significance of his appearance can be perceived on the basis of the "prophetic writings." When Philo of Alexandria speaks of the "prophetic word" (*Plant.* 117) and 2 Pet. 1:19 takes up this manner of speaking, they mean the Spirit-filled word of the prophets of the Old Testament. Accordingly, the "prophetic writings" are—in correspondence to 1:2—the books of the prophets of the Holy Scripture, including their promises pointing to Christ, which, in doing so, also include the Gentiles (cf., e.g., 9:33; 11:26f.; and 15:12). Guided by the witness of the prophets, the salvific turning point of human history may and should now be made known to "all the Gentile peoples" (cf. the allusion to the command to baptize and go forth from Mtt. 28:19f.!). This turning point, moreover, has taken place in accordance with the will "of the eternal God" (cf. Gen. 21:33; 1QH 7:31), which in turn has been carried out through the sending of the apostle by the resurrected Christ (cf. 1:4f.; 10:14f.). This announcement is to inaugurate the obedience of faith among the Gentiles (cf. 1:5). With his work, therefore, Paul has participated decisively in this missionary event (cf. 11:13f.; 15:16). Colossians 1:25ff.; Eph. 1:7–10; 3:5, 9f.; 2 Tim. 1:9f.; Tit. 1:2f.; 1 Pet. 1:20; together with 2 Thess. 2:17; 3:3; and 1 Pet. 5:10, show that the manner of expression found in these two verses gained adherents far beyond the letter to the Romans. This language was probably made available to the apostle (and to other New Testament authors) from the early Christian liturgy, concerning which, unfortunately, we have only a fragmentary orientation (cf., e.g., Col. 3:16).

[27] With v. 27 Paul brings his doxology to a close. It applies to the "only wise God" (cf. 1 Enoch 63:2). For in his creative wisdom God has arranged all things through Christ to bring about salvation (cf. 1 Cor. 1:30; 2:6ff.; 8:6; Col. 1:15–20). Therefore praise is due him, by virtue of which he is recognized in his glory. Paul's "amen" (which means, "So be it!"), and that of all those who repeat and join in with his praise, then concludes the doxology.

Select Bibliography

Scholarly Commentaries

Barrett, C. K. *A Commentary on the Epistle to the Romans*, BNTC, ²1962.
Best, E. *The Letter of Paul to the Romans*, CNEB, 1967.
Black, M. *Romans*, NCeB, 1973.
Bruce, F. F. *The Epistle of Paul to the Romans*, TNTC, ²1985.
Cranfield, C.E.B. *The Epistle to the Romans*, ICC, I 1975, II 1979.
Dunn, J.D.G. *Romans*, Word Biblical Commentary 38A/38B, 1988.
Käsemann, E. *An die Römer*, HNT 8a, ⁴1980.
Kuss, O. *Der Römerbrief*, I ²1963, II ²1963, III 1978.
Leenhardt, F. J. *L'Epître de Saint Paul aux Romains*, CNT 6, ²1981.
Lietzmann, H. *An die Römer*, HNT 8, ⁵1971.
D. Martin Luthers Werke, Weimarer Ausgabe 56: *Der Brief an die Römer*, 1938.
Luther, Martin. *Vorlesung über den Römerbrief* 1515/1516 Latin-German Edition, ed. M. Hofmann, I/II, 1960.
Michel, O. *Der Brief an die Römer*, KEK ¹⁴/⁵1978.
Nygren, A. *Der Römerbrief*, ⁴1965.
Schlatter, A. *Gottes Gerechtigkeit. Ein Kommentar zum Römerbrief*, ⁵1975.
Schlier, H. *Der Römerbrief*. HThK VI, ²1979.
Schmidt, H. W. *Der Brief des Paulus an die Römer*, ThHK 6, ³1972.
Schmithals, W. *Der Römerbrief. Ein Kommentar*, 1988.
Wilckens, U. *Der Brief an die Römer*, EKK VI, 1 ²1987; VI, 2 ²1987; VI, 3 1982.
Zeller, D. *Der Brief an die Römer*, RNT, 1985.

Other Commentaries

Althaus, P. *Der Brief an die Römer*, NTD 6, ¹³1978.
Barth, K. *Kurze Erklärung des Römerbriefes*, ³1964.

NOTE: Most of the abbreviations used here may be found in the list by S. Schwertner in *Theologische Realenzyklopädie*, Berlin, 1977–.

Cranfield, C.E.B. *Romans: A Shorter Commentary*, 1985.
Gaugler, E. *Der Brief an die Römer* (Prophezei), Zurich, I ²1958, II 1952.
Kertelge, K. *Der Brief an die Römer*, Geistliche Schriftlesung 6, 1971.
Luther, Martin. *Vorlesung über den Römerbrief 1515/1516*; tr. E. Ellwein, 1957.
D. *Martin Luthers Epistelauslegung*, vol. 1: *Der Römerbrief*, ed. E. Ellwein, 1963.
Pesch, R. *Römerbrief*, NEB.NT 6, 1983.
Schlatter, A. *Der Brief an die Römer*, Erläuterungen zum NT 5, 1974.
Shields, B. *Romans*, Standard Bible Studies, 1988.

Monographs and Essays

Aune, D. "Romans as a Logos Protreptikos in the Context of Ancient Religious and Philosophical Propaganda," in *Symposiumsband Tübingen–Durham*, WUNT, 1989.
Balz, H. R. *Heilsvertrauen und Welterfahrung*, BEvTh 59, 1971.
Barth, G. *Die Taufe in frühchristlicher Zeit*, BThSt 4, 1981.
Bartsch, H.-W. "Die historische Situation des Römerbriefes," StEvIV(TU 102), 1968, 281–291.
Berger, K. "Abraham in den paulinischen Hauptbriefen," in MThZ 17, 1966, 47–89.
———, *Formgeschichte des Neuen Testaments*, 1984.
———,"Hellenistische Gattungen im Neuen Testament," ANRW II 25, 2, 1984, 1031–1432.
Betz, H. D. "Das Problem der Grundlagen der paulinischen Ethik (Röm 12, 1–2)," ZThK 85, 1988, 199–218.
Blank, J. *Paulus. Von Jesus zum Christentum*, 1982.
Bornkamm, G. *Das Ende des Gesetzes*, BEvTh 16, ⁵1966.
———, *Studien zu Antike und Urchristentum*, BEvTh 28, ³1970.
———, *Geschichte und Glaube*, Teil 1/2, BEvTh 48/53, 1968/1971.
———, *Paulus*, UB 119, ⁴1979.
Brandenburger, E. *Adam und Christus*, WMANT 7, 1962.
———, *Fleisch und Geist*, WMANT 29, 1968.
———, "Paulinische Schriftauslegung in der Kontroverse um das Verheissungswort Gottes (Röm 9)," ZThK 82, 1985, 1–47.
———, "Pistis und Soteria," ZThK 85, 1988, 165–198.
Breytenbach, C. *Versöhnung*, WMANT 60, 1989.
Bultmann, R. *Theologie des Neuen Testaments*, ⁷1976.
———, *Exegetica* (ed. E. Dinkler), 1967.
Conzelmann, H. *Grundriss der Theologie des Neuen Testaments*, ⁴1987, rev. H. Lindemann.
———, *Theologie als Schriftauslegung*, BevTh 65, 1974.

Dahl, N. A. "Formgeschichtliche Beobachtungen zur Christusverkündigung in der Gemeindepredigt," in *Neutestamentliche Studien für R. Bultmann zu seinem 70. Geburtstag*, BZNW 21, ²1957, 3–9.

Deichgräber, R. *Gotteshymnus und Christushymnus in der frühen Christenheit*, StUNT 5, 1967.

Dietzfelbinger, C. *Die Berufung des Paulus als Ursprung seiner Theologie*, WMANT 58, 1985.

Dinkler, E. "Prädestination bei Paulus. Exegetische Bemerkungen zum Römerbrief," in *Signum Crucis*, 1967, 241–269.

Donfried, K. P. (ed.), *The Romans Debate*, 1977.

Dunn, J.G.D. "Paul's Epistle to the Romans: An Analysis of Structure and Argument," ANRW II 25, 4, 1987, 2842–2890.

Eckstein, H. J. *Der Begriff Syneidesis bei Paulus*, WUNT II 10, 1983.

Eichholz, G. *Die Theologie des Paulus im Umriss*, ²1977.

Ellis, E. E. *Paul's Use of the Old Testament*, ²1981.

Friedrich, J., W. Pöhlmann, and P. Stuhlmacher (eds.), *Rechtfertigung*, FS E. Käsemann, 1976.

———, "Zur historischen Situation und Intention von Röm 13, 1–7," ZThK 73, 1976, 131–166.

Friedrich, G. *Die Verkündigung des Todes Jesu im NT*. BThSt 6, 1982.

Haacker, K. *Exegetische Probleme des Römerbriefes*, NT 20, 1978, 1–21.

Hafemann, S. *Suffering and the Spirit*. WUNT II 19, 1986.

Hahn, F. "Das Gesetzesverständnis im Römer- und Galaterbrief," ZNW 67, 1976, 29–63.

———, "Das Verständnis der Taufe nach Römer 6," in *Bewahren und Erneuern*, FS T. Schaller, 1980, 135–153.

Haubeck, W. *Loskauf durch Christus*, 1985.

Heiligenthal, R. *Werke als Zeichen*, WUNT II 9, 1983.

Hengel, M. "Der vorchristliche Paulus," in *Symposiumsband Tübingen–Durham*, 1989.

Hermisson, H.-J., and E. Lohse, *Glauben*, 1978.

Hofius, O. "Das Evangelium und Israel—Erwägungen zu Römer 9–11," ZThK 83, 1986, 297–324.

———, "'Rechtfertigung des Gottlosen' als Thema biblischer Theologie," JBTh 2, 1987, 79–105.

Hübner, H. *Das Gesetz bei Paulus*, FRLANT 119, ³1982.

———, *Gottes Ich und Israel*, FRLANT 136, 1984.

Jeremias, J. "Zur Gedankenführung in den paulinischen Briefen," in *Abba* (collected essays), 1966, 269–276.

———, "Einige vorwiegend sprachliche Beobachtungen zu Röm 11, 25–36," in L. de Lorenzi (ed.), *Die Israelfrage nach Röm 9–11*, 1977, 193–205.

Jüngel, E. "Das Gesetz zwischen Adam und Christus," in *Unterwegs zur Sache*, BEvTh 61, 1972, 145–172.

Käsemann, E. *Exegetische Versuche und Besinnungen*, I/II, 1960/1964 (I/II 61970).

————, "Erwägungen zum Stichwort 'Versöhnungslehre im Neuen Testament,'" in E. Dinkler (ed.), *Zeit und Geschichte* (FS R. Bultmann), 1964, 47–59.

————, *Paulinische Perspektiven*, ²1972.

Kertelge, K. "'Rechtfertigung' bei Paulus," NTA NF 3, ²1971.

Kettunen, M. *Der Abfassungszweck des Römerbriefes*, AASF 18, 1979.

Kim, S. *The Origin of Paul's Gospel*, WUNT II 4, ²1984.

Klaiber, W. *Rechtfertigung und Gemeinde*, FRLANT 127, 1982.

Klauck, H.-J. *Hausgemeinde und Hauskirche im frühen Christentum*, SBS 103, 1981.

Klein, G. *Rekonstruktion und Interpretation*, BEvTh 50, 1969.

Kleinknecht, K. T. *Der leidende Gerechtfertigte*, WUNT II 13, ²1988.

Koch, D.-A. *Die Schrift als Zeuge des Evangeliums*, BHTh 69, 1986.

Kümmel, W. G. "Römer 7 und die Bekehrung des Paulus (1929)," in *Römer 7 und das Bild des Menschen im Neuen Testament*, TB 53, 1974, 1–160.

Kuss, O. *Paulus*, ²1976.

Lampe, P. *Die stadtrömischen Christen in den ersten beiden Jahrhunderten*, WUNT II 18, 1987.

Lohfink, G. *Wie hat Jesus Gemeinde gewollt?*, 1982.

Lübking, H.-M. *Paulus und Israel im Römerbrief*, EHS.T 260, 1986.

Lührmann, D. *Das Offenbarungsverständnis bei Paulus und in den paulinischen Gemeinden*, WMANT 16, 1965.

————, *Glaube im frühen Christentum*, 1976.

Luz, U. *Das Geschichtsverständnis des Paulus*, BEvTh 49, 1968.

————, "Zum Aufbau von Röm. 1–8," ThZ 25, 161–181.

Martin, R. *Reconciliation*, 1981.

Mattern, L. *Das Verständnis des Gerichts bei Paulus*, AThANT 47, 1966.

Merk, O. *Handeln aus Glauben*, MThSt 5, 1968.

Michel, O. *Paulus und seine Bibel*, BFChTh II 18, ²1972.

Müller, C. *Gottes Gerechtigkeit und Gottes Volk. Eine Untersuchung zu Römer 9–11*, FRLANT 86, 1964.

Munck, J. *Paulus und die Heilsgeschichte*, Acta Jutlandica XXVI, no. 1, 1954.

Mussner, F. *Traktat über die Juden*, 1979.

Neugebauer, F. *In Christus*, 1961.

Ollrog, W.-H. *Paulus und seine Mitarbeiter*, WMANT 50, 1979.

Osten-Sacken, P. von der. *Römer 8 als Beispiel paulinischer Soteriologie*, FRLANT 112, 1975.

Paulsen, H. *Überlieferung und Auslegung in Römer 8*, WMANT 43, 1974.

Räisänen, H. *Paul and the Law*, WUNT 29, ²1987.

————, "Römer 9–11: Analyse eines geistigen Ringens," ANRW II 25, 4, 1987, 2891–2939.

Reinmuth, E. *Geist und Gesetz*, ThA 44, 1985.

Ridderbos, H. *Paulus. Ein Entwurf seiner Theologie*, 1970.

Riekkinen, V. *Römer 13*, AASF 23, 1980.

Rolland, R. *Épitre aux Romains. Texte Grec Structuré*, 1980.

Röhser, G. *Metaphorik und Personifikation der Sünde*, WUNT II 25, 1987.

Sanders, E. P. *Paul and Palestinian Judaism*, 1977.

————, *Paulus und das palästinische Judentum*, 1985.

————, *Paul, the Law and the Jewish People*, 1983.

Sandnes, K. O. "Paul—One of the Prophets?," Dissertation, Oslo, 1988.

Schäfer, P. *Studien zur Geschichte und Theologie des rabbinischen Judentums*, AGJU 15, 1978.

Schmithals, W. *Der Römerbrief als historisches Problem*, StNT 9, 1975.

Schnelle, U. *Gerechtigkeit und Christusgegenwart*, GthA 24, 1983.

Schrage, W. *Ethik des Neuen Testaments*, NTD Supplement 4, 1982.

Siegert, F. *Argumentation bei Paulus*, WUNT 34, 1985.

Smend, R., and U. Luz, *Gesetz*, 1981.

Soards, M. L. *The Apostle Paul*, 1987.

Stendahl, K. *Paul among Jews and Gentiles*, 1976.

Stowers, S. K. *The Diatribe and Paul's Letter to the Romans*, SBL Diss. Ser. 57, 1981.

Stuhlmacher, P. *Gerechtigkeit Gottes bei Paulus*, FRLANT 87, ²1966.

————, *Versöhnung, Gesetz und Gerechtigkeit*, 1981.

————, "Sühne oder Versöhnung?" in *Die Mitte des NTs* (FS E. Schweizer), ed. U. Luz and H. Weder 1983, 291–316.

————, (ed.), *Das Evangelium und die Evangelien*, WUNT 28, 1983.

————, "Evangelium," EKL² I, 1217–1221.

————, "Paulus und Luther," in *Glaube und Eschatologie* (FS W. G. Kümmel), ed. E. Grässer and O. Merk, 1985, 285–302.

————, *Paul's Understanding of the Law in the Letter to the Romans*. SEÅ 50, 1985, 87–104.

————, "Der Abfassungszweck des Römerbriefes," ZNW 77, 1986, 180–193.

Synofzik, E. *Die Gerichts- und Vergeltungsaussagen bei Paulus*, GthA 8, 1977.

Theissen, G. *Studien zur Soziologie des Urchristentums*, WUNT 19, ³1989.

Vögtle, A. *Das Neue Testament und die Zukunft des Kosmos*, KBANT, 1970.

Walter, N. *Zur Interpretation von Römer 9–11*, ZThK 81, 1984, 172–195.

Wedderburn, A.J.M. *Baptism and Resurrection*, WUNT 44, 1987.

Wilckens, U. *Rechtfertigung als Freiheit*, 1974.

Zeller, D. "Sühne und Langmut," ThPh 43, 1968, 51–75.

————, *Juden und Heiden in der Mission des Paulus*, FzB 8, ²1976.

Index of Names and Subjects

(Compiled by Jürgen Schwarz and Edda Weise)

Abba, Father   p.129; Rom. 8:15
Abraham   p.69, 70, 76; Rom. 8:3;
    p.125, 138; Rom. 9:4, 6; p.166;
    Rom. 11:18, 27; 15:27
  as Father   Rom. 4:22; 11:27
  as "Root"   p.166; Rom. 11:17
Adam   p.83f.; 106ff.; 124; Rom. 8:29;
    p.190f.
Apostle   Excursus 1 (20ff.); Rom.
    10:13; p.159; Rom. 15:16, 19
  to the Gentiles   Rom. 1:14; Rom.
    11:14; p.184
Atonement   p.58f.; Rom. 3:25; 5:9;
    p.82, 99
  death of atonement   p.64; Rom.
    6:7; 8:34; 11:27
  Jesus' death of atonement   p.47;
    Rom. 5:16; p.123
  sacrifice of atonement   p.58f.

Baptism   p.64, 90; Rom. 6:3;
    Excursus 9 (97ff.); Rom. 8:15;
    12:2; 13:11
  exhortation at   Rom. 14:17
  preaching of   p.97; Rom. 7:5;
    p.185
  tradition   Rom. 8:28ff.
Baur, Ferdinand Christian   p.3
Blood   p.58
Boasting/Boast   p.65f.; Rom. 4:2

Body   Rom. 6:6; 8:13
  of Christ   p.190; Rom. 13:14

Catechism   p.218
Christ   Rom. 2:16; 3:25; 10:2; 11:26;
    Rom. 15:9
Christians   p.98
  in Rome   Rom. 7:1; p.144, p.192;
    Rom. 15:13, 14; p.242f.; Rom.
    15:31; 16:17, 19
Circumcision   p.49; Rom. 2:25; 3:25;
    p.70; Rom. 4:9; p.182, 220;
    Rom. 15:8
  to be circumcised   p.69
Clean and Unclean   Rom. 14:14
Collection, the   p.241
Composition of Romans
  circumstances of   p.3ff.
  purpose of   p.239; Rom. 16:16
Confession   p.90; Rom. 10:12
  formula of   p.18; Rom. 4:25
  tradition of   p.117
Congregation (church)   Rom. 14:19
  exhortation to   p.186; Rom. 12:1;
    p.211; Excursus 14 (214ff.);
    Rom. 15:13
  house churches in Rome   p.191,
    195, 201; Rom. 13:2; p.219, 247
Conscience   p.42: Rom. 2:15; 12:5;
    p.221

Covenant   p.70, 117f.; Rom. 8:4; 9:4;
    11:27
  New   p.124, 125
Creation   Rom. 8:19
Crucifixion   p.182f.

Death   Rom. 5:17; *see also* Atone-
    ment: death of; Sacrifice
  inherited   Rom. 5:12
Decalogue   Rom. 1:18; 3:20; p.107,
    125, 194, 209; Rom. 13:10;
    p.217; Rom. 14:5
Decree of Election   Rom. 11:36
Depravity, Catalog of   Rom. 1:31;
    p.212; Rom. 13:13
Diatribe   p.39
Doctrine   Rom. 6:17; p.100, 186;
    Rom. 16:17
  doctrinal formula   p.18
  doctrinal statement   p.113f.; Rom.
    8:18; 9:16
  doctrinal tradition   p.57f.; Rom.
    12:7

Edict of Claudius   p.7, 191, 221, 247,
    249
Edification   Rom. 14:19
Election   Rom. 8:29; 11:16, 29

Faith   Rom. 1:17; 3:22; p.64; Rom.
    4:6-8; Excursus 7 (76ff.); Rom.
    6:9; 12:3; 14:1, 23
  from faith alone   Rom. 3:28
  fides ex auditu   p.77
  sola fide   Rom. 3:28
  righteousness of   Rom. 4:13; Rom.
    10:7
  obedience of   Rom. 1:5; 6:16
  tradition   Rom. 4:25
Fathers   p.70; Rom. 4:22; 9:5; 11:27
Flesh   p.102; Rom. 7:14, 25b; p.118;
    Rom. 8:4, 18
"Full Number"
  of the Gentiles   p.166; Rom.

11:25; 15:19
  of Israel   p.166

Gentiles   Rom. 6:19; 16:26
Glosses   p.42; Rom. 2:16; p.113, 158
  Rom. 13:1-7   p.199
  Rom. 16   Excursus 15 (244f.)
God-fearers   p.7, 69; Rom. 7:1; p.143
Godless   Rom. 4:5; 5:6
Gospel   p.9, 10; Rom. 1:2; Excursus
    2 (22ff.); p.26f.; Rom. 1:16; 2:16;
    6:17; p.100f., 105, 142; Rom.
    11:15; 13:10; p.236f.; Rom.
    15:19, 28; p.256f.; Rom. 16:25
Grace   Rom. 5:2
  election of   Rom. 8:28; p.147

Hardening   Rom. 11:8, 27
History of Salvation   Rom. 11:24, 36
Holy Days, setting apart of   Rom.
    14:5
Homosexuality   Rom. 1:26f.

"I"   Excursus 10 (114ff.)
Imminent Expectation   Rom. 13:12;
    p.218
Impulse   p.118
  good and evil   p.109f.; Rom. 7:23;
    8:6
  evil   p.109
Isaac, Binding of   p.71, 138
Israel   p.142; Rom. 9:4, 32; 10:21;
    11:32; Excursus 12 (177ff.)

James   p.6, 123, 181, 220
  letter of   p.9, 78
Jealousy   Rom. 10:19; p.184
Jerusalem   Rom. 15:19; p.241; Rom.
    15:24
Jesus   Rom. 1:4; p.24; Rom. 3:25;
    p.65f.; Rom. 4:25; p.77; Rom.
    5:6; p.84f., p.98, 126f., 129;
    Rom. 9:24; 11:27; p.218f.; Rom.
    14:9, 14; 15:3, 7, 8, 12

sending of p.117
Jesus-tradition p.24f.
behavior and model Rom. 12:21
Jews Rom. 2:17-19; 2:28f.; 3:1
and Gentiles Rom. 1:16; p.40;
    Rom. 15:8f.
Judgment Rom. 1:16; p.35; Rom.
    1:24; 2:5; 2:13; p.45; Rom. 2:25;
    p.138; Rom. 8:34; 11:11; 12:19
of God Rom. 14:10
final judgment Rom. 13:12
according to works Excursus 5
    (45ff.); p.128
final justification p.100
judgment of the world p.218
Junia p.247f.; Rom. 16:7
Justification Rom. 3:20, 25; 4:3, 24;
    p.100; Rom. 8:33; p.147, 179,
    215
in Paul's thought Excursus 6
    (61ff.)
and Reconciliation Excursus 8
    (82ff.)
final justification p.100
to justify Rom. 11:16

Käsemann, E. p.2, 32
Kingdom of God, reign of God
    Rom. 14:17
Kiss, Holy Rom. 16:16
Knowledge of God, natural
    Excursus 4 (44f.)

Law p.42, 46f.; Rom. 3:20; p.65f.;
    Rom. 4:13; 5:12, 20; p.105, 106;
    Rom. 7:7, 14; 8:2; Excursus 11
    (122ff.); Rom. 9:4; 13:10
end of the Rom. 10:4
joy in the p.110
of Christ p.126f., 216; Rom. 15:1
and Gospel p.123
Love p.201
of God Rom. 5:8; 8:39; 12:9
for one's brother Rom. 12:10

for one's enemy Rom. 12:14; p.216
for God p.216
of one's neighbor p.209, 216
love command Rom. 13:8
Lucius/Luke Rom. 16:21
Luther p.1, 32

Man p.42, 109; Rom. 8:29
outer/inner p.109
Man/Son of Man p.84, 85, 99; Rom.
    8:20; p.190
the "Many" Rom. 5:19
Melanchthon p.2
Mission p.24, 26; Rom. 1:14; p.143;
    Rom. 11:31; p.181, 235; Rom.
    15:19; p.239; Rom. 16:23, 26
contramission p.6, 143, 237
missionary to the Gentiles p.178
to the Gentiles p.143; Rom. 9:24;
    11:32; p.181
to the Jews p.142f.; Rom. 9:24;
    10:16; p.180
plans Rom. 1:15
world mission Rom. 15:24
Mystery p.170; Rom. 11:25
Mystery Cults p.99

Opponents, Critics, Slanderers p.5f.,
    8, 21, 50, 51; Rom. 3:7, 8, 9, 31;
    p.69; Rom. 4:13; p.89; Rom. 6:1,
    5, 15; p.101; Rom. 7:7; 8:4;
    p.123, 143, 149, 181; Rom.
    13:10; p.242f.; 252
contramissionaries p.5f., 143,
    220, 237
Original Sin Rom. 5:12; 6:11

Paraklesis See Congregation:
    exhortation to
Parousia (Second Coming) p.35f.;
    Rom. 11:26
Passions (Lusts) Rom. 6:12; 7:5, 7;
    13:14
to lust Rom. 1:24

Paul   p.5f.; Rom. 1:1; p.20, 22, 62,
97, 113f., 115, 126, 142; Rom.
9:3; 10:2; 11:1, 14, 32; p.177,
205, 243f.
Peace   p.79; Rom. 12:18; 14:17
Peter   p.6, 123, 142, 180, 181, 220
Phoebe   p.246
Pilgrimage of the Nations   p.170f.
Prayer of Thanksgiving   Rom. 14:6
Preaching   p.22f.; Rom. 10:17
   of the Gospel   Rom. 12:1
Preaching of Conversion   p.34, 97
Prisca and Aquila   p.220, 249; Rom.
16:3f.
Promise   p.144; Rom. 9:6; 11:24;
p.179

Reader in Rome   Rom. 11:13
Reason, understanding   Rom. 1:28;
7:23; 12:2; p.216
Reconciliation   Rom. 5:10; 11:9
   justification and   Excursus 8 (82ff.)
   to reconcile   Rom. 5:10
Redemption   Rom. 3:24; 8:23; p.162;
Rom. 11:15
Remnant   Rom. 9:28; p.162, 163;
Rom. 11:32
Repentance
   prayer of   p.178
   texts of   p.109
   tradition of   Rom. 7:18
Righteousness   Rom. 6:16; 14:17
   service on behalf of   Rom. 6:19;
p.123f., 185
   of faith   Rom. 4:13; 10:7
   of God   p.10; Rom. 1:17; Excursus
3 (29ff.); p.35; Rom. 3:8, 25;
10:3; 11:32
Root   p.166; Rom. 11:17
Romans, Letter to the   p.8, 235,
242f., 244, 254, 256

Sacrifice   Rom. 12:1; see also
Atonement: sacrifice of

Sacrificial Act   Rom. 8:4
Sacrificial Death   Rom. 8:27
Sanctification   Rom. 6:19; p.218f.
   sanctified   p.100
   saints   p.205
Schlatter, Adolf   p.2, 31, 32
Scripture   Rom. 3:10, 27; 4:6-8;
p.152; Rom. 11:27; p.230
   Holy   Rom. 3:21; p.147, 149, 153;
Rom. 14:11; 15:4; 16:26
Servant of God   p.64, 71; Rom.
8:32f.; p.159, 215
Sin   Rom. 1:32; p.47; Rom. 3:20;
p.58; Rom. 5:12; 6:16; 7:7, 13
   Fall into sin   p.132
   sinner and righteous at the same
time   p.115
   sacrifice for sin   Rom. 8:3
Son   Rom. 8:3
Son of God   Rom. 1:3
Sons, children of God   p.129
Sonship   p.129
Spirit   p.101; Rom. 8:9, 26
   of life   Rom. 8:2
   of sonship   Rom. 8:15
   Holy Spirit   Rom. 5:5; 8:23, 38
   and flesh   p.102; Rom. 7:14, 25b;
p.118; Rom. 8:4, 18
State   Rom. 13:2
   power of the state   Excursus 13
(205ff.)
Stephen   p.65, 126
   Stephen-circle   p.59, 127
Strong and the Weak   p.219f.; Rom.
14:1f., 13; 15:7
Suffering   p.79; Rom. 8:17; p.132;
Rom. 8:18; p.138; Rom. 8:31, 35

Teacher   p.113
Ten Commandments   (see
Decalogue)
Tertius   p.254
Timothy   Rom. 16:21

Torah   p.209, 216
Tradition   p.9, 132

Weizsäcker, Carl   p.5
Wisdom   p.34f., 44; Rom. 5:13;
    p.102, 106, 117; Rom. 12:2
Woes, messianic   p.132
Women   p.246; Rom. 16:12

Works   p.45; Rom. 4:4; 8:34
    evil/good   p.215
    of the Law   p.45; Rom. 3:20; p.215
Worship   Rom. 9:4; 12:1; p.201
    reasonable   p.187; Rom. 12:1
Wrath of God   p.35; Rom. 3:8

Zion   p.171; Rom. 11:25f.; p.242